PREFACE TO
CRITICAL
READING

PREFACE TO CRITICAL READING

Richard D. Altick

SIXTH EDITION

Revised by

Andrea A. Lunsford
The University of British Columbia

HOLT, RINEHART AND WINSTON .

New York   Chicago   San Francisco   Philadelphia
Montreal   Toronto   London   Sydney
Tokyo   Mexico City   Rio de Janeiro   Madrid

Library of Congress Cataloging in Publication Data

Altick, Richard Daniel, 1915–
  Preface to critical reading.

  Includes bibliographical references and index.
  1. English language—Rhetoric. 2. Reading.
I. Lunsford, Andrea A., 1942–   II. Title.
PE1408.A56   1984   808'.0427   83-12912
ISBN 0-03-061373-6

CBS COLLEGE PUBLISHING
Holt, Rinehart and Winston
The Dryden Press
Saunders College Publishing

PREFACE

Preface to Critical Reading has now passed its thirty-seventh birthday, and so is older than most of the students who use it — an unusual distinction for a textbook, and one that imposes a special obligation upon the authors, who seek to ensure that the book will continue to have immediate value to new generations of students with their changed outlooks and needs.

Because the basic approach adopted in these pages has served well through five editions, in the course of which it was repeatedly refined and modified in the light of many teachers' experience, it has not been altered radically in this fresh revision. The overall structure has also been retained, though in some cases the discussion within chapters has been reordered or expanded. The order of the chapters and of the materials within them is not sacrosanct in any case, and some teachers will undoubtedly prefer to follow another sequence.

For this sixth edition, all illustrative and exercise material has been freshly evaluated. As a result, "dated" passages, examples, and exercises have been deleted and replaced with others. We have particularly included several entire pieces of discourse so that students may go beyond the excerpt or the paragraph to study the effects of the whole piece. And for the first time, we have included several reproductions of advertisements, so that students may analyze their visual as well as verbal effects. But much material which has proved serviceable across the years has been retained, both because teachers still like to use it and because equally satisfactory replacements are hard to find. Once again, we have included more exercises than any one class will have time to handle. Because this book is used in courses enrolling students with a great range of preparation and ability, our aim has been to make it as flexible as possible. The variety of the exercises, some of which are designed to approach the same subject from different angles or on different levels of sophistication, will enable the instructor to adapt the book to the special needs of each class and to the time available. Like its forerunners, the present edition has been designed to encourage innovations and departures. There is no single "best" way to use it.

We have added a concise glossary and expanded the index. The sources of all quotations are listed in the back of the book (pages 334–349), except for those few passages whose copyright owners have requested acknowledgment on the same page as the quotation itself. Once more it is a pleasure to thank the companies which have consented to our reproducing their advertisements, as well as the owners of other copyright material who have given their permission to quote.

In preparing *Preface to Critical Reading* for this newest edition, we have been aided by a number of readers. In particular, we wish to thank Lisa Ede, Stephen

Lunsford, and Cheryl Draper, who offered valuable assistance in revising the exercises, as well as our many reviewers: Walter Beale, University of North Carolina at Greensboro; Alma Bryant, University of Southern Florida; Janice Cline, York College, CUNY; Joseph Comprone, University of Louisville; Edward P. J. Corbett, Ohio State University; Kathleen Dubs, University of San Francisco; Charles Duke, Murray State University; Prescott Evarts, Monmouth College; John Gage, University of Oregon; Helen Gilbart, St. Petersburg Junior College; Vincent Gillespie, Kansas State University; David Hibbard, Kent State University; James C. Hines, Charles Stewart Mott Community College; William Irmscher, University of Washington; William J. Johnson, Augusta College; Elaine Kleiner, Indiana State University; Nevin Laib, Texas Tech University; Elaine Langerman, University of the District of Columbia; Ken Lauter, University of Missouri at St. Louis; Erika Lindemann, University of South Carolina at Columbia; Valerie Lister, Portland Community College; Randall Miller, Ricks College; Roberta Pritchard, Texas Christian University; Robert Siegle, University of North Carolina at Chapel Hill; and Marilyn Sternglass, Indiana University.

R.D.A.
A.A.L.

CONTENTS

If we think of it, all that a University, or final highest School can do for us, is still but what the first School began doing, — teach us to read.

Thomas Carlyle, "The Hero as Man of Letters"

First Question: Is this true?

It is the business of the critical power . . . to see the object as in itself it really is.

Matthew Arnold, "The Function of Criticism at the Present Time"

Second Question: What has "the critical power" to do with reading and writing?

INTRODUCTION: THE PROCESS OF CRITICAL READING

This book is meant to help you learn to read. And if you carefully apply the lessons learned here, you will improve your writing too.

Of course, everybody knows how to read, in one sense. From newspapers, magazines, advertisements, directions for use, and product guarantees we absorb a barrage of printed words. In general we know what is being said, and we believe that we could report the gist of the writing. On any given day, we do a great deal of such reading: we may scan the newspapers for important stories, sort through job application forms and directions for completing them, read a newly printed city bus schedule, consult a recipe for vegetable curry. This kind of reading demands fluency—the ability to read quickly for immediate information. This ability is important for much of the workaday reading we must do.

But critical reading demands far more than speed or simple fluency. So, for that matter, does truly incisive writing. Both talents are generated by the critical spirit, which, as our second epigraph says, is the determination to see things clearly and truly. We are talking, then, about the communication of ideas: how they are embodied in language and how effectively and accurately they are conveyed.

Examine this short speech. Read it first at your normal speed, and then reread it more slowly, pausing to decide what each sentence says. What are the speaker's ideas? What, presumably, are the speaker's purposes? How plainly and effectively are they presented? And—most important—just what does the whole speech mean?

Mr. Chairman, Ladies and Gentlemen:

It is indeed a great and undeserved privilege to address such an audience as I see before me. At no previous time in the history of human civilization have greater problems confronted and challenged the ingenuity of man's intellect than now. Let us look around us. What do we see on the horizon? What forces are at work? Whither are we drifting? Under what mist of clouds does the future stand obscured?

My friends, casting aside the raiment of all human speech, the crucial test for the solution of all these intricate problems to which I have just alluded is the sheer and forceful application of those immutable laws which down the corridor of Time have always guided the hand of man, groping, as it were, for some faint beacon light for his hopes and aspirations. Without these great vital principles we are but puppets responding to whim and fancy, failing entirely to grasp the hidden meaning of it all. We must readdress ourselves to these questions which press for answer and solution. The issues cannot be avoided. There they stand. It is upon you, and you, and yet even upon me, that the yoke of responsibility falls.

What, then, is our duty? Shall we continue to drift? No! With all the emphasis of my being I hurl back the message No! Drifting must stop. We must press onward and upward toward the ultimate goal to which all must aspire.

But I cannot conclude my remarks, dear friends, without touching briefly upon a subject which I know is steeped in your very consciousness. I refer to the spirit which gleams from the eyes of a newborn babe, that animates the toiling masses, that sways all the hosts of humanity past and present. Without this energizing principle all commerce, trade, and industry are hushed and will perish from this earth as surely as the crimson sunset follows the golden sunshine.

Mark you, I do not seek to unduly alarm or distress the mothers, fathers, sons, and daughters gathered before me in this vast assemblage, but I would indeed be recreant to a high resolve which I made as a youth if I did not at this time and in this place, and with the full realizing sense of responsibility which I assume, publicly declare and affirm my dedication and my consecration to the eternal principles and receipts of simple, ordinary, commonplace *justice*.

If you didn't get much out of this speech, even after careful rereading, you did not miss anything. To borrow the old wisecrack, there is less here than meets the eye. The speech is, in fact, a blast of hot air. The speaker's only discernible point is that he is in favor of justice, which is not surprising, since everybody is in favor of justice, just as everybody is opposed to sin.

But the speech as a whole isn't about justice. It isn't really about anything. It opens (paragraph 1, sentence 2) with a platitude, a statement of the obvious expressed in worn-out language. Then it asks a series of questions to which we might reasonably expect to get the answers before the speaker finishes. We never get them. Nor do we ever find out what is meant, in paragraph 2, by "all these intricate problems," "those immutable laws," "these great vital principles," "these questions which press for answer and solution," "the issues." "We" (who?)

are said to be "drifting," but we must keep working toward "the ultimate goal" (what?). A "spirit" is mentioned in paragraph 4; it is also an "energizing principle." But again — to what does the speaker refer?

The speech, looked at in this critical way, consists of five paragraphs of high-sounding but empty language. The unwary might jump to the conclusion that the speaker is a deep thinker, uttering undying truths. Actually, the speech is like a child's soap bubble. It has pretty colors, for the moment; its words ("mist of clouds," "faint beacon light," "the spirit which gleams from the eyes of a new-born babe," "the crimson sunset," "the golden sunshine") may please us, just because we are accustomed to react in certain ways to such language. But when we prick the bubble with our critical intelligence, its substance proves so frail that it simply vanishes.

Look at the first sentence in paragraph 2. Analyze it logically, word by word. If we take "casting aside the raiment of all human speech" at face value, or literally, we must assume that the speaker is no longer going to use "human speech." What, we may ask, does he plan to use instead? What is meant by "the crucial test for the solution of all these intricate problems" to which he says he has "just alluded"? What sort of picture does the reference to the hand of man groping for a *beacon* light evoke?

We could say much more about this pompous speech. It is filled with trite phrases ("a great and undeserved privilege," "the corridor of Time," "the yoke of responsibility," "onward and upward," "the toiling masses," "this vast assemblage"). It employs a variety of cheap oratorical tricks ("dear friends," "with all the emphasis of my being I hurl back the message No!"). It uses both short sentences (paragraph 3) and a long one (paragraph 5) to produce certain effects upon the audience. But since these opening pages are intended as a preview, and we shall go into such matters more thoroughly in the chapters to come, we shall not linger here for further analysis.

The point of the questions we have raised, however, is this: by keeping a few pertinent considerations in mind, and by taking a questioning attitude as you read, you can strip away the pretensions of such vague, seemingly "impressive" language. When you do so, you discover that the actual content of the speech — what content there is — is worthless. This book is intended to show you how you can recognize honestly used language and distinguish it from language that has the power to deceive. Critical reading involves reading and then *rereading*, digging beneath the surface, attempting to find out not only what a writer is saying but also *why* he or she is saying it, what the intent is, and what further implications the message may hold. When you can answer these questions, you will be on the way to becoming a *critical* reader as well as a fluent one.

We turn now to an excerpt from another speech, but one which uses language to convey an important message. The "philosophical habit of thought" which the speaker mentions is that critical spirit which this book can help you develop.

There is an immense and justified pride in what our colleges have done. At the same time there is a growing uneasiness about their product. The young men and women who carry away our degrees are a very attractive lot—in looks, in bodily fitness, in kindliness, energy, courage, and buoyancy. But what of their intellectual equipment? That too is in some ways admirable . . . Yet the uneasiness persists. When it becomes articulate, it takes the form of wishes that these attractive young products of ours had more intellectual depth and force, more at-homeness in the world of ideas, more of the firm, clear, quiet thoughtfulness that is so potent and so needed a guard against besetting humbug and quackery. The complaint commonly resolves itself into a bill of three particulars. First, granting that our graduates know a good deal, their knowledge lies about in fragments and never gets welded together into the stuff of a tempered and mobile mind. Secondly, our university graduates have been so busy boring holes for themselves, acquiring special knowledge and skills, that in later life they have astonishingly little in common in the way of ideas, standards, or principles. Thirdly, it is alleged that the past two decades have revealed a singular want of clarity about the great ends of living, attachment to which gives significance and direction to a life. Here are three grave charges against . . . education, and I want to discuss them briefly. My argument will be simple, perhaps too simple. What I shall contend is that there is a great deal of truth in each of them, and that the remedy for each is the same. It is larger infusion of the philosophic habit of mind.

Our initial reading of the opening of this speech suggests that it has substantial content. It makes important points and conveys ideas that listeners have every reason to consider carefully. Unlike our experience with the first effusion, a careful rereading confirms our first impression. The author states the problem as he sees it clearly and succinctly, summing it up in three charges brought against college education. He then presents his solution to the problem, a "larger infusion of the philosophic habit of mind." If we turned to the rest of his remarks, we would find "philosophic habit of mind" examined in detail. The message presented in the opening withstands the test of our critical intelligence.

At this point you may be somewhat alarmed by the implications of what we have said so far. "Must I read everything critically and carefully?" you ask. The answer is "Yes." For the time being, in order to sharpen your ability to detect deviousness or emptiness in language and to appreciate their opposite, you should read carefully, questioning and challenging each statement and analyzing what is being said. Only such practice in criticism and analysis can train you to recognize the pitfalls that await superficial, hasty readers: not only the too-easy acceptance of anything in print, but the deliberate tricks of the manipulator of language.

We do not mean to say, however, that you will have to pore laboriously over every text for the rest of your life. After all, you will be reading for many reasons and hence in different ways. You will probably not give the same careful attention to reading a grocery list or a television listing that you will to a major political address or to a contract you must sign. There is no reason why you should. But if you develop now the habit of critical reading, of watching for certain devices of style and logic as clues to the true meaning of what you read and hear, the lesson will remain with you. Such skills will give you control over the material you read and, in fact, may turn out to be the most valuable benefit you receive from your formal education. Critical reading can permanently improve the workings of your mind.

The advice and practice offered here are of more immediate value as well, for careless reading frustrates the entire aim of college education. Consider how many of your courses presuppose the ability not merely to read but also to read with accuracy, comprehension, and discrimination. In how many courses would your performance not be improved if you could do a better job of reading your textbooks and library assignments? What this book teaches can be applied in almost every course you take. Thus the time spent now in improving your skill in critical reading will be repaid many times over.

Most college students have already had some practice in intensive reading, even though they may not have known it at the time. Mortimer Adler, in *How to Read a Book*, says,

> If we consider men and women generally, and apart from their professions or occupations, there is only one situation I can think of in which they almost pull themselves up by their bootstraps, making an effort to read better than they usually do. When they are in love and are reading a love letter, they read for all they are worth. They read every word three ways; they read between the lines and in the margins; they read the whole in terms of the parts, and each part in terms of the whole; they grow sensitive to context and ambiguity, to insinuation and implication; they perceive the color of words, the odor of phrases, and the weight of sentences. They may even take the punctuation into account. Then, if never before or after, they read.

The necessity for careful reading is not limited to affairs of the heart or to the completion of college assignments. Uncritical reading habits cost us money. When we read an advertisement in a magazine or newspaper, we are being influenced to buy something. The art of writing advertising copy for both the print and electronic media is based wholly upon the skillful use of language especially chosen to flatter us, to whet our interest, to entice us to buy. How often do we buy a product on the strength of the advertiser's persuasive language when we should have bought another brand that is both cheaper and better? We are prone to forget that the product most attractively packaged in words may well be inferior to other brands. If you question these judgments, spend a half-hour sometime with the current report of one of the consumers' research organizations, which rank various brands on the basis of laboratory and field tests.

The skillful use of language for commercial purposes is peculiarly a phenomenon of the modern age. But virtually as old as society is the use of language to affect the destiny of nations. The English critic and teacher F. L. Lucas has written,

> No doubt strong silent men, speaking only in gruff monosyllables, may despise "mere words." . . . [But] consider the amazing power of mere words. Adolf Hitler was a bad artist, bad statesman, bad general, and bad man. But largely because he could tune his rant, with psychological nicety, to the exact wave length of his audiences and make millions quarrelsome-drunk all at the same time by his command of windy nonsense, skilled statesmen, soldiers, scientists were blown away like chaff, and he came near to rule the world. If Sir Winston Churchill had been a mere speechifier, we might well have lost the war; yet his speeches did quite a lot to win it.
>
> No man was less of a literary aesthete than Benjamin Franklin; yet this tallow-chandler's son, who changed world history, regarded as "a principal means of my advancement" that pungent style which he acquired partly by working in youth over old *Spectators;* but mainly by being Benjamin Franklin. The squinting demagogue, John Wilkes, as ugly as his many sins, had yet a tongue so winning that he asked only half an hour's start (to counteract his face) against any rival for a woman's favor. . . . Cleopatra, that ensnarer of world conquerors, owed less to the shape of her nose than to the charm of her tongue. Shakespeare himself has often poor plots and thin ideas; even his mastery of character has been questioned; what does remain unchallenged is his verbal magic. Men are often taken, like rabbits, by the ears. And though the tongue has no bones, it can sometimes break millions of them.

The capacity of words to stir people to fateful decisions was never stronger or more crucial than it is in our own day. As citizens in the nuclear age whose very lives are at the mercy of world events, we witness and react to the daily occurrences in the world that promise to determine our future. These events are reported and "interpreted" to us by the powerful mass media—big-circulation newspapers and magazines, radio and television, and to some extent, popular paperback books. It is a commonplace to say that we live in the "information society," and in certain respects we are better informed about current events and issues than were preceding generations. The speed, efficiency, and resourcefulness of contemporary communications systems are to be welcomed, not deplored. But one very disturbing, indeed alarming, accompaniment to the rise of mass-consumption journalism, whether printed or electronic, has been the decreasing opportunity to hear and respectfully consider dissenting or minority opinions.

Not too many decades ago, for instance, people living in large towns were informed by a number of independent local newspapers, uttering diverse opinions on the various local, national, and international matters which affected them. But by 1970, fewer than seventy of the 1,500 largest American cities and towns had competing newspapers. Today, that number has fallen to fifty-five or less. In most big cities, the newspapers are under one ownership. This decline in the number of competing newspapers inevitably has resulted in a decrease of vigorous editorial discussion, and the lack has not been filled by radio or television, notwithstanding the latter's frequently effective and visually dramatic presentation of current problems and issues. The same economic "facts of life" which continue to shrink the number of daily newspapers place similar restrictions on the number of weekly and monthly magazines which ideally could provide a wide marketplace for the exchange and evaluation of conflicting viewpoints.

The vast opinion-molding agencies are in the hands of relatively few owners and editors—and of the advertisers who supply most of the profit margin. As a result, millions of people who depend on them for the knowledge and opinions they acquire are the losers. They are encouraged to adopt ready-made but possibly mistaken opinions, to form oversimplified ideas about complex issues, to think in terms of misleading words and images instead of accurate ones, and in other ways to substitute conditioned reaction for independent thought. As unwitting participants in the phenomenon that has been called "mass think," they are constantly tempted to cease being individuals intent upon analyzing every issue for themselves on the basis of sound and adequate information. Instead, they submit to the dictates of the unreasoning "mass mind." Equipped with these false or misleading ideas alone, they mark their ballots, confide their off-the-cuff views to inquiring pollsters, and write letters to their public officials, thus helping directly or indirectly to affect the nation's—and in some measure the world's—destiny.

Every mature man and woman has the urgent obligation to resist the easy temptation to fall automatically into step with the mass of people. An unfailing mark of truly educated people is their insistence on weighing all aspects of an issue, on avoiding oversimplification and unwarranted generalization, on applying the tools of critical analysis to the materials presented to them. Their responsibility as citizens and members of society, in short, obligates them to be critical readers and thinkers.

In recent years, conflict among nations has become increasingly ideological. Most battles are fought at conference tables and, more important in the long run, in the various organs of propaganda and discussion which influence the minds of people. The ammunition now is such emotive, easily manipulated words and phrases as *aggression, provocation, mutual security, national interest, third world, peace loving, nuclear deterrent, balance of power, neutralist, intervention, containment, self-defense capability.* The word *democracy* has been bandied about by proponents of communist, fascist, and nontotalitarian societies until it has come to mean merely what each user wants it to mean. Obviously the term as used in the name of the German Democratic Republic (East Germany) or as implied in the People's Republic of China does not contain the same idea it possesses when applied to the North American and western European systems of government. Multiply such instances of ambiguous word use in thousands of speeches, pronouncements, broadcasts, and editorials—and you see quickly enough why the state of the world today demands close and critical reading. Language is the key to the ceaseless battle for people's minds.

In addition to helping you apply your native intelligence in such diverse roles as purchaser of consumer goods and responsible citizen, this book is designed to increase your understanding and enjoyment of good reading. Whether it is a fictional piece in *Esquire* or the *New Yorker*, a travel article in *Gourmet*, a complex report in *Scientific American*, a best-selling novel, or a supposedly hard-to-crack "classic," everything you read with close attention to substance and to implication will prove to have more in it than you would earlier have suspected. And the writer's purposes will be more evident. Although this book is not directly concerned with the reading of imaginative literature or the development of individual literary taste (a long, continuous process which requires sustained and discriminate reading), it will point out some of the elements of style, organization, and logic that always distinguish good writing from poor. By the time you reach the end of this book, you should be more impatient with careless, hack writing, produced for people who read with their mental eyes shut. In addition, you should have a more acute sense of what genuinely good writing is.

At present you are probably still reading material which for the most part has been written especially for you. Writers of popular literature — fiction and non-fiction — assume that the great reading public is made up of persons who want to be amused and instructed without effort or obligation. What they write must be aimed at the "average" person; it must contain few unfamiliar words, few allusions to anything not learned in high school, few ideas which require deep thought. You could go through life quite easily reading nothing beyond this wide but still very limited area of material. But you would sacrifice acquaintance with the great writers of the past whose pertinence is still felt today. They have written for their intellectual equals, in language as complex as the expression of their ideas requires. Seldom have they "written down" to reach a mass audience. They have rightly supposed that, if they reached those of superior education, they would have achieved success enough for their purposes. This is also true of many of today's most respected thinkers. They too refuse to make concessions, to put complex ideas into oversimple language. To them this sort of dilution is a form of intellectual dishonesty. Thus we must rise to meet them, recognizing that critical reading is not a passive activity. On the contrary, a truly critical reader is an active and involved participant. Writers set down the words and ideas, but it is readers who realize those ideas, test them, and put them to use in their lives. The purpose of this book is to offer some guidelines for becoming a more active, demanding, critical reader.

Now, a final word before we get down to specifics. If the following pages have the effect upon you that they are meant to have, somewhere before the middle of the book you will become worried because you no longer believe most of what you read. Wherever you turn you will be noticing the sly misuse of language or logic — sometimes both. This will be a matter not for concern but for congratulation, because it will mean that you have begun to cultivate the "philosophic habit of mind" that the second speaker recommended. You will have lost your faith in many false gods which you may have unknowingly served at the cost of true understanding. The question mark will loom larger in your mind than it ever has before.

At such a point, you will be halfway through the process of becoming an intelligent reader—the half in which the thought-inhibiting clutter of old lazy habits is swept away. The other, constructive half will see you establishing positive critical standards by which you can detect what is good, credible, and sincere in what people write and say. This new but wiser faith may come slowly, but it will come if you allow it to do so. No one need be, or should be, a mere cynic who maintains that all words are meant to deceive. But to recognize the true, you must first be able to recognize the false. In the end, as Thomas Carlyle once put it, you "will understand that destruction of old forms is not destruction of everlasting substances; that Scepticism, as sorrowful and hateful as we see it, is not an end but a beginning."

1

DENOTATION AND CONNOTATION

Incidents like this happen every day: a teacher in a college English course has returned a student essay on a poem. One sentence in the essay reads, "Like all of Keats's best work, the 'Ode to Autumn' has a sensual quality that makes it especially appealing to me." The instructor has underscored the word *sensual* and in the margin has written "Accurate?" or "Diction?" or perhaps "right word?" The student has checked the dictionary and comes back puzzled. "I don't see what you mean," she says. "The dictionary says *sensual* means 'of or pertaining to the senses or physical sensation. And that's just what I wanted to say. Keats's poem is filled with words and images that suggest physical sensation."

"Yes," replies the instructor, "that's what the word means — according to the dictionary." And then, taking a copy of the *American Heritage Dictionary*, the teacher turns to the word *sensual* and points to a passage just after the definition and forms of the word:

Synonyms: *sensuous, sensual, luxurious, voluptuous, sybaritic, epicurean.* These adjectives refer to satisfaction of the senses. *Sensuous* can refer to any of the senses but more often applies to those involved in aesthetic enjoyment of art, music, nature, and the like. *Sensual* specifically applies to gratification of the physical senses, particularly those associated with sexual pleasure. *Luxurious* in this comparison is applicable to gratification of physical comfort, aesthetic fulfillment, or sense of extreme well-being. *Voluptuous* refers principally to satisfaction of physical senses and stresses indulgence in pleasure. *Sybaritic* suggests devotion to pleasure and luxury even more strongly. *Epicurean* stresses gratification of a taste for good food and drink.

1

The student reads the passage carefully and sees that the word *sensual* carries with it a shade of meaning, an association with sexual pleasure, that she did not intend. The word she wanted was *sensuous*. This student has just had a lesson in the dangers of taking dictionary definitions uncritically. And she has recognized the vital difference between connotation and denotation.

The difference between these terms is briefly stated in small-print paragraphs of explanation such as this, taken from another dictionary:

> *Denote* implies all that strictly belongs to the definition of the word, *connote* all of the ideas that are suggested by the term; thus, "home" *denotes* the place where one lives with one's family, but it usually *connotes* comfort, intimacy, and privacy. The same implications distinguish *denotation* and *connotation*.

The denotation of a word is its dictionary definition. According to the dictionary, *sensuous* and *sensual* have the same general denotation: they agree in meaning "experience through the senses." Yet they suggest different things. And that difference in suggestion constitutes a difference in connotation.

As another example, take the word *tabloid*, which refers by denotation to small size. For that reason, newspapers such as the *National Enquirer*, with pages half as large as regular newspaper pages, are regularly called tabloids. But the average tabloid newspaper emphasizes the racy and the bizarre in its attempts to appeal to readers. As a result, the word's connotation introduces the idea of sensationalism. Thus *tabloid*, not surprisingly, is often applied to newspapers in a negative sense. In the same way, many words take on additional meanings from common experience and usage. The term *chauvinism* refers, strictly speaking, to extreme devotion to one's country. By what process has it come to be applied to a certain kind of person, with no reference to national pride?

Good critical readers are sensitive to connotation. Only when we possess such sensitivity can we understand both what writers mean, which may be quite plain, and what they want to suggest, which may actually be far more important than surface meaning. The difference between reading an essay for immediate, literal meaning and reading it for suggested meaning is the difference between listening to the latest electronic music on a beat-up old transistor radio and listening to it on a sophisticated quadraphonic system. You may recognize the basic tones on the old radio, but only the full system brings out special shades of sound that are important to appreciation of the music.

Being aware of the connotative power of words is also vital to writers. Their task is to select the words which will create the exact effects they are after. Practiced writers, like practiced readers, know that although many words may have almost the same denotation, few have exactly the same connotation. Inexperienced writers, forgetting this, often go to a book like Roget's original *Thesaurus*, where they find whole sets of synonyms. Such books can be helpful only if the writer already knows the shades of meaning which differentiate each word in a set from all the others. If you want to refer to the familiar expressions of wisdom in the Bible, for example, you might think of "old sayings." The *Thesaurus* lists these synonyms for *saying: maxim, aphorism, dictum, proverb, epigram, saw*, and *motto*. But if you choose *saw* or *epigram*, you choose the wrong word, because neither of these words is a suitable label for biblical quotations. (Can you explain why?) The way to avoid picking the wrong word from a list is to refer to those paragraphs in the dictionary that describe the connotative differences among words in a closely related group. (If the definition of the word you are looking for is not followed by such a paragraph, look for a cross-reference to the place where the differentiation is made. The *American Heritage Dictionary* entry for *denote* refers readers to the entry for *mean* for a discussion of synonyms.) If you need more help, consult the fuller discussions, including examples from good writers, in *Webster's New Dictionary of Synonyms* or S. I. Hayakawa's *Modern Guide to Synonyms and Related Words*. Avoid cheap pocket and desk dictionaries in any work involving word choice. These are often misleading because they oversimplify entries that are already simplified, even in the larger, more reliable dictionaries.

We do not mean that the good reader or writer must take up every single word he or she proposes to use and examine it for implied or subsurface meanings. Many words—such as *and, but, that*, or *where*—have no connotative powers at all. They are used to connect other words or to show some relationship between them. Still other words, such as scientific or technical terms, have few connotations and do not call forth vivid pictures or emotional responses. *Psychomotor* and *pulmonary* are neutral words in this sense; so are *acetylsalicylic acid* (aspirin) and *crustacean* (shellfish). The single word *genetics* is a neutral term compared with the words for some of its concerns: *cloning, human engineering, biological warfare*. Still, most words have some connotation, however limited. Even neutral technical words take on more and more connotation, especially when they affect our everyday lives: *dyslexia, chemotherapy, anorexia nervosa, nuclear reactor*, or *meltdown*.

(Exercises: pages 31–33)

CONNOTATIONS: PERSONAL AND GENERAL

Connotations may be either personal or general. Personal connotations result from individual experience. How we react to ideas and things, and to the words that refer to them (which is why the ideas and things are often called *referents*), is determined by all our personal associations with those ideas or things. Taken together, the connotations that surround most words in our vocabularies make up a complex and intimate record of our lives. Our reactions to a word may be the combined result of all our experiences with the word and its referent. In the case of another word, our reactions may have been formed once and for all by an early memorable experience with it.

Your reaction to the word *teacher*, for instance, may be determined by all your experiences with teachers, which have merged in the course of time into a single image or emotional response. The single image includes memories of the first-grade teacher who dried your tears after a hard fall; of the sixth-grade teacher who bored pupils with repeated stories of a trip to Mexico many years earlier; of the high-school gym teacher who merely laughed at the angry red brush burns left by your inexpert slide down a rope; of the college professor who packed mountains of information into lectures that seemed too entertaining to be instructive. On the other hand, when you think of *teacher*, you may think of one particular teacher who made an especially deep impression — perhaps the chemistry teacher in high school who encouraged you, by example and advice, to make chemistry your life's work.

A moment's thought will show the relationship between personal and general connotations as well as make clear the fact that no firm line divides the two types. General connotations result when the great majority of people react to a specific word in substantially the same way. The reasons one word should have a certain connotation, whereas another word has a quite different connotation, are complex. We shall spend a little time on that subject later. At this point we will say only that differences in general connotation have at least two major causes. For one thing, a single writer or book may have great influence over our language and over the exact shade of meaning words may have. The King James version of the Bible, for instance, is responsible for many connotations. People first came to know a given word from its occurrence in certain passages in the Bible. Thus the word came to connote to them on all occasions what it connoted in those biblical passages, and the word was permanently colored by particular associations. Such words include *trespass*, *money changers*, *manger*, *Samaritan* (originally the name of a person living in a certain region of Asia Minor), *salvation*, *vanity*, *righteous*, *anoint*, and *charity*. The same is true of many words used in other widely read works, such as Shakespeare's plays, which influenced the vocabularies of following generations. We can easily think of recent examples: Alex Haley's use of *roots* and the *Star Wars Saga*'s use of the *Force* both exemplify the way in which popular current works can subtly change the connotations of words.

But general connotation is not always a matter of literary or artistic development. It can result also from the experience a social group has with the ideas the words represent. The word *defoliation* carried only neutral descriptive connotation until recently. The *Oxford English Dictionary* defines it as "loss or shedding of leaves." The Vietnam war, however, brought television images of "defoliated" wastelands, dead landscapes brought about by devastating chemical warfare. The *American Heritage Dictionary* now notes the chemical sprays we associate with the war in its discussion of the word *defoliation*. *Additive* is another word whose inoffensive connotations have recently changed. Studies linking chemical additives and preservatives with diseases in animals led to growing negative connotations. Now many packaged foods proclaim "No Additives" and use the positive phrase "All Natural" to reinforce this claim.

All general connotations grow out of private connotations—personal, individual, but generally shared reactions to words and the ideas they are linked to. But later, after general connotations have been established, the process works the other way: the individual, who may have had no personal experience with the idea represented by a given word, may acquire a personal attitude toward the idea by observing how society in general reacts to the word. Men and women not yet born when Winston Churchill was delivering his famous Second World War speeches in Britain, when Adolf Hitler was presiding over mass killings of the Jews, or when Franklin D. Roosevelt was broadcasting his "fireside chats" probably will continue to react to the connotations evoked by their names. In addition, some words pass into and then out of connotative "atmospheres." The word *quisling* probably means nothing to students today. Yet not very long ago *quisling* was synonymous with *traitor*, in reference to Vidkun Quisling, head of the State Council of Norway during the German occupation of 1940–1945, who served as a puppet (what does the word connote?) of the enemy forces.

Writers must always remember the distinction between general connotations and personal ones. The general ones—those which readers probably share—do the main work of conveying an accurate message. Writers who use words that have private connotations run the risk of writing in a private shorthand or language no one else will understand. Since no clear line divides general and personal connotations, it is unrealistic to require writers to confine themselves completely to general connotations. But in most forms of everyday communication, writers are well advised to use words whose connotations are approximately the same to most readers.

(Exercises: pages 33–35)

THE USES OF CONNOTATIONS

What forms do our reactions to words take? As we have observed, not all words evoke any clear emotional response; *delusion* and *illusion*, for instance, probably do not do so for most people. Here the response is largely an intellectual one: the two words are customarily used in different contexts and imply slightly different things.

But the most important words are often those which appeal to the emotions, words which stir people to strong (but not always rational) judgment and may arouse them to action. Mention of *militarist* or *atheist* or *capitalist* or *socialist* or *fundamentalist* can evoke deep-seated prejudice, either for or against the ideas or beliefs behind the words or the people who are called by those names. Until 1945, the word *nuclear* was a purely technical term in physics. Today, *nuclear* carries a variety of connotations—on the one hand, of global war and ultimate destruction, and on the other hand, of a certain measure of hope for human progress through medical applications and increased sources of energy.

Many words lose much of their clear connotation, and in some instances much of their evocative power, through indiscriminate application. The word *guru* has been so overused that now it covers nearly any form of popular leader. The term today has only vague and sometimes negative connotations instead of the much stronger and positive associations with highly respected Hindu spiritual teachers. In the same way, *programmed* seems to be losing its once powerful associations with computer technology. Today, washing machines, weed eaters, and fountain pens are all "programmed" to perform efficiently. One cosmetics chain even offers "programmed" skin-care advice. The related term *programming*, frequently used to mean *brainwashing*, and its counterpart *deprogramming* also reflect the shift in associations. Three decades ago *space age*, which became current when the Russians orbited their first sputnik, called up thoughts of man's most awesome achievements. But within a decade of its introduction, *space age* was being applied to everything from athletic equipment to stereo systems. The inevitable result: the initial power of the phrase was entirely lost. *Space age* became merely another too-handy, threadbare word in the vocabulary of advertising and journalism. The word *holocaust* is currently in danger of much the same fate. Before the Second World War, its regular meaning was "wholesale devastation by fire," including loss of life. But later, that meaning was overshadowed by the term's association with Jewish genocide. Now the powerful connotations surrounding *holocaust* are being weakened by using the word to refer to almost any kind of fatal event.

Often the connotative power of a word is dependent on circumstances: who uses it, who is intended to read or hear it, and where. The connotations associated with *women's liberation* can be positive or negative depending on the speaker's intention. *Designer fashions* means one thing to New York socialites and another to a family ordering clothes from a mail-order catalogue. *Conservationist* carries very different connotations to a member of the National Wildlife Federation and to the president of a big logging and lumber operation. *Social assistance, aid to the needy, welfare, handout,* and *the dole* mean basically the same thing, but one or two have more unpleasant connotations than the others. Who is likely to use which term, and why?

Intimately associated with emotional response are the images that many words inspire in our minds. The most common type of image is the visual: that is, a certain word habitually calls forth a certain picture. Mention of places we have seen and people we have known produces a visual memory of them. Of course the kind of experience we had with the original persons or places determines the exact content of these "pictures." *Mary* may recall not the picture of a childhood sweetheart but a picture of a pink ribbon Mary must have once worn in her hair. *Los Angeles* may recall only the picture of an automobile accident, if that is the most vivid memory carried away from that city. Examining these mental images spontaneously conjured up by words is a fascinating game. Equally rewarding is the attempt to explain why many words evoke images which on first thought seem so completely irrelevant to their denotations.

Not only words referring to concrete objects have this power of evoking imaginative responses. Our picture-making faculty also enables us to see abstractions in concrete terms — and it sometimes gets us into trouble on that account. Abstractions often mean little unless we can anchor them in mental images. But we must take care not to allow abstractions, once visualized, to become distorted by preconceptions or ingrained prejudices. *Dictator* denotes a person who has absolute authority in any state; it does not necessarily mean a tyrannical megalomaniac. But the most memorable dictators of recent history — Mussolini, Hitler, Perón, Idi Amin — have also been egotists and demagogues. And so our understanding of the abstract word *dictator* is colored by a composite picture: we perhaps envision a strutting, ranting military figure, mesmerizing a crowd with emotional appeals to national pride and hatred of enemies. The truth is that most dictators, such as Spain's General Franco, have been far less colorful than those previously mentioned. And in any case, personal flamboyance is not nearly as significant as a dictator's substantive actions. Our mental image of the dictator, then, is composed of what really amounts only to irrelevant window dressing. The word *dictator* serves to pull out many emotional stops in our minds; and emotion clouds any reasonable response we might be able to make to the idea. Therein lies the danger of connotation.

As a further example, consider the following passage, which includes a telling description of the power of connotation. Asked how he pictured a *dropout*, an executive who has worked hard to find jobs for teenagers said, "When I hear the word *dropout*, I have this image in my mind of a kid sitting across from me in the subway car: he's smoking a cigarette; he has a radio the size of a grand piano, and he keeps turning up the volume; his legs are stretched out so nobody can pass; he is staring at me with a look I can only describe as hate. I know that's not fair or accurate because I've hired many of them. Still, I can't help thinking of that kid in the subway." As the executive notes, such an image obviously is not fair. It is a stereotype, a stock response built up in our minds by many books, movies, and television shows. Stereotypes that often rule our ideas about gender, nationality, race, party, profession — in fact, all kinds of groups — and our attitudes toward them grow out of similar materials. We shall meet stereotypes again on page 18.

In addition to visual responses in the imagination, words evoke responses associated with the other senses. Many words have connotations that appeal most directly to our inward ear: *tick-tock, boogie, slap, whir, squeak, splash, trumpet, shrill, thunder, shriek, boom*. Others appeal to our sense of touch: *greasy, gritty, woolly, slick, silky, spongy, velvet, ice-cold, scalding, hairy, furry*. Another class invites responses involving taste: *peppery, creamy, mellow, sugary, olive oil, menthol, salty, bitter*. Another brings the sense of smell into play, as in *burning rubber, incense, new-mown grass, pine forest, rancid, coffee roaster, ammonia, stench, diesel fumes, coal smoke*. Many words, of course, appeal to two or more senses at once: in addition to some of the above (which ones?) there are, for instance, *dry, effervescent, satin, lather, plastic, mossy, winy, slimy, wrinkle, sewage, frothy, sea breeze, misty*.

Because our sensory experiences may be either pleasant or unpleasant, the words that remind us of those experiences have the power to make us accept or reject an idea. "Now, one of nature's richest treasures . . . Aloe Vera, is revealed in our shampoo and conditioner. For cleaner, fuller, more manageable hair that shines like the desert sun. It's beauty pure and simple." So writes the advertiser who wants us to buy a brand of shampoo, and the advertiser is clearly counting on the fact that we will have pleasant associations with "nature's richest treasures," "desert sun," and "beauty."

In some of the following pages, we shall concentrate on this persuasive power of words, especially in advertising and political discussion. There is perhaps no simpler or better way of showing how connotation works. But this preliminary emphasis on the ways language may be used for selfish purposes must not lead us to believe that all, or even most, writers have wicked designs on their readers. On the contrary, the greater part of what people read has the primary goal of informing or entertaining them. And here connotation heightens the effectiveness, the accuracy, and the vividness of the writer's communication. But whether the goal is to sell a car or to explain the principles of DNA, a writer's tools are words. Those words, with their denotative and connotative meanings, provide the basis on which we decide to accept — or to reject — the message.

Take the best of today's journalism — not routine newspaper reporting but, say, feature stories and magazine articles. Really good descriptive journalism requires a high degree of skill in the use of words; and the more skillfully and attentively we read, the greater will be our reward. The following paragraph introduces readers to a government-supported work program. (We have italicized words that help to build up the central impression.)

It is a *frigid* February morning, and the Wildcat Skills Training Center, on West Thirty-seventh Street, is *locked*. The members of the class known as basic typing 27, or BT-27, who attend the training center for seven months and work at an actual job site for the remainder of the one-year program, are part of a five-year nationwide experiment that is known as supported work. The Wildcat Service Corporation, like other nonprofit corporations set up to manage supported-work programs around the country, attempts to reach members of the American underclass and *bring them back* into the mainstream of society and the world of work. This experiment was supervised by the Manpower Demonstration Research Corporation, of Manhattan, which received much of its funding from the federal government and from foundations. Today, the members of BT-27 congregate in the lobby of the training center and *complain* about the previous Friday, when the building was so *cold*—despite the presence of three portable heaters—that they *walked out* in midafternoon. Wildcat officials told them they would be *docked* a day's pay. Now, on top of this *threat*, they can't get into the classrooms they are paid to learn in. The *threat* of lost pay, the *cold* classrooms, the *waiting around* for the center to open—all fuel the sense of *exploitation* they have had, in *prison* or on *welfare* or in their dealings with the "helping professions" that often *dominate* their lives and contribute to this sense of *victimization*.

Here, in carefully chosen everyday words, the writer has produced an impression of frustration. He is clearly troubled by what he sees at the Center, and he means us to feel troubled too. If we read on past the opening paragraph, we would find that the words *frigid, locked*, and *threat* are all part of his master plan, for the entire article builds on the conflicts caused by the sense of hopelessness that pervades the atmosphere at the Center.

In the same way, poets also use the connotative potentialities of language. They employ words lovingly, wishing to delight and move the reader by imparting their own vivid experience:

> You take my hand and
> I'm suddenly in a bad movie,
> it goes on and on and
> why am I fascinated
>
> We waltz in slow motion
> through an air stale with aphorisms
> we meet behind endless potted palms
> you climb through the wrong windows
>
> Other people are leaving
> but I always stay till the end
> I paid my money, I
> want to see what happens.
>
> In chance bathtubs I have to
> peel you off me
> in the form of smoke and melted
> celluloid
>
>   Have to face it I'm
> finally an addict,
> the smell of popcorn and worn plush
> lingers for weeks

Or

> I have known the inexorable sadness of pencils,
> Neat in their boxes, dolor of pad and paper-weight,
> All the misery of manila folders and mucilage,
> Desolation in immaculate public places,
> Lonely reception room, lavatory, switchboard,
> The unalterable pathos of basin and pitcher,
> Ritual of multigraph, paper-clip, comma,

Endless duplication of lives and objects.
And I have seen dust from the walls of institutions,
Finer than flour, alive, more dangerous than silica,
Sift, almost invisible, through long afternoons of tedium,
Dropping a fine film on nails and delicate eyebrows,
Glazing the pale hair, the duplicate grey standard faces.

CONNOTATIONS IN ADVERTISING

If advertising copywriters were less skillful masters of word connotations, we should spend far less money than we do on the products they recommend. They know how to create pleasant pictures that make us long for what we lack — and all without our being aware of it. They also have a formidable list of taboos — words which must never be mentioned because they have negative connotations of one sort or another. In recommending a product because (they say) it doesn't cost very much, they never use the word *cheap: cheap* connotes shoddiness as well as stinginess. And so they appeal to our sense of thrift, a respected virtue in a society that is trying to learn that less can sometimes be best. A large-size package is always the *budget economy size* — "You save when you buy it!" *Fat* is never used except in reducing-course ads; one could never sell clothes by calling people fat. Instead, there are clothes for the *larger figure*. In the same way, *old* is carefully avoided in favor of *mature* or *senior*.

One copywriter has identified two particular kinds of "weasel words" used in advertising. The word *help*, he says, is a weasel word that "means things it really doesn't mean." It actually means *"aid* or *assist.* Nothing more. Yet, *help* is the single word which ... has done the most to say something that couldn't be said.... *Helps* keep you young. *Helps* prevent cavities. *Helps* keep your house germ free.... And the most fascinating part of it is, you are immune to the word. You don't hear the word *help*. You only hear what comes after it." This writer goes on to say that the second kind of weasel words most often used in advertising are words that have no specific meaning. All cereals, he says, "have one thing in common: they're all *fortified....* Fortified means *added on to*. But *fortified*, like so many other weasel words of indefinite meaning, simply doesn't tell us enough. If, for instance, a cereal were to contain one unit of vitamin D, and the manufacturers added some chemical which would produce two units of vitamin D, they could then claim that the cereal was *fortified with twice as much vitamin D*. So what? It would still be about as nutritious as sawdust."

You can easily find out how advertising language works: a half-hour with one or two current magazines, keeping in mind the powers of connotation, will supply many examples of the way products are always presented in the best light. Here are a few instances chosen at random. In parentheses are inserted alternative words which the writer of each advertisement could have considered. Which of the words do you think the writer actually chose, and for what reasons?

1. Cheese (supplements, adds, throws in) a slice of life. Slice of (zesty, tasty, piquant, tangy) Cheddar or mozzarella. Or the (smooth, bland, mellow, flavorful) goodness of American, Monterey Jack, or Gouda. And you'll add (energetic, lively, gay, brisk, spirited) flavor to sandwiches, salads, snacks. Your store is (advertising, pushing, highlighting, featuring) your favorite cheeses today. So stock up and enjoy a (delectable, scrumptious, sumptuous, palatable, splendid, delicious) slice of life!

2. No one has been able to (duplicate, equal, match, replicate, imitate, copy) our (atypical, uncommon, unusual, one-of-a-kind, unique*) (look, appearance, style, image). Our women's shoes are (manufactured, fabricated, built, made, benchcrafted) by (clever, skilled, cunning, adroit, ingenious, nimble) hands. They aren't rolled off the assembly line. They never will be.

3. Each fine (pen, writing instrument, stylograph, writing tool) is a mastery of (elementary, effortless, simple, facile, delicate, easy) balance and unique (plan, design, contrivance, arrangement)—a (distinctive, well-defined, clear-cut, particular, definite) gift or (beloved, cherished, adored, prized, revered) personal possession. Each piece or set is (nicely, attractively, handsomely, luxuriously, pleasingly) gift-boxed. Write for a full-color (pamphlet, brochure, booklet, flyer).

The precise words a copywriter chooses depend to a great extent on the audience to whom the message is addressed. Confronted with several choices, all of which are generally pleasing, the writer selects the one most likely to appeal to a particular group of people. Thus an ad intended for the widely diversified audience of the *Reader's Digest* uses words whose connotations have the widest acceptance; but one for *Scientific American,* let us say, or *Field and Stream* or *Gourmet* may use a completely different set of words. We shall have more to say later about this matter of writing for a specific audience.

All this is very interesting; but is it important? The answer is a decided "Yes." How often do we buy something on the strength of words, rather than on the actual merits of the product? Perhaps we really do not need it, but the magic words of the advertiser (*luxurious . . . elegant . . . money-saving . . . figure-flattering . . . rare*) have tempted us so much that we buy it. Or perhaps we do need it; but why buy Brand A instead of Brand B? Perhaps Brand A's advertising writer did a better job with words (*not a hotel, a resort . . . first-class, south-of-the-border taste . . . a world-class gift . . . a lot more than you expect a compact car to be . . .*). But how much that is really worth knowing have we learned from Brand A's advertisements? Or has the writer been playing on our weak spots—our vanity, our envy, our fear of not being in style, our desire for greater personal beauty

---

*Are these words, in fact, synonyms of *unique*? See a dictionary.

or more leisure or more friends? We can find out very easily if we analyze the advertiser's words for their connotative overtones.

(Exercises: pages 36–39)

CONNOTATIONS IN POLITICAL PERSUASION

Now consider the reader not as a consumer, a buyer of goods temptingly advertised in magazines and on television, but as a citizen of a free society, whose personal opinions, when joined with those of millions of other citizens, constitute public opinion. Every day, representative men and women are interviewed for public opinion polls. They are asked what they think about a current issue. Where and how do they get their opinions?

Public opinion is formed wherever and whenever one person expresses views on a topic to others. Unless the hearers or readers have already made up their minds and see no reason to change, they will be influenced by what they are told. Thus, where before there was only one person who believed such and such, now there are several. And as in advertising, in persuasion designed to make someone think a certain way about an issue, the emotion-producing powers of words are a potent force for good or evil. Used in one way, they are a means of spreading and intensifying the basest sort of prejudice and bigotry; used in another, they are a means of stirring the human spirit to heights of courage and nobility. The Old Testament prophets' denunciations of godlessness and idolatry, Pericles' funeral oration, Milton's *Areopagitica*, Wordsworth's "Milton! thou shouldst be living at this hour," Emily Dickinson's poems on the nature of friendship, Robert Frost's "The Gift Outright," Martin Luther King's "I Have a Dream," Doris Lessing's *Notebooks*, Maya Angelou's *I Know Why the Caged Bird Sings*—all are, in one way or another, pieces of persuasion or inspiration. They are designed primarily to stir people to serious thought or to constructive action by appealing to their loftiest emotions, emotions of compassion, honor, fairness, or courage.

But much emotive language operates on a considerably lower level, appealing to intolerance, vanity, desire for status, suspicion of the new or different, jealousy, or fear. All of us, whether we admit it or not, are prejudiced. We dislike certain people, certain activities, certain ideas—in many cases, not because we have reasoned things out and found a logical basis for our dislike, but rather because those people or activities or ideas affect our less generous instincts. Of course we also have positive prejudices, by which we approve of people or things—perhaps because they give us pleasure or perhaps because we have always been taught that they are "good" and never stopped to reason why. In either case, these biases, irrational and unfair though they may be, are aroused by words, principally by name-calling and the use of the glittering generality. Both of these techniques depend on the process of association, by which an idea (the specific person, group, proposal, or situation being discussed) takes on emotional coloration from the language employed.

Name-calling is the device of arousing an unfavorable response by such an association. A speaker or writer who wishes to sway an audience against a person, group, or principle will often use this device.

> The bleeding-heart liberals are responsible for the current economic crisis.
> The labor union radicals keep honest people from honest work.
> Environmental extremists can bankrupt hard-pressed companies with their fanatical demands for unnecessary and expensive pollution controls such as chimney-scrubbers.

Name-calling is found in many arguments in which emotion plays a major role. It rarely is part of the logic of an argument but instead is directed at personalities. Note how the speakers here depend on verbal rock throwing in their attempt to win the day:

> He's no coach, but a foul-mouthed, cigar-chomping bully who bribes high-school stars to play for him.
> The Bible-thumping bigots who want to censor our books and our television shows represent the worst of the anti-intellectual lunatic fringe.
> Mayor Leech has sold the city out to vested interests and syndicates of racketeers.
> City Hall stinks of graft and payola.

The negative emotional associations of the "loaded" words in these sentences have the planned effect of spilling over onto, and hiding, the real points at issue, which demand — but fail to receive — fair, analytical, objective judgment. Generating a thick emotional haze is, therefore, an effective way for glib writers and speakers to convince many of the unthinking or the credulous among their audience.

The *glittering generality* involves the equally illogical use of connotative words. In contrast to name-calling, the glittering generality draws on traditionally positive associations. Here, as in name-calling, the trouble is that the words used have been applied too freely and thus are easily misapplied. Many writers and speakers take advantage of the glitter of these words to blind readers to real issues at hand. *Patriot, freedom, democracy, national honor, Constitution, God-given rights, peace, liberty, property rights, international cooperation, brotherhood, equal opportunity, prosperity, decent standard of living:* words or phrases like these sound pleasant to the listener's ear, but they can also divert attention from the ideas the speaker is discussing, ideas which are usually too complex to be fairly labeled by a single word.

> The progressive, forward-looking liberal party will make certain that we enjoy a stable and healthy economy.
> The practical idealists of the labor movement are united in supporting the right of every person to earn an honest living.
> Dedicated environmentalists perform an indispensable patriotic service for us all by keeping air-polluting industries' feet to the fire.

He's a coach who is a shining light to our youth. He believes that football helps to build the character, stamina, and discipline needed for the leaders of tomorrow.

The decent, God-fearing people who want to protect us from the violence and depravity depicted in books and on television represent the best of a moral society.

Mayor Leech has stood for progress, leadership, and vision at a time when most cities have fallen into the hands of the corrupt political hacks.

These two categories in no way exhaust the methods by which words can be used to condemn or endorse without reference to proof. You will be able to find many pieces of persuasion in which there is not a single example of name-calling or one glittering generality. These devices have been singled out for notice at this point because they are very common and because their unfairness is so easily seen. (Several more devices will be discussed and illustrated in Chapter 5.)

The irrationality of the use of such words and the injustices and harm that result from it can be illustrated by a brief analysis of the actual process:

THE SPEAKER: "X [a university student, a government official, a writer, a college professor, an artist, a scientist, a television performer] is a radical and a troublemaker."

THE EVIDENCE: None. As a matter of fact, X, although a member of an antinuclear group, has never been involved in violent demonstrations or trouble of any kind.

PERSON IN THE CROWD: "I don't like radicals. You say this bum is a radical troublemaker? All right, throw him in jail . . . get rid of him!"

What are the principal errors here? One is that the speaker calls X a radical troublemaker without producing any evidence to support the accusation; a second is that the listener translates "radical troublemaker" into "criminal"—a very common habit, because people love to simplify, to distort, and to exaggerate; a third is that the listener reacts promptly and vehemently to a phrase, without stopping to ask by what right the speaker uses it. What does *radical* mean to the listener? Plainly it has some strong and unpleasant connotation. But if asked to explain why the word touches off such a disagreeable reaction, the listener might have only the vaguest idea of what *radical* represents. This person belongs to the large group of people who react to words rather than to the ideas behind them. If proof is needed, just stop twenty people at random in, say, a shopping center and ask them to define *radical* (or any other political term that arouses strong feelings) and then to explain why they feel as they do about what the word supposedly means.

As thoughtful persons, we are horrified that so many are ready, even eager, to condemn an individual or party or philosophy on the strength of a word alone, without knowing what it means, or with only the faintest idea of its meaning, or with a positively wrong idea of its meaning. And just as dangerous to the successful operation of a democratic society is the willingness to accept an unsupported accusation. The listener quoted above may have substantial reasons for hating radicals; he may be able to list, on request, a large number of sound arguments against radicalism. Yet if he censures a person on someone's mere say-so, he is as unthinking and unjust as the people who admit they don't know exactly what *radical* means but still have an opinion to offer.

Not only in politics, however, but in every sphere of life — campus, factory, home, office — we run across such groundless denunciations and irrational responses. To paste a ready-made label on a bottle is far easier than going to the trouble of analyzing its contents.

Try the same analytic procedure with the second device, the glittering generality:

THE CANDIDATE: "We must protect our nation's greatest asset—a dynamic economy."

FIRST LISTENER (a machine operator): "Right! Dynamic economy—high wages, more fringe benefits, cost-of-living increases, labor unions protected by law, equal chance to get ahead. . . . I'll vote for that candidate!"

SECOND LISTENER (owner of a factory): "My sentiments exactly! Dynamic economy—government keeps its hands off business, gives us tax breaks, keeps unions off our backs. With brains and aggressiveness, I can make a million dollars and it'll be my own. . . . I'll vote for that candidate!"

Who is going to be disappointed after the candidate takes office and begins making decisions on specific issues? The elected official cannot serve two masters (at least not at the same time and certainly never to the complete satisfaction of both); yet both people voted for the candidate who favored what they favored — or so the vague phrase about a "dynamic economy" seemed to promise. The words are bound to please all people as long as they remain undefined and vague. The simple test to apply to every such word or phrase is this: What, in particular, concrete terms, does it mean to the person who utters it? Is the idea as beautiful in application as it looks on paper or sounds from the campaign platform? Would we agree with the sentiment if we knew the specific things the speaker proposed to do? The danger in all such easygoing use of language is lack of definition, which allows the emotions and prejudices free play. Wrenched loose from what it "stands for" — its strict dictionary definition — or from specific applications, a word can be used as inaccurately as the speaker chooses. Imagine the effect a single vocal, alert critic would produce by interrupting such a speaker with the question "Would you care to define 'dynamic economy' for us?"

The point is well made in the following excerpt from a talk by Alistair Cooke entitled "Justice Holmes and the Doffed Bikini":

One day last summer a young woman sunning on a public beach decided to take off her bikini and lie naked on the sand. Pretty soon the families lolling nearby came awake. Husbands began to dive for their cameras and in no time wives were diving for their husbands.

One husband, at the instigation of his wife, called the police. The young woman was arrested and last week she appeared before a judge.

That's all. Or that would have been all a few years ago. But the young woman was furious over her arrest. She is a product of the 1970's. She is therefore not a law-breaker but an evangelist. She maintained, as a daring and original proposition, that the naked human body is decent and that she was causing no harm, only going about her decent business of sunning in the nude. . . .

The word "decent" is another victim of the habit, common both to politicians and to their enemies, of using noble or impressive words not for thinking with but for raising, like those boards they hold up before television audiences, as invitations to applaud. Vice President Spiro Agnew simply proclaims that something is indecent, and the cheers ring out on the Right. A girl takes her clothes off and says the human body is decent, and there is an ovation from the Left. The word "decent" means "becoming," and the question surely is: becoming to whom and in what place? It was Bernard Shaw, I think, who defined evil as "matter out of place."

Twenty years ago, United States Representative Morris K. Udall of Arizona prepared (but did not mail — why?) a reply to constituents who wrote to complain about "federal spending." The complaints depended, wrote Udall, on what each person meant by the term, on the context in which it was used, and, of course, on *where* the federal money would be spent.

If, when you say "federal spending," you mean the billions of dollars wasted on outmoded naval shipyards and surplus airbases in Georgia, Texas and New York; if you mean the billions of dollars lavished at Cape Kennedy and Houston on a "moondoggle" our nation cannot afford; if, sir, you mean the $2 billion wasted each year in wheat and corn price supports which rob Midwestern farmers of their freedoms and saddle taxpayers with outrageous costs of storage in already bulging warehouses; if you mean the $4 billion spent every year to operate veterans hospitals in other states in order to provide 20 million able-bodied veterans with care for civilian illness; if you mean such social-istic and pork-barrel projects as urban renewal, public housing and TVA which cynically seek votes while robbing our taxpayers and weakening the moral fiber of millions of citizens in our Eastern states; if you mean the bloated federal aid to education schemes calculated to press federal educational controls down upon every student in this nation; if you mean the $2 billion misused annually by our Public Health Service and National Institutes of Health on activities designed to prostitute the medical profession and foist socialized medicine on every American; if, sir, you mean all these ill-advised, unnecessary federal activities which have destroyed states' rights, created a vast, ever-growing, empire-building bureaucracy regimenting a once free people by the illusory bait of cradle-to-grave security, and which indeed have taken us so far down the road to socialism that it may be, even at this hour, too late to retreat—then I am unyielding, bitter, and four square in my opposition, regardless of the personal or political consequences.

But, on the other hand, if when you say "federal spending" you mean those funds which maintain Davis-Monthan Air Force Base, Fort Huachuca and other Arizona defense installations so vital to our nation's security, and which every year pour hundreds of millions of dollars into our state's economy; if you mean the Truman-Eisenhower-Kennedy-Johnson mutual security program which bolsters our allies along the periphery of the Iron Curtain, enabling them to resist the diabolical onslaught of a Godless Communism and maintain their independence; if you mean those funds to send our brave astronauts voyaging, even as Columbus, into the unknown, in order to guarantee that no aggressor will ever threaten these great United States by nuclear blackmail from outer space; if you mean those sound farm programs which insure our hardy Arizona cotton farmers a fair price for their fiber, protect the sanctity of the family farm, ensure reasonable prices for consumers, and put to work for all the people of the world the miracle of American agricultural abundance; if you mean those VA programs which pay pensions to our brave soldiers crippled in mortal combat and discharge our debt of honor to their widows and orphans and which provide employment for thousands of Arizonans in our fine VA hospitals in Tucson, Phoenix, and Prescott; if, sir, you refer to such federal programs as the Central Arizona Reclamation project which will, while repaying 95 percent of its cost with interest, provide our resourceful people with water to insure the growth and prosperity of our state; if you mean the federal education funds which build desperately needed college classrooms and dormitories for our local universities, provide little children in our Arizona schools with hot lunches (often their only decent meal of the day), furnish vocational training for our high school youth, and pay $10 million in impact funds to relieve the hard-pressed Arizona school property taxpayers from the impossible demands created by the presence of large federal installations; if you mean the federal medical and health programs which have eradicated the curse of malaria, small-pox, scarlet fever and polio from our country, and which even now enable dedicated teams of scientists to close in mercilessly on man's age-old enemies of cancer, heart disease, muscular dystrophy, multiple sclerosis, and mental retardation that afflict our little children, senior citizens and men and women in the prime years of life; if you mean all these federal activities by which a free people in the spirit of Jefferson, Lincoln, Teddy Roosevelt, Wilson and FDR, through a fair and progressive income tax, preserve domestic tranquillity and promote the general welfare while preserving all our cherished freedoms and our self-reliant national character, then I shall support them with all the vigor at my command.

Quite obviously, the connotations of a simple two-word phrase such as *federal spending* vary with its application.

When a word refers to a large concept or group of people (as is often the case with name-calling and the glittering generality), it can be used with equal effectiveness to condemn or to praise, depending on the writer's purpose. *Computer technology* is a typical dual-purpose term. Those who fear that computers will replace people and thus increase unemployment use the term to arouse a negative reaction based on its association with mechanical, "nonhuman" elements. Other writers, however, might use *computer technology* to evoke the favorable connotations associated with efficient modern businesspeople who have the good of both employees and public at heart. Again, what is *labor:* a clique of racketeering union bosses, with criminal convictions in their past and no doubt also in their future, or honest and intelligent leaders who are devoted to the welfare of the rank and file? Or what is the *civil service:* a large group of efficient government employees, dedicated to the ideals of a democratic society, or a mass of overpaid incompetents who do a minimum of work for a maximum of benefits, including short work weeks and luxurious pensions?

Such omnibus words are by no means useless. On the contrary, they are indispensable, because otherwise we could not talk about large entities such as parties, religions, institutions, philosophies. But the duty of intelligent people is plain and urgent: we must not allow our minds to become cluttered with stereotypes— mental images of certain groups that are based on oversimplification, misunderstanding, or handed-down prejudices. These stereotypes inhibit true understanding and clear reason when we are called on to form opinions. Furthermore, they can lead to the intolerance and irrational bias which trouble much of modern society. By keeping aware of the process by which an inoffensive-looking word can touch off illogical prejudice, we can help prevent the spread of ignorance and bigotry.

Persuasive writing cannot do without these special effects of words, but critical readers can learn to know when they are used fairly. Look, for instance, at the preceding paragraph, which is intended to persuade you to be alert to the uses of connotation we have discussed. Our words *intelligent people, cluttered, handed-down prejudices, stereotypes, modern society, ignorance,* and *bigotry* all carry strong connotative appeals. But have we been unfair in our use of them? This question cannot be answered simply by noting that they have emotional connotations. You must rather ask yourself whether we have earned the right to use these connotations, whether they are justified by our entire analysis of words thus far.

(Exercises: pages 40–42)

CONNOTATIONS IN LITERATURE

When we turn from these aspects of practical persuasion to imaginative writing — poetry, drama, fiction, factual descriptive or narrative pieces — our duty as intelligent readers is different. Here the writer usually has no ax to grind, no product to sell, no vote to win, no policy to put over. A literary text is indeed persuasive insofar as it brings us to experience a scene, a character, or a pure emotion as fully as we possibly can; it invites us to take part in a vivid experience, the essence of which is the transmutation of actual life into an imaginative adventure. A writer may wish to present a person or event with as much clarity and "truth" as possible or to create a certain attitude toward life, death, or courage. Whatever the writer's precise intention as an observer and interpreter of life, one of his chief ways to make us see and hear and think and feel is the skillful use of word connotations. And now, instead of being alert to deceptive or oversimplified uses of language, we must become receptive to its subtleties and complexities, using the words the author wrote to re-create the meaning of the work within ourselves.

Much of the pleasure of reading poetry is due to the manner in which the poet is able to fill the reader's mind with a rapid series of impressions, which the poet may select and control in order to produce a single powerful effect. In "Dolor," quoted on pages 9–10, Theodore Roethke seeks to produce a single impression of sorrow, and he does so by the careful selection of words which connote that feeling. Sometimes a poet relies on the connotative quality of words to transport the reader from the world of actuality into a realm of pure imagination, a land of enchantment created solely by language. (At this point, don't concern yourself with the poem's meaning. Simply examine the author's use of richly connotative words.)

Now as I was young and easy under the apple boughs
About the lilting house and happy as the grass was green,
    The night above the dingle starry,
        Time let me hail and climb
    Golden in the heydays of his eyes,
And honoured among wagons I was prince of the apple towns
And once below a time I lordly had the trees and leaves
        Trail with daisies and barley
    Down the rivers of the windfall light.

And as I was green and carefree, famous among the barns
About the happy yard and singing as the farm was home,
    In the sun that is young once only,
        Time let me play and be
    Golden in the mercy of his means,
And green and golden I was huntsman and herdsman, the calves
Sang to my horn, the foxes on the hills barked clear and cold,
        And the sabbath rang slowly
    In the pebbles of the holy streams.

All the sun long it was running, it was lovely, the hay
Fields high as the house, the tunes from the chimneys, it was air
    And playing, lovely and watery
        And fire green as grass.
    And nightly under the simple stars
As I rode to sleep the owls were bearing the farm away,
All the moon long I heard, blessed among stables, the nightjars
    Flying with the ricks, and the horses
        Flashing into the dark.

And then to awake, and the farm, like a wanderer white
With the dew, come back, the cock on his shoulder: it was all
    Shining, it was Adam and maiden,
        The sky gathered again
    And the sun grew round that very day.
So it must have been after the birth of the simple light
In the first, spinning place, the spellbound horses walking warm
    Out of the whinnying green stables
        On to the fields of praise.

And honoured among foxes and pheasants by the gay house
Under the new made clouds and happy as the heart was long,
    In the sun born over and over,
        I ran my heedless ways,
        My wishes raced through the house high hay
And nothing I cared, at my sky blue trades, that time allows
In all his tuneful turning so few and such morning songs
    Before the children green and golden
        Follow him out of grace.

Nothing I cared, in the lamb white days, that time would take me
Up to the swallow thronged loft by the shadow of my hand,
    In the moon that is always rising,
        Nor that riding to sleep
    I should hear him fly with the high fields
And wake to the farm forever fled from the childless land.
Oh as I was young and easy in the mercy of his means,
        Time held me green and dying
    Though I sang in my chains like the sea.

Often a single line or two may contain a wealth of suggestiveness. To those living with the constant threat of global destruction, T. S. Eliot's lines

        This is the way the world ends
        This is the way the world ends
        This is the way the world ends
        Not with a bang but a whimper

evoke emotions implicit in a society plagued by anxiety and a sense of meaninglessness. Take a minute to study the way in which the connotations of the separate words in the following lines merge to produce a simple but powerful emotional effect:

> Your low voice tells how bells of singing gold
> Would sound through twilight over silent water.

Of course, not only poets make literary use of word connotations. The writer of imaginative prose uses them just as often, and for the same reasons. Here is a brief excerpt from the prologue to June Goodfield's book on scientific discovery, *An Imagined World*, in which the writer, by presenting a succession of connotative images, evokes the flavor of the day-to-day work of a scientist:

You want to know what science is? I will tell you. I'll tell you what I did today. After getting in through a corridor of smells, I got myself a little corkboard and the cages of mice. Cages and cages of mice were injected, controls and all; the injected ones with one shot on Sunday. I handled surgical instruments, petri dishes, sterile bottles of medium, sterile bottles of lymph-node cell suspensions. And this is what science is made of.

Oh, it is fine, the great idea, and the best of creative activity, but the day-by-day brickwork is mouse bites which sometimes draw blood; mouse stinks (atoms may not stink, but mice do); the irritating noise of the deep freeze that has gone wrong; sterile bottles, millions of them, washed and autoclaved by the washing-up ladies. Petri dishes, hypodermics, pipettes, packed in some dull chain manipulated by people I do not know; sterile syringes made in some anonymous mass-production system, by people who are not told what the hell I'm going to do with them! They—the technicians, the photographers, and Mrs. Wiggins who washes up our glassware. She looks over sixty and looks as though she has always looked over sixty. She makes up the fantastic infrastructure that we take for granted, that makes it all possible and easy for me.

Without this infrastructure these days there is very little a scientist can do. And if your book manages to tell people just that, to me that is enough. If the man or the woman in the chain who cleans the floor, or who packs the syringe or the needle, hears from your book that by the time it got into the dustbin in this disposable era, their effort wasn't altogether a waste, then your book is worth writing.

The importance of connotation in imaginative literature may be illustrated by a paraphrase of a lyric by Shelley. Note that the paraphrase closely reproduces the denotations contained in the original. But the emotional qualities, supplied by words of rich and powerful associations, have completely evaporated. What is left is a dull, drab string of words.

(a)	(b)
My soul is an enchanted Boat,	My inner self resembles a marine craft under a spell,
Which, like a sleeping swan, doth float	Which like a dormant member of the subfamily Cygninae of ducks, is suspended
Upon the silver waves of thy sweet singing;	On the light-reflecting grayish undulations of your agreeable vocalism;
And thine doth like an angel sit	And yours is seated like a supernatural being
Beside the helm conducting it,	Next to the steering apparatus guiding it,
Whilst all the winds with melody are ringing.	While all the air currents reverberate with a pleasant succession of sounds.
It seems to float ever, for ever,	It appears to remain permanently, yes permanently, on the surface,
Upon that many-winding river,	On that circuitous water-filled channel,
Between mountains, woods, abysses,	Between rocky elevations, dense arboreal growths, precipitous gaps,
A Paradise of wilderness!	A euphoria-producing but imaginary area comprising uncultivated tracts!
Till, like one in slumber bound,	Until, like a hypnotized individual,
Borne to the ocean, I float, down, around,	Transported to a large body of saline H_2O, I proceed, simultaneously dropping and spinning,
Into a sea profound, of ever-spreading sound.	Into (metaphorically speaking) an aqueous region of considerable depth, made up of interminably diffusing auditory sensations.

The pale, labored, and sterile paraphrase is exaggerated, but not much. The reason for its failure is simple: although the poet has used word connotation with utmost skill, the writer of the paraphrase, though preserving the right denotation, has drained off the suggestive power inherent in the original language.

Preserving denotation is a task computers are now equal to. The Bell Laboratories have produced a series of programs, *Workbench*, that will analyze a text for certain features and produce a revised (and supposedly improved) sample. The computer essentially "reads" the writing of scientists or businesspersons and suggests ways to make their prose more clear. Recently, *Discover* magazine asked *Workbench* to analyze and revise some imaginative prose, including the opening of Charles Dickens's *Tale of Two Cities:*

> It was the best of times, it was the worst of times, it was the age of wisdom, it was the age of foolishness, it was the epoch of belief, it was the epoch of incredulity, it was the season of Light, it was the season of Darkness, it was the spring of hope, it was the winter of despair, we had everything before us, we had nothing before us, we were all going direct to Heaven, we were all going direct the other way—in short, the period was so far like the present period, that some of its noisiest authorities insisted on its being received, for good or for evil, in the superlative degree of comparison only.

Here is what the computer had to say about Dickens's prose:

Workbench Analysis

Readability: 46.1. A very high (i.e., poor) score for this type of document. Good training materials average close to the tenth grade level, even though the audience has more education than that.

Revised Version

The times were the best and worst, wise and foolish. The era was one of belief and disbelief, light and darkness, hope and despair. Before us lay everything and nothing. We were all going direct to heaven or straight to hell. The period was so much like today that its loudest critics could describe it only in superlatives.

In the revision, which essentially tightens up the prose, the computer has done a very good job of retaining denotative meaning. But the connotative power of much of the passage, to say nothing of the rhythm, is lost.

(Exercises: pages 42–45)

HOW CONNOTATION CHANGES

One of the chief difficulties in reading literature written a hundred or more years ago is that we encounter words which, although still in daily use, look strange or inappropriate as they are used by their authors. For example, the diary-keeper Samuel Pepys, writing in 1660, described the execution of a leader of the Puritan rebellion of 1649. "I went out to Charing Cross," Pepys writes, "to see Major-general Harrison hanged, drawn, and quartered; which was done there, he looking as cheerful as any man could do in that condition." Immediately we stop short at the word *cheerful*. Is it likely that a man who was in the process of being hanged, drawn, and quartered would be "cheerful"? Obviously Pepys meant nothing of the sort. In his day, *cheerful* meant something unlike what it connotes today. To him it suggested "tranquil," "calm," "resigned," not "full of good spirits," "happy," or "optimistic." Such instances can be multiplied without end. We encounter them on every page of Shakespeare, Milton, Pope, Johnson, Wordsworth, or Ruskin. Consider the lines in which Wordsworth is praising his wife for her many virtues:

> A creature not too bright or good
> For human nature's daily food;
> For transient sorrows, simple wiles,
> Praise, blame, love, kisses, tears, and smiles.
>
> And now I see with eye serene
> The very pulse of the machine.

The word *machine* jolts nearly every reader who comes to it; what business has such a word, with its suggestion of steel and gears and motors, in such a poem? What has machinery to do with Mary Wordsworth? The answer is that to Wordsworth and his contemporaries *machine* had a much more general meaning. The line might be paraphrased, "The very pulse (or heart) of her intricate being." The word *engine*, incidentally, causes similar trouble to modern readers who run across it in older literature. What does "two-handed engine" mean in Milton's "Lycidas" (line 130) or "the fatal engine" in Pope's "The Rape of the Lock" (Canto III, line 149)? With poetry this problem of "dated" meanings is intensified by the fact that many poets have used what in their time was already archaic or outdated language, because they considered it more picturesque or connotative. Thus the phrase "the meanest flower that blows" (Wordsworth's "Ode: Intimations of Immortality," line 202) does not, as a reader might think, refer to a "most bad-tempered flower that is blown by the wind" or (if one remembers *Moby-Dick*) spouts like a whale. The flower is simply the "humblest" one that "blooms."

Connotations are in a constant state of flux. In this respect, the writings of our own contemporaries will be as troublesome to readers a century or two from now as the older English classics sometimes are to us. We have already seen the reasons words acquire certain agreed-upon connotations: the practice of the most influential authors and the attitude of society toward the ideas which certain words have come to represent. But these general connotations are by no means permanently established. After all, few writers remain influential indefinitely, and all social attitudes undergo some change. Although the usage of Addison and Steele, influential eighteenth-century essayists, stabilized many connotations in their own day, the time came when other writers had more influence. And thus, very gradually, Addison and Steele's use of words began to seem old-fashioned.

The effect of social attitudes on connotations is well illustrated by the history of *Roman Catholic*. This term was brought into use when the older words used to refer to members of that faith (*Romanist, Roman,* and *Papist*) had acquired such negative associations that a substitute was needed, one which lacked the bad connotations the other words held in Protestant England. The subsequent career of *Roman Catholic* is, in effect, a history of shifting winds of feeling. In England it eventually lost the stigma it acquired as a substitute for *Papist*. But wherever there is anti-Catholic feeling, the term retains its negative connotations. The histories of such words as *Methodist* and *Quaker* offer similar illustrations of the evolution of social feelings.

Thus a word with an established denotation can acquire a new connotation which in time becomes as well established as the denotation itself. If we begin to use the word only in the sense implied by this new connotation, the original denotation may be forgotten, and the dominant connotation becomes the new denotation. In brief, change of connotation, if carried far enough, results in change of actual denotative meaning. Since no sharp line divides denotation and connotation, just when a change in connotation has such an effect is impossible to say. But it has happened to thousands upon thousands of words, whose meanings have been completely altered by a series of shifts in connotation. These changed meanings, of course, introduce further difficulties in the reading of older literature. Take as an example of both types of change the opening sentences of Bacon's essay "Of Studies" (1597):

> Studies serve for delight, for ornament, and for ability. Their chief use for delight is in privateness and retiring; for ornament, is in discourse; and for ability, is in the judgment and disposition of business. For expert men can execute, and perhaps judge of particulars, one by one; but the general counsels, and the plots and marshalling of affairs come best from those that are learned. To spend too much time in studies is sloth; to use them too much for ornament is affectation; to make judgment wholly by their rules is the humour of a scholar.

Readers can grasp the general sense at first reading, but only because enough of the words Bacon uses retain the denotations they had in his day to give us clues. Yet no one will say that this is modern English, or even close to it. What if we are asked to rewrite the passage and to take out every trace of its late sixteenth-century origin? *Delight* is too strong a word for this context; we might use *pleasure* instead. *Ornament* is no longer used in Bacon's sense of "social advantage"; *ability* stands for our modern "practical profit" or "usefulness." *Privateness* has gone almost completely out of use; taken together with *retiring* (people of Bacon's day liked to couple two virtually synonymous words) it means "our personal, or home, life." *Expert* to Bacon suggested "accomplished, competent" in general; in our time its use is restricted to "special skill in certain particular areas." And so on. Scarcely a noun of Bacon's could be retained if the passage were to be made intelligible to, let us say, a prospective student in a correspondence course.

We can see that connotations keep changing if we note the considerable alteration some words have undergone in the last hundred years. In the vocabulary of the nineteenth-century Victorians, who laid great stress on moral uprightness, there was no stronger word of praise than *manly*, applied to a man's character or actions or to the spirit that pervaded a book he had written. *Manly* connoted courage, frankness, modesty, seriousness, control of feelings — all the qualities the Victorians admired in a Christian gentleman. But partly because the word was grossly overused, and partly because a later age, more aware that women also can possess such virtues, has not wholeheartedly accepted the Victorians' standards, *manly* today is seldom used.

Another instance of fairly recent semantic change is *lover*. For centuries this word had, in ordinary usage, simply the meaning of "sweetheart." Now, however, it carries the connotation of sexual relations; one cannot refer to another as "lover" without suggesting more than one may intend! A closely analogous fate has befallen the verb phrase *to make love*. Until recently, it was wholly innocent of the specific meaning it now carries. *Mistress*, too, has undergone a radical shift of meaning. The sense in which it occurs in older love poems ("O mistress mine, where are you roaming?") has largely disappeared from present-day usage, and another, largely derogatory, meaning has taken over.

Saloon has had a curious career in North America. Originally the common word for a drinking establishment was *tavern*, but eventually this acquired an unsavory connotation, so *saloon* was imported from England where it had a genteel flavor, suggesting an elegantly furnished room where people met for social converse. In time, however, *saloon* came to have connotations at least as disagreeable as *tavern*, a process assisted by the formation of the much-publicized Anti-Saloon League. Thus, when prohibition was repealed in 1933 and drinking places became legal again, the industry had to find various words with respectable connotations to substitute for *saloon*. Ironically, one of the choices was *tavern*, which by this time had had a long rest and had been cleansed of its former associations.

Recognizing shifts of connotation as we read calls for constant care, but the result is worth the effort. We instinctively fear the strange and the seemingly forbidding, as we may fear an austere-looking new instructor on the first day of classes. But as acquaintance increases and strangeness wears off, we cease to dread and instead look forward to conversation. So too with writing from previous centuries. If we approach it with patience and understanding, we can unlock the mysteries of the long-dead author's prose. How can you improve your ability to read material written in previous centuries? First, refuse to be frightened by it. And second, read more of it. If a child has much contact with a very old great-grandparent who uses English words in ways that were proper two or three generations ago, the child will gradually acquire a "feeling" for such usages, and they will seem entirely natural. Likewise, an adult who reads more widely in older literature than is customary nowadays will gradually acquire a similar feeling. Vocabulary habits will accommodate themselves to those of Shakespeare or Milton; such frequently used words as *humor* will no longer cause puzzlement by the oddness of their use. The reader will begin to think comfortably in the language of the author.

Because he made such highly individual and inventive use of the English language, Shakespeare is harder to read than some of his contemporaries. Today, therefore, his plays are nearly always read in annotated editions, with the troublesome words or phrases explained in footnotes. But except in textbooks, most of the other great authors of the past must be read without such easily available help. Really inquisitive readers can turn to the *Oxford English Dictionary*, an immense encyclopedia of the history of English words. The *OED*, as it is usually called, lists and gives examples of all the meanings a word has had throughout its history. Your education won't be complete until you have traced the history of a few selected words in the pages of the *OED*.

(Exercises: pages 45–48)

THE IMPORTANCE OF CONTEXT

The pages to follow have been anticipated by the preceding discussion and by the earlier demonstration of how the purpose or use of a word can determine which particular one to choose from a group of synonyms. Thus we had brief glimpses of the usefulness of *context*, which means the portions of a sentence or passage that precede and follow a particular word or phrase.* These portions not only have their own meanings, but by their proximity to the word in question they necessarily somewhat modify its meaning and on occasion actually determine it.

Many English words have two or more distinct meanings, and context is often the only way to learn which one is intended:

"She's mad."
"What's she mad about?"
"She's mad—locked up in a padded cell."
"Oh! *That* 'mad.'"

Note these variant uses of the same words:

The King *executed* his opponents.
He *executed* the *dive* with masterly precision.
The police raided the *dive*.

In each case, the immediate context determines the denotation of the italicized word. Though the middle sentence shares one word with each of the other sentences, in that one sentence *execute* and *dive* have meanings appropriate to it and not to the others. Similarly, the meaning of *fix* in the footnote below is only one of a dozen meanings that word possesses, depending on where it is found. (How many others can you think of?)

---

*Context also has a broader meaning: the sentences that precede and follow a particular sentence in a paragraph, or the whole tendency of thought in a passage, which can help fix the meaning of an individual statement.

The extract from Bacon's essay on page 25 illustrates how context can help us interpret a passage of older writing. Context is equally helpful in reading modern prose and poetry. Here again the meaning of a certain word is often hinted at by the words that surround it. The momentum of the preceding thought may carry us right to the explanation we require. Or if we are still puzzled, it often pays to go past the word in question to scc what follows. Perhaps the sentences immediately following will throw light on the troublesome word's meaning.

Of course, this method of trying to guess the meanings of words is not foolproof. Mere guessing can lead readers far astray. Therefore, a dictionary should always be kept close at hand to help resolve difficulties. Under the word in question are often found a number of definitions. The trick is to select from the list the meaning which best fits the context. Often it may be difficult to decide which of two or three meanings, each apparently fitting the context, the author meant. Readers should then return to the context, rereading the whole passage more carefully, until they can reject certain definitions as not being precisely what the author meant and emerge with the one meaning which in their judgment adequately conveys the author's intention.

Here is part of the conclusion of Loren Eiseley's "The Creature from the Marsh":

I had spent so many years analyzing the bones of past ages or brooding over lizard tracks turned to stone in remote epochs that I had never contemplated this possibility before. The thing was alive and it was human. I looked uneasily about before settling down into the mud once more. One could make out that the prints were big but what drew my fascinated eye from the first was the nature of the second toe. It was longer than the big toe, and as I crawled excitedly back and forth between the two wet prints in the open mud, I saw that there was a remaining hint of prehensile flexibility about them.

Most decidedly, as a means of ground locomotion this foot was transitional and imperfect. Its loose, splayed aspect suggested inadequate protection against sprains. The second toe was unnecessarily long for life on the ground, although the little toe was already approximating the rudimentary condition so characteristic of modern man. Could it be that I was dealing with an unreported living fossil, an archaic ancestral survival? What else could be walking the mangrove jungle with a foot that betrayed clearly the marks of ancient intimacy with the arboreal attic, an intimacy so long continued that now, after hundreds of thousands of years of ground life, the creature had squiggled his unnecessarily long toes about in the mud as though an opportunity to clutch at something had delighted his secret soul?

We can understand this passage at first reading. Yet a number of words are no doubt unfamilar to many readers: *prehensile, splayed, mangrove, arboreal, squig-*

gled are those which probably attract attention first. Read through the passage again, writing the definition of these five words and of any others unfamiliar to you as you understand them from the context. Then look up the words in your best dictionary, and see whether or not this additional information alters your understanding of the passage.

Here is part of an older and hence more difficult passage, taken from the conclusion of Henry James's essay on Ralph Waldo Emerson. James is commenting on a biography of Emerson written by J. E. Cabot.

> It has not, however, been the ambition of these remarks to account for everything, and I have arrived at the end without even pointing to the grounds on which Emerson justifies the honors of biography, discussion, and illustration. I have assumed his importance and continuance, and shall probably not be gainsaid by those who read him. Those who do not will hardly rub him out. Such a book as Mr. Cabot's subjects a reputation to a test—leads people to look it over and hold it up to the light, to see whether it is worth keeping in use or even putting away in a cabinet. Such a revision of Emerson has no relegating consequences. The result of it is once more the impression that he serves and will not wear out and that indeed we cannot afford to drop him. His instrument makes him precious. He did something better than anyone else; he had a particular faculty, which has not been surpassed, for speaking to the soul in a voice of direction and authority.

Again, we can understand the general sense of this passage at first reading. James is saying in effect that the test of a great man's permanent worth is whether his fame can survive a biography like Cabot's. James says that Emerson triumphantly passes the test. (The fourth and fifth sentences say as much.) But a careful reader will wish to know more. Since James presumably wrote each sentence for a particular purpose—to advance his earlier argument, to clinch a point, to prepare for a new idea—each sentence should be considered and understood. And on closer examination we find a number of words which need explanation:

Ambition: "Remarks" are not usually thought of as having ambition; normally we think only of people as having it. But the meaning is clear from context: "design," "purpose," "intention."

Illustration: Since James has already used the word in the same sense earlier in the essay, the careful reader will already have discovered its meaning: "quotation," "the selection of examples to clarify certain aspects of the subject."

Continuance: By "importance and continuance" James means "his present and future importance," or as we should say, more simply, "his continuing importance."

Gainsaid: The context suggests the idea of opposition. The conjunction *and* implies agreement or similarity between the two parts of the sentence. Therefore, the second part should be in harmony with the first. "I have thought so-and-so," says James, "*and* others will probably agree with me." *Gainsaid* is more commonly used to mean "denied" ("The assertion will not be gainsaid"). But its meaning here ("I shall probably not be opposed") is clearly similar.

Revision: This can be attacked in two ways. Here the word does not mean "change (of opinion)" or "new edition." Readers with a smattering of Latin will recognize the prefix *re* (again) and the root *vis* (seeing, looking — as in *vision, visual, visionary*). They then realize that James is using the word in its literal sense of "looking over again." And if they review the context, they will find that the preceding sentence had already explained the word.

Relegating: Latin is of some help here, but again the context is sufficient; "putting away" in the preceding sentence is the literal meaning of *relegating*. In other words, in the preceding sentence James has said in Anglo-Saxon-derived words what he now says in Latinized diction.

Serves: One definition of *serve* is "to answer a purpose." But that meaning can be inferred from the following "and will not wear out."

Instrument: This is explained by what follows. "Not *what* he said so much as *how* he said it."

By using such a combination of methods as this, you can arrive at the full meaning of a passage. Analyzing a few paragraphs, word by word, for complete meaning will impress on you the importance of each individual word in context. The best writing contains no superfluous words or sentences. Each small brick in the structure has its own special function and cannot be removed without loss.

In performing such analysis, readers who have at least a nodding acquaintance with foreign languages enjoy a marked advantage over those who have none at all, because their knowledge of root words, especially Greek and Latin, can help them over many obstacles. Moreover, they are not as easily daunted when they encounter foreign words which have been imported into our own language. One cannot go through an issue of a magazine published for a well-educated audience without finding words like *élan, charisma* (much overused lately), *Weltanschauung, raison d'être, finesse.* One unmistakable mark of an educated person is a vocabulary of foreign expressions (*manqué* and *détente*, for example) which embody meanings that cannot be expressed in single English words. (Use of foreign words where English would serve just as well is, of course, merely affectation.) And foreign words, too, can often be translated from the context: "There was a palace *coup* in the South American country, and now a military *junta* is in charge." For *coup* read "sudden (perhaps also violent) takeover" and for *junta* read "ruling council" or "ruling committee," and the sense is complete. Seen often enough and understood, such words enrich readers' vocabularies, providing them with still more words that are of constant service in both reading and writing.

Thus — to sum up the argument of this chapter — cultivating a critical attitude toward what you read and developing a clearer and more accurate prose style depend initially on how sensitive you are to the shades of meaning that determine the individuality of words. Knowing that the English vocabulary has very few strict synonyms, that words which mean roughly the same thing are actually set apart by their differences in suggestion and connotation, is the first step toward becoming a critical reader and a good writer.

EXERCISES ══════════

DENOTATION AND CONNOTATION

1.1 Explain why the italicized words in the following sentences reflect the writer's insensitivity to connotation. In each case, supply a more appropriate word.

1. We all wanted to go swimming, but Father *combated* the idea.
2. I am pleased with your *drastic* improvement in this course over the past few weeks.
3. A remake of *Gone With the Wind* can be successful only with *crafty* direction and seasoned, mature actors.
4. The young man was really very *comely*, for he had wavy hair, a great tan, and a winning smile.
5. The evangelist does not intend his crusades to make money; they are *merely* to improve the religious lives of the people.
6. Although she was well into her forties, there was a certain *childishness* in her manner which delighted everyone who met her.
7. Handle this old phonograph record with extreme care. It's very *tender*.
8. What strikes newcomers most is the absolute *smoothness* of the countryside.
9. By simplifying many daily operations, small business computers have made such transactions much less *entangled*.
10. Although it looked like a first-rate job, I decided to *spurn* the offer and look for some other position.
11. I've been taking aspirins by the carload, but they haven't *healed* my headache.
12. The judge heard the case with a good deal of *mildness*, since he was disposed to sympathize with the defendant.
13. The concert was so terrific, we all felt *gay* for several days afterward.
14. I was glad to see by his *agile* walk as he strode down the street that he was fully recovered from the accident.
15. What I *pined* for above all was a thick, juicy hamburger with plenty of onions and a side order of French fries.

1.2 Explain the differences in connotation among the members of each of the following groups of words. Then make up sentences that use the words in the groups accurately. As an alternative exercise, make up sentences in which some of the words are conspicuously *misused.*

1. corpulent, plump, obese, pudgy, heavy-set, fleshy, fat, paunchy, burly, overweight, rolypoly, bulky, portly, beefy
2. mansion, abode, dwelling, domicile, residence, house, home, habitat
3. hurl, throw, pitch, chuck, toss, fling, cast
4. friendly, open, sociable, jovial, approachable, affable, chummy, ingratiating, companionable, genial
5. arrogant, stuck-up, conceited, cocky, vain, proud, self-satisfied, egotistical, overbearing, supercilious
6. cheat, phony, con man, fraud, charlatan, operator, crook, impostor, quack, swindler
7. dislike, resent, lament, hate, scorn, disapprove, decry, deplore, oppose, regret
8. naked, nude, stripped, bare, unclothed, in the buff
9. bizarre, singular, far out, outlandish, off the wall, curious, odd, unusual, extraordinary, remarkable, noteworthy, strange, eerie
10. grasp, clutch, hold, cling, clamp, clasp, grip
11. titter, giggle, chuckle, laugh, guffaw, roar, snicker, snigger, cackle
12. saving, tight, miserly, frugal, economical, careful, penurious, thrifty, penny-pinching, budget-minded, prudent, mean
13. shrewd, calculating, clever, sly, adroit, knowing, astute, cunning, skillful, smooth, slick
14. dilapidated, ramshackle, ruinous, neglected, tumbledown, deteriorated, shabby, run down, derelict, tatty, seedy
15. honest, straight, on the level, veracious, guileless, unaffected, artless, genuine, candid, truthful, sincere
16. buff, enthusiast, amateur, fan, hobbyist, bug, connoisseur
17. pig-headed, stubborn, obdurate, adamant, stiff-necked, rigid, obstinate, unalterable, changeless, dogged, steadfast
18. sullen, taciturn, glum, withdrawn, down, silent, reticent, wordless
19. concise, pointed, laconic, terse, bare bones, economical, pithy, compressed, brief, boiled down
20. steal, purloin, pinch, rip off, filch, embezzle, burglarize, rob, hold up, snatch, grab, help oneself to, appropriate

1.3 Often two words roughly "mean" the same thing, except that one has an unfavorable, the other a favorable, connotation. Thus, although you may like to think of yourself as an *idealist*, people who do not sympathize with your attitudes might call you a *dreamer*. For the following pairs of terms, write short explanations of why you might like to be described by one term but not by the other.

slender/skinny
high-strung/freaked out
trusting/gullible
firm/stubborn
reckless/adventurous
flexible/wishy-washy
relaxed/flaked out

hypocritical/diplomatic
hard worker/workaholic
assertive/pushy
playboy/eligible bachelor
original/weird
plodding/methodical
scholar/bookworm

CONNOTATIONS: PERSONAL AND GENERAL; THE USES OF CONNOTATION

1.4   A study has shown that the following nouns and adjectives are among those most frequently used by English poets in the past five hundred years. They are part of the basic vocabulary of poetry. How many of them possess particularly strong connotations today? Why have poets made extensive use of such terms?

good, great, day, God, heart, king, life, lord, love, man, thing, time, soul, youth, long, light, spirit, cruel, dear, fair, high, old, poor, sweet, true, beauty, death, eye, fortune, gold, hand, heaven, lady, night, pain, word, world, earth, bright, dark, happy, new, rich, blood, face, fire, grace, name, nature, power, sin, son, sun, tear, year, soft, air, friend, joy, divine, proud, tender, vain, art, breast, fate, flower, head, hour, land, maid, sky, song, virtue, deep, dim, holy, child, dream, father, hope, mother, prayer, sea, star, white, black, green, bird, leaf, moon, nothing, stone, tree, water, wind

1.5   What are the present connotations of the following terms? Compare your answers with the answers of others. How can you explain the differences as well as the similarities among the responses?

welfare state, leftist, censorship, brainwashing, hippie, commune, astrology, racist, thermonuclear warfare, executive, big business, multinational, astronaut, cult, concentration camp, street person, night person, police state, law and order, conservation, defense, genocide

1.6   What is the difference in connotation between *slum* and *ghetto?* Trace the earlier history of the word *ghetto* in the *Oxford English Dictionary* and then try to account for its present application, especially in the United States. How does the term *inner city* relate to these words?

1.7 **(a)** What reaction, if any, do you have when you hear or read the name *Florrie?* Do you see any specific picture in your mind? How can you explain it? Ask yourself the same questions about the following names: *Ida Mae, Percy, Lu Ann, Bobby Joe, Evelyn, Clyde, Bertha, Clarence, Elmer, Jo-Jo, Clem, Daphne, Lance, Guinevere.*

(b) Account for the slight differences in connotation among the variants of the following common names. Compare your reactions to the reactions of others.

James, Jamie, Jimmy, Jim
Elizabeth, Beth, Liz, Lizzie, Bessie, Liza, Bess
Robert, Rob, Robbie, Bob, Bobby
Katherine, Kay, Kathy, Kate, Kitty, Kit
Edward, Eddie, Ned, Ed, Ted, Teddy
Margaret, Margie, Meg, Marge, Peggy, Peg, Maggie

1.8 Try to account for the connotative quality of the following words. Is it due to the word's sound, the picture called to mind, or both? Does the word have connotative value even though the meaning may not be precisely fixed in your own mind?

maggot, retch, funk, phlegm, miasma, raucous, gobbet, clot, bombast, reek, prestidigitator, udder, colossal, blitz, brillig, slithy, toves, mimsy

Now make up a new word (for example, *glert, manspac, parakine, stonk*), assign it a meaning, and write several sentences using it. Read the sentences aloud to others and compare the images and associations the word brings to their minds with the definition you devised.

1.9 Explain, as accurately and in as concrete detail as possible, the pictures and reactions that are evoked for you when you read each of the following terms. Try to describe the personal associations and experiences that have resulted in the word's present cluster of connotations to you.

debutante, mangled, beer, acid rain, monster, bust, slither, cram, bus depot, gurgle, sopping, cathedral, stereo, classy, hike, dawn, mess, endurance, disco, chocolate, orchid, Frisbee, tea, bleak, airport, heavenly, prima donna, emporium, wrinkled, executive suite

1.10 By virtue of your chronological age, you may be eligible to be described by a number of the following terms: *teenager, adolescent, youth, young person, juvenile, preadult, youngster, boy,* or *girl.* Or you may be eligible to be described as *mature, middle-aged, over thirty, in the prime of life.* How do you respond to these terms? In what ways do you like or dislike them? Why? What does each connote? Are there any terms you prefer to describe your age group?

As an alternate exercise, consider the term or terms you use to refer to some class of people, for example, those with high incomes. What are the connotations of the term you most frequently use for that group of people? What are some alternative terms (for example, *rich, well off, affluent, comfortably fixed, wealthy, rolling in dough, loaded*) and their connotations to you?

1.11 The following words have distinct connotations for many people. Select two or three that arouse particularly strong reactions in you and explain why each affects you as it does.

virgin	Christmas
old-timer	macho
red-neck	sophistication
cancer	puritanical
addict	punk
atheist	filth
cheater	Hiroshima
pornography	poverty

1.12 (a) Below is a sampling of cover blurbs* from some modern bestsellers. Why do you think the publisher's advertising writer chose the words he or she did in each case?

1. "An ardent young girl's thrilling struggle to win her place in the world of high finance."
2. "The best-selling novel that has become an affair of state . . . 'DEVASTATING.'"
3. "Secrets we've all kept hidden, even from ourselves—for the first time the stunning truth revealed!"
4. "A brass-knuckled thriller for those who like fast action and a surprise ending."
5. "A girl, a gun, a gunfighter . . . fast-paced action that will keep you riveted."

(b) Bring to class for analysis a similar set of blurbs collected during your inspection of the books on the display racks in a drugstore or supermarket.

(c) Choose a book or story you are familiar with and write a cover blurb for it which uses connotation to attract potential readers.

---

*Like some of the words in Exercise 1.8, *blurb* is a coinage (see a dictionary). Why do you think the man who invented it chose that particular sound?

CONNOTATIONS IN ADVERTISING

1.13 The following advertisement appeared in magazines directed toward people with higher than average incomes. From each group of alternatives, choose the word you think the copywriter actually used.

> Beauty culture is what's happening . . . at every Charles of the Ritz Beauty Salon. Because our (innovating, novelty-conscious, original, avant garde, trend setter) (experts, beauticians, technicians, hairdressers, beauty operators, glamour consultants) know beauty is the most (remarkable, notable, famous, important) fashion (implement, additive, supplement, accessory) of all. They'll (attend, attend to, take care of, dispose of, fix) you with the same (imagination, creative effort, ingenuity, cleverness, inventiveness) you'd expect of a (couturier, dressmaker, garment designer, seamstress). Your hair will be (shaped, arranged, coiffed, fashioned), not just "done."

1.14 The following are all brand names for the same kind of product. What connotative values do the names have? What might the product be?

Rave	Come Alive
Spring Feeling	Adorn
Enhance	Original Glow

1.15 After reading the following three advertisements, published in 1923, 1939, and 1982 respectively, identify the chief selling points the copywriter wishes to impress upon the reader. What are the connotative values of the words the writer uses to stress those selling points? What are the major differences between the selling points in the first advertisement and those in the second and third? Are there any words in the older advertisements that no longer have favorable connotations? Finally, how much straightforward *information* is contained in the advertisements?

1.   **Where Town and Country Meet.**

> Chevrolet enables the city housewife to buy vegetables, eggs, poultry and small fruits, direct from the farmer's wife, fresh and cheap.
>
> Each woman benefits by the exchange as the low prices paid by the city woman are much higher than the farmer can get on wholesale shipments.
>
> In like manner, Chevrolet enables the farmer's wife to buy dry goods, groceries and household appliances not available in country stores. In time and money saved and health and happiness

gained a Chevrolet more than pays for itself; therefore every family, in city or country, can afford to own one and should have it.

2.   **Here is a "Close-up" of the Style Setter for 1940.**

Presenting a totally new conception of high-styling in the field of motor car design, the Pontiac Torpedo Eight is a thrilling invitation to all lovers of the beautiful.

Here are seventeen feet of blue-blooded distinction—long, low and superbly lithe . . . with a front end like some gigantic jewel out of Tiffany. Here are interiors equally unique in restrained richness, created about a glamorous new instrument panel highlighted in plastic and chrome. Here, in brief, is the luxury of the perfect gem in the perfect setting—radiant style wedded to superb performance.

For Pontiac designers—inspired by the enthusiasm of owners for Pontiac's remarkable eight cylinder power plant and famous trouble-free chassis—created the Torpedo to be the *first and only fine car* wherein luxury is divorced from extravagance! The Torpedo is the largest and most powerful Pontiac ever built. On the basis of what it *is,* what it *does,* and what it *costs,* it should be seen and driven by everyone accustomed to the best.

3.   **The Most Astounding Car In The German Auto Show Was A Ford.**

The Probe III, an experimental Ford, drew some of the biggest crowds at the Frankfurt Auto Show. And it got great press. Germany's leading automotive publication, *Auto Motor and Sport,* called it "a dream car—sleek as a futuristic study in aerodynamics."

Aerodynamics is what the Probe III is all about. The airstream over the car does not symbolize the wave of the future, rather it shows how the Probe III looks in a wind tunnel.

It looks spectacular. A completely enclosed underbody, unique twin deck biplane rear spoiler (to maximize aerodynamic efficiency), sculptured door mirrors and flat wheel covers all contribute to Probe III's aerodynamic excellence.

Compare it to most '82 European models and you get a glimpse of the near future. Drag coefficient is reduced by 50%, which conceivably could result in a 27% rise in fuel efficiency at higher speeds.

But aerodynamics is not merely a future concern of Ford Motor Company. It's a science in which we are assuming a leading role right now.

Our Ford Escort and Mercury Lynx, here in America, for example, have less wind resistance than the VW Rabbit, Mercedes Benz 300D, and Audi 5000.

So the Ford Probe III is not a beginning, it's another move forward.

There's A Ford in America's Future.

1.16 **(a)** Write an advertisement for one or more of the following products, selecting words appropriate for the magazine indicated or others in the list. Begin by considering who would normally read the particular magazine, what specific qualities of the product you want to stress, and what connotations you want to emphasize.

bath soap	*Mother Earth News*
home computer	*Time*
camera	*National Geographic*
breakfast cereal	*Reader's Digest*
automobile	*Psychology Today*
mouthwash	*Cosmopolitan*
video game	*Rolling Stone*
stereo system	*Smithsonian*
yogurt maker	*Organic Gardening*

(b) Rewrite the advertisement you have written, this time for a different magazine.

(c) In the following piece, the author, Bruce McCall, is making fun of a particular sort of advertisement. What is the point he wants to make? Identify and analyze as many of the words and phrases used to "hype" the products as you can. Why might these terms and others like them be fashionable among advertising copywriters at this time? How does McCall deflate the fictitious copywriter's language?

Rolled in Rare Bohemian Onyx, Then Vulcanized by Hand

Dear Eminent Patron of the Mail Order Arts,
Imagine a collector's item so exquisitely detailed that each is actually invisible to the naked eye. Think of an heirloom so limited in availability that when you order it, the mint specially constructed to craft it will be demolished. Ponder an item so precious that its value has actually tripled since you began reading this.

Kiln-Fired in Edible 24-Calorie Silver

Never before in human history has the Polk McKinley Harding Coolidge Mint (not a U.S. Government body) commissioned such a rarity.

Consider: miniature pewterine reproductions, authenticated by the World Court at The Hague and sent to you in moisture-resistant Styrofoam chests, of the front-door letter slots of Hollywood's 39 most beloved character actors and actresses. . . .

12 Men Died to Make the Ingots Perfect

But why, as a prudent investor, should you spend thousands of dollars, every month for a lifetime, to acquire this 88-piece set of Official Diplomatic License Plates of the World's Great Governments-in-Exile? One Minnesota collector comments: "I never expected to buy an item so desirable that it has already kept its haunting fascination forever." But even this merely hints at the extraordinary investment potential of the Connoisseur's Choice selection of Great Elevator Inspection Certificates of the World's Tallest Buildings. Molded in unobtainable molybdenum, each is precision ejected from a flying aircraft to check a zinc content that must measure .000000003 per cent or the entire batch will be melted down, discarded, and forgotten. . . .

Registered with the Department of Motor Vehicles

A dazzling proposition, you will agree. If you do not, your 560-piece set of Belgium's Most Cherished Waffle Patterns, together with your check or money order, will be buried at sea on or before midnight, April 15 . . . the anniversary, college-trained historians tell us, of the sinking of the R.M.S. Titanic, one of the 66 Great Marine Disasters commemorated in the never-yet-offered series, each individually bronzed, annealed, Martinized, and hickory-cured by skilled artisans working under the supervision of the Tulane Board of Regents. . . .

(d) Find several examples of the type of "collectibles" advertisement parodied in the preceding passage. Identify and analyze the connotative words and phrases used in these advertisements. In what ways do they differ from those used in the parody? Then compare both the parody and the advertisements you find with the one reprinted on page 265.

1.17 With as much precision and detail as possible, analyze a single television commercial for the variety of ways in which it "speaks" to the prospective consumer. Watch the advertisement several times to pick up as many clues as you can to the intended audience of the advertisement (consider the time it is shown; what characters, if any, appear in the advertisement; the clothing they wear and the way they speak; the setting; musical accompaniment; and so on). How do the images and the mode of speech, including that of the "voice over" if there is one, supplement the impression made by the words themselves?

CONNOTATIONS IN POLITICAL PERSUASION

1.18 Count up and analyze individually all the emotive words found in this quotation from a national political figure. When all the language is reduced to a simple straightforward statement, what is this person saying?

> Public debt mounts to astronomical heights and cannot be paid off except by ruinous inflation or repudiation. The federal debt is a time bomb hanging over the security of our people. . . . Have you ever seen such outrageous taxation, such a staggering national debt, such waste of public money, such a pyramid of Government subsidies, such dangerous inflation, so many lavish political promises, such a gigantic federal bureaucracy, so much Government favoritism to special groups, such moral laxity and so little responsibility in public life?

1.19 Name-calling and glittering generalities are often encountered in the kind of writing commonly called *propaganda*. However, as a book on *How to Understand Propaganda* says, "Propaganda is not all lies. It can be the simple truth. It can be safe or dangerous. By all odds, the thing that should concern the consumer is the way he permits himself to react to propaganda."

(a) What connotations does *propaganda* have for you? How can you account for your present attitude? What is the word's denotation?

(b) Propaganda can be used for or against any cause—whether the cause is "good" or "bad." Collect some examples of what you consider to be "good" and "bad" propaganda. What standards do you use in classifying each example? Can there be "good" propaganda for a "bad" cause and vice versa? How so?

(c) Someone has remarked that all writing is propaganda. In what sense could this statement be true?

(d) One writer identified the key to the success of propaganda as the ability to use "God" and "Devil" terms. Writing some thirty years ago, this author identified *democracy* and *progress* as major "God" terms and *communism* as the major "Devil" term. What would you identify as the most effective "God" and "Devil" terms today?

1.20 Make a list of the catchwords and catchphrases most in favor with politicians and their publicists at the moment. What are the most commonly used terms of approval or disapproval? What are the connotations of these terms? Can any of the terms be interpreted in differing ways, depending on which connotations you consider to be most important?

1.21 (a) Record some of the slogans of today's leading activist groups, such as are included in the following list. Analyze the language for its emotive appeal. Why were some words chosen instead of others which might have been clearer or more explicit about the aims of the group? Are there any examples of glittering generalities, stereotypes, or omnibus words in the slogans or in the names of the groups themselves?

antiabortionists	marine ecologists
survivalists	labor unionists
civil rights activists	antinuclear demonstrators
atheists	feminists
religious traditionalists	guerrilla revolutionaries (= terrorists?)

(b) Make a list of the terms used to refer to the preceding groups by their opponents, and then analyze those terms.

(c) Make a list of some of the immediate issues or causes championed by some of these groups, or choose another group if you wish. Assume that you have been asked to write slogans for placards to be carried in a demonstration by the group or for bumper stickers. Write the slogan (no more than six to eight words) and then explain why you chose the words you did and what emotional effects you tried to create.

(d) Now write slogans to be carried on placards by a group opposing the causes just championed. Which slogans, of the ones you have written thus far, tell the "truth"?

1.22 (a) Write a short description of the characteristics you associate with a person in one of the following classes. To what extent is your description based on actual observation and experience, and to what extent on opinions you have heard expressed by others?

1. Russian, New Yorker, Yankee, reservation Indian, French Canadian, Midwesterner, Italian, Oriental
2. lawyer, pacifist, hard hat, lumberjack, preacher, Hollywood director, rock star, Wall Street economist, military officer, Boy or Girl Scout, soap opera actress or actor, philosopher, mechanic, used-car salesman, English teacher
3. a member of the Loyal Order of Moose, Alcoholics Anonymous, Moral Majority, teamsters' union, chamber of commerce, local bridge club, Audubon Society, Salvation Army, Kiwanis Club, NAACP, B'nai B'rith

(b) Compare your descriptions with those of the same category written by others. How have your experiences or opinions differed and thus controlled your choice of descriptive words and phrases?

1.23 You undoubtedly belong to some group identified by various labels. Choose one such label for yourself and your group and make a list of characteristics you think apply to that label. Compare your list with one for the same label prepared by someone else, preferably someone who is not in the group.

CONNOTATIONS IN LITERATURE

1.24 Analyze the literary uses of connotative words in the following passages. You might begin by listing the words or phrases which bring to mind some sensory image, such as a sight, smell, or touch; briefly describe the images as they affect you; then consider, perhaps, the effect of substituting your descriptions for the original words and phrases in the passages. Finally, do the images as a group suggest any pattern or theme that the author of each passage may have been trying to create?

1.   Lamb, what makes you tick?
    You got a wind-up, a Battery-Powered,
    A flywheel, a plug-in, or what?
    You made out of real Reelfur?
    You fall out the window you bust?
    You shrink? Turn into a No-No?
    Zip open and have pups?

    I bet you better than that.
    I bet you put out by some other outfit.
    I bet you don't do nothin.
    I bet you somethin to eat.

2.   The public liked the atomic bomb as little as we did, and there were many who were quick to see the signs of future danger and to develop a profound consciousness of guilt. Such a consciousness looks for a scapegoat. Who could constitute a better scapegoat than the scientists themselves? They had unquestionably developed the potentialities which had led to the bomb. The man in the street, who knew little of scientists and found them a strange and self-contained race, was quick to accuse them of a desire for the power of destruction manifested by the bomb. What made this both more plausible and more dangerous was the fact that, while the working scientists felt very little personal power and had very little desire for it, there was a group of administrative gadget workers who were quite sensible of the fact that they now had a new ace in the hole in the struggle for power.
    At any rate, it was perfectly clear to me at the very beginning that we scientists were from now on to be faced by an ambivalent

attitude. For the public, who regarded us as medicine men and magicians, was likely to consider us an acceptable sacrifice to the gods as other, more primitive publics do. In that very day of the atomic bomb the whole pattern of the witch hunt of the last eight years became clear, and what we are living through is nothing but the transfer into action of what was then written in the heavens.

3. Standing on our microscopic fragment of a grain of sand, we attempt to discover the nature and purpose of the universe which surrounds our home in space and time. Our first impression is something akin to terror. We find the universe terrifying because of its vast meaningless distances, terrifying because of its inconceivably long vistas of time which dwarf human history to the twinkling of an eye, terrifying because of our extreme loneliness, and because of the material insignificance of our home in space—a millionth part of a grain of sand out of all the sea-sand in the world. But above all else, we find the universe terrifying because it appears indifferent to life like our own: emotion, ambition and achievement, art and religion all seem equally foreign to its plan.

4. He knew the street and indeed the whole neighborhood: the boarding house from which he had moved was not far; until now, however, the street had revolved and glided this way and that, without any connection with him; today it had suddenly stopped; henceforth it would settle down as an extension of his new domicile.

Lined with lindens of medium size, with hanging droplets of rain distributed among their intricate black twigs according to the future arrangement of leaves (tomorrow each drop would contain a green pupil); complete with smooth tarred surface some thirty feet across and variegated sidewalks (hand-built, and flattering to the feet), it rose at a barely perceptible angle, beginning with a post office and ending with a church, like an epistolary novel. With a practiced eye he searched it for something that would become a daily sore spot, a daily torture for his senses, but there seemed to be nothing of that sort in the offing, and the diffuse light of the gray spring day was not only above suspicion but promised to mollify any trifle that in more brilliant weather would not fail to crop up; this could be anything, the color of a building, for instance, that immediately provoked an unpleasant taste in the mouth, a smack of oatmeal, or even halvah; an architectural detail that effusively caught one's attention every time one passed by; the irritating sham of a caryatid, a hanger-on and not a support, which, even under a lighter burden would crumble into plaster dust; or, on a tree trunk, fastened to it by a rusty thumbtack, a pointless but perpetually preserved corner of a notice in longhand (runny ink, blue runaway dog) that had outlived its usefulness but had not been fully torn off; or else an object, in a shop window, or a smell that refused at the last moment to yield a memory it had seemed ready to shout, and remained instead on its street corner, a mystery withdrawn into itself.

5. One could not have passed him on the street without feeling his great physical force and his imperious will. Not much taller than the Bishop, in reality, he gave the impression of being an enormous man. His broad high shoulders were like a bull buffalo's, his big head was set defiantly on a thick neck, and the full-cheeked, richly colored, egg-shaped Spanish face—how vividly the Bishop remembered that face! It was so unusual that he would be glad to see it again; a high, narrow forehead, brilliant yellow eyes set deep in strong arches, and full, florid cheeks,—not bland areas of smooth flesh, as in Anglo-Saxon faces, but full of muscular activity, as quick to change with feeling as any of his features. His mouth was the very assertion of violent, uncurbed passions and tyrannical self-will; the full lips thrust out and taut, like the flesh of animals distended by fear or desire.

1.25 Writers and publishers often use the power of connotation in book titles. What does each of the following titles suggest to you about the dominant feeling or tone of the book to which it refers?

All the King's Men
Elephant in Flight
*The Kandy-Kolored Tangerine-
   Flake Streamlined Baby*
Brave New World
The Rebel Angels
The Grapes of Wrath
Who Has Seen the Wind?
I Heard the Owl Call My Name
Tender Is the Night
The Heart Is a Lonely Hunter

The Power Brokers
Pale Fire
How Green Was My Valley
The Plough and the Stars
Daughters of Copper Woman
The World According to Garp
Manchild in the Promised Land
Wise Blood
Ship of Fools
The Edible Woman
For Whom the Bell Tolls

1.26 Check the current local or national bestseller list in the newspaper or in a bookstore. Write a brief analysis of the connotations of some of those titles.

1.27 Some fiction writers give their characters names that influence the reader's attitudes toward them. What sort of connotations do the following names have?

Mrs. Slipslop
Molly Brazen
Mr. Feathernest

Major Major Major
The Reverend Lucas Honey-
   thunder

Luke Skywalker

Lord Byron Jones

Sir Toby Belch

Rawdon Crawley

Heathcliff

Count Smorltork

Lord Frederick Verisopht

Grace Ardent

Lady Wishfort

Flem Snopes

Captain Ahab

Osbie Feel

Hamm

Magnus Eisengrim

HOW CONNOTATION CHANGES

1.28 Each of the following words has changed considerably in connotation—and some even in denotation—through the centuries. Using either an etymological dictionary or the *Oxford English Dictionary*, summarize the changes one of the following words has undergone. Be sure to include the connotations you associate with the word and your reasons for them. Where applicable, use quotations from important writers who have used the word distinctively or differently.

curious

quaint

privy *(adjective)*

churlish

cheer

complaint

tax *(verb)*

rude

honest

doom

sue

awful

vulgar

conversation

romance

artist

silly

undertaker

apprehend

stuff *(noun)*

matter

shift *(noun)*

disposition

testify

1.29 Some connotations (and denotations as well) change from year to year. Words which have undergone changes in connotation in the last few years include

pill

gay

contract

missile

jog

gross

roommate

satellite

godfather

sting

trip

sexy

Try to identify some changes in connotation that have occurred in your own vocabulary, pinpointing, if you can, what caused the changes.

1.30 In the following quotations, the meaning of each italicized word differs from the meaning it has in today's common usage. Determine the meaning of each word by fitting it into the general sense of the sentence. Then check your answers by referring to the *Oxford English Dictionary.*

1. An ant is a wise creature for itself, but it is a *shrewd* thing in an orchard or garden; and certainly men that are great lovers of themselves *waste* the public. (Bacon, 1612) [In the sentence, *shrewd* is a pun. What makes it so?]
2. "I fear," replied Neander, "that in obeying your commands I shall draw some *envy* on myself." (Dryden, 1668)
3. Most of the quarrels I have ever known have proceeded from some valiant coxcomb's persisting in the wrong, to defend some prevailing folly, and preserve himself from the *ingenuity* of *owning* a mistake. (Steele, 1709)
4. But most by *numbers* judge the poet's song:
And smooth or rough, with them, is right or wrong. (Pope, 1711)
5. A good that seems at an immeasurable distance, and that we cannot hope to reach, has therefore the less influence on our *affections.* (Cowper, 1786)
6. The language was not only *peculiar* and strong, but at times knotty and contorted, as by its own impatient strength. (Coleridge, 1817)

1.31 First, write down the usual meaning(s) each of the following words has today: *head, extravagant, probation, cousin, admiration, doubt* (verb), *eager, fee, toys* (noun), *lets.* Then, using an annotated edition of *Hamlet*, find out what each word meant in Shakespeare's time, in the particular passages from Act One of that play:

Scene One: line 106 *(head)*, 154 *(extravagant)*, 156 *(probation)*.
Scene Two: line 64 *(cousin)*, 192 *(admiration)*, 256 *(doubt)*.
Scene Four: line 2 *(eager)*, 65 *(fee)*, 75 *(toys)*, 85 *(lets)*.

1.32 The following passage contains a number of words whose connotations, and sometimes denotations, have changed since it was written in the seventeenth century. Rewrite the passage in clear, readable modern English. Refer to the *Oxford English Dictionary* for help in understanding the seventeenth-century meaning of any words that puzzle you. You are free to modernize sentence structure or make other necessary changes, as long as you retain the meaning of the original passage.

The general use of speech is to transfer our mental discourse into verbal; or the train of our thoughts into a train of words, and that for two commodities; whereof one is, the registering of the consequences of our thoughts, which being apt to slip out of our memory and put us to a new labor may again be recalled by such words as they are marked by. So that the first use of names is to serve for marks or notes of remembrance. Another is, when many use the same words, to signify (by their connection and order), one to another, what they conceive or think of each matter, and also what they desire, fear, or have any other passion for. And for this use they are called signs. Special uses of speech are these: First, to register what by cogitation we find to be the cause of anything, present or past, and what we find things present or past may produce or effect: which in sum is acquiring of arts. Secondly, to show to others that knowledge which we have attained, which is, to counsel and teach one another. Thirdly, to make known to others our wills and purposes, that we may have the mutual help of one another. Fourthly, to please and delight ourselves and others by playing with our words, for pleasure or ornament, innocently.

To these uses there are also four correspondent abuses. First, when men register their thoughts wrong, by the inconstancy of the signification of their words; by which they register for their conceptions that which they never conceived, and so deceive themselves. Secondly, when they use words metaphorically—that is, in other sense than that they are ordained for—and thereby deceive others. Thirdly, when by words they declare that to be their will which is not. Fourthly, when they use them to grieve one another: for seeing Nature hath armed living creatures, some with horns, and some with hands, to grieve an enemy, it is but an abuse of speech to grieve him with the tongue, unless it be one whom we are obliged to govern; and then it is not to grieve, but to correct and amend.

In these two paragraphs, the author touches on several basic principles of language, its purposes, and its effects. Which of the ideas he expresses are discussed or reflected in this chapter?

1.33 Because of technological and other developments, new words are constantly being added to our vocabularies. Words associated with space exploration, for instance, have come into our vocabulary within the last few decades — *countdown, interorbital, payload.* The electronic information-processing sciences have brought in a host of others, for example, *printout, on-line, software;* and physics and microbiology have contributed many others, such as *quark,* black hole, clone.* Within a very short time most such terms acquire some connotative value.** Find out the scientific or technical denotations of the terms in the fol-

---

*The word *quark,* now a scientific term, has its origin not in science but in literature, in James Joyce's *Finnegans Wake.*

**Sometimes, when the scientific term for a new development or concept is not readily adaptable to ordinary writing, the media invent their own term. What is the equivalent, in medical language, of *test-tube baby?* What does the term itself connote?

lowing list and then explain any connotative values that have come to be attached to them.

psychedelic	quasar
laser	extraterrestrial
infrastructure	binary
frogman	cursor
pollutant	dioxin
digital	floppy disc
CAT scanner	microchip

REVIEW

1.34 In the following passages, two authors, writing a century apart, record their memories of schoolrooms in which they sat and the emotions they associate with their memories. The differences in effect between the two accounts are partially due to each writer's choice of connotative words. Define the differences of mood and feeling in the two passages that are caused by the connotative qualities of specific words.

1. Here I sit at the desk again watching his eye—humbly watching his eye, as he rules a ciphering book for another victim whose hands have just been flattened by that identical ruler, and who is trying to wipe the sting out with a pocket-handkerchief. I have plenty to do. I don't watch his eye in idleness, but because I am morbidly attracted to it in a dread desire to know what he will do next, and whether it will be my turn to suffer or somebody else's. A lane of small boys beyond me, with the same interest in his eye, watch it too. I think he knows it, though he pretends he doesn't. He makes dreadful mouths as he rules the ciphering book; and now he throws his eye sideways down our lane, and we all droop over our books and tremble. A moment afterwards we are again eyeing him. An unhappy culprit, found guilty of imperfect exercise, approaches at his command. The culprit falters excuses and professes a determination to do better to-morrow. Mr. Creakle cuts a joke before he beats him, and we laugh at it—miserable little dogs, we laugh, with our visages as white as ashes, and our hearts sinking into our boots.

    Here I sit at the desk again on a drowsy summer afternoon. A buzz and hum go up around me, as if the boys were so many blue-bottles. A cloggy sensation of the luke-warm fat of meat is upon me (we dined an hour or two ago), and my head is as heavy as so much lead. I would give the world to go to sleep. I sit with my eye on Mr. Creakle, blinking at him like a young owl; when sleep overpowers me for a minute, he still looms through my slumber, ruling those ciphering books, until he softly comes behind me and wakes me to plainer perception of him with a red ridge across my back.

2. All my early life lies open to my eye within five city blocks. When I passed the school, I went sick with all my old fear of it. With its standard New York public-school brown brick courtyard shut in on three sides of the square and the pretentious battlements overlooking that cockpit in which I can still smell the fiery sheen of the rubber ball, it looks like a factory over which has been imposed the facade of a castle. It gave me the shivers to stand up in that courtyard again; I felt as if I had been mustered back into the service of those Friday morning "tests" that were the terrors of my childhood.

It was never learning I associated with that school: only the necessity to succeed, to get ahead of the others in the daily struggle to "make a good impression" on our teachers, who grimly, wearily, and often with ill-concealed distaste watched against our relapsing into the natural savagery they expected of Brownsville boys. The white, cool, thinly ruled record book sat over us from their desks all day long, and had remorselessly entered into it each day—in blue ink if we had passed, in red ink if we had not—our attendance, our conduct, our "effort," our merits and demerits; and to the last possible decimal point in calculation, our standing in an unending series of "tests"—surprise tests, daily tests, weekly tests, formal midterm tests, final tests. They never stopped trying to dig out of us whatever small morsel of fact we had managed to get down the night before. We had to prove that we were really alert, ready for anything, always in the race. That white thinly ruled record book figured in my mind as the judgment seat; the very thinness and remote blue lightness of its lines instantly showed its cold authority over me; so much space had been left on each page, columns and columns in which to note down everything about us, implacably and forever. As it lay there on a teacher's desk, I stared at it all day long with such fear and anxious propriety that I had no trouble believing that God, too, did nothing but keep such record books, and that on the final day He would face me with an account in Hebrew letters whose phonetic dots and dashes looked strangely like decimal points counting up my every sinful thought on earth.

1.35 Make a list of some emotive and connotative words you associate with your early school years. Compare those words and your associations with those of the preceding two writers. In what major ways would your description of experiences at school either be like or unlike the ones just given?

DICTION

Probably nothing reveals more about us than the language we use, that web of words which reflects our attitudes toward ourselves, others, and the world around us. In an essay written early in Hitler's career, the critic Kenneth Burke analyzed Hitler's use of language and showed how it revealed complex hidden assumptions and attitudes, assumptions which later became all too terrifyingly clear. We may not be prepared for a complicated analysis such as Burke's, but we regularly draw much information — inferences — from the words speakers and writers choose.

To illustrate, let us do a little detective work.

1. "When I told Dad how I'd screwed up that exam, he literally blew his top." *Who is writing (or speaking)? In what country? At the present time, or at some time in the past? How carefully does this person choose words?*
2. "There was a constable on point duty just where we stopped, and he came over and lifted the bonnet and made ineffectual motions with a spanner. And then — what do you think? — we found we were out of petrol!" *What is the nationality of the speaker?*
3. "We don't keep nothin' like that here, but maybe we could order it for you special. Not in a hurry for it, was you?" *How formally educated is the speaker?*
4. "I had him on the ropes in the fourth, and if one of my short rights had connected, he'd have gone down for the count. I was aiming for his glass jaw, but I couldn't seem to reach it." *What activity has the speaker been engaged in?*
5. "A close examination and correlation of the most reliable current economic indexes justify the conclusion that the next year will witness a continuation of the present upward market trend, though this may be accompanied by seasonal fluctuations in respect to certain areas of the economy." *How much of a gift for clear, concise expression has this writer? What makes this passage difficult to read?*
6. "We were loading hay in the west forty when we saw the twister in the distance." *From what section of North America does this speaker probably come?*

7. "Both the Oriental romance and the picaresque narrative have been favorite vehicles for the satirist, the romance because it permits a handy and vivid way of contrasting western manners with those of a very different culture, the picaresque tale because the hero's adventuresome career, spiced as it is with all sorts of roguery, gives an excellent excuse for pungent comment on the errant ways of mankind." *What can you infer about the educational and professional interests of this person?*

8. "In fine, could a machine be invented which would instantaneously arrange on paper each idea as it occurs to us without any exertion on our part, how exactly useful would it be considered!" *Is it likely that this sentence was written in modern times? How can you tell?*

9. "The ominous final movement begins with a toccata in the horns, punctuated by glissando effects in the tympani, and then develops, in the middle section, into a lyric coda." *How much does this person know about music?*

10. "Okay, so there was this one checker at the store who was a real loser, had a put-down for everybody, that guy did." *Is this spoken or written discourse? Is the situation formal or informal? How do you know?*

If we have a fairly dependable sense of language, we should be able to answer these questions somewhat as follows:

1. The use of a contraction *(I'd)* and slang *(screwed up, blew his top)* and the content all suggest that this sentence probably was spoken, not written. Contractions and colloquial or slang expressions are used in popular journalism and advertising, of course, but they are even more typical of oral speech patterns. Still, the sentence could have occurred in a letter. The reference to an exam and the use of current slang suggest that the speaker is young, as does the reference to "Dad." We find no evidence, however, of whether the speaker is a man or a woman. He or she is probably North American and speaking at the present time. Finally, the use of *literally* indicates some carelessness in language, though it is an error common to many people, including professional writers. If Dad "literally blew his top," he was lucky to escape with his life. *Literally* does not belong with an expression intended as a figure of speech, as *blew his top* is. The correct adverb, if any is needed, would be *figuratively*. Keep this in mind when you read, and you will soon collect your own set of amusing misuses. ("The audience literally sat on its hands throughout the whole show." "The tennis champion literally blasted his opponent out of the court." "The children literally ate everything in sight.")

2. The speaker is British. A *constable on point duty* is an English traffic cop; *bonnet, spanner,* and *petrol* are, respectively, the British equivalents of the American *hood* (of a car), *wrench,* and *gasoline.*

3. This speaker either does not know, or has chosen to ignore, rules of standard English. Although such usage may be perfectly acceptable in some regions and in informal spoken discourse, use of the double negative *(we don't keep nothin')*, use of an adjective *(special)* where an adverb is in order, and mismatching of subject and verb *(was you)* all suggest that the speaker has little formal education.

4. The person is, or has been, a boxer: note the use of five terms associated with that sport.

5. This writer has no gift for plain communication. What forty-five words convey could be said far more clearly in sixteen: "Present signs indicate that stock prices will continue to rise, though certain stocks may temporarily decline." The original sentence is an example of wordiness or inflated writing.

6. The speaker—or writer—is from the west. *Forty* designates a forty-acre tract, a customary division of land in that region, and *twisters* (tornadoes) are most common in the Midwest.

7. The writer probably has a university education, has a strong interest in various types of literature, and writes clearly. He or she may be a professional critic or literary historian. The sentence, though long, is very well constructed. Note how the opening clause (down to *satirist*) is developed by what follows—two parallel elements, the first expanding on the idea of the Oriental romance, the second on the idea of the picaresque tale. The words chosen are familiar to a reasonably experienced reader and convey accurately the writer's main point.

8. This sentence was written at least a hundred years ago; certainly not in recent times. *In fine* is no longer used to convey *finally*. and the word *machine* is used in an old-fashioned way. In addition, the inverted word order—*could a machine . . . how exactly useful would it be*—characterizes eighteenth- and nineteenth-century prose more than it does contemporary style.

9. Readers with a basic knowledge of musical terms will recognize this sentence as nonsense. A *toccata* is a "touch-piece" designed to exhibit the dexterity of an organist or a pianist, not of a horn player; nor is it likely to appear in an "ominous" passage. Tympani cannot produce *glissando* effects. A *coda*, being the concluding portion of a composition, would not occur in the middle section.

10. This is almost surely spoken discourse in an informal situation. The use of slang *(loser, put-down)* and the loosely organized sentence pattern suggest both informality and speech.

From these examples, we can draw one major conclusion. Words not only carry connotations and denotations. They also give us valuable clues to the background, personality, and often the attitudes and intentions of the writer or speaker.

Some of the following material appears in college composition textbooks under the heading of "Diction" or "Word Choice." There it is primarily used to show how to achieve a good written style through the selection of words and phrases appropriate to situation and speaker. Here the chief purpose of this material is to suggest how you can gather more information from what you read and at the same time infer possibly unstated purposes of the author. Of course, the two aims are closely associated; in fact, they are two sides of the same coin. Choosing words and phrases that will carry your precise meaning is closely related to the ability to infer meaning from the words and phrases another person has chosen. Just as the preceding chapter stressed the need for precise word choice, so this chapter will point out ways in which writing can be made more clear and economical—and more accurately suited to your prospective readers.

ELEMENTARY CLUES OF DICTION

Geographical Clues

Though all are "English," the British, United States, Canadian, and Australian vocabularies differ considerably. No reader of British essays or fiction can long remain unaware that the North American *grain* is the British *corn.* In Britain, a *subway* is a subterranean passage for pedestrians only; the American *subway* is the Londoner's *tube* or *underground.* The long line that the American stands in is a *line-up* in Canada and a *queue* in Britain. In British and Australian schools, the students play *rounders;* in Canada and the United States the game is *softball.* An English *biscuit* is a *cracker* in the United States and much of Canada (but one of the largest producers of crackers in the United States is the National Biscuit Company). At the same time, *biscuits* served with breakfast in the United States are popular as *scones* in many other parts of the English-speaking world. Idioms (phrases peculiar to a particular language group) also differ. A student in the United States is taking courses at the university or going to the hospital, but in British and Canadian usage the *the* is dropped.* In Australia the student would probably be said to be studying *at uni.*

Similarly, vocabularies differ among various regions of a country. In Boston, a milk shake is a *frappe* (pronounced as one syllable). In certain parts of the Midwest, a cola drink is a *soda,* but in many areas of the South it is simply a *cold drink.* New England *johnny cake* becomes the Midwesterner's *cornbread* and the Southerner's *corn pone.* A New England *stone wall* is a *stone row* in northern New Jersey, a *stone fence* in Pennsylvania, and a *rock fence* from West Virginia southward. And the center of a cherry or a peach will contain a *pit,* a *seed,* or a *stone,* depending on the regional dialect of the speaker.

Occupational Clues

Every profession and occupation has its own slang as well as its own technical vocabulary. A person on *O.B.* duty is probably a nurse or doctor in the obstetrical section of a hospital. (However, someone else using the same abbreviation may turn out to be a school psychologist; *O.B.* is also an abbreviation for "orthogenic-backward" or "problem" children.) In the United States, at least, a *G.I.* could be a soldier or a gastrointestinal specialist. Mention of *tolerance* or *round-stock* identifies the lathe operator; *sleeper cab* or *rig,* the trucker; *modem, byte,* and *disk drive,* the computer specialist; *shagging* or *sinker,* the baseball player. To a sailing enthusiast, being *in shackles* is losing headway after attempting to put a boat on

---

*Long and interesting lists illustrating this difference are printed in H. L. Mencken's *The American Language,* 4th ed. (New York, 1936), pp. 233–237; and in *Supplement One* thereto (1945), pp. 457–487. Mencken's work is also available in an abridged and revised edition by Raven I. McDavid, Jr. (New York, 1963).

another tack. *The Linguistic Atlas of the United States and Canada* reveals that even the way farmers call certain animals is part of their distinct occupational vocabulary. Thus various trades and occupations coin new terms or appropriate words from the general vocabulary and give them special significance.

Often, however, what begins as a term used by one occupation or another ends up in everyday language. *On the beam*, which in the sense of "in the right direction" originated in radio air navigation, later became common slang; *network*, borrowed from the general vocabulary of the 1920s to designate a "hook-up" of radio stations, returned to the general vocabulary with its new special meaning broadened to apply to any widespread organized system, such as a network of brokerage offices or a professional women's network. *Top brass*, originally a military term, is widely used for high executives (what attitude is implied by its use?). *Snafu*, the account of whose origins makes entertaining reading, was in the beginning a military term for a mixup resulting from conflicting or suddenly changed orders. Now it refers to any snarl in administration. *Tailgating* is another example of a word originally peculiar to a certain occupation (which one?) but now in general use, though in this case the meaning remains unchanged. The terms *input* and *interface*, earlier the possession of the computer scientists, have been taken over by the general public. Sometimes, therefore, what seems at first glance to be a clue to a person's occupation may have no value as such.

Educational Clues

Grammatical choices, as illustrated in example 3 on page 50, reveal a great deal about the educational background of a writer. Using an objective form in the subject position *(him and me went out)* or using singular subjects with plural verbs *(she don't)* generally reflects lack of formal education, though such habits do not necessarily reveal anything about intelligence.

Modern standards, however, allow the literate person generous leeway in English usage. Only those who hold unnaturally rigid views of language condemn the person who splits an infinitive or ends a sentence with a preposition. Probably no reputable grammarian denies that "It is me" is perfectly acceptable colloquial English, or that in many situations *not* splitting an infinitive is awkward (often it is simply a matter of sound). Sometimes dialect differences are responsible for our grammatical choices. Both *dived* and *dove* are used by educated speakers as past tense of the verb *to dive*, but *dived* is the choice in one region and *dove* in another. When writers use structures not shared by a large group of educated persons, however, their language indicates a lack of formal education.

Grammatical choices offer the most immediate clues to a person's educational background. Another important clue is vocabulary. The writer or speaker who uses words appropriately and accurately, as does the writer of example 7 on page 51, is well educated. One who often misuses words or phrases is not soundly educated, because a major purpose of education is to teach people to use their native language with accuracy. In fact, a major part of your college experience should involve vocabulary development. How well you are able to assimilate and use the vocabulary of your various courses will reflect not only the level of your education but also how well you have learned the concepts involved.

Imperfect command of language sometimes results in a *malapropism* (from the name of Mrs. Malaprop, the hilarious misuser of words in Richard Sheridan's eighteenth-century play *The Rivals*)—the accidental confusion of two words with similar sounds but different meanings. Most teachers have treasured files of such "mistakes": "My goal in life is to be a success, and when I retire I want to devote my money to philandering"; "The young Studs Lonigan was well acquainted with the steamy side of life"; "It sure is a doggie dog world"; "Some drugs are known to lower your eye cue." Much of the humor of *All in the Family* rested on Archie Bunker's use of malapropisms. Archie often claimed that his prejudice was only a "pigment of the imagination." In the following sentence, he managed three malapropisms: "I come home and tell you one of the greatest antidotes of all times, an item of real humane interest, and you sit there like you're in a comma." Such slips are always funny—as long as someone else makes them. The best way to ensure that we don't sound like a Mrs. Malaprop or an Archie Bunker is to read widely, attentively, and retentively among good writers, to consult the dictionary when necessary, and to practice using words accurately in writing and in speech. The only way we can be fair judges of another's use of language is to be precise users of language ourselves.

Time Clues

We have already seen, in Chapter 1, how words shift in meaning through the years. Many other words, once commonly used, now appear only in historical references, either because the objects they named have vanished *(Dundreary whiskers, sponging house, carpet bag, gig)* or because other words took their places *(rubber-neck wagon, watering place, deadbeat, pantaloons, counting house, jitterbug)*. A word used in an obsolete sense, or a word that is itself obsolete, helps to date a particular passage. If we know approximately when the word, or the old meaning, was current, we can roughly date the passage. The *Oxford English Dictionary*, the *Dictionary of American English*, and the *Dictionary of Canadian English* are standard sources of information on this subject.

Slang and colloquialisms also give important clues to the time background of a passage. A letter in which a young man speaks of a fraternity stag party or a musical comedy as having been "bully" can be dated with fair accuracy at around the beginning of the twentieth century. Theodore Roosevelt was particularly fond of *bully* as a general mark of enthusiastic approval. In the 1930s, *swell* served the same purpose. (What are the most current terms?) *Hooch, lounge lizard, tin lizzie, sheik, the cat's pajamas, banana oil,* and *the bee's knees* suggest that a piece of writing dates from the 1920s. In dialogue, however, those words may simply show that a contemporary author wants to give the flavor of slang in that era. Words like *handle, ten-four,* and *CB* would tell us a piece of writing had been produced recently. It might be fun to gather a list of all the words that have been used, at one time or another, for the activity once known as *sparking* or *spooning,* later as *pitching woo*, still later as *smooching*, and more recently as *necking*, *making out*, or *getting it on*. What are the current slang terms? And while we are on this topic, what terms currently express strong approval or disapproval of a member of the opposite sex? In the 1920s, for example, saying that a *flapper* had plenty of *it* was high praise. *It* later became the somewhat more specific *sex appeal*. More recently, a young woman might call a man a *hunk* if he had sex appeal and a *drip* if he didn't. For his part, he might call her either a *fox* or a *dog*. What are the current terms that you would use? Because such words pass out of vogue almost as fast as they are adopted, they offer very good clues to the time period of a quoted speaker or a piece of writing.

CLUES TO PERSONALITY AND INTENTION

Although they must be used carefully, the clues discussed so far throw some light on the social, occupational, and educational background of the writer or speaker. But language also contains subtle clues to character, personality, and intention. "Language," as Shakespeare's contemporary Ben Jonson wrote, "most shewes a man: speake that I may see thee. It springs out of the most retired, and most inmost parts of us, and is the Image of the Parent of it, the mind." Certainly the words we use and the manner in which we use them reflect more of our attitudes and values than we are usually aware. Some linguists note that terms used to designate or describe women carry images of passivity and powerlessness and are often associated with animals, in direct contrast to similar words for men. Does your listing of current terms for the opposite sex (above) support this argument? In the preface to the *Dictionary of American Slang*, Stuart B. Flexner says that words used by drinkers to refer to being drunk can reveal motivations: "*clobbered* may indicate that a drinker is punishing himself, *high* that he is escaping . . . and *paralyzed* that he seeks punishment, escape, or death." Educators have long realized that students whose language reveals lack of confidence and poor self-image are more likely to fail than are those who are self-confident. Thus, we can learn much about ourselves and our motivations and attitudes as well as about others by a careful analysis of the language we use.

For example, compare the two ways in which a person could express the desire to borrow some money: (1) "Hey, good buddy, how about loaning me a ten for a couple of days? I'm in a bind. You'll get it back Friday." (2) "I'm very sorry to impose on you, but I'm in a bit of a predicament, and I need ten dollars just until payday. I'd be extremely grateful." The language of the first appeal suggests that slang is the normal means of expression for this speaker. The meaning of the second appeal is identical, and the general approach is the same. But whereas the first speaker is forthright and unembarrassed, the other seems hesitant and apologetic. The personalities of the two seem as different as the connotations of *bind* and *predicament*. Would it be safe to say that the first person is used to borrowing from friends, whereas the second is embarrassed to do so? Or is the seeming hesitancy of the latter just an affectation? We would have to know more about the language patterns of these two speakers to answer such questions definitely.

In Chapter 1 we saw how connotations lead us to a judgment of a given person or idea. Connotations also reveal the writer's or speaker's own judgment, often without his or her knowledge or desire. This characteristic relates to one of the most valuable uses of critical reading — analyzing a person's language to discover true feelings and attitudes and values. We often find that even though someone denies prejudice in a certain matter, the choice of words betrays that prejudice. Or we find that a person's true feelings on a question, as reflected by diction, are the direct opposite of his *alleged* feelings. Examining diction, therefore, can help us see the truth despite an attempt to conceal it. In Jane Austen's *Pride and Prejudice* we read a letter written by the foolish and self-righteous clergyman William Collins. Mr. Collins is supposedly writing a letter of condolence to Mr. Bennet, whose daughter Lydia has eloped with an "unsuitable" character. Notice how Mr. Collins's language reveals his smug satisfaction over the "downfall" of Lydia, whose sister has turned down his own offer of marriage.

MY DEAR SIR,—

I feel myself called upon, by our relationship, and by my situation in life, to condole with you on the grievous affliction you are now suffering under, of which we were yesterday informed by a letter from Hertfordshire. Be assured, my dear sir, that Mrs. Collins and myself sincerely sympathise with you and all your respectable family, in your present distress, which must be of the bitterest kind, because proceeding from a cause which no time can remove. No arguments shall be wanting on my part that can alleviate so severe a misfortune—or that may comfort you, under a circumstance that must be of all others most afflicting to a parent's mind. The death of your daughter would have been a blessing in comparison of this. And it is the more to be lamented, because there is reason to suppose, as my dear Charlotte informs me, that this licentiousness of behaviour in your daughter has proceeded from a faulty degree of indulgence; though, at the same time, for the consolation of yourself and Mrs. Bennet, I am inclined to think that her own disposition must be naturally bad, or she could not be guilty of such an enormity, at so early an age. Howsoever that may be, you are grievously to be pitied; in which opinion I am not only joined by Mrs. Collins, but likewise by Lady Catherine and her daughter, to whom I have related the affair. They agree with me in apprehending that this false step in one daughter will be injurious to the fortunes of all the others; for who, as Lady Catherine herself condescendingly says, will connect themselves with such a family? And this consideration leads me moreover to reflect, with augmented satisfaction, on a certain event of last November; for had it been otherwise, I must have been involved in all your sorrow and disgrace. Let me advise you then, my dear sir, to console yourself as much as possible, to throw off your unworthy child from your affection for ever, and leave her to reap the fruits of her own heinous offence.—I am dear sir, etc., etc.

Although Mr. Collins no doubt thinks of himself as a Christian shepherd, a true servant of God, his language reveals him as a self-serving hypocrite.

(Exercises: pages 84–87)

TALKING THE LANGUAGE OF THE AUDIENCE

In Chapter 1 we pointed out that every writer who wants to be understood must choose words whose connotations reader and writer share. Otherwise, the message will not be received as intended. Not only must words be used whose connotations will carry shades of meaning from writer to reader. In addition, the writer's vocabulary must be that of the audience, and the way the writer says things — uses or avoids slang, for example — must accommodate the audience. Shared connotations and vocabularies always help to establish a link between writer and reader.

The way vocabulary reflects the needs of the audience can be seen in the obvious differences among history books written for fourth-graders, for high-school students, for college students, and for historians. As you read the following excerpts from four such books, try to discover how each differs from the others in simplicity or complexity of vocabulary. Do the authors accurately adapt their language to their respective audiences? Are any words or phrases too difficult for the intended readers? On the other hand, do any words or phrases suggest over-simplification or "talking down"?

1. [For fourth grade]

The army camped at Valley Forge. During the terrible, cold winter of 1777–1778, Washington and his men were camped in a few log cabins on the snowy plains of Valley Forge, just twenty miles outside of Philadelphia.

The men were half starved, for their food was nearly gone. They were cold, for their uniforms were ragged and thin, and their shoes were torn. Their feet were cut and bleeding and often left tracks in the snow. The soldiers wrapped their feet in old cloth or papers when they could, but this was not warm or comfortable. Hundreds of soldiers lay wounded or sick. There were only a few doctors and very little medicine to help them.

Washington was indeed saddened at his men's sufferings. When would the states send him the supplies he and his soldiers needed so badly? He could not wait. He spent thousands of dollars of his own fortune to buy provisions, and wrote many letters to his friends begging for help.

Things seemed to be going from bad to worse for the Americans, so they decided to look for help outside their own country. Benjamin Franklin went to France to ask for help.

2. [For high school]

The spot which Washington chose for his winter encampment on the Schuylkill River, twenty miles above Philadelphia, has become a name to immortalize the sufferings and endurance of the American army. While the British were making the winter gay with balls and pageants in the captured city, Washington's eight thousand men, housed in rude huts which they built from trees of the surrounding forests, shivering from lack of clothing and blankets, and leaving their bloody footprints on the snow as they toiled, dragging the cannon or foraging for firewood, presented a harrowing picture of distress. Valley Forge was a terrible test of their great commander's courage too. Not only did he suffer from the hardships of his soldiers but he had to endure also personal humiliation. The Congress (which had fled to York before Howe's army) criticized him for retiring from Philadelphia. This treatment drew from Washington one of his few sarcastic replies to Congress: "I can assure those gentlemen that it is much easier and less distressing to draw remonstrances in a comfortable room by a good fireside than to occupy a cold, bleak hill, and sleep under frost and snow without clothes or blankets." Odious comparisons were made between the failures at Brandywine and Germantown and Gates's brilliant success at Saratoga. A group of generals and members of Congress joined in a cabal against Washington headed by the Inspector-general Conway, to supplant him by Gates. His repeated supplications for supplies went unheeded.

3. [For college]

During the winter of 1777–1778 Washington's army was quartered at Valley Forge. While here the soldiers were subjected to extreme hardships owing to a shortage of food and clothing. These sufferings could have been avoided if proper arrangements had been made for bringing in supplies; for there was an adequate stock of food in the country. The failure to meet the needs of the army was due mainly to a lack of transportation facilities, and this handicap was aggravated by the inefficiency of Congress. Another cause was the depreciated paper money. British gold enabled Howe's army in Philadelphia to live in luxury, whereas the Pennsylvania farmers refused to supply Washington's soldiers with food in exchange for their cheap paper money. Over this scene of unnecessary distress, Washington's grandeur of character shed the one bright gleam of splendor. He was daily confronted with the sufferings of a justly complaining army, the intriguing efforts of some of his subordinate officers to displace him, the impotence of the government, and the unconcern and lack of patriotism exhibited by the civilian population. In this atmosphere of envy and selfishness he stood erect and exhibited a faith and composure which stamped him as one of the world's noblest characters.

4. [For historians and well-educated general readers]

Through the worst of the ordeal, even in the dreadful third week of February, 1778, Washington had retained outwardly his unshaken composure, his "calm and firm behavior," as one officer styled it; and he did not lose that self mastery as the days of later winter dragged by, and the hour-by-hour uncertainty and concern over provisions were aggravated by a hundred vexations in the problems of things material and in the management of men. His was the task of planning for the victorious long life of an Army that might die of starvation the very next week. Washington had, fortunately, the companionship of Martha who lightened the long evenings and directed the spartan entertainment at headquarters, where, on occasion, she had the assistance of Mrs. Nathanael Greene, Lady Stirling, Lady Kitty Stirling and others. Simple as were the diversions of officers' quarters, they represented some unhappy hours because they were in heartrending contrast to the life of the soldiers. Washington made the best of what he could not change, and as his duties multiplied, he used increasingly the service of a staff he now was free to augment as he saw fit though actually he added no members. Col. Alexander Scammell, the new Adjutant General, proved competent and highly diverting as a humorist but he had to confess that his duties were intolerably heavy.

Nearly every book — textbook, novel, or how-to manual — addresses a particular audience. So also do magazines and newspapers. In fact, such publications go to great lengths to gather information about their readers, and their writers and editors carefully choose language with which readers are most at home. *Ranger Rick, Cricket, National Geographic World,* and *Odyssey: The Young People's Magazine of Astronomy and Outer Space* all use vocabulary and sentence structure appropriate for young readers. Magazines aimed at those in their early teens, such as *Tiger Beat* or *16 Magazine,* use current slang, colloquialisms, and comic book language (like *ZAP!*) to speak directly to their readers. A close look at the vocabulary of *Ms., Playboy, The Mother Earth News, Scientific American, Rolling Stone, Bon Appétit,* or *Field and Stream* can tell you much about the readers of each publication.

Choosing words that reflect the tastes and habits of readers is most important when a writer wants to move those readers to a course of thought or action. The most effective way to do so is to speak in their language. "Now you're talking my language" is no empty compliment. It means that the listener or reader identifies in some way with the speaker or writer and that they both share a common goal or background. Suppose a politician addresses a meeting of a steelworkers' union. If he speaks in formal academic language, or in bureaucratic language, his chances of persuading the steelworkers are slim. If, however, he has a knack of talking their own language, without ever "talking down" to them, success is much more likely. As they leave the hall, they will be saying what a good talk it was, even for a politician — no "hot air" (or its less printable equivalent), just "straight-from-the-shoulder talk." And most important, they will be inclined to react favorably not only to the manner of speaking but also to whatever action (such as voting or contributing to a campaign fund) the politician wanted them to take.

The use of appropriate diction to establish rapport between writer or speaker and an audience can often become abuse. Just as with words of highly emotional connotation, words designed to promote rapport between two parties can turn attention away from the reasonableness of any argument. "We're friends, we see eye-to-eye, so of course you'll believe what I'm telling you."

Consider the following advertisement, which accompanied a picture of a Will Rogers-looking fellow wearing cowboy shirt, boots, and jeans:

The Unsinkable Mr. Brown Shoots the Breeze with Wrangler

My full name is Warren Granger Brown. But you probably won't print that. Everybody just calls me Freckles. Which is just fine with me.

Had a bunch of freckles once, and when this man hired me out on my first job, it was a ranch in Wilcox, Arizona, he started it all. I said, my name's Warren Granger Brown. And he said, "Anything you say, Freckles." Well, it has sure stuck. But you could hurt your eyes trying to find any freckles on me now. I reckon all those bulls over the years just shook off all my freckles.

Maybe all that shaking hasn't done my brains any good either. People keep telling me I've got no business playing horsey with 3000 pounds of irritated beef. Leastways, not at my age. I just turned 52. Have to say I've been lucky over the years, and thank the Lord, I feel fine. Work out a lot. Watch my weight.

Of course, I got a few mementos here and there. Broke my leg 3 times in a space of 13 months once. Got a piece of hip bone in my neck to replace what they took out after I broke it. Also got a pin in my shoulder and a screw in my ankle. I'm a walking hardware store. Starting to worry about getting by those metal detectors they're using at the airports. . . .

You know a funny thing? I came to New York so Mr. Penn could take my picture and something very interesting is happening. Used to be, walking around in my Wranglers I stuck out a lot more. Now everybody's starting to look like me. New York is starting to wise up.

Me and Wrangler are old friends. I've got no time for people who don't know what they're doing. Wrangler sure as hell knows how to put together a piece of clothes. If I was put together as good as their clothes, I'd be riding till I was a hundred. And they've been nothing but great to us rodeo people over the years. . . .

Wrangler Western Wear. Wremember the "W" is silent.

The person responsible for this ad had a message to deliver: buy Wrangler clothes. The intended audience is made up of "plain folks," who share the values of individuality, physical courage, and home-grown wisdom that Mr. Brown represents. Note the free use of colloquialisms, slang, and informal phrases—from "Shoots the Breeze" in the title to "Me and Wrangler" and "nothing but great" at the end. Sometimes the speaker omits the subject of a sentence, as we often do in informal talk *(Work out a lot)*. Note, too, the short sentences and the use of contractions *(everybody's; I'm; they're; they'll)*. After convincing readers that he is a friendly, trustworthy, everyday kind of guy, Mr. Brown comes to the point: "Me and Wrangler are old friends." The conclusion we are to draw is that Wranglers are honest, tough, trustworthy, down-to-earth clothes—just like good old Freckles Brown.

The reasoning is weak, however. The advertiser's care to speak in just the language he or she thinks will make us feel most at home has little to do with the soundness of the ideas. The advertiser may be 100 percent right about the value and durability of Wrangler clothes, but do we have any proof, any solid reasons, to believe this ad? Homely, familiar talk can often be a device for evading or concealing the real issue, for inducing us to relax our vigilance and take ideas on faith alone. If we do, we are in danger of buying a worthless package just because it is attractively wrapped—or because someone we admire offers a "testimonial" to it.

In recent times, the marriage of politics and advertising has been remarkably close. Media experts now package and sell a candidate for national office in much the same way they do jeans or soap. So successful are some politicians in "speaking the language of the people" that citizens must be very careful to analyze speeches thoroughly before deciding to "buy" what the politician and the media specialists are selling.

(Exercises: pages 87–93)

CLUES OF UNNECESSARILY DIFFICULT LANGUAGE

The principle that all writers who want to communicate successfully must speak to the audience in its own language may suggest to you that the obligation is all on the writer's side, that as readers all we have to do is allow writers to impart information and arguments to us in our own terms. Such a conclusion, however, would be wrong. Readers must go halfway to meet writers in creating meaning. As should be abundantly clear by now, intelligent reading is in no way passive absorption. Good readers aren't like sponges. Instead, critical reading is an active and demanding process. On the other hand, though, every reader may expect writers to express themselves as clearly and directly as possible. Whenever we encounter language which seems unnecessarily difficult or obscure, we should try this procedure:

1. Try to find out what is said: use what we know already about the subject, the context, the dictionary — and our brains. (Perhaps try to outline or summarize the piece of writing.)

2. Try to restate the meaning in simpler terms, without using much more space or, if possible, using less — and without changing or omitting any essential idea. If this experiment is successful, two preliminary conclusions may follow: (a) The difficult or obscure language is not justified because it saves space. Sometimes big words are chosen because the ideas they embody can otherwise be expressed only by awkward, space- and time-consuming clauses or sentences. Rightly used, this is a perfectly legitimate kind of shorthand. But if the big words can be replaced by short synonyms, obviously no space has been saved. Furthermore, if some words or phrases can be left out without loss, space is being wasted. (b) The difficult language is not called for by the complexity of the idea. In a technological culture like ours, many ideas cannot possibly be expressed by the familiar, short words of our everyday vocabulary. They require the use of longer, less common words, many of which were created just to stand for such ideas. If, however, the paraphrase does preserve the sense of the passage, it is fair to conclude that the language is unnecessarily complicated.

If, on the other hand, conscientious effort fails to simplify the passage, we may conclude that the difficult language probably was necessary. Then we have no choice but to dig in and try to understand the writer's terminology. If the writer cannot come any further to meet readers, they must move to meet the writer by expanding their vocabulary and understanding of the concepts involved.

But suppose the experiment proves that the author's use of difficult language was not justified — what then? Several inferences may follow:

1. The lack of clarity and precision in the writing reflects lack of clarity and precision in thinking. If a writer's thinking on a particular issue is muddled, the writing is likely to be muddled too.

2. The writer may be a fairly incisive thinker but honestly assumes that the ideas involved can only be conveyed by the use of outsized words, roundabout expressions, and knotty syntax. In this case, we may find the ideas valuable, but we are justified in wishing they were presented more clearly.

3. The writer is using difficult language in an attempt to impress the audience. The uncritical reader may, in fact, be impressed. But the critical reader will be impatient and suspicious: "Why are you wasting my time? I could write like that too, but I know better."

4. The writer is deliberately using such language to hide something — perhaps uncertainty or ignorance, perhaps an idea the audience would not approve if it were expressed clearly and directly.

A fifth inference may well accompany any of the preceding four. That is, the writer who uses an unnecessarily wordy or obscure style may have little sensitivity to the beauty and power of language. Writing that is full of polysyllabic words and hard knots and clusters of phrases is likely to offend not only the intellect but also the ear. We will say more about the sound of language later, and again in Chapter 4. But in reading the examples of bad writing in this chapter, notice how jagged, heavy, and ugly-sounding the sentences often are, and try to find the cause of this unpleasantness.

The following are among the most common characteristics of unnecessarily difficult and obscure language:

Wordiness

Most books on composition include at least one section on getting rid of excess words. "Dead wood" — words and phrases that add nothing to meaning or could be drastically simplified — is the most apparent form of wordiness. Strewn carelessly across the straight highway of thought, dead wood forces constant and unnecessary detours. "It is not incorrect to say that the condition of redundancy and repetition that exists in such a very great number of themes which are produced by college undergraduates in schools today should be eliminated by every means that lies at the disposal of the person who teaches them." That sentence is full of dead wood. Such phrases as *It is not incorrect to say, the condition* (or *fact*) *of, the quality of, the state of, the nature of* can nearly always be omitted without loss. *That exists, situated in, serve to,* and many similar phrases are usually redundant. *Such a very great number of* is a roundabout way of saying "so many." *Which are produced by* in this case means "written." And *that lies at the disposal of* and the concluding phrase and clause can be greatly condensed. Revised, the sentence could read, "The redundancy found in so many college students' themes should be eliminated by every means known to the teacher." This sentence, though much improved, is still not perfect. We will return to it before long for further simplification.

One form of wordiness, stereotyped phrases, clutters up far too much writing. Among the most common space-wasters are *due to* (or *in view of, owing to, in light of,* or *considering*) *the fact that* (= *because*), and *despite* (or *regardless of* or *notwithstanding*) *the fact that* (= *although*). The simple *the fact that* often is equally superfluous (*the fact that he was ill* = *his illness*). Here are some other chunks of dead wood, together with their simple equivalents:

in an efficient manner	efficiently
in the matter of (in respect to, in reference to)	about
a long period of time	a long time
at that point in time	then
in the capacity of	as
resembling in nature	like
in many instances	often
in the event that	if

One especially common sort of wordiness employs a whole verb phrase where a single verb would do as well or better:

avail oneself of	get, use
make an attempt	try
reach a decision	decide
have the effect of making	make
met with the approval of	was approved by
signed an agreement providing for	agreed to
announced herself to be in favor of	said she favored
it is believed*	he believes
paid a compliment to	complimented
is in the process of being	is being
exhibits a tendency	tends
inform us of the reason	tell us why
has the opportunity to	can

Such roundabout expressions seldom completely block understanding. But they waste space and the reader's time and eyesight. And when writers or speakers habitually clog discourse with unnecessary words and phrases, we are justified in two conclusions: (1) they are inefficient; (2) they are slaves to custom. Having absorbed these stereotyped phrases from associates and routine reading, they are using such expressions without examining or criticizing them. What a refreshing experience it would be to break away from the stereotypes and say things more simply, tersely, directly!

Big Words, Stock Words, Pompous Diction

Another enemy of clarity is the use of big words where shorter ones would do as well. Because many people suspect all big words, let us repeat what we said on pages 62–63. Short words are not always better than long ones. Many ideas cannot possibly be conveyed in words from the common vocabulary, whether long or short. In addition, although one short word and one long word may seem synonymous, practiced readers and writers know that their connotations differ substantially. Therefore, if the longer word conveys the idea more precisely than does the shorter one, good writers will choose it. No open-minded reader shies away from a book that contains long words because he or she thinks they are merely ostentatious. Perhaps they are. But in the use of language, as in the eyes of the law, a writer is presumed innocent until proven guilty. If we resent a writer's use of big words, we must show that we could say the same thing *more effectively* with short words.

---

*Note that opening a sentence with an impersonal construction such as *It is believed* is a device often used to transfer responsibility from an individual to an unspecified group. See below, pages 78–79.

The wordy writer, however, is fatally fascinated by words which carry an impression of importance and weightiness, of high-level thought and action. Pompous diction, in brief, overdignifies the commonplace idea it expresses. Thus we read *activate* instead of *form* or *begin*, *effectuate* instead of *do*, *operationalize* instead of *start*, and *entry-level position* instead of *lowest-paying job*. Hiring new help is *personnel procurement*. A list of an employee's duties is a *job description*. An order, in pompous diction, is always a *directive*. It is carried out or *implemented* or *instrumentalized* by a *coordinator* or *facilitator*, assisted perhaps by one or two *liaison officers*, who will *finalize* the arrangements. A somewhat softened *directive*, implying (no doubt falsely) that the receiver has some leeway in interpretation, is *guidelines*. To hurry up is *to expedite*; to find out is *to ascertain*; to work on or attend to is *to process*; to join or adjust (as in advertising campaigns, company plans, or policies) is *to integrate*. Standards for judging become *criteria for evaluating*, and the simple act of acquainting someone with a new activity is dignified beyond its deserts when presented as an *orientation procedure*.

Such stock words, large and small, appear on demand in the offices of administrators of all kinds, from operators of tiny businesses to the upper echelons of government, to save them the trouble of having to think of the plainest and most exact word for each situation. *Key factors, upgrade, optimum, in depth, maximize, functionalize, time frame* — such terms are nearly always verbal crutches. All too familiar is the grossly abused *setup*, which fills the gap left by the more accurate *scheme, situation*, or *plan*. Another is *picture* ("Do you get the picture?" = "Do you understand?" "Let me fill you in on the overall picture" = "Let me summarize").

Although such terms flourish perhaps most lavishly in business and government, hardly any occupation that uses language constantly is immune from them. And indeed, an important trait of such language is its contagion. A term that begins in one field may soon appear in half a dozen others. The use of *Operation* as a code formula for a large military project in the Second World War ("Operation Sea Lion") bred what is now a customary way of designating — and supposedly giving importance to — any business, civic, or charitable campaign ("Operation Sales Boom"; "Operation Safety"). Some civilian *Operations* have been widened (*escalated*) into *Wars* (on Poverty, for example). Since *top priority* is given to *crash programs*, it is conceivable that we may soon witness *crash wars* on this or that social problem, seeking to *accomplish several basic objectives* (= do several things). These "wars" will continue to a certain point, at which they will be *reevaluated* or *reassessed* by a *task force* (the old-fashioned *committee*) and then, as a result of a *high-level policy decision*, either *retained on an ongoing basis* or *phased out*.

Other overworked, and therefore decreasingly effective, stock words include many that once had metaphorical value, such as *bottleneck, pipeline, geared, ceiling, breakthrough, focus, angle, polarity, clinic* (for example, *salesmanship clinic*), and *workshop* (*teachers' workshop**). Particularly popular are words con-

---

*Both *workshop* and *conference* are now often used as verbs or participles, so that we hear of "workshopping" or of teachers who "conference" with students.

noting dramatic action. A useful byproduct of a larger enterprise, for example, is a *spinoff*. We read also of *population explosions, technological explosions, information explosions, cultural explosions, economic explosions,* even *video-game explosions.* In such a manner, a single metaphorical noun may be put to numerous uses, steadily losing its original picture-making power in the process. The word *gap*, once used to dramatize an alleged difference in military strength (the *missile gap*) has since reappeared in *generation gap* or *communications gap* (= *lack of understanding*) and *credibility gap* (= *distrust*). In addition, many non-metaphorical words have lost their former precise meaning through constant misuse. *Format* is an example. Until a few years ago, the word referred exclusively to the physical makeup of a book (page size, type, binding, arrangement of contents). Now it is applied to almost any kind of plan, such as the *format* of a television show, a meeting, or a computer program.

To those sensitive to language, stock words and phrases are as impersonal as something stamped out by a die. Individuality, freshness, even humanity itself are rigidly excluded. Such words and phrases suggest that the human touch is inappropriate, that people who write and talk in the course of their work must be as mechanized as a production line. Because such language can depersonalize both the user and the audience, we should be especially alert to its use.

Some stock words become "trend words" that are grossly overused. Such fashionable words include *dialogue*, used now as a verb as well as a noun to designate any sort of discussion; *thrust*, a term from jet propulsion technology which has replaced the standard *direction, purpose, tendency, effect*; the verb *to program*, borrowed from the computer laboratory, which is the trendy substitute for *to plan*; and *parameter*, taken from mathematics and now used for any kind of limit or boundary ("the parameters of our deal").

Through overuse and misuse, words which once held strong positive meaning can lose their integrity. *Fantastic* has been misused so often that its meaning of "unreal" or "strikingly unusual" is almost always lost, as people use it to refer to any perfectly ordinary event or item ("that was a fantastic hamburger"). Another instance of overuse is *excellence*. It used to designate genuinely high quality, especially in regard to abstractions such as academic standards and achievements. But then it became a fashionable word, first among educators — every college and university president bandied it about in speeches and appeals for funds — and then among everybody who had a product to sell. Through sheer overuse and indiscriminate application, *excellence* lost its former dignity and power. No longer a forceful expression of high resolve or accomplishment, it has been vulgarized into an adman's term. A recent *Time* essay asks, "Has a quality called Excellence gone under like Atlantis in an inundation of the third-rate, a deluge of plastics, junk food, bad movies, and trashy thought?" If so, our use — and misuse — of the word reflects that loss.*

When stock words and phrases, such as those we have been discussing, litter a writer's pages, critical readers may well suspect (1) lazy vocabulary, accompanied

---

*Another word that has undergone similar debasement is *professional* (or *pro*). What did it once mean as a term of approbation, and in what circumstances is it now applied?

by imitativeness; (2) indifference to precise meaning and usage; (3) excessive tolerance for language worn down and weakened by misuse or overuse; or even (4) deception. We will return to the deceptive uses of stock language soon.

Clichés and Other Stereotyped Language

Thus far we have seen that we, as readers, can reasonably demand that those who write for us express themselves as clearly as the subject matter allows. Those who fail to do so lay themselves open to charges of windiness, cloudy thinking, egotism, pomposity, or deliberate deception. We have also noted a common characteristic among users of excess words and stock phrases: they are all imitators. Unable or unwilling to choose their own words carefully, and thus to give individual distinction and force to what they have to say, they blindly adopt the phrasing that others use, regardless of how effective or apt it is.

Many of the stock expressions we have cited were preliminary examples of the large treasury of clichés, to which we must now pay more specific attention. The word *cliché* is French for "stereotype," a metal plate cast from a page of type. Before the advent of photographic printing processes, a printer used stereotypes to produce more copies of a book without the expensive and time-consuming work of resetting all the type. To reissue a book, the printer simply put the plates on the press and touched a button. In English usage, by a neat transfer of meaning, *cliché* means a ready-cast, or stereotyped, expression—a prefabricated phrase. Clichés save a writer or speaker the trouble of inventing a fresh way of saying something.

At first glance, the cliché might seem an admirable device, because it economizes on time and effort. But good writing is not merely economical: it is effective. It must bear the marks of being written for a particular occasion. The big drawback of even the best form letters is that they fail to meet these requirements of individuality and immediacy; and clichés are nothing more than form letters in miniature. Those who use clichés to excess write mechanically; their phrases suggest the products of a copying machine.

Nor is fondness for the cliché a sign simply of indifference. A writer's affection for threadbare words may be a clue to the quality of his or her thought. In the first place, fresh ideas by their very nature require fresh language. They cannot be expressed in any other way. Ready-made language can be fitted only to ready-made thoughts. Thus a writer who fails to recognize stale terms may also fail to recognize stale ideas, and the same is true of readers. If we can quickly detect hackneyed phraseology, we are forearmed against tired or stereotyped thinking. A commencement speaker who addresses graduates as the "leaders of the future" and urges them to put their "shoulders to the wheel" so that the "sky is the limit" only suggests, inadvertently, that he has little to say. During a recent economic slump, the Canadian Prime Minister Pierre Trudeau announced that those in "dire straits" would certainly receive government aid. Recognizing the meaninglessness of such a tired cliché, one town quickly changed its name to "Dire Straits" and notified the government that it was waiting for the promised assistance.

Use of trite language, then, suggests that a writer or speaker is intellectually as well as verbally imitative. A writer does not have to coin flamboyant "original" phrases that might be published in the "Quotable Quotes" department of the *Reader's Digest*. Indeed, one can err almost as far in that direction as in the other. But readers have a right to expect that a writer's style will provide traction for their minds, rather than allow them to slide and skid on a slippery surface paved with slick, well-worn phrases.

Insisting that good writers never, never use clichés would be foolish; let those who have never sinned cast the first stone. But good writers, if they use clichés, use them with caution. In informal speech, of course, clichés are almost indispensable. When we are relaxing with friends, we do not want to be bothered to find new ways of saying things. We rely on our ready supply of clichés, and if we do not overdraw our account, no one thinks the worse of us. So long as we succeed in conveying the everyday ideas we have in mind, no harm is done.

When does an expression become a cliché? There can be no definite answer, because what is trite to one person may still be fresh to another. But many expressions are commonly agreed to be so threadbare as to be useless except in the most informal discourse. They have been loved not wisely but too well. A good practical test is this: if we can accurately predict the exact words a speaker or writer is going to use next, that person is using clichés.

According to the report of earnings for last quarter, our company is not yet in desperate   ("straits," we expect, and lo and   , there it is). We have, on the one hand, some ground for ("optimism," we correctly anticipate). But to be frank, I must lay it ("on the line": we win again). Let's put all our cards (yes, of course, "on the table"). We are locked in fierce ("competition") with no ("holds barred"). But we can learn to roll ("with the punches"). We have a lot of lost ground ("to recover") and it will be an uphill ("fight"—but "battle" would serve just as well) all the way (we can now say it in unison). In the end, I am willing to bet my ("bottom dollar") and stake my ("reputation") on our emerging from the struggle ("victoriously").

Clichés, in brief, are paint-by-the-numbers language, phrases whose words come in a sequence as predictable as the events in the formula plot of a third-rate spy thriller or romance. The degree to which we are aware of clichés depends directly on the scope and sensitivity of our previous reading. If we have read widely, and have carefully observed authors' styles, we are probably quite alert to trite language. But if our experience of books has been limited, we will not recognize so many overripe expressions. In the eyes of such readers, most clichés still have the dew on them.

Many (but by no means all) familiar clichés are figures of speech. Now a figure of speech is useful only as long as it makes an idea more vivid, enabling the reader to visualize an abstract concept in concrete terms. If a figure of speech no longer stimulates the imagination, however, it has no more value than a nonfigurative expression. And that is what has happened to many such images, which might have been clever and appropriate long ago. Now they are almost lifeless. Some are similes (direct comparisons): *hungry as a bear, cold as ice, pale as a ghost, right as rain, tough as nails, smart as a whip, pretty as a picture, slow as molasses in January, soft as silk, green as grass, sold like hotcakes, a mind like a sieve. . . .* Some are metaphors: *the fickle finger of fate, the long arm of the law, the salt of the earth, throw caution to the winds, nip a plot in the bud, burn one's bridges behind one, water over the dam, the lion's share, tower of strength, talk off the top of one's head, a face that could stop a clock, a tongue-lashing, a cold shoulder, a beady eye, leap from the frying pan into the fire, till hell freezes over, a finger in every pie, keep one under one's thumb, on top of the world, fly into a rage.* How many can you add?

The number of clichés that compare people and animals is humorously illustrated by this paragraph from a leaflet once issued by the Columbia University Press. Occasionally we will omit a word to show how automatically our minds can supply the missing element in a cliché:

"Man," says *The Columbia Encyclopedia,* "is distinguished from other animals by his brain and his hands." But there the difference would seem to end because he is chicken-livered, lion-hearted, pigeon-toed. He is treacherous as a snake, sly as a fox, busy as a   , slippery as an   , industrious as an ant, blind as a bat, faithful as a dog, gentle as a   . He has clammy hands, the ferocity of the tiger, the manners of a pig, the purpose of a jellyfish. He gets drunk as an owl. He roars like a   ; he coos like a dove. He is still as a mouse; he hops around like a sparrow. He works like a horse. He is led like a sheep. He can fly like a bird, run like a deer, drink like a   , swim like a duck. He is nervous as a cat. He sticks his head in the sand like an   . He acts like a dog in a manger. He is coltish and kittenish, and stubborn as a   . He plays possum. He gets hungry as a bear, and wolfs his food. He has the memory of an   . He is easily cowed. He gets thirsty as a camel. He is strong as an   . He has a catlike walk, and a mousy manner. He parrots everything he hears. He acts like a puppy, and is as playful as a   . He struts like a rooster, and is as vain as a   . He is as happy as a   and as wise as an owl. He has a whale of an appetite. He has a beak for a nose, and arms like an ape. He has the eyes of a   and the neck of a bull. He is slow as a tortoise. He chatters like a magpie. He has raven hair and the shoulders of a buffalo. He's as dumb as an ox, and has the back of an ox—he is even as big as an ox. He's a worm. His   is cooked. He's crazy like a bedbug (or a fox or coot). He's a rat. He's a louse. Of course, he is cool as a cucumber, fresh as a   , red as a beet, etc.—but *The Columbia Encyclopedia* doesn't suggest that he differs in any way from vegetables and other flora, so we won't go into that.

Another large category of clichés includes those which link a particular adjective with a particular noun. Some examples: *hasty retreat, encyclopedic learning, crashing bore, voracious reader, mad scramble, cutting edge, landslide victory, marathon* (or *round the clock*) *bargaining session, slim chance, rude awakening, runaway* (or *spiraling*) *inflation, cruel fate, crushing blow, quantum leap.* Other common types of clichés include verb and noun phrases. The former are typified by *add insult to   , arm to the   , bite off more than   , lead a   life, come to the end of one's rope,   over spilled   , follow in the footsteps of, heave a   of relief, lend a helping hand.* Among the noun phrases which have outlasted their freshness (and therefore their usefulness) are *a fly in the   , the tip of the tongue, the apple of her   , a bull in a china shop, hand in hand, a labor of   , the milk of   , a pillar of the church or community, a dog in a manger, last but not least.* Clichés often arrive and grow old and feeble as twins or even triplets: *leaps and   ; hopes and   ; first and foremost; head and shoulders; short and   ; to all intents   ; body and soul; part and parcel; bag and baggage; safe and   ; tired but happy; tooth and   ; lock,   , and barrel; once and for all; hop, skip, and jump; Tom,   , and Harry; wine, women, and song; hook, line, and   ; cease and desist; to have and to hold; each and   ; aid and comfort.*

Clichés are especially deadly in descriptive and narrative writing, which depends on freshness and exactness to communicate impressions to a reader. A sure mark of the inexperienced writer is the willingness to describe settings and characters in clichéd terms. "He walked with catlike tread" . . . "they were drenched by mountainous waves" . . . "the moonbeams danced on the water" . . . "the fighter sprang into action" . . . "the child was bubbling over with happiness" . . . "there was a blinding flash" . . . "he made a convulsive grab for the rope" . . . "they heard a rustle of leaves" . . . "the flowers nodded in the gentle breeze" . . . "the shadows were lengthening" . . . "Kim had a glassy stare." The only delight we can find in such writing is that of seeing old familiar faces. Surely we are allowed to join in no new experience. We cannot see things from any new angle or receive a fresh interpretation of meaning. A "creative" writer who depends on clichés is really not creating anything, but merely recycling worn-out words and phrases.

Whether we realize it or not, many of our clichés come from books which have influenced our common speech. *To kill the fatted calf, to cast the first stone, covers a multitude of sins, the spirit is willing but the flesh is weak, the wages of sin, the blind leading the blind, the parting of the way, voice crying in the wilderness*—all have their source in the Bible, even though in most cases their original biblical contexts have been forgotten. Few people now react to them as deeply as did those to whom the English Bible was a new and wonderful book, the phrases shining like coins from the mint.

The alert reader can watch clichés in the very process of being made. For example, words associated with atomic developments are now standard clichés in many sorts of usages. The verb *to mushroom* was a fairly common cliché many years ago, when it meant "to grow as fast as mushrooms" or "to assume a mushroom shape" ("the suburbs of the city mushroomed"; "the bullet mushroomed against the steel plate"). But once the cloud produced by an atomic explosion was described as *mushroom-shaped,* the cliché achieved new popularity and in the process lost its metaphorical suggestions. Today *mushrooming* applies to everything from a dam under construction to a sudden burst of public sentiment on some issue. *Chain reaction,* originally a technical term in nuclear physics, now is an all too handy way to describe a series of events that are (or are supposed to be) causally connected, in the manner of a bowling ball knocking down the head pin, which in turn knocks down pins two and three, and so on.* Observe also how the verb *to trigger,* first applied to the action of an atomic bomb in setting off the far greater explosion of the hydrogen bomb, has become a tiresome cliché to describe any similar action, no matter how remote the resemblance: "The protest of the home owners' delegation *triggered* a full investigation by City Council." *Bottom line,* by contrast, has entered the general vocabulary from accounting, where it referred to the bottom line of a ledger, indicating either a net profit or loss. Now we hear of *bottom line issues* or the *bottom line word* on something. What additional words can you list that are undergoing a similar change?

Clichés and stereotyped language are especially apparent in news reports, where writers work against strict deadlines. Some newspapers such as the *New York Times,* the (London) *Guardian,* or the *Christian Science Monitor* and a few news programs on public broadcasting networks take pride in the quality of their language. But most of us, used to our local newspapers and local news reports, will recognize the following sample of clichés. We've added their simpler equivalents in the right-hand column.

The death toll rose to ten today in the wake of the disastrous fire. . . .	Four more people died as a result of the fire. . . .
The mercury soared to a record high for the year (or plummeted to a new low). . . .	Today was the hottest (or coldest) day of the year. . . .
At an early hour this morning the identity of the victim had not yet been established. . . .	Early this morning the body was still unidentified. . . .
The traffic was snarled (or paralyzed or at a standstill or moved at a snail's pace or crept bumper to bumper or ground to a halt) as snow blanketed the metropolitan area. . . .	Snowfall slowed traffic. . . .
Local police, aided by volunteers, today combed the area adjacent to Center City in search of clues that might lead to the solution of the bizarre murder-kidnapping mystery. . . .	Local volunteers and police were looking for the person who kidnapped and murdered. . . .

*How does this differ, if at all, from the cliché *domino effect,* a term used in reference to (anticipated) geopolitical events?

Three persons suffered injuries when the automobile in which they were traveling figured in a head-on collision with a large truck. . . .	Three persons were hurt when their car hit a large truck. . . .
As he completed the investigation, the coroner said it was his opinion that death was instantaneous. . . .	The coroner said he thought the person died instantly. . . .

Many single words, especially epithets and verbs, seem indispensable to news reporting. Any bigger-than-ordinary fire or auto accident is *spectacular;* an unusual accident must be *tragic,* a *freak,* or both. When public officials approve of something they *hail* it; when they disapprove of it they *attack* it; and when they want something they *urge* it. When two factions have a disagreement they *clash;* when anything is announced it is *made public.*

The language of weather and sports reporters seems particularly susceptible to cliché. Every hurricane *howls,* swollen rivers *rage,* high winds *lash,* storms *buffet,* and rains *pound* a region *relentlessly.* Sportswriters, perhaps because they deal with lively, entertaining matters that seldom have serious implications, have greater freedom, and indeed a greater necessity, than do other reporters to find colorful new ways of saying things. Sport reports overflow with metaphorical language. When first used, such terms add a welcome novelty to what are, after all, fairly routine events. (One hockey game differs from another in details but not in general pattern.) But like all clichés, these terms soon lose their vividness through overuse. We took the following passage from a local newspaper: "The Beavers *handed a setback* to the Bills as they *breezed to victory* today. The Beavers *capped a six-game winning streak* as *slugger* Jake Peters *clubbed* a two-run *homer out of sight* in the sixth, *driving in* veteran Phil Smithe. The great *knuckleballer* Sam Jefferson *hurled a grueling seven straight* in his *longest stint* since July, and the crowd *roared their approval* in an *extravaganza of fan fever.*" Such formulaic writing may help out the writer facing a deadline, but it is flat, dull, and predictable to most readers.

Circumlocution, Euphemism, and Doublespeak

Clichés and stereotyped diction may — and should — bore readers. But selected diction can also, in the form of circumlocution, euphemism, or doublespeak, actually obscure the truth. All three can be forms of verbal cowardice, of unwillingness to put hard-to-face facts in forthright language. A *circumlocution* is a roundabout expression which takes one on a pleasant detour around a disagreeable idea. A *euphemism* is a device, usually consisting of a single word, by which the disagreeable idea is given a more attractive appearance. *Doublespeak,* the name given by the novelist George Orwell to the language of Big Brother in 1984, is the extensive use of such language, especially by governmental or military groups, to hide or blunt the truth.

Abundant illustrations of such whitewashing devices come to mind at once. In fact, such expressions reveal much about the values, attitudes, or fears of a culture. We use a host of euphemisms to soften the idea of death (*to expire, to pass away, to enter into eternal rest, to be deceased, to go to one's reward,* and—a favorite of insurance salesmen—*to be out of the picture;* and the less sentimental ones, *to kick the bucket, to cash in one's chips, to give up the ghost, to check out*). How many others can you add? We are sensitive about bodily functions; hence our numerous expressions for toilet or bathroom (*rest room, lounge, powder room, lavatory, can, head, john, W.C.*—the British water closet). Other euphemisms gloss over unpleasant truths relating to disease (*mental illness, rest home, retirement villa, respiratory affliction, terminal patient*). Still others attempt to cover up particularly unappealing aspects of life (*halitosis* for bad breath, *blemish* for pimple, *intemperate* or *tipsy* for drunk, *marital infidelity* for adultery, *incarceration* for jail, *corrective institution* for prison).

Euphemisms often refer to occupations, where they serve either to conceal unpleasantness or "upgrade" social status. *Bookkeepers, dogcatchers, undertakers, garbage collectors, janitors, teachers of physical education,* and *members of the "Mob"* are now, respectively, *account executives, canine control officers, morticians* (or *funeral directors* or, currently, *bereavement counselors*), *sanitation engineers, custodians, instructors of human kinetics,* and *members of career offender cartels*. In one large school system, the person who checks up on students who stay away from school, once called the truant officer, holds the dignified title of *director of pupil personnel*. A used-book dealer may advertise as an *antiquarian book specialist* or *consultant*.

Business euphemisms and circumlocutions are not limited to names for occupations. *Termination of employment* (the British call it *declaring staff redundant;* in Canada, teachers who lose their jobs are *made surplus*) is a common euphemism for firing. Unsuccessful applicants are often told that they are *overqualified* or that *opportunities are limited* or that they have been *deselected* rather than that they didn't get the job.

The language of merchandising and sales takes full advantage of euphemisms. The *budget* or *economy shops* of department stores dispose of cheap goods; the installment plan is *deferred payment;* a kitchenware shop is a *gourmet boutique;* the complaint desk is the *customer service center;* fake material is *simulated;* a clerk is a *salesperson;* a used-car lot is a *preowned vehicle center*. As we saw in Chapter 1, advertisements are filled with such attempts to build on positive connotations.*

Circumlocutions and euphemisms are very useful ways to oil the wheels (cliché) of social relationships. They are often the best friends we can have in situations that call for tact and courtesy instead of bluntness. They are soft words that can turn away anger or save hurt feelings. Not long ago, a faculty committee in a New York City junior high school compiled a list of phrases to convey their complaints about pupils to parents without causing offense:

---

*See the lively pages on euphemisms in Mencken's *The American Language,* 4th ed., pp. 284–294, and Supplement One thereto, pp. 565–595; and Paul Stevens's discussion of advertising "weasel words" in *I Can Sell You Anything* (1972).

is awkward and clumsy	appears to have difficulty with muscular coordination
does all right if pushed	accomplishes tasks when interest is frequently stimulated
is too free with fists	resorts to physical means of winning a point or attracting attention
could stand more baths; is dirty	needs guidance in development of good habits of hygiene
lies	shows difficulty in distinguishing between imaginary and factual material
steals	needs help in learning to respect the property rights of others
cheats	needs help in learning to adhere to rules and standards of fair play
is insolent	needs guidance in learning to express respect
is lazy	needs ample supervision in order to work well
is rude	needs to develop a respectful attitude toward others
is selfish	needs help in learning to enjoy sharing with others
is coarse	needs assistance in developing social refinement
is noisy	needs to develop quieter habits of communication

In the same list of tactful expressions, the teachers recommended ways to tell parents a child had poor table manners, was a bully, was babyish, hung around with gangs, was disliked by others, was often late, or skipped school. What expressions can you think of for each case?

Of course, the elaborate phrases seem more polite and genteel than their shorter, more direct equivalents. On the other hand, they can suggest pussyfooting, or beating around the bush. (Note the metaphors.) And certainly the loss of directness may be a high price to pay for delicacy. Putting aside the question of hurt feelings, which expression—the direct one or the indirect one that uses euphemisms—is more likely to stir the parents to action?

Carried to their logical extreme, circumlocution and euphemism often cloak ideas that are drastically opposed to surface meaning. They not only dress up unpleasant concepts in more agreeable clothes; sometimes they actually disguise them. The iron fist of true meaning is concealed, sometimes not too subtly, in the velvet glove of elegant phraseology. Thus the sign in a hotel, "For your convenience, please consult the cashier concerning credit needs before departing," means in blunt language "Don't leave without paying the bill, and don't pay with a bad check either." An overdue bill that concludes "Perhaps in the rush of events you have allowed the matter to escape your attention" is a thinly veiled warning that the next notice you get will be from the collection agent. And the editor's rejection letter which begins "Your manuscript has received our careful attention and we are not unaware of its merits. Unfortunately our backlog of material is so large . . ." may conceal the sentiment, "This is garbage; we wouldn't touch it." In such cases tact, which is always desirable, is corrupted into hypocrisy.

Language, so used, becomes the vehicle of dishonesty. Euphemisms of this type are particularly dangerous and demand special vigilance on the part of readers and listeners. When *limited peace offensive* means "heavy bombing," when *negative growth* means "bankruptcy," when *reeducation center* means "concentration camp," or when a leak in a nuclear reactor is called an *unscheduled event* — then euphemism enters the realm of doublespeak. The extensive use of such verbal deception led the National Council of Teachers of English to form a special Doublespeak Committee, whose task is to alert citizens to this brand of linguistic concealment and to promote the use of honesty and clarity in public language. Each year, this group gives a Doublespeak Award to individuals or groups most guilty of using euphemisms to deceive others or to make it somehow easier to do or accept the unthinkable. Military groups or leaders from several different countries have received tongue-in-cheek "awards" for their widespread use of terms which mask brutal destruction. One year the award went to a U.S. Air Force colonel who said to reporters covering the American bombing raids in Cambodia: "You always write it's bombing, bombing, bombing. It's not bombing! It's air support." Another year the award went to Yasir Arafat, leader of the Palestine Liberation Organization, for this statement: "We do not want to destroy any people. It is precisely because we have been advocating coexistence that we have shed so much blood." As you read newspapers and magazines and listen to television or radio news reports, watch out for the use of doublespeak. You may want to start keeping a list of such deceptive euphemisms. If you do, you are invited to submit a nomination for a Doublespeak Award. Just write down the example, including the place of publication, and send it to the Committee on Public Doublespeak, National Council of Teachers of English, Urbana, Illinois, 61801.

Overworked Nouns

Another cause of unnecessarily difficult language is the tendency to overuse nouns, or nouns in phrases, and to neglect verbs. The prime mover in language, whether spoken or written, is the verb. Single action verbs carry more power than linking (copulative) verbs. If the verb in a sentence is of the latter kind, it has the hard task of dragging along a train of inert nouns. "The effect of the overuse of nouns in writing is the placing of too much strain on the inadequate number of verbs and the resultant prevention of movement of the thought." There is only one verb, *is*, and you can count the nouns for yourself. Forms of the verb *to be* are hard workers, but they cannot possibly do everything demanded of them by people who rely too heavily on them. (You may want to take a sample of your own writing and count the number of *to be* verbs. If the number is over 35 percent of your total verbs, you are probably overworking them, and as a result, your writing is probably not very forceful.) As in the quoted sentence, the copulative (any form of the verb *to be*) too often must pull a subject loaded down with nouns and noun phrases; at the same time, it must push a predicate that is also loaded with nouns. The result is a sentence that creaks and groans when it moves. The presence of so many nouns forces the writer to use many prepositional phrases, especially *of* phrases, to the detriment of smooth rhythm. An intelligent writer will replace some of the noun phrases with clauses, adding verbs which will help share the load: "One who overuses nouns in writing places too much strain on the verbs and thus prevents the thought from moving along." Note that revising the sentence converted the static nouns *overuse* and *prevention* to the motion verbs *overuses* and *prevents*. The revision also significantly reduces the number of prepositional phrases. Circle the prepositions in the following sentence and then see how many you can eliminate in a revision: "For children, the constant watching of the medium of television is harmful because it results in the acceptance of violence and in the tendency toward passivity."

Much dull and turgid writing, especially in government and business, prefers a noun derived from a verb instead of the verb itself: *information* (inform), *determination* (determine), *assessment* (assess), *resistance* (resist), *development* (develop). As a result, the statement becomes less direct than it should be. "The decision on evaluation of student fees takes place at the presidential level" does not have the same force as does "The President decides when to raise student fees." At its worst, overusing nouns results in nonsense. Here is a sentence taken from a governmental news bulletin: "The rationale for the alteration in administration is the maintenance of one of the beneficial features of the former system—the equalization principle." When writing becomes this weighted down with vague nouns, we simply can't understand it.

The practice of headline writers may well encourage the overuse of nouns in prose. Often they pile noun upon noun into a tottering wall of heavy words. We might forgive the headline SLUM PROJECT FINANCE PLAN ANSWER SOUGHT because the copy editor had to cram a complex idea into the small space of two or three lines at the head of a column. But what of the jarring phrase "Mortgage Protector Disability Income Insurance Plan" in a brochure which presumably has as much space as it needs? Because such strings of nouns are very hard for readers to understand, they usually convey little meaning. In addition, they are ugly: *industry mechanization potential*, for example, has little to recommend it by way of either sound or sense. Perhaps more intelligible, but hardly lovelier, is the term *program audience size measurement service* to designate the Neilsen and other "surveys" which lead to television ratings. *Simply Stated*, the newsletter of the Document Design Center, which reports on efforts to promote the use of "plain English" in government and business writing, recently called for examples of such noun strings. The longest, with seven nouns, came from the *Commerce Business Daily:* "Roof Rock Bolt Bond Integrity Tester Development." Can you top this score?

Overused Passives

Passives can also make writing unnecessarily difficult to read. "A letter is dictated" is not as easy to understand as "Professor Ashdown dictates a letter." The first instance fixes our attention on the act itself, which is hard to picture, since apparently no one is around to perform it. The letter is just there, being dictated. But the second instance fixes our attention not on the abstract idea of the act itself but on the concrete presence of someone who is performing it.

You will recall that we did not finish correcting a sentence we were working on (page 64). We left it in this form: "The redundancy found in so many college students' themes should be eliminated by every means known to the teacher." We already omitted the empty negative "It is not incorrect to say." We now get rid of ("eliminate") the weak passive, and the sentence becomes much more vigorous: "The teacher should use every method he or she knows to get rid of the redundancy found in so many college students' themes."

Like all grammatical constructions, the passive voice has its uses. In particular, it allows a writer to highlight certain words or ideas and to express ideas without attributing them to a specific general source. For that reason, journalism, government communications, and scientific writing use it constantly. Those who do not want to take personal responsibility for their statements find an easy "out" by saying "It is directed that you be relieved of your duties" or "it has been proven" instead of "I direct that you be fired" or "my research proves"; or even "It is recommended that you begin radiation therapy" instead of "I recommend that you. . . ." Readers must distinguish carefully between those writers who use the passive voice for valid stylistic reasons, as scientists do, and those who use it merely out of habit or as a means of avoiding responsibility.

As an example, read the opening of the dispatch the *New York Times* writer Tom Wicker filed when John Kennedy was assassinated in 1963:

> Dallas, Nov. 22—President John Fitzgerald Kennedy was shot and killed by an assassin today.
>
> He died of a wound in the brain caused by a rifle-bullet that was fired at him as he was riding through downtown Dallas in a motorcade.
>
> Vice President Lyndon Baines Johnson, who was riding in the third car behind Mr. Kennedy's car, was sworn in as the 36th President of the United States 99 minutes after Mr. Kennedy's death. . . .
>
> Shortly after his assassination, Lee H. Oswald, who once defected to the Soviet Union and who has been active in the Fair Play for Cuba Committee, was arrested by the Dallas police. Tonight he was accused of the killing.

The crucial verbs in Wicker's opening are passive, and with good cause. Readers were primarily interested in the facts and in Kennedy; the important thing was that Kennedy was shot, not that an assassin killed him. In the same way, the Vice President is more important in sentence three than who swore him in, just as

Oswald's arrest is more important in the next sentence than the fact that the Dallas police arrested him. Note also that we are unaware of the writter. We know that a newspaper reporter is writing the story, but we are not interested in hearing that "Tom Wicker reported that the President. . . ."

A month later, Wicker wrote an article about the same day for *Times Talk*, a *New York Times* house publication. The different audience and purpose dictated a very different use of verbs. Here is the opening of that report on Kennedy's assassination.

> I think I was in the first press bus. But I can't be sure. Pete Lisagor of the Chicago *Daily New* says he *knows* he was in the first press bus and he describes things that went on aboard it that didn't happen on the bus I was in. But I still *think* I was in the first press bus.
>
> I cite that minor confusion as an example of the way it was in Dallas in the early afternoon of Nov. 22. At first no one knew what happened, or how, or where, much less why.

In this opening, all the verbs are active, because the focus here is on Wicker and on *his* activities and experiences that day.

We should not, then, condemn the use of passive verbs in general. But we should recognize that legitimate use of the passive can easily turn into abuse. When stories or reports constantly employ passives or impersonal constructions which do not require an agent ("it was learned," "it was revealed," "it was reported," or "progress was indicated"), then the critical reader rightly asks "*who* learned, or revealed, or reported, or indicated?" A similar device for passing on news without giving a source is the use of the mysterious *officials who asked that their names be withheld, spokespersons*, or *informed* (or *highly placed* or *reliable*) *sources*.

Two paragraphs on the same topic provide a good way to sum up what we have said so far about the forms wordiness and difficult language take—and the need to avoid them. The first paragraph is about as easy to get through as ankle-deep mud. Read it and see how many examples of wordiness and sheer bad writing you can spot.

> In addition, attention must be called to the places of habitation, which were decidedly uniform in appearance and street-front alignment. Their condition was badly deteriorated, the substructure of a number of them having settled out of the perpendicular and developed an unsteadiness on their foundations, their exterior walls deficient in respect to cleanliness and exhibiting the negative effects of climatological conditions on the paint. The doors were conspicuous for the evidence they displayed of prolonged and abusive misuse, their surfaces being severely mutilated by the repeated and wanton application of various damaging instruments; the vertical posts abutting on these doors had lost the stability they had previously possessed, and

the stucco that in former times had provided a cover for their surface had at some considerable distance in the past eroded away; it was only with difficulty that they provided a means of support to a minimum degree for the equally vibratory doors of which the hinge mechanisms, having been oxidized by sustained exposure to adverse weather, were no longer capable of upholding a weight of any substantial size. The windows were rendered opaque by strata of adhesive powdery particles which had been borne upward from the unmaintained thoroughfare below. Ubiquitous unsanitary conditions and physical disability were the obvious evidence of unsatisfactory economic circumstances on the part of the occupants and of the disappearance of the hope of these occupants of an eventual amelioration of their present mode of living. These disadvantaged persons purchased the lowest-priced aliment that would sustain life, whether it was food with a high ratio of starch such as potatoes, the most common nonalcoholic beverage, edible forms of the general category of compounds of fatty acids and glycerol, or the flesh of various animals with high protein content; and they spent in inactivity the interval until previously fresh bread had become desiccated to an extent sufficient to warrant the commercial purveyor's marketing it at a reduced figure. Even residue from their economical repasts was utilized to the utmost degree. The lengthy streets were abundant with indications of decomposition, dilapidation, and decrepitude. It was not within the realm of possibility to activate a memory of the period at which this particular thoroughfare was the domicile of some who were numbered among the most affluent and well-born members of this urban center's society. It was many years since the final survivor of this society, a female of superior social status, had reached the conclusion of her life in the single remaining residence which preserved the dignity of that society. It is a fact that not even solar rays appear to penetrate this area. The intangible suggestion of monetary wealth and social elevation by which it was once characterized has now evanesced to a virtually total extent. Neither flora of any description nor birds of any nature are able to flourish in this vicinity; it is impossible for even so adaptable an ornithological specimen as the common sparrow to find sufficient nutritional value in the food to be discovered here; as a matter of fact, the prevailing conditions are inhospitable even to the genus Cirsium. It is difficult if not impossible to conceive of the possibility that any member of the literary profession was ever motivated toward visionary exultation and verbalized statement in this environment.

This is, of course, a very bad, indefensibly long, and unnecessarily wordy paragraph. Its dull, lackluster words hide whatever sense impressions it might have conveyed. In fact, you probably "read" it without understanding much of it. Extensively rewritten, with attention to direct statements and concrete language, the result might be something like the following passage from the autobiographical writings of the Irish playwright Sean O'Casey:

> There were the houses, too—a long, lurching row of discontented incurables, smirched with the age-long marks of ague, fevers, cancer, and consumption, the soured tears of little children, and the signs of disappointed newly-married girls. The doors were scarred with time's spit and anger's heavy knocking; the pillars by their sides were shaky, their stuccoed bloom long since peeled away, and they looked like crutches keeping the trembling doors standing on their palsied feet. The gummy-eyed windows blinked dimly out, lacquered by a year's tired dust from the troubled street below. Dirt and disease were the big sacraments here—outward and visible signs of an inward and spiritual disgrace. The people bought the cheapest things in food they could find in order to live, to work, to worship: the cheapest spuds, the cheapest tea, the cheapest meat, the cheapest fat; and waited for unsold bread to grow stale that they might buy that cheaper, too. Here they gathered up the fragments so that nothing would be lost. The streets were long haggard corridors of rottenness and ruin. What wonderful mind of memory could link this shrinking wretchedness with the flaunting gorgeousness of silk and satin; with bloom of rose and scent of lavender? A thousand years must have passed since the first lavender lady was carried out feet first from the last surviving one of them. Even the sun shudders now when she touches a roof, for she feels some evil has chilled the glow of her garment. The flower that here once bloomed is dead forever. No wallflower here has crept into a favoured cranny; sight and sign of the primrose were far away; no room here for a dance of daffodils; no swallow twittering under a shady eave; and it was sad to see an odd sparrow seeking a yellow grain from the mocking dust; not even a spiky-headed thistle, purple mitred, could find a corner here for a sturdy life. No Wordsworth here wandered about as lonely as a cloud.

(Exercises: pages 93–102)

THE USES AND ABUSES OF TECHNICAL LANGUAGE

Since every trade and profession has its own special ideas, methods, materials, and tools, it must also have its own special vocabulary.* The medical vocabulary, which may seem unintelligible to most of us, is essential to doctors. It enables

---

*The vocabulary of a special field is often called *jargon*. We will use *technical language* to avoid the strong negative connotations of *jargon*.

them to speak concisely and accurately of diagnoses, medicines, surgical procedures, courses of treatment, and clusters of symptoms which could otherwise be
described only by indirect and time-wasting paragraphs. Furthermore, some medical terms have an antiseptic freedom from emotional connotations—a great
advantage in the field of human anatomy and physiology, where many of the
common words used to describe parts, functions, and diseases of the body involve
problems of modesty, taste, or even revulsion. Thus a doctor can speak briskly of
palpating a patient's abdomen, when the word *feeling* might arouse irrelevant
responses. And to the layman, at least, *carcinogenic* is a less disturbing word than
cancer-causing; and a *cerebral episode* somehow is less alarming than a *stroke.*

So it is with all other men and women who have their own occupational vocabularies—the electronic engineer, the fashion designer, the computer programmer,
the psychologist, the food chemist. Their special vocabularies enable them to
think more precisely and to communicate with their colleagues more easily and
exactly. This is, after all, a logical extension of our earlier principle that we must
speak the language of the audience whenever possible.

By the same token, the use of technical language in addressing a nontechnical
audience is inappropriate, inefficient, and perhaps even dishonest. The willful use
of technical doubletalk is important to the success of quacks in every field. Every
person who caters to the real or fancied emotional ills of readers of popular "self-
help" books depends on such terms as *neurosis, frustration, adjustment, inhibi-
tion, drive, sublimation, fixation, compensation, phobia, complex*—terms which
have prestige with the public because they are associated with the "mystique" of
the psychoanalyst's couch. Ideally, only a trained psychologist or psychiatrist
should use such terms, because they represent extremely complicated ideas.
Nevertheless, they have become part of the popular vocabulary, even though
their meanings are seriously distorted and oversimplified in common usage.

Thus technical language should be kept for a specific technical audience, for
times when it provides the best means of concise, exact communication. It should
not be used just because it is easy to use, because it impresses others, or because
it excludes others from the knowledge it hides.

Here is a classic anecdote on the subject:

> A plumber wrote to the Federal Bureau of Standards that he had
> found hydrochloric acid did a good job of cleaning out clogged
> drains.
> The bureau wrote: "The efficacy of hydrochloric acid is indisputa-
> ble, but the corrosive residue is incompatible with metallic
> permanence."
> The plumber replied he was glad the bureau agreed.
> Again the bureau wrote: "We cannot assume responsibility for the
> production of toxic and noxious residue with hydrochloric acid and
> suggest you use an alternative procedure."
> The plumber was happy again at bureau agreement with his idea.
> At last the bureau wrote: "Don't use hydrochloric acid. It eats hell
> out of the pipes."

Many writers in scientific and technical fields use a clear professional language which conveys meaning with utmost precision and economy. Other writers, however, often grossly misuse their technical vocabulary. To the sociologist such words as *status, ethnic, mobility, institution, ecological,* and *culture* embody basic and necessary sociological concepts. Although students may be irritated by the constant use of such terms in textbooks, they must learn exactly what such words mean or they can learn little about sociology. Every field of study and almost every job demand that students or new workers master certain basic terms and concepts. But sometimes writers in these fields go to unwarranted extremes in the use — or misuse — of technical language. The following passage appeared in a journal for sociologists and social psychologists:

> The purpose of this article is to demonstrate that media influence is a function of the receptiveness of message recipients to communication in general. It is also to show that this receptiveness is a scalable pre-dispositioning attitude which is directly and positively correlated with the number of types of media to which message recipients are exposed, the impact these media have, and the overt behavior induced by media exposure and contact.

Which, being interpreted, means: "I intend to show that newspapers and television and other 'mass media' influence people who pay attention to them, and that the more people are bombarded with any given message, the more they will respond to it." A truism is all that lurks behind the wordiness and technical language.

Now try your hand at translating this further paragraph:

> From a socio-psychological point of view, a person's attitudes toward certain events in his life space are conditioned by the norms of his associates and of his positive reference groups. Data from sample interview surveys on international attitudes do not usually provide evidence directly relevant to this general hypothesis, for three reasons: First, the number of persons from any particular interacting group who fall into the sample is generally too small to permit adequate assessment of the group's norms. Second, there are too few groups for which the area of foreign affairs is sufficiently salient to encourage the development of norms. Finally, it is difficult to disentangle a respondent's perception of a reference group norm from his tendency to project his own attitudes onto persons he likes. For these reasons, sample interview surveys are probably not the most appropriate device for the study of social influences from the standpoint of reference group therapy. Preferable approaches are provided by experimental manipulation of artificial groups or long-term study of complete natural groups.

Educators are guilty of misusing technical language in much the same way as the sociologists just quoted. We find writers for educational journals speaking of *learning facilitators* and *instructional personnel* instead of teachers. Professional books and articles are filled with such terms as *acceleration, integration, visually aided instruction, life adjustment progress, relatedness, subskills measurement,* and a host of unnecessarily difficult terms drawn from statistics. Use of such words is justified only if the audience belongs to the same specialized group and if the words stand for well-defined concepts that cannot be described in simpler language. Too often today, we hear of pupils *verbalizing a felt need* instead of asking for something; or of taking home a *skill-concepts progress chart* rather than a report card. In the *classroom situation learning environment,* the teacher (more probably the *facilitator*) *optimizes learning potential* and *gives corrective feedback.* Students are either *underachievers* or *overachievers;* who ever heard of a mere *achiever?*

Although we have emphasized the misuse of technical language by social scientists and educators, writers in every field — government, business, the physical sciences, and the arts (critics of literature, music, painting, architecture, film) — are often guilty of the same errors of judgment. Many such writers seem either unwilling or unable to achieve clear communication, even with colleagues in their own field. The books and articles of some contemporary literary critics are full of pompous diction, incomprehensible terminology, and convoluted sentences, and as lacking in grace and clarity as anything a social scientist might turn out. And once readers have cut their way through the tangled jungle of words, they often find that what the writer has to say is actually fairly simple. Little wonder, then, that effective writers with liberal arts backgrounds are in growing demand — in the sciences, government, industry, and certain professions. They often possess a valuable talent: the ability to turn wordy, overblown, unnecessarily difficult language into clear, concise English and hence to interpret specialist to specialist — and to the public as well.

(Exercises: pages 102–104)

EXORCISES

ELEMENTARY CLUES OF DICTION; CLUES TO PERSONALITY AND INTENTION

2.1 Use clues of diction to infer as much as you can about the author of each of the following statements.

1. It's been real, eh?
2. I've had a pleasant time; thank you ever so much.
3. Gotta scram, Sam; thanks for the jam.
4. What a blast!
5. The evening has proved most entertaining. I extend my deepest thanks.

6. Basically, I mean fun-wise, this really blew me away.
7. Most enjoyable, old fellow.
8. Dee-lightful, dearie; loved every teenie weenie minute.
9. Gotta blow. Thanks for the burgers 'n' suds.
10. Crazy, daddy-o, crazy.
11. Just our luck. Don dug the obit out of the morgue a week ago and we had it in type, all ready for word from Mac, who was standing the death watch at the hospital. So what happens? He calls ten minutes after the last edition has gone to bed.
12. I rang through to the theatre, but they couldn't give me anything but two seats in the stalls a fortnight from Boxing Day.
13. Oh, Doris! What a thrilling surprise! I hadn't known you were coming to the reunion. My dear, why haven't I heard from you? It's been oodles of years!
14. Despite the dark and ominous clouds that seem to hover every-where we look, we can forge ahead to ever greater achieve-ments if we but retain our faith in the eternal verities to which our grandparents clung and refuse to be daunted by the proph-ets of gloom and doom.
15. Can't tell them young folks nothin'. They figger as how they knows it all. The big city, ain't nothin' for 'em but they'll be want-in' to go to the big city anyways and get into all sorts of tomfoolery.
16. Look you, forsooth, I am, as it were, bound for the land of matri-mony; 'tis a voyage, d'ye see, that was none of my seeking. I was commanded by father, and if you like of it mayhap I may steer into your harbour. How say you, mistress? The short of the thing is, that if you like me, and I like you, we may chance to swing in a hammock together.
17. My young men shall never work. Men who work cannot dream, and wisdom comes in dreams.

    You ask me to plow the ground. Shall I take a knife and tear my mother's breast? Then when I die she will not take me to her bosom to rest.

    You ask me to dig for stone. Shall I dig under her skin for bones? Then when I die I cannot enter her body to be born again. You ask me to cut grass and make hay and sell it, and be rich like white men. But how dare I cut off my mother's hair?
18. As the reservoir of knowledge becomes obese and the momen-tum of data production catapults geometrically, man finds him-self in a strangely deluded self-perception: he perceives himself as omniscient. This aberration of self-focusing, this self-delusion, has spawned another grotesque optical disfiguration—man now imagines himself as omnipotent. Armed with this new dazzling chromeplated rhinestone of knowledge, "stoned" over the power of his "toy technology" and developing an incontinent

will for self-restraint, man has gleefully immersed himself into his perceived task: conquering and domesticating what is left of nature and then going full speed in "making her perfect" by peeling away at her tresses and learning her structural body secrets.

19. My friends, peace be on this house! On the master thereof, on the mistress thereof, on the young maidens, and on the young men! My friends, why do I wish for peace? What is peace? Is it war? No. Is it strife? No. Is it lovely and gentle, and beautiful and pleasant, and serene, and joyful? O yes! Therefore, my friends, I wish for peace, upon you and yours.

20. There has come to be recognized a situation where the input-output capacity of the intradepartmental information distribution system has fallen behind demand-use pressures. To facilitate rectification of this matter, a study team will be directed to submit proposals for consideration.

2.2 What can you infer about the personality, education, and attitudes of the speaker who made the following comments?

The czars exiled misfits to Siberia. The Soviets do that, too. The Siberian exiles will eventually break away. Alaska is the place for misfits from the Lower Forty-Eight. And we will eventually break away. Alaskans are inheritors of determinative genes that took people out of Europe to the New World. Alaska attracts construction workers who are wild hairs, willing to take a chance. The Gelvins would be misfits somewhere else. They're doers. They don't destroy. They build. They preserve. They are conservationists in the true sense of the word. They have killed wolves right and left. They are responsible for many moose being alive today. That Ginny—she's a hell of a gunner. She can take a Browning and shoot the hell out of wolves.

2.3 The members of each of the following groups of words and phrases, although having the same general denotation, vary in connotation. Consider who would use each term in what circumstances, and what the user's attitude is toward whatever the term refers to.

1. belly, stomach, abdomen, trunk, torso, nether regions, gut, breadbasket, midriff, tummy, midsection, paunch
2. heavy drinker, alcoholic, alky, toper, sot, lush, inebriate, drinking man, tosspot, drunkard, dipsomaniac, drunk, wino, rummy, winebibber, barfly, problem drinker
3. rollback, recession, inventory adjustment, decline, depression, slump, dip, leveling off, hard times, distress
4. cinema, movies, flickers, flicks, motion pictures, picture show, film

5. tall tale, whopper, fib, lie, story, prevarication, misrepresentation, misleading statement, gross exaggeration, stretching the truth, fantasy, invention, fairy tale, hype
6. senior citizen, old-timer, old fogey, codger, oldie, oldster, geezer, gaffer, octogenarian, patriarch or matriarch, old-age pensioner, retiree, old gentleman, elderly gentleman
7. village, small community, crossroads, whistle stop, jerkwater town, hole in the road, rural settlement, backwoods town, bush community, small town, hick town, boondocks
8. nonintellectual type, slow learner, underachiever, late bloomer, dope, plodder, backward student, dullard, dull pupil, knucklehead, dunce, member of the less advanced group, dummy
9. undergarments, lingerie, unmentionables, underwear, scanties, underthings, undies, intimate wear, intimate feminine apparel
10. peace officer, law enforcement officer, policeman, cop, copper, flatfoot, the law, the Man, gendarme, fuzz, smokey
11. colleague, ally, associate, sidekick, partner, mate, comrade, buddy, accomplice, cohort, companion, co-worker, collaborator, henchman, business associate

TALKING THE LANGUAGE OF THE AUDIENCE

2.4 How effectively does the following advertisement convey its message to today's audience? Can you suggest any improvements in the wording or content?

The Floor Where Lives Eternal the Embers' Ruddy Glow.

Just as Maple gives you the spirit of sunlight in a floor, so do Beech and Birch hold in themselves the richer coloring of the embers which glow on the autumn hearth.

Natural colors are these—the pleasing effects which you secure when you finish these three beautiful flooring woods with clear varnish or wax. But if you wish the darker tone of walnut or mahogany—if you wish to harmonize the color of your floor with the decorative scheme of your whole room—you may accomplish precisely the effect you desire by using a stain on a floor of Beech or Birch.

Thus do floors of Maple, Beech or Birch round out their sphere of universal usefulness.

2.5 Suggest ways to rewrite each of the following messages to make it more easily understood by the audience indicated in brackets.

1. [Workers in a small factory]
   It has been decided to issue this Bulletin on a quarterly basis for the time being, until such time as there is sufficient input to warrant a more frequent schedule of publication.

2. [Local real estate agents]
   No person who is appointed to manage, sell, lease, or otherwise dispose of surrendered lands or who is an officer or servant of the government employed in the Department may, except with the approval of the appropriate government office, acquire directly or indirectly any interest in surrendered lands.

2.6 What requirements of diction should be observed in preparing the following? Consider the reader's or listener's interests, as well as the purpose of the writing or talk.

1. An advertisement for a new "wonder drug" to be published in the *Journal of the American Medical Association;* the same advertisement, tailored for *Good Housekeeping.*
2. A booklet on high-scoring techniques for a video game.
3. A booklet entitled "So You're Going to Have a Baby by Natural Childbirth," to be given to participants in a prenatal clinic.
4. A story entitled "So You're Going to Have a Little Baby Brother or Sister," intended for kindergarten children.
5. A talk on "Meeting the Needs of Youth," to be delivered at a luncheon meeting of the Kiwanis Club.

2.7 Write a letter to a former teacher or employer giving a brief description of this book (first two chapters only). Then write a letter to your best friend describing the same thing. Compare the two letters, noting major differences in diction.

2.8 To what group of people does the following advertisement attempt to appeal? Is the diction appropriate and effective for that audience? What weakness, if any, can you detect in the reasoning presented? How effectively is connotation used?

> Has America forgotten how it feels to live without
> saccharin, PPG-14 Butyl ether, and FD & C Yellow dye #5?

Why do we have to put up with things like saccharin and blue dye in our toothpaste? And preservatives in our shampoos? And artificial bactericides in our deodorants?

When you stop and think about it, these ingredients don't make sense. Not when you can accomplish clean teeth, beautiful hair and a sweet smelling body another way. Tom's of Maine is doing just that with natural personal care products designed for people who are concerned about their health.

Take toothpaste. Most leading brands contain artificial flavors, preservatives and dyes. And all of them have saccharin. Not Tom's toothpaste. It's made from a natural calcium base containing a mild coconut oil cleanser, vegetable glycerin, seaweed, pure spearmint oil for flavor and fluoride for those who want decay prevention. So, you get the benefits of your present brand with none of the artificial ingredients.

All Tom's natural products contain the things people used before we got so fancy and technical. They're good, sensible ingredients. So you'll never worry from one day to the next about what you put in your mouth, on your hair, or next to your skin. And you'll feel better too, knowing you used your head when you bought them.

Tom's of Maine. Someone has to care.

2.9 **(a)** Compare the writing in a national news magazine, such as *Time* or *Newsweek*, with the writing in your local newspaper. What differences in diction are most noticeable? Does the diction indicate any difference in intended audiences or purposes?

(b) Compare articles with roughly the same subject matter found in two different sorts of magazines, such as *Playboy* and *Reader's Digest*. What are some of the most conspicuous differences in word choice, sentence length, and treatment of the subject? What do these differences tell you about the intended audiences of the two magazines?

2.10 The following statement on plagiarism was handed to each student of fresh-man composition at a large university for a number of years. It was carefully worded to make clear what plagiarism is and what penalties the plagiarist incurs. A revised form, which was later adopted, is printed after the original. Examine each statement, sentence by sentence. Which would be more successful in reaching its intended audience? Which appears more conciliatory? Which leaves less room for doubt as to the definition of plagiarism and the procedure to be followed in cases of cheating?

TO THE STUDENT:
The purpose of this statement is to help and protect you by defining what sorts of aid you may or may not receive in preparing your themes for freshman English. This has proven a vexing problem for students faced for the first time with the writing of many papers, so we ask you to read this statement with care.

Clearly you have come to this university to exchange ideas with oth-ers as well as to take in new ideas from your teachers and from books. But unless these ideas are proven in your experience—that is, unless you make them your own by thinking them through and finally devel-oping them into your own language—they are worthless. There is no objection, then, to your discussing the topic of a paper with others; indeed this can be a broadening experience if there is a real *inter-change* of ideas. Nor do we object to your considering ideas gained from reading—if your teacher feels that you must read to complete the assignment—provided you put these ideas to original use and further develop them. But you cannot use and develop these ideas unless you first express them adequately and literally in your own words; only then can these ideas begin to become your own. If you do thus make use of ideas or material taken over from other persons or documents, published or otherwise, you must be sure to acknowledge specifically in the paper your sources of information. However, the basic ideas of any paper, the formulation and extension of the ideas derived from reading, the writing of the paper, and the preparation of the final draft must be your own work. In this way alone can we begin to fulfill the purpose of the course: *to teach you to express yourself.*

If you are to do an intellectually responsible job, then, you must never passively accept the ideas or the words of others. Conceivably we could grade the *Reader's Digest,* if that is the source of a paper, or the friend on whose ideas a paper is based, or the wife who may have written it, but what value would this have for the student? He can learn and the teacher can teach only when the student's own abilities and difficulties are made clear in the student's own work. For the same reason we insist that you prepare and correct your own drafts of each paper: the corrections of your family or your friends cannot reflect your own knowledge. If someone types your paper for you, have him type exactly what you have given him. The paper you give your instructor must be entirely yours.

We do not list these many qualifications to bedevil you but to protect you, because to hand in work as your own that is not your own or to help another student improperly—according to any of the conditions detailed above—lays you open to charges of cheating or plagiarism. These are harsh words, but the reality is harsher still. For the disciplinary action required in such cases by *University Rules and Regulations* can include a statement on the student's permanent record and may mean dismissal from the university. The permanent record is read by all prospective employers and consulted by all graduate schools which the student might want to attend; in short, the record haunts him for the rest of his life. This may seem severe to you. In affairs of cheating and plagiarism, however, the integrity of the university, which depends on the integrity of its individual students, is at stake.

Finally, we realize that only a minute percentage of students willfully involve themselves in plagiarism or cheating, though a small percentage may mean a large number in a big university. But some students can become innocently entangled by not understanding quite what plagiarism and cheating consist in or quite what risks they are running. It is to prevent such misunderstandings and to define the conditions of work required in freshman English that we are distributing this statement to you.

PLAGIARISM

Every student will be held responsible for reading and understanding the following statement.

Because the purpose of Freshman English is to improve your ability to express yourself in writing, your themes and exercises must be your own work. To submit to your instructor a paper that is not truly the product of your own mind and skill is to commit plagiarism. To put it bluntly, plagiarism is the act of stealing the ideas and/or the expressions of another and representing them as your own. It is a form of cheating and a kind of academic misconduct which can incur severe penalties. It is important, therefore, that you understand what it consists of, so that you will not unwittingly jeopardize your college career.

Plagiarism, as the English Department defines it, can take several forms. The most obvious form is a word-for-word copying of someone else's work, in whole or in part, without acknowledgment, whether that work be a magazine article, a portion of a book, a newspaper piece, another student's essay, or any other composition not your own. Any such verbatim use of another's work must be acknowledged by (1) enclosing all such copied portions in quotation marks and (2) giving the original source either in the body of your essay or in a footnote. As a general rule, you should make very little use of quoted matter in your themes. The theme topics in Freshman English are so designed as to make it unnecessary for you to consult anything but your own mind.

A second form of plagiarism is the unacknowledged paraphrasing of the structure and language of another person's work. Changing a few words of another's composition, omitting a few sentences, or changing their order does not constitute original composition and therefore can be given no credit. If such borrowing or paraphrase is ever necessary, the source must be scrupulously indicated by footnotes.

Still another form of plagiarism is more difficult to define. It consists of writing a theme based solely on the ideas of another. Even though the language is not the same, if the thinking is clearly not your own, then you have committed plagiarism. If, for example, in writing a theme you reproduce the structure and progression of ideas in an essay you have read, or a speech you have heard, you are not engaging your own mind and experience enough to claim credit for writing your own composition.

How, then, you may ask, can I be original? Am I to learn nothing from others? There are several answers to such questions.

Of course you have come to the University to learn, and this means acquiring ideas and exchanging opinions with others. But no idea is ever genuinely learned by copying it down in the phrasing of somebody else. Only when you have thought through an idea in terms of your own experience can you be said to have learned; and when you have done that, you can develop it on paper as the product of your own mind. It is your mind we are trying to train and evaluate. When, therefore, you are given a theme assignment, do not consult books or articles or friends' themes in search of something to say. If an assignment baffles you, discuss it with your instructor. And if you are directed to use printed sources, in English or in other courses, consult your instructor about how to proceed. There is an art to taking notes for research; careless note-taking can lead to plagiarism.

Why be so concerned about plagiarism? Because it defeats the ends of education. If a student were given credit for work that is not his own, then his course grades would be meaningless. His college degree would become a mere sheet of paper and the integrity of the University would be undermined. To protect the conscientious student, therefore, and to guarantee the quality of his education, the University assesses heavy penalties against those who plagiarize. By Faculty Rules, penalties for plagiarism range from an "E" grade in the course to dismissal from the University; and the penalty given may be noted on the student's permanent record, for prospective employers or other interested persons to read. If these penalties seem severe, remember that your integrity and the integrity of the University itself are at stake.

Finally, the English Department cannot prevent a student from plagiarizing, but it can make sure that he knows what plagiarism is, what the penalties for it are, and in what jeopardy it places his future career. Hence this statement. Read it carefully. If you do not understand it fully, consult your instructor. AND, IF YOU HAVE ANY DOUBTS ABOUT THE ORIGINALITY OF A PAPER YOU HAVE WRITTEN, SEE HIM BEFORE YOU TURN IT IN.

2.11 Every writer of textbooks faces the problem of suiting his or her style to the needs and capacities of a particular audience and of avoiding both oversimplification and overcomplexity. To help authors with clear, comprehensible college textbooks, a publishing firm issued a series of brochures called "If You Are Writing a Book," from which the following excerpts are taken:

The fact is that if you are a good teacher, you can probably write a clear, simple book. For if you are a good teacher, you are sufficiently aware of the learning situation and the student level to use, vividly and forcefully, simple words and simple sentences, and you know that your goal is to teach the student rather than to impress your colleagues with your general brilliance.

Simplicity does not, of course, mean words of one syllable used in sentences of idiot-child, "see-the-tree" construction. A textbook must be geared to the level of the subject matter and the student, and such a sentence as "College glee clubs may be classified in three distinct categories: (1) those which contain only male members; (2) those which contain only female members; and (3) those which contain both male and female members" is quite as undesirable as one which can be understood only with the aid of a dictionary and grammar. Simplicity depends also on context. In a general biology text, the sentence "All ontogeny recapitulates phylogeny" is anything but simple when it opens the second chapter. But it may be crystal clear as the last sentence of the tenth.

★   ★   ★   ★   ★

Perhaps the most common temptation . . . is to indulge—in text and footnotes—in scholarly pyrotechnics. These are likely to dazzle the author's colleagues, but they are equally likely to strike the students stone-blind. Other authors try to achieve rapport with the student through a kind of slangy colloquialism and the use of situations and analogies that they fondly believe to be "really at the level of the student." But this sort of writing is so "loose" as to be valueless in communicating concepts with any degree of precision. Perhaps more important, many students are almost hypochondriacally sensitive to being talked down to, and they don't expect a textbook author to sound like one of their classmates airing his views at the local Coke bar.

(a) Using what you have learned in this chapter as well as the criteria provided by the preceding excerpts, write short reviews of the textbook you like best and the one you like least among those you have recently used or are using now, emphasizing how well or how little the authors have succeeded in reaching you, the intended audience.

(b) Describe the qualities you think a good textbook should have, especially noting qualities of diction.

(c) Write a short review of the tone of this book. Is the style unnecessarily difficult? Could the authors have used simpler language? Do they "talk down" to you? If they sometimes use unfamiliar words, do they seem to do so for a purpose? What does the diction of this text tell you about the authors and their purpose?

CLUES OF UNNECESSARILY DIFFICULT LANGUAGE

2.12 Each of the following passages is stuffed with unnecessary words and phrases. Rewrite it in the most economical and easy-to-understand form possible.

1. In this little twelve-line poem, which is entitled "Nothing to wear?" and was first published in the volume *Brimming Over*, dated 1965, the author, Meighan Bruce, points out the fact that

some members of the female sex, particularly those in the younger age brackets, take an exaggerated and really undue interest in the clothes they wear. Writing in a lighthearted, satirical vein, he seems to want to make the point that in the course of anybody's life, there are some things that are in actual reality of much greater importance than the question of how an individual looks. To take only one example out of many that come to mind, a young woman should also have a sincere and honest concern in the direction of cultivating her mental equipment so that she does not ever have to fear being called a brainless beauty. This is the point which the author of this poem, which is in a rather rollicking style of verse, is bent upon making, and it is one which in my humble estimation is well worth making.

2. In the circumstance that the government leaders of all the various countries of the world with all their different interests should have the hitherto unprecedented opportunity to meet together and discuss with one another their number one priorities relative to supplies of foodstuffs, then the aware observer would without a doubt come to notice two distinct occurrences. First and foremost, no single individual country will be found to be entirely and completely independent as regards food supply. And second, and not least important of the two observations, agreement between individual countries and groups of countries sharing similar food supply needs will not take the direction of unilateral cooperation in meeting those needs.

3. In regard to your welcome inquiry of recent date, I want to take this opportunity to make what might be called an interim report. You will understand that this must not be regarded as the final and definitive answer to the question you raised, since certain key members of our research staff happen to be on vacation or are at present engaged in assignments which have been given high priority. This case is such that it would be unwise to be content with a snap judgment. However, based upon such information as is available at this moment, I think I can say with some confidence that the side effects you report some of your patients have noticed in connection with the oral administration of Diathorazanarcotomine are not due to the nature of the drug itself, which was subjected to two full years of clinical testing before being released to the medical profession. Our best consensus of opinion, at least for the time being, is that the side effects must be derived from the circumstance that the patients are also taking some other type of medication in addition to our product, and that the conjunction of the two would result in the kind of side effects you describe. However, the entire matter will be examined more thoroughly in the next week or ten days, and I trust you will bear with us until I can

return a fuller report to you on the basis of these further discussions.

4. The failure of the Landlord to insist in any one or more instances upon a strict performance of any of the covenants of this lease or of the rules and regulations or to exercise any option herein contained shall not be construed as a waiver or relinquishment for the future of such covenant, rule, regulation or option, but the same shall continue and remain in full force and effect.

5. Pursuant to the recent memorandum issued August 9, 1979, because of petroleum exigencies, it is incumbent upon us all to endeavor to make maximal utilization of telephonic communication in lieu of personal visitation.

2.13 Written in pompous and unnecessarily difficult language, the familiar saying "Honesty is the best policy" looks like this: "Adopting the practical point of view, it is justifiable to conclude that for every individual the conformity to a standard of behavior which stresses integrity and lack of dissimulation as the key factor has the optimum probability of producing satisfactory end results." Try to write the following common sayings in the same inflated style.

Beauty is only skin deep.
A penny saved is a penny earned.
Practice makes perfect.
You can't judge a book by its cover.
A fool and his money are soon parted.
Absence makes the heart grow fonder.
Waste not, want not.
A bird in the hand is worth two in the bush.

2.14 What familiar saying or quotation is hidden in each of the following sentences?

1. Irrespective of its substandard physical condition and lack of appurtenances which would place it, and therefore its inhabitants, in a higher socioeconomic bracket, the structure in which a family pursues its domestic routine, and which the familial group associates with its mutual emotive attitudes, has a unique status.

2. When an operator of any motor vehicle approaches a point on a public highway which is intersected by the right-of-way of a railroad, he is required by law to bring said motor vehicle to a complete standstill, and having done so, to verify by ocular inspection whether or not a train or other factor in a potential collision is approaching from either direction along the aforementioned right-of-way, as well as to substantiate the evidence thus obtained by being attentive to the auditory warning of such approach pro-

duced by whistle, horn, bell, or other device designed for the purpose of emitting an appropriate signal in such circumstances.

4. In a situation in which there exists the potentiality of further deterioration unless immediate remedial and preventive action is instituted, it is without exception advisable that such steps be taken as are required, before the occurrence of the anticipated additional damage has the opportunity to eventuate.

5. Theologians have in their dialogue about the human element in civilization ascertained that the proclivity toward erroneous activity is a characteristic of *homo sapiens,* whereas the habituated tendency to exonerate or exculpate is characteristic of an Immanent Will or Being on a much higher level of existence.

2.15 Here is a list of current terms which attempt to embody concepts in a kind of shorthand, useful to some occupational group to be sure, but confusing to others because they either oversimplify meaning or fail to express it clearly. Explain what each means, using a single, more common word or a whole, clear sentence.

price rollback	first strike capability
reorientation	nuclear family
debriefing	intelligence quotient
pilot study	wage indexing
arms buildup	learning disability
sanitized	down time
capsulized	social mobility
docudrama	high tech industry

2.16 In a humorous column poking fun at the tendency of journalists to use stock phrases to describe situations, a writer says that every time "a heat wave started going well the newspapers sent out photographers to take pictures of somebody frying an egg on the sidewalk. 'Hot enough to fry an egg,' was the invariable picture caption." Look through several newspapers and make a list of the stock phrases, descriptions, or catchwords that you find. In what way do these standardized expressions affect your understanding of the events being reported? Try your hand at rewriting one such article, replacing the stock phrases in each case.

2.17 (a) Make a collection of sportswriters' stock terms from the pages of your local newspaper; then translate the following into sports-page terminology:

made a successful shot (in basketball)
struck out
touchdown
prevented the other team from scoring by holding firm on the two-yard line
a close finish (in various sports)

a win by a large margin (again, in various sports)
winner of the three major American horse races
the team coach
withdrawn from the game
last place in the league
scored three goals in one game
an outstanding play (or player)

(b) Choosing a newspaper or magazine article on a sport you are unfamiliar with, identify any terms which you do not understand fully and try to assign meanings to them. Have someone familiar with the sport assign meanings to these same terms and then compare lists. How accurate were your assigned meanings? How much did context count?

2.18 (a) Translate each of these headlines into a clear sentence that even someone who hardly ever reads the newspapers could understand:

SUMMIT PARLEY ENDS: NORTH-SOUTH PACT OFF
MISTRIAL CALLED: COURT RAPS D.A.
COPS NAB SLAYING SUSPECT AFTER WILD CHASE
DAD PACES WRONG HOSPITAL FLOOR AS STORK ARRIVES
POLICE RAID LOCAL HANGOUT: BIG DRUG HAUL
OPPOSITION ORDERS JUNKET PROBE: CONSIDER FOREIGN TRAVEL CUTOFF
CRONIES DENY BACK ROOM DEAL: COVERUP CHARGES FLY
REPORT HAMMERS WINDFALL PROFITS: OIL REPS MUM
FEDS EYE NEW DEAL FOR PREGNANT WORKERS

(b) Translate the following facts into attention-getting, paper-selling headlines. Use no word of more than three syllables; select the most dramatic verbs and nouns possible. Try to use no more than eight words.

1. A fire badly damaged a downtown department store, and six firemen were treated for smoke inhalation.
2. A jury acquitted a woman accused of trying to poison her husband.
3. The local municipal government approved the biggest yearly budget ever.
4. Union leaders and federal government negotiators failed to reach agreement on wage and benefit increases.
5. The attorney general refused to consider intervention in the scheduled execution of the murderer of a police officer.
6. The discoverer of a new vaccine denied secretly testing the vaccine at a local university medical center.
7. A taxi driver was still alive after being shot four times in the chest; his assailant was arrested.

(c) Comb current newspapers for examples of stock words used to "color" the news. Try to find examples of such words as *plot, rap* (disapprove of), *flay, fear, nab, probe, vice ring, assail, plea, bolster, doom* (verb), *gear* (verb), *alert* (verb), *stage* (verb), *menace, smash, deadlock, expose, edict, grill, demand, block, seek, warn, grab, storm, around-the-clock, razor-thin* (majority), *vigil, love triangle, front* (in nonmilitary uses), and so on. Substitute words with less dramatic connotation and determine how far each substitution affects your reaction to the news.

2.19 (a) Fill in the blanks:

Her meteoric   was only a flash in the   . Since then she has had a checkered   .

Financially, we bit off more   . After a while we began to   to pay Paul. Now we avoid time payments like the   .

My life has been pretty hectic. I've been burning the   at both ends, and at exam time, when the day of   finally arrives, I find that to meet the acid   , I have to burn the   .

What they say has neither   nor reason. They always make a   out of a   .

Since they got married after a whirlwind   , things have gone from   to   until now their marriage is on the   . I've moved   and   to reconcile them, but I'm afraid their relationship is on its last   .

Perhaps I'm whistling in the   or indulging in wishful   , but the   that be have   me the nod. So things may start looking up and give me a new lease on   . Until recently, I've been living from   to mouth and have been as poor as   . But now I'm putting all my eggs in   and banking on my business to grow by   and   .

(b) Complete each expression:

The Midas
A shadow of your
Spending money like it's
Warm as
Doing a   business
Fit as a

Flat as a
Brown as a
     flowed like water
     as greased lightning
Fiddle while
Fight   and nail
The   of one's brow
Hit below the
The naked
By hook or
A tempest in a
A miss is as good as
The name of the
The grass is
Turn a   ear
Keep one's shoulder to the
Keep one's nose to the
No news is
A bolt from the
Better safe than
Better late than
Trials and

(c)   The cliché has been discussed in this book primarily from the viewpoint of trite language. But since tired language and tired thoughts generally are inseparable, the term *cliché* also refers to the statement of an obvious idea. In this sense, it is roughly synonymous with *commonplace, truism, platitude,* and *bromide.* (For ways in which their connotations differ, see *Webster's New Dictionary of Synonyms* under *commonplace.*) Many familiar sayings—aphorisms, proverbs, adages, and so on—are clichés. Whether or not they have considerable truth in them, they have been so overworked as to have lost much of their force: "Still waters run deep," "Spare the rod and spoil the child," "Christmas has become too commercialized," "The artist is lost in modern society," "There's nothing new under the sun." How long a list can you make of similar platitudes? Examine several newspaper or magazine articles for more.

(d)   We often hear of "clichéd situations" or "clichéd characters" in movies, plays, novels, or television programs ("sitcoms"). What do these terms mean? Give some examples of situations or characters that are clichés, and point out the features that make them clichés.

(e)   Many clichés of any given moment are derived from the mass entertainment media—the sports page, comic strips, movies, popular songs, radio, and television. Make a list of such clichés which are now circulating among your friends and acquaintances, and try to indicate the probable origin of each.

2.20 Identify the "plain English" synonyms of the following terms:

cosmetologist	waste material contractor
tree surgery service	security officer
landscape engineer	hearing-impaired
demolition engineer	burial couch
inurnment	instructional resources
self-destruction	disciplinary action
criminal assault	investment counselor
sanitary landfill	health problem
hearing impaired	surgical procedure
controlled substance abuse	service technician

2.21 Analyze as thoroughly as possible the connotations of each of the following terms, and then decide how many of them are euphemisms:

almsgiving, welfare, poor relief, charity, dole, succor, public assistance, aid for the needy, handout, benevolence, philanthropy, entitlement, negative income tax

2.22 The following words all mean roughly the same thing (that is, someone who buys a product or receives a service), yet their appropriateness varies with the context. Consider who would use each of the following terms, and in what kind of circumstances. (For example, an undertaker would not be very likely to welcome his client with "Hello, shopper!")

customer, buyer, purchaser, client, patient, guest, consumer, patron, shopper, subject

2.23 (a) Rank, in ascending order of presumable elegance, the following terms. How does each term differ in connotation from the others?

motel	inn
motor inn	motor lodge
tourist court	motor hotel
resort	bed and breakfast

(b) What is the difference, if any, between the following paired terms?

grease job	lubrication service
girdle	foundation garment
field underwriter	insurance salesman
underarm deodorant	antiperspirant

house trailer	mobile home
family planning	birth control
industrial park	factory district
physical (in contact sports)	rough
shop teacher	industrial arts instructor
paraprofessional	helper
slum clearance	urban renewal
toothpaste	dentifrice
embezzlement	accounting irregularity
insurance	risk management
polygraph	lie detector
housewife	homemaker

2.24 (a) Why is the word *institute* often used to designate establishments devoted neither to education nor to research, as in *Good Housekeeping Institute* and *American Iron and Steel Institute?*

(b) Why is the word *family* frequently used in the advertisements of large corporations when referring to their employees or to the subsidiary companies of which the corporation is composed? And why do some large firms refer to their employees as *associates?*

(c) "And now, a brief message from our sponsor." Why *brief message* rather than *advertisement, commercial,* or *plug?*

(d) What kind of film entertainment is implied in the terms *art theater* and *adult picture?* How would you define *adult entertainment* in this context? Does *adult* have the same meaning in the term *adult book,* as used by librarians?

(e) What do the phrases *equal opportunity employer* and *affirmative action employer* mean in help-wanted advertisements?

(f) In educational contexts, what is meant by *exceptional child?*

2.25 Among connoisseurs of doublespeak, the term *therapeutic misadventure* is readily understood as the more familiar *medical malpractice* (or even a *doctor's mistake*). Try to identify the common meanings of the following frequently encountered doublespeak terms from the military vocabulary:

radiation enhancement device
counterfactual proposition
mutual assured destruction
protective reaction
incomplete success
incursion
pacification

2.26 Try to make up doublespeak expressions for some of the following terms (for example, *negative growth = economic slump*):

high property taxes	fraud
a company's losing money	fixing an election
getting fired	causing an accident
cheap labor	mechanical failure
government lying	political corruption
bigot	politicians taking vacations at taxpayers' expense

2.27 The following sentences all include overworked nouns. Identify the nouns which have been derived from verbs, and then rewrite the sentences by using active verbs which clarify the meaning. (For example, "If problem occurrence necessitates action, decision making should follow with immediacy" is changed to "If a problem occurs, quickly decide what to do.")

1. Failure to follow these directions will result in disqualification of the applicants.
2. Incurrals of business expense should have complete documentation.
3. Responsibility is placed on the intending applicant for the completion of the program.
4. Utilization of this card constitutes acceptance of the terms and conditions set forth upon issuance of said card.
5. Receipt of a check does not indicate a termination of legal proceedings.

THE USES AND ABUSES OF TECHNICAL LANGUAGE

2.28 The following passages are from articles in various professional journals. Try to identify the overworked nouns and passive verbs and the unnecessary technical language used in each. Then rewrite each passage simply and clearly — as if, for example, you were writing for a family reference book.

1. The behavior of the restricted dogs in their cages indicates that sensory and neural maturation had provided the necessary substrate for the restricted dogs to react adaptively. It seems, therefore, that well-organized experience of the environment in which emotion-provoking objects will appear is necessary for the emergence of adaptive emotional behavior such as avoidance and aggression. The fact that considerable diffuse excitement was manifested by the restricted dogs after almost a year of normal laboratory environment indicates that organized perceptual expe-

rience of a new environment is acquired through long, continued periods of sensory stimulation. The present experiment also provides evidence that in the course of emotional development avoidance appears before aggression.

2. The urban centers caught within the web of metropolitan decentralization have an advantageous ecological position for both population growth and central-place function expansion. Most of the small centers grow by attracting central-city commuters and their families. A few of these rural-marketing centers attract some of the decentralizing employing activities, and their transition is from service to employment, drawing to themselves each day workers from other segments of the metropolitan area. Many of the suburban communities take on an increased central-place function as new suburban shopping centers emerge. These new retailing complexes place the suburb in a favorable position to compete for retail trade with the large metropolitan center and with the agricultural service centers at the periphery of the metropolitan area.

3. The foregoing data on recovery of vision after optic nerve regeneration in six different species of anuran amphibians support the previous conclusions based on visual recovery in the urodele *Triturus*. These conclusions and their logical basis are, briefly, as follows: Since stimulation of different retinal areas evokes different responses, each retinal locus must possess functional connections with the brain centers differing from those of all other areas. After optic nerve regeneration these differential relations between retinal and visual centers are systematically restored in their original form, as shown by tests of optokinetic responses and visual localization of small objects.

4. There has long been resistance to the basal proposition that the effectiveness of methods and teachers must be measured in terms of the results secured. Those responsible for evaluating teachers have exalted procedures in teaching and have seldom examined the products, that is, the efficiency of the teacher as indicated by what his pupils can do following instruction. However, we are beginning to see an increasing number of bold proposals founded on the assumption that the American public expects results from schooling. As public support of education increases, there will be greater insistence on judging a teacher in the light of his ability to enhance the learning of pupils.

2.29 Rewrite the following statements, substituting simpler words, active verbs, and so on.

1. The changing nature of our social controls makes it absolutely necessary for the entire police department to be trained in the understanding of ethnic groups, which will help them to over-

come their own inclinations to participate in the cultural conflict by expressing in words or actions their contempt of the culturally different.

2. An integral part of the total educational experience involves the student's adjustment to a new living environment. Guidelines for behavior are indispensable to assist the maturation process. For this reason, the dean for student relations has requested the counselors in the first-year women's living facilities to assist their residents in familiarizing themselves with the desirable mores of the university family by making sure that the security hours posted for the benefit of all are strictly observed.

3. Activity in this sector was at a minimum until approximately 1430 hours this date, when it was sharply increased by a forward movement of the hostile forces upon several outlying posts occupied by our troops. The engagement, which lasted five hours, resulted in 76 casualties. The 50 wounded personnel were evacuated by helicopter to a rear area. To consolidate the situation, troops in the forward areas were withdrawn to a more tenable position. Reinforcements have been dispatched to strengthen this sector in anticipation of possible renewed enemy action.

REVIEW

2.30 The following five versions of a famous American speech illustrate many of the points made in the present chapter. For what audience and what sort of medium might each have been designed? Try to characterize the major differences in diction among the various versions in as much detail as you can. Which version do you find most effectively communicates its message? (The original speech is presented at the end so that you can compare it with the others.)

1. Friends, it is now eighty-seven years since our beloved nation saw the light of day. Behind it was a new idea, the idea that one man is as good as another and every man deserves the blessings of liberty. We are met here today while the war clouds hang over us. Our brothers, husbands, and sons are giving their all to defend the sacred principles upon which our country was founded. On this solemn occasion it is our purpose to do homage to them by setting aside a portion of the rolling countryside around us, in which they were recently locked in mortal combat, as a last resting place for the departed heroes.

   When we give way to reflection, however, it becomes plain that we, who have not fought and bled here, are not the ones to "dedicate" this cemetery. It has already been dedicated by the valorous warriors who clashed in fierce struggle here last July. Our program today will not go down in the annals of time. That honor is reserved, and justly so, for the magnificent deeds of those soldiers. Let us turn our thoughts instead to the unfinished business remaining before us. We must carry on, with every ounce of determination at our command, so that the great ideals that our fallen brethren cherished in their stout hearts shall be fulfilled. Let us therefore partake of fresh inspiration from the sacrifices they have made. Let us make a solemn vow that their deaths were not in vain. The finest monument we can erect to them will be the triumph of the high cause for which they laid down their lives—the cause of democratic government. Then we can rest assured that they are gone but not forgotten.

Eighty-seven years ago, our grandfathers created a free nation here. They based it on the idea that everybody is created equal. We are now fighting a civil war to see if this or any similar nation can survive. On this battlefield we are dedicating a cemetery to those who died for their country. It is only right. But in another sense, the task is impossible, because brave men, living and dead, dedicated this place better than we can.

Hardly anyone will notice or remember what we say here, but nobody can forget what those men did. We shall continue the work they began, and make sure they did not die in vain. With God's help we will have freedom again, so that the people's government will endure.

The present occasion of commemoration and dedication is an appropriate moment at which to offer several observations. These are as follows: (1) The current state of belligerency between two sections of the nation is traceable to a regrettable divergence of opinion as to whether the aforesaid nation has an indefinite life expectancy, predicated as it is upon certain novel principles laid down 8.7 decades ago, viz.: that all members of the commonwealth are (a) equal in status and (b) entitled to freedom of intellect, expression, and action. (2) The ceremonies attendant on the allocation, in perpetuity, of the acreage environing us as a memorial to the casualties of the late battle, while they are indisputably honorable in intent, nevertheless must not detract attention from the fact that the memorializing has already been implemented by the sanguinary activities which occurred here last July. (3) In view of this circumstance, it is highly desirable that our motivations be directed instead toward the finalization of the procedure which is already under way. (4) Such finalization should consist of an intensified application to the program for insuring the future stability of the nation, namely, for guaranteeing that the principles of liberty shall be resuscitated and that the concept of government, deriving its authority from, and operating through, the agency and in behalf of the best interests of the constituents shall be indefinitely preserved.

4. **In Memoriam**

Today, in the typically American countryside of Gettysburg, Pa., a soldiers' cemetery is being dedicated.

Think what that means. Only a few months ago, a great battle was fought here. A battle that probably marked the fateful turning point of the war—a war fought to preserve a free America—an America that owes its very being to the sacrifice of our grandfathers who believed, as we do, that all men are brothers.

The ceremonies at Gettysburg are a fitting gesture, but still only a gesture. We mustn't flatter ourselves that they are history-making. History has already been made there, and we can't possibly match that.

The *real* dedication must take place within ourselves.

The soldiers of the Union Army have done a wonderful job. But they can't do it all. We, who survive, must become, in a sense, their comrades-in-arms.

Every patriotic American must take a greater part in the affairs that concern us all. Every public-spirited citizen must contribute, in the way he is best fitted, to furthering the cause of freedom and democracy.

Join the great crusade—*today!*

5. I haven't checked these figures but 87 years ago, I think it was, a number of individuals organized a governmental setup here in this country, I believe it covered certain Eastern areas, with this idea that they were following up based on a sort of national independence arrangement and the program that every individual is just as good as every other individual is. Well, now, of course, we are dealing with this big difference of opinion, you might almost call it a civil disturbance, although I don't like to appear to take sides or name any individuals, and the point is naturally to check up, by actual experience in the field, to see whether any governmental setup with a basis like the one I was mentioning has any validity and find out whether that dedication by those early individuals will pay off in lasting values and things of that kind.

Well, here we are, at the scene where one of these disturbances between different sides got going. We want to pay our tribute to those loved ones, those departed individuals who made the supreme sacrifice here on the basis of opinions about how this thing ought to be handled. And I would say this. It is absolutely in order to do this.

But if you look at the over-all picture of this, we can't pay any tribute—we can't sanctify this area, you might say—we can't hallow according to whatever individual creeds or faiths or sorts of religious outlooks are involved about this very particular area. It was those individuals themselves, including the enlisted men, very brave individuals, who have given this religious character to the area. The way I see it, the rest of the world will not remember any statements issued here but it will never forget how these men put their shoulders to the wheel and carried out this idea.

Now frankly, our job, the living individuals' job here, is to pick up the burden they made these big efforts here for. It is our job to get on with the assignment—and from these deceased fine individuals to take extra inspiration for the same theories for which they made such a big contribution. We have to make up our minds right here and now, as I see it, that they didn't put out all that blood, perspiration and—well—that they didn't just make a dry run here, and that all of us here, under God, that is the God of our choice, shall beef up this idea about freedom and liberty and those kind of arrangements, and that government of all individuals, by all individuals, and for the individuals shall not pass out of the world-picture.

6.   *(The Original Version)*

Fourscore and seven years ago our fathers brought forth on this continent a new nation, conceived in liberty and dedicated to the proposition that all men are created equal.

Now we are engaged in a great civil war, testing whether that nation, or any nation so conceived and so dedicated, can long endure. We are met on a great battle-field of that war. We have come to dedicate a portion of that field as a final resting-place for those who here gave their lives that that nation might live. It is altogether fitting and proper that we should do this.

But in a larger sense, we cannot dedicate—we cannot consecrate—we cannot hallow—this ground. The brave men, living and dead, who struggled here, have consecrated it far above our poor power to add or detract. The world will little note nor long remember what we say here, but it can never forget what they did here. It is for us, the living, rather, to be dedicated here to the unfinished work which they who fought here have thus far so nobly advanced. It is rather for us to be here dedicated to the great task remaining before us—that from these honored dead we take increased devotion to that cause for which they gave the last full measure of devotion; that we here highly resolve that these dead shall not have died in vain; that this nation, under God, shall have a new birth of freedom; and that government of the people, by the people, for the people, shall not perish from the earth.

2.31 In the spirit of the preceding exercise, select a paragraph or two from a famous speech or historical document and rewrite it for an audience other than that of the original—for example, a feminist gathering, a group of eighth-grade students, or a company of soldiers. Explain, as well, exactly what you have done to adapt the original for its special audience.

2.32 Each of the following quotations relates to topics discussed in this chapter. Identify those, and then go on to examine the language and content of each passage for what it reveals about the author's personality and intention, and the time of writing.

1. There is a busybody on your [newspaper] staff who devotes a lot of his time to chasing split infinitives. Every good literary craftsman splits his infinitives when the sense demands it. I call for the immediate removal of this pedant. It is of no consequence whether he decides to go quickly or quickly to go or to quickly go. The important thing is that he should do it at once.

2. By the way, would you convey my compliments to the purist who reads your proofs and tell him or her that I write in a sort of broken-down patois which is something like the way a Swiss waiter talks, and that when I split an infinitive, damn it all, I split it so it will stay split, and when I interrupt the velvety smoothness of my more or less literate syntax with a few sudden words of barroom vernacular, this is done with the eyes wide open and the mind relaxed but attentive. The method may not be perfect but it is all I have.

3. Do but take care to express yourself in a plain, easy manner, in well-chosen, significant, and decent terms and to give an harmonious and pleasing turn to your periods; study to explain your thoughts, and set them in the truest light, laboring, as much as possible, not to leave them dark nor intricate, but clear and intelligible.

4. How can an answer in physics or a translation from the French or an historical statement be called correct if the phrasing is loose or the key word wrong? Students argue that the reader of the paper knows perfectly well what is meant. Probably so, but a written exercise is designed to be read; it is not supposed to be a challenge to clairvoyance. My Italian-born tailor periodically sends me a postcard which runs: "Your clothes is ready and should come down for a fitting." I understand him, but the art I honor him for is cutting cloth, not precision of utterance.

5. *Too* startling words, . . . *too* just images, *too* great displays of cleverness are apt in the long run to be as fatiguing as the most overused words or the most jog-trot cadences. That a face resembles a Dutch clock has been said too often; to say that it resembles a ham is inexact and conveys nothing; to say that it has the mournfulness of an old smashed-in meat tin, cast away on a waste build-

ing lot, would be smart—but too much of that sort of thing would become a nuisance.

6. It is a natural, simple, and unaffected speech that I love, so written as it is spoken, and such upon the paper as it is in the mouth, a pithy, sinewy, full, strong, compendious and material speech, not so delicate and affected as vehement and piercing. Rather difficult than tedious, void of affectation, free, loose, and bold, that every member of it seems to make a body; not pedantical, nor friarlike, nor lawyerlike, but rather downright, soldierlike.

2.33 In the following passage, Samuel Johnson, the great eighteenth-century critic and author of the first modern dictionary of English, discusses some marks of good diction. Read the passage carefully, and then revise it so that the word choice and sentence structure accord with modern usage. Which of Johnson's observations have their counterparts in the text of this chapter?

Every man speaks and writes with intent to be understood; and it can seldom happen but he that understands himself might convey his notions to another, if content to be understood, he did not seek to be admired; but when once he begins to contrive how his sentiments may be received, not with most ease to his reader, but with most advantage to himself, he then transfers his consideration from words to sounds, from sentences to periods, and as he grows more elegant becomes less intelligible.

It is difficult to enumerate every species of author whose labors counteract themselves; the man of exuberance and copiousness, who diffuses every thought through so many diversities of expression, that it is lost like water in a mist; the ponderous dictator of sentences, whose notions are delivered in a lump, and are, like uncoined bullion, of more weight than use; the liberal illustrator, who shows by examples and comparisons what was clearly seen when it was first proposed; and the stately son of demonstration, who proves with mathematical formality what no man has yet pretended to doubt.

There is a mode of style for which I know not that the masters of oratory have found a name; a style by which the most evident truths are so obscured that they can no longer be perceived, and the most familiar propositions so disguised that they cannot be known. Every other kind of eloquence is the dress of sense, but this is the mask by which a true master of his art will so effectually conceal it, that a man will as easily mistake his own positions, if he meets them thus transformed, as he may pass in a masquerade his nearest acquaintance. This style may be called the terrific, for its chief intention is to terrify and amaze; it may be termed the repulsive, for its natural effect is to drive away the reader; or it may be distinguished, in plain English, by the denomination of the bugbear style, for it has more terror than danger, and will appear less formidable as it is more nearly approached.

2.34 Go to the library and look up one of the following books. Choose a chapter that deals with word choice or diction and prepare a summary of that chapter to share with the class: Walker Gibson, *Tough, Sweet, and Stuffy* (1966); Martin Joos, *The Five Clocks* (1967); Virginia Clark, ed., *Language: Introductory Readings*, 3rd ed. (1981); Peter Farb, *Word Play* (1973).

3

OTHER
DETERMINANTS
OF TONE

Almost everything we have talked about in the previous chapters works together to create *tone*, which is the total effect of a piece of writing. Connotation and diction, sentence length and rhythm, and the form of paragraphs (to be discussed in Chapter 4) all contribute to tone. As we have seen, one important function of language is to shape a reader's attitude toward the subject discussed. Tone is largely responsible for affecting the attitude of a reader, just as inflection of voice affects a listener.* We all know that "Thanks a lot!" can suggest gratitude, disgust, or sarcasm—all depending on the tone in which the words are spoken.

A writer's attitude toward a subject may not be the same as the response the writer wants to produce in the reader. Writers of advertisements, for instance, may be completely indifferent to their subject or may have very different views from those they communicate in print. But their job is to make readers feel a certain way toward the product or service, so they write in the ways they think are most likely to evoke that feeling. The people who write the advertisements for Levis may well hate blue jeans. And we often suspect that the celebrity telling us how delicious Brand X coffee is secretly despises it. Thus readers must understand such practices and take them into account before making or acting on a decision. That is one practical reason to know what tone is and how it is created.

This knowledge does more than enable us to recognize and make allowance for the strategies of advertisers and other "hidden persuaders." More important, it can enrich our enjoyment of imaginative writing. If we understand how tone

---

*Tone is sometimes distinguished from *voice*, which characterizes a writer's stance toward the audience. Because we are focusing on the act of reading, rather than the act of writing, we will use the term *tone* to cover most of the aspects of voice as well.

is achieved, we can clarify to ourselves the attitude a writer displays toward a subject: is it serious, playful, sympathetic, outraged, sarcastic, bitter, humorous? Sometimes, especially when we are dealing with ironic writing, the writer's apparent attitude suggests quite a different one, which we shall have to discover. And when we have determined a writer's true position, we may not want to share it. That is all right. As independent-minded readers, we are perfectly free to disagree. But once we commit ourselves to read a piece of writing critically, we are obligated to "listen" carefully, to absorb the argument in its own terms, and to reflect on its worth. Then we are free to accept or reject it. In any event, we have nothing to lose and everything to gain by remembering that tone influences us.

The preceding paragraph should sound familiar, because it essentially restates what was said in the Introduction. By this time, we have seen ample demonstrations of the general power of words. We shall now examine the influence on tone of three special sorts of language—metaphors, symbols, and allusions—and then briefly discuss some other aspects of tone.*

METAPHORICAL LANGUAGE

On pages 6-10 we described at some length skilled writers' use of highly connotative words to intensify readers' experiences by appealing to their senses as well as their minds. This "visualizing" principle lies at the heart of connotative language. And specifically metaphorical language is a logical extension of the same principle.

The way metaphorical language operates is easy enough to understand. The basic function of a metaphor is to suggest an analogy or comparison. A writer who wishes to make something clearer and more vivid draws into the discussion, if only by a word or two, some concrete image which brings to mind qualities of the idea which need illustration. Note the use that William Golding makes of metaphorical language in this sentence: "Where a satirist like Pope destroys his victims with flashes of lightning, Miss Jane Austen often roasted her victims over a fire so slow and nicely judged that the thick-skinned feel no discomfort on their behalf at all but only a gentle tickling."

Writers of imaginative literature are not the only ones to use metaphorical language. Indeed, although we usually think of scientific writing as "objective" or "plain," scientists sometimes draw on the power of metaphor. James Watson and Francis Crick, who won the Nobel Prize for their work on the structure of DNA, used the metaphor of a double helix to describe the DNA chain. They also used the zipper as a metaphor to describe how the two strands of the molecule could separate during cell division. Another metaphor basic to the field of molec-

---

*How would you characterize the tone of these opening paragraphs? Do we sound uninterested and distant, friendly and helpful, or as though we were "lecturing" you? In whatever way you characterize it, how do you *respond* to the tone?

ular biology is embodied in the notion that a messenger transmits a code laden with bits of genetic information from one generation of cells to another. Without such basic metaphors, scientists would have difficulty explaining many of their ideas to anyone other than a fellow scientist.

Metaphor-making, in fact, is one of the oldest and most elemental habits of the human mind. From the beginning of time, human beings seem to have searched for patterns in the universe, a process which led them to discover links between objects and ideas that were superficially unlike. Metaphors are the linguistic embodiment of these links. Furthermore, metaphors have always helped people perform one of the most difficult intellectual tasks: that of making an abstract notion understandable in terms of ordinary experience and of explaining the mysterious in everyday language. Metaphors, in short, are psychologically indispensable to our comfort in a complicated and often baffling world.

Thus the history of language is, in one respect, largely a history of words called into being by our search for resemblances and relationships in the midst of apparent chaos, for simplicity in the midst of complexity. They are a record of the attempt to relate one thing to another. One contemporary psychologist argues that "the metaphors of mind are the world it perceives." As examples, he notes that each age describes consciousness itself in metaphors that reflect the major concerns of the age. In ancient Greece, where citizens enjoyed remarkable freedom of speech and action, he argues, Heraclitus described consciousness as "an enormous space whose boundaries . . . could never be found out. . . . The first half of the nineteenth century was the age of the great geological discoveries in which the record of the past was written in layers of the earth's crust. And this led to the . . . idea of consciousness as being in layers which recorded the past of the individual, there being deeper and deeper layers until the record could no longer be read. . . ." The way we use metaphors thus reflects much about the way we see the world.

The very use of language inevitably involves words that originated as metaphors, even though their metaphorical significance is no longer realized. But in addition, we can hardly write or speak without using metaphorical expressions. We talk of *nipping a plot in the bud, of getting our act together, of blowing a project sky-high, marching to a different drummer, throwing in the towel, floating on cloud nine, seeing red, smelling a rat, drawing a blank, turning a deaf ear, talking with tongue in cheek, tightening our belts, rolling in the aisles*—without ever meaning that we really perform any of these acts. We are using such expressions metaphorically, or figuratively, to refer to some other action or attitude which, through familiar use, each depicts.

As we saw in Chapter 2, the use of figures of speech is one of our most deeply ingrained language habits. In casual conversation, as well as in writing, we use hundreds every day, most of them clichés. But more importantly, metaphorical language is one of the most frequent and influential means by which practiced writers convey their attitudes to us. The following paragraph from an essay by Jonathan Miller offers an unusually rich example of this practice.

Television is a vast, phosphorescent Mississippi of the senses, on the banks of which one can soon lose one's judgment and eventually lose one's mind. The medium itself is depressing. The shuddering fluorescent jelly of which it's made seems to corrode the eye of the spectator and soften his brain. It's quite different from the movies, which seem to be made of nothing except the images themselves. In television, the bodies and faces, the dances and games are suspended in a coldly glowing magma that must surely be repulsive to the touch: at once palpable and intangible—quite uncanny. It is like ectoplasm, in fact, which makes the term "medium" doubly appropriate. Television is a low-grade domestic seance in endless session, and the set goes to it with a vengeance, mouthing its gobbet of luminous cheesecloth until the tube burns out. Like a seance, too, it has a curiously limited repertoire, and it is certainly banal in the same way. There are no epiphanies to be had on television. There are none of the sometimes shattering apocalypses that one can get, even with the worst movies, in the dreamy caverns of the cinema. Possibly it's because Telly is so small and stingy. How could one ever hope to get an epiphany from it? Movies start with the advantage of an oceanic form, which can at least engulf the spectator and force him into delicious surrender. Telly, on the other hand, is a mean, fidgeting irritant, far smaller than one's own field of vision, flickering away in the corner of the eye like a dull, damaged butterfly. It would be mad, perhaps, and certainly unfair, to expect consistent marvels from such a mingy* little electronic membrane as this. Not to mention all the other drawbacks of the instrument—the frame rolls, the flickers, the snowstorms, the ghosts, the warps, the jumps, the judders, the chronic vibrato. Not to mention the commercials, which inhabit the crevices of programs like vile, raucous parasites, jumping out all over the living room, nipping, tweaking, and chattering unforgivably about joints, armpits, skin wrinkles, bowels, and blocked-up nasal passages. And not, furthermore, to mention the way in which Telly slithers into the home and stays in one corner of the room like a horrible electronic gossip.†

*Mingy and judders (three lines below) are not in the common vocabulary, though both appear in the dictionary. Even though we may never have seen them before, they are accurately defined by context. Both are portmanteau words—words formed from two other ones, whose meanings are thereby merged. Mingy evidently derives from mean and stingy, both of which appear earlier in the paragraph; some readers may also detect a suggestion of mangy. Judders combines jerk and shudders, with possibly a hint of jitters. They cleverly support the general effect of the paragraph. Telly is an expression used in Britain but not in North America.

†Jonathan Miller, "The Air," New Yorker, Nov. 16, 1963. Note that since this article was written in the days of black and white television, the author uses no references to color. What other changes in television might affect his description? We also note that in the twenty years since this article appeared, Mr. Miller, a physician as well as an actor and director, has starred in and directed television shows of his own, including a series on the human body.

Here the writer's case against television develops largely through his expert selection and arrangement of metaphor. Plainly, he is outraged by television, at least as television now exists; and his purpose is to make us share his disgust. On first reading, we are perhaps most conscious of the lively diction which establishes the tone of sardonic humor — humor unaccompanied by genial laughter. The connotative words the writer chooses are invariably powerful; they have not lost their force through overuse. Although a few (*magma, ectoplasm, gobbet*) are perhaps unfamiliar, their harsh sound goes well with caustic criticism, and so we accept them simply for the contribution their sound makes to the general atmosphere. Another word which may be unfamiliar, *palpable*, is clarified by its association with *intangible*. In the same way, *epiphanies* is defined in context by its contrast to the more familiar term *apocalypse*. Nevertheless, readers may have to look up several words in the dictionary.

On second reading, we can detect whole patterns of images which are more effective in condemning television than a long series of abstract assertions would be. In fact, even if the author used much more space he would be hard put to manage his surprising turns of thought and original linking of ideas without metaphor. The case against television has often been stated, but seldom in such vivid or entertaining terms. If we assent to Miller's argument, it is largely because he appeals to our intellect by way of our sensory experience. And the power of his statement is intensified by the way the several patterns of picture-making language unite in a single overall impression.

First are the figures which suggest thick liquid, jelly, protoplasm: television as a long river (*Mississippi* possibly connoting, in addition, muddiness) contrasted with the grander oceanic form of motion pictures; *phosphorescent* (suggesting the dull glow that emanates from decaying matter at night); *coldly glowing magma* (phosphorescence is also "coldly glowing"); *shuddering fluorescent jelly; softened brains; electronic membrane.*

Second are the terms which relate to the miraculous, the supernatural: *quite uncanny; medium; low-grade domestic seance,* complete with *luminous cheese-cloth* and *ectoplasm; epiphanies; apocalypses; marvels; ghosts.*

Third, an extraordinary sequence of words relating to unpleasant sensory experience describes the quality of television itself and relates to the physical reactions of the unhappy viewer: *corrode the eye; repulsive to the touch; mouthing its gobbet* (when we consider that the word *gobbet* connotes food that has been chewed and even partially digested, the repulsiveness of the image accords perfectly with the surrounding effects); *shuddering; mean, fidgeting irritant . . . flickering away in the corner of the eye; raucous; nipping, tweaking,* and *chattering.* The same purpose underlies the concluding references to those parts of the body that are the special concern of "commercial messages": *joints, armpits, skin wrinkles, bowels,* and *blocked-up nasal passages.* The commercials themselves, we should note, are described as nasty household pests crawling out of the woodwork *(the crevices of programs)* and filling the living room with their half-obscene chatter. Television as a whole is personified in the final sentence (metaphor often takes the form of *personification,* giving human qualities to an inanimate object). In a sense, television is commercials writ large — an adult, family-size intruder, slithering into the room as do insects, and chattering meanly, like a gossipy neighbor.

Even the most avid television fan will admit that the many expressions which describe what happens when a set is turned on ring true: *phosphorescent, coldly glowing, fluorescent, luminous, flickering, fidgeting, raucous.* A long sequence of words, all of them metaphorical to a greater or lesser degree, represents the "endless session" of a malfunctioning television set and conveys the writer's growing exasperation: *the frame rolls, the flickers, the snowstorms, the ghosts, the warps, the jumps, the judders, the chronic vibrato.* But although the paragraph certainly presents a graphic portrayal of experience, its intent is not so much to describe as to pronounce a value judgment. Every descriptive term is loaded against television. Thus, although readers sympathetic to television agree that the words accurately reflect their denotative role, they might well protest the loaded connotations of the metaphors, which work together to excite feelings against television. And they would, of course, be right. The author has done several things, all for one purpose. He has transferred to television people's general revulsion against jellylike substances. He has, in fact, gone much further, to present television as irritating all the senses, either figuratively (despite the images, television does not literally offend the specific sense of touch) or actually (the senses of sight and hearing). On another level, the imagery which suggests change and gradual erosion combines the short-lived nature of television programs with the effect on the viewer: the senses are corroded, the brain softened by the senseless and depressing flickering.

Seizing upon the double meaning of *medium*, Miller declares that television's "mystery" is of no higher quality than a spiritualist's séance, in which ghosts are called forth in a dark room. A séance is a form of deception, and so, the writer suggests, is television. But television cannot even boast the attractions of a dignified séance; instead, it is "low-grade" and "domestic." It has a dreamlike unreality, its performances featuring "dances and games" (both literally and metaphorically) rather than flesh-and-blood people and real life. Its dreams are not, however, the kind to be sought after. Viewers are always disappointed if they expect genuine "epiphanies," "apocalypses," and "marvels," for what they get is an eerie artificiality that offends both the senses and the mind. Perhaps the final impression we receive, indeed, is of the meanness, the triviality, of television. Metaphors and nonmetaphorical language both convey this idea: *low-grade; mingy little; curiously limited; so small and stingy; far smaller;* and *mean* itself.

This analysis by no means exhausts the rich metaphorical language of the paragraph. Among its other fine qualities is its freshness. The writer never employs stale imagery. Instead of calling television a "vast wasteland" (the reigning cliché at the time this piece was written), he strikes out in a new direction immediately by beginning with "vast" (which momentarily suggests he is going to use the cliché) and then surprising readers by replacing the expected "wasteland" with "phosphorescent Mississippi." This deliberate, specific departure from the cliché is typical of his whole method. The persuasiveness of his argument is directly proportional to the originality and appropriateness of his metaphors.

In our discussion of clichés (pages 68–73), we saw one way in which use of metaphor may give us a clue to thought processes. If, unlike Miller, writers depend on hackneyed figures of speech to convey meaning, they probably are thinking in stereotypes. By being aware of trite language, we arm ourselves against writers who seek to influence us with second-hand ideas as well as with second-hand language.

But metaphors may also tell us other things about writers and their attitudes, as well as about the attitudes they wish us to adopt. Ordinarily, metaphors should fulfill two requirements: they should be appropriate to the subject, the tone, and the occasion; and they should be consistent. Consider, for instance, the opening of James Baldwin's essay "The Uses of the Blues."

> The title "The Uses of the Blues" does not refer to music; I don't know anything about music. It does refer to the experience of life, or the state of being, out of which the blues come. Now, I am claiming a great deal for the blues; I'm using them as a metaphor—I might have titled this, for example, "The Uses of Anguish" or "The Uses of Pain." But I want to talk about the blues, not only because they speak of this particular experience of life and this state of being, but because they contain the toughness that manages to make this experience articulate. I am engaged, then, in a discussion of craft or, to use a very dangerous word, art. And I want to suggest that the acceptance of this anguish one finds in the blues, and the expression of it, creates also, however odd this may sound, a kind of joy. Now joy is a true state, it is a reality; it has nothing to do with what most people have in mind when they talk of happiness, which is not a real state and does not exist.

Even though the metaphor of blues music seems inappropriate at first glance, Baldwin goes on to relate the themes and substance of blues songs to the American black's experience of life and ultimately to "the universal challenge, the universal hope, the universal fear," the paradox expressed in the blues song: "The very time I thought I was lost/My dungeon shook and my chains fell off."

Baldwin's essay is a serious one, and he uses the central blues metaphor consistently to create a tone of seriousness and urgency. Not all writers, of course, use only one main metaphor. Jonathan Miller uses a number of differing metaphors which join to create a negative image of television. The writer of the following lighthearted article also uses several which converge in one concept: an obsession with chocolate.

> For millions of people, the product of the cacao bean is not so much a feast as a fix. . . . In stores that cater to chocolate freaks, the bounty is endless and bewildering. Chocoscenti quibble as they nibble over the respective merits of, say, Switzerland's Bachmann, France's

Debauve et Gallais and Belgium's Neuhaus. Some buy the immodest slogan of London's Charbonnel et Walker: "probably the best chocolate in the world." Passionate pilgrims trek all the way to 42 Cours Franklin Roosevelt, Lyon, in central France, to sample the exquisite specialties of Bernachon, which are sold nowhere else. Fans of Godiva, the Belgian firm that was acquired by the Campbell Soup Company and now makes its chocolates in Reading, Pa., are unbudgeable votaries.

The tone of the whole article on chocolate (not reprinted here) is humorous but informative. The writer reports on how much money people in various countries spend on it and on the psychological effects of an insatiable craving for chocolate. He maintains the humorous tone by using a number of metaphors which refer to devotion (*passionate pilgrims, fans, votaries*—usually people who have taken vows to live lives of personal deprivation and religious service) and addiction (*fix, freaks*). Taken together, the metaphors help create the amusing picture of crazed chocoholics dashing from country to country in pursuit of the ultimate chocolate "experience."

Here is another brief example of the use of a number of different metaphors, this time a less successful one. The excerpt comes from a newspaper article about one of the original stars of the popular television series *Star Trek.*

James Doohan (Scotty) was nothing so much as a Celtic teddy bear, soft and endearing. . . . He makes you think of Paddington and Pooh and all things warm and comforting. He is a little heavier today than he was 16 years ago. The locks on his head have silvered a bit with the years and the creases are etched a little deeper around the eyes when he laughs, but he, perhaps of all the Star Trek originals . . . is the one to whom time has been the kindest. . . . Time may have been kind to Doohan but the business has been more obstreperous since Star Trek went into the hyperdrive of space syndication. He, like the others in the supporting cast, has been typecast and the work has not fallen upon his head like manna from heaven. Only William Shatner and Leonard Nimoy seem immune to this fate. Doohan, on the other hand, seems doomed to be cast as a Highlander forever.

In the next paragraph, Doohan is described as a "chameleon" and later still as a "loony." In this case, the different metaphors do not converge toward a central image or concept. Rather, they clash and produce a confusing picture of Doohan, who has gone from a teddy bear to someone with silvered locks and deep creases to someone who is "immune" to manna from heaven, and then to a Scottish Highlander and later a chameleon. Such a hodgepodge of metaphors does little to reinforce the tone established by the writer's choice of words in general.

Metaphorical language which seems unsuited to the general tone of the passage may suggest that the writer simply does not have a clear idea of his or her purpose or of the way to achieve it. But a writer may deliberately use incongruous metaphors for a particular purpose. Writers often use just such an unexpected and apparently inappropriate metaphor for the sake of contrast. Many modern poets, for example, add extra meaning to their work by introducing language, and especially metaphors, whose connotation pulls in a direction opposite to that in which the poem as a whole is moving. This stress, or "tension," allows the writer to make an oblique, often ironic, comment and leads readers to entertain two simultaneous attitudes toward the poem's ideas: the one encouraged by the general tone and direction, and the quite different one suggested by the seemingly inappropriate or contradictory metaphor. Sylvia Plath's long poem "Tulips" uses the flowers as a metaphor not for the goodness and naturalness of life but for death. The tulips have filled up her hospital room and are "eating" her oxygen. Here is a stanza from the poem:

> The tulips are too red in the first place, they hurt me.
> Even through the gift paper I could hear them breathe
> Lightly, through their white swaddlings, like an awful baby.
> Their redness talks to my wound, it corresponds.
> They are subtle: they seem to float, though they weigh me down,
> Upsetting me with their sudden tongues and their color,
> A dozen red lead sinkers around my neck.

If we carefully consider the appropriateness of metaphor, we can throw light on the writer's attitude toward a subject and our own attitude toward it as well. In the same way, we can find significance in the consistency, or lack of consistency, of the metaphors in a passage. The extended or repeated use of concrete language calls up a series of pictures to us. Just as we retain a retinal "afterimage" when we close our eyes after looking at a bright light, so does the "eye" of our imagination (a metaphor in itself). When we read at normal speed, the picture that appears in our minds is not instantly blotted out. Instead, it lingers for a brief moment in our short-term memory. If another image occurs before the first fades, the result can be a sort of double exposure. Unless the two images are of the same type, so that they harmonize or converge, they will clash. And the total effect will be one of confusion.

See what happens to metaphors in the course of this paragraph from a recently published short story:

> I remember when she opened the door the evening we first met. She was the most striking woman I'd ever seen—a sort of wild combination of Audrey Hepburn and one of Gaugin's [sic] Polynesian nymphets. She was tall, probably five-ten or so, with huge eyes of Coke-bottle green, cheekbones high and gentle as an Olympic downhill slope, mouth a perfect, irresistible Lolita rosebud. The mahogany-auburn mane made her look like a lioness in training. She was adorable—and snobbish, frigid, unsociable, a real rich brat.

Here we have a glorious riot of unconnected imagery and mixed metaphors. The writer begins with allusions, to a movie star (Audrey Hepburn) and to a subject of the nineteenth-century French painter, Gauguin. Allusions, as we shall note later, can be both clever and illuminating. But here they are neither, because any power that might have come from such an odd combination of images is immediately lost in the ensuing description. Here the woman has eyes the color of Coke bottles, cheeks like Olympic downhill slopes, and a mouth like (of course) a rose. Her mouth is also likened to Lolita's, an allusion to Vladimir Nabokov's very young and very alluring character who, again, is far removed both from Audrey Hepburn and from Gauguin's natives. (Lolita is, in fact, more appropriately called a "nymphet" — a pubescent girl regarded as sexually desirable — than are the women in Gauguin's paintings.) In the next sentence, the woman is compared to a tree (mahogany) and a horse or lion (mane). Even the "lioness" of this sentence is ironically inappropriate, for only *male* lions have manes. The final evaluation — that she was "adorable" — can only strike us as odd. The whole jumble of unrelated pictures creates an impression which is blurred to the point of ludicrousness.

Other writers use metaphors more carefully, with constant attention to the contribution each can make to the whole argument. Their figures are not mere patchwork but coherent pictures. Often a skilled writer can lend unity to an entire passage by using an extended metaphor. Here the poet Edwin Arlington Robinson reminisces about his youthful pursuit of expressive language:

> In those days time had no special significance for a certain juvenile and incorrigible fisher for words who thought nothing of fishing two weeks to catch a stanza, or even a line, that he would not throw back into the squirming sea of language where there was every word but the one he wanted. There were strange and iridescent and impossible words that would seize the bait and swallow the hook and all but drag the excited angler in after them, but like that famous catch of Hiawatha's, they were generally not the fish he wanted. He wanted fish that were smooth and shining and subtle, and very much alive, and not too strange; and presently, after long patience and many rejections, they began to bite.

In this passage, the metaphorical language is as clear as the pool which the author implies. His words, like the fish, gleam with intrinsic and reflected meaning, with denotation and connotation. Even more important, the metaphor is suitable to its theme. The aspiring poet fishes for words just as he must countless times have angled for fish. Both fish and words — at least the kind worth catching — are elusive, and one must develop some expertise, as well as patience, before the coveted ones can be landed with any success.

We find numerous examples of extended metaphor in the speeches and essays of Martin Luther King, Jr. Here is one:

In a sense we have come to our nation's capital to cash a check. When the architects of our republic wrote the magnificent words of the Constitution and the Declaration of Independence, they were signing a promissory note to which every American was to fall heir. This note was a promise that all men would be guaranteed the unalienable rights of life, liberty, and the pursuit of happiness.

It is obvious today that America has defaulted on this promissory note insofar as her citizens of color are concerned. Instead of honoring this sacred obligation, America has given the Negro people a bad check; a check which has come back marked "insufficient funds." But we refuse to believe that the bank of justice is bankrupt. We refuse to believe that there are insufficient funds in the great vaults of opportunity of this nation. So we have come to cash this check—a check that will give us upon demand the riches of freedom and the security of justice.

The promissory note and bad check metaphors are especially appropriate because of their association with both our legal and our financial systems. The bad check especially suggests financial exploitation, which fits in well with King's theme.

In poetry, too, a sustained metaphor can sometimes contain almost the whole meaning a writer has in mind. W. B. Yeats's "A Coat" sums up in just ten lines how he feels about the use others have made of his poems (his song, or coat):

> I made my song a coat
> Covered with embroideries
> Out of old mythologies
> From heel to throat;
> But the fools caught it,
> Wore it in the world's eyes
> As though they'd wrought it.
> Song, let them take it,
> For there's more enterprise
> In walking naked.

Thus the use of a single metaphor can reveal an agile mind, one that can make a single analogy suggest a very broad concept, such as all of Yeats's poetry. But overdeveloped metaphors can be dangerous in the hands of the less skilled. In Ely Cathedral, in England, stands a tablet erected over a century ago to celebrate the memory of two men who were killed while working on the railroad line:

The Spiritual Railway

> The Line to heaven by Christ was made,
> With the heavenly truth the Rails are laid,
> From Earth to Heaven the Line extends,

To Line Eternal where it ends.
Repentance is the Station then,
Where passengers are taken in,
No fee for them is there to pay,
For Jesus is himself the way.
God's Word is the first Engineer,
It points the way to Heaven so clear,
Through tunnels dark and dreary here
It does the way to Glory steer.
God's Love the Fire, his Truth the Steam,
Which drives the Engine and the Train,
All of you who would to Glory ride,
Must come to Christ, in him abide
In First, and Second, and Third Class,
Repentance, Faith and Holiness;
You must the way to Glory gain
Or you with Christ will not remain.
Come then poor Sinners, now's the time
At any Station on the Line,
If you'll repent and turn from sin
The Train will stop and take you in.

Although the sentiment of this poem is obviously sincere, the stretching of the railroad analogy to cover so many religious ideas is unsuccessful. It may move a reader, but only to laughter. Extended, elaborated metaphors, even when used by more skillful writers, should always be carefully examined. Sometimes they work out well, as does John Donne's use of the drawing-compass figure in his poem "A Valediction Forbidding Mourning." Sometimes, however, they carry the reader from the first ground of similarity, which is perfectly acceptable, to other suggested similarities which are not, in fact, present. The reader who accepts the analogy as first presented may be induced to accept every other application of the analogy, whether sound or not.

For practice in examining extended metaphors, read the following passage. Are the analogies sound at every point? Or does the writer at any time strain the metaphor when he applies it to everything being said?

I find the great thing in this world is not so much where we stand, as in what direction we are moving: to reach the port of heaven, we must sail sometimes with the wind and sometimes against it—but we must sail, and not drift, nor lie at anchor. There is one very sad thing in old friendships, to every mind that is really moving onward. It is this: that one cannot help using his early friends as the seaman uses the log, to mark his progress. Every now and then we throw an old schoolmate over the stern with a string of thought tied to him, and look—I am afraid with a kind of luxurious and sanctimonious compassion—to see the rate at which the string reels off, while he lies there bobbing up and down, poor fellow! and we are dashing along with the white foam and bright sparkle at our bows;—the ruffled bosom of prosperity and progress, with a sprig of diamonds stuck in it! But this is only the sentimental side of the matter; for grow we must, if we outgrow all that we love.

Don't misunderstand that metaphor of heaving the log, I beg you. It is merely a smart way of saying that we cannot avoid measuring our rate of movement by those with whom we have long been in the habit of comparing ourselves; and when they once become stationary, we can get our reckoning from them with painful accuracy. We see just what we were when they were our peers, and can strike the balance between that and whatever we may feel ourselves to be now. No doubt we may sometimes be mistaken. If we change our last simile to that very old and familiar one of a fleet leaving the harbor and sailing in company for some distant region, we can get what we want out of it. There is one of our companions;—her streamers were torn into rags before she had got into the open sea, then by and by her sails blew out of the ropes one after another, the waves swept her deck, and as night came on we left her a seeming wreck, as we flew under our pyramid of canvas. But lo! at dawn she is still in sight—it may be in advance of us. Some deep ocean-current has been moving her on, strong, but silent—yes, stronger than these noisy winds that puff our sails until they are swollen as the cheeks of jubilant cherubim. And when at last the black steam-tug with the skeleton arms, which comes out of the mist sooner or later and takes us all in tow, grapples her and goes off panting and groaning with her, it is to that harbor where all wrecks are refitted, and where, alas! we, towering in our pride, may never come.

We may admire the ingenuity or sheer persistence it takes to stretch a metaphor so far, but we must conclude that here the metaphor is overextended and hence strained. The picture of the fleet of ships being towed into the heavenly port (past the pearly seawall?) by the grim black tugboat of Death adds nothing to the passage's effect. In fact, we learn nothing that could not be said more efficiently in a single concise nonmetaphorical paragraph. As critical readers, our judgment of metaphors should depend primarily on their function rather than their mere appearance. Metaphors, as Aristotle noted long ago, are a major part of the pleasure of learning. By linking the unknown or unfamiliar to something known and familiar, they lead us to new insights. Thus, if a writer uses metaphors accurately and appropriately, and if their significance is readily interpreted, they fulfill a very important purpose. Metaphorical language, indeed, is indispensable to both writers and readers.

(Exercises: pp. 159–167)

SYMBOLS

Until now, we have concerned ourselves with metaphors as instruments of analogy or comparison. The significance of each metaphor to the writer and its effects on the reader sometimes depend on personal and private experience. D. H. Lawrence uses a snake in one of his poems to represent "one of the lords of life," but the reader who has been bitten by snakes or who has always feared them may "read" this poem in a personal or private way. To a large extent, however, a metaphor's significance depends not on private experience but on traditional associations and on the context in which the symbol is used. The following passage describes a librarian, a man who has only dreamed of life's passions. Here he is on the beach, watching a woman fishing, a woman who appeared in his village after a shipwreck and whom the villagers think of as "a gift from the sea." In the context of this passage, the sea suggests to the librarian the passionate potential in life that has so far eluded him.

> She cast that line like a spell out over the sea, and stood motionless . . . to wait for the spell to take. She raised them up and reeled them in, one after the other, raised them up to reel them in, and stopped only long enough for her quick white hands to do with them whatever it was she did before she stood again to cast her spell another time. Pure goddess, and Larry, hidden in the cold wet brush, was himself spellbound. He felt himself rise every time to her lure and leap with it, and he felt all his body pulled towards her again and again, sliding through water, towards her and back and towards her again, completely in her power. . . .
>
> The next day when she set out it was without a rod and he followed her all the way . . . to the open sea. There, in a small bay where the breakers spread out like foamy lace on the level sand, she stood barefoot amongst the sea-carved driftwood and stranded intertidal life to look out across the waves. . . . What will you raise up here? And Larry half expected sunken ships and old whales to burst free into light.

In this passage, the sea is in fact the "sea of life." But the sea means many things to many writers. For instance, to Dante on occasion it suggested fierce sound: "I came into a place void of all light, which bellows like the sea in tempest, when it is combated by warring winds." Shakespeare adopted in another way the same association of turbulent sea and strife when he had Hamlet use the sea to emphasize the troubles that, like an army, besiege him:

> Whether 'tis nobler in the mind to suffer
> The slings and arrows of outrageous fortune,
> Or to take arms against a sea of troubles,
> And by opposing end them?

In *Macbeth*, Shakespeare used the sea's vastness to intensify the hopelessness of Lady Macbeth's attempts to cleanse herself of guilt:

> Will all great Neptune's ocean wash this blood
> Clean from my hand? No, this hand will rather
> The multitudinous seas incarnadine,
> Making the green one red.

—that is, turning the whole green ocean to one uniform blood-red color.

Isaac Newton, the great eighteenth-century scientist, used the sea to suggest the vast regions of scientific knowledge he would "swim in": "I do not know what I may appear to the world, but to myself I seem to have been only like a boy playing on the sea shore, and diverting myself in now and then finding a smoother pebble or a prettier shell than ordinary, while the great ocean of truth lay all undiscovered before me."

Other writers have used the enormous, almost limitless, size of the sea to make explicit comparisons. One, for instance, employs it to illustrate the amplitude of life: "Give me fullness of life like unto the sea and the sun; give me the fullness of physical life, mind equal and beyond their fullness." And another uses it, with exaggeration, to set a standard by which a dead naval hero's celebrity is to be measured:

> The waters were his winding-sheet, the sea was made for his tomb;
> Yet for his fame, the ocean sea was not sufficient room.

The metaphorical uses of the sea are as numerous as the sea's own qualities and moods: broad, deep, tempestuous, serene, rolling, salty, wet, green, blue, gray, protective ("rocked in the cradle of the deep"), death-dealing.

> Sunset and evening star,
> And one clear call for me!
> And may there be no moaning of the bar,
> When I put out to sea.

*   *   *   *   *

> Whereto answering, the sea,
> Delaying not, hurrying not,
> Whisper'd me through the night, and very plainly before daybreak,
> Lisp'd to me the low and delicious word death.

*   *   *   *   *

> The people along the sand
> All turn and look one way.
> They turn their back on the land.
> They look at the sea all day. . . .

> They cannot look out far.
> They cannot look in deep.
> But when was that ever a bar
> To any watch they keep?

*   *   *   *   *

> A current under sea
> Picked his bones in whispers. As he rose and fell
> He passed the stages of his age and youth
> Entering the whirlpool.

In these instances, in contrast to the preceding ones, the sea suggests more than a specific comparison. Rather, it functions here as a symbol, representing the essential quality of a complex or basic concept. Like all figurative language, the symbol expresses one thing (usually an abstraction) in terms of something else (usually a concrete object). But it operates not so much by analogy as by association. Feelings aroused by the sea, the elements, the sky and stars, a tree or a river—these have been part of people's imaginative experience since before language began. Whether or not we are aware of it, our cultural heritage has led us to respond in certain ways to natural objects and phenomena like the sea, and also the language which brings them to mind. In the examples just cited, the sea suggests nature's great continuum of time and creation, of life and death. Its rhythm is that of life itself, with its ebbs and flows. To seafaring people such as the Inuit of the far north or the Vikings of Norway, the sea has always been the source both of livelihood (and hence of life) and of sudden death. The sea, therefore, is thought of as the center of life, the source of being. But it also represents the darker forces of death, dissolution, and ultimate formlessness. These are some of the attitudes which people have acquired from looking or thinking about the sea. And these attitudes have become part of folk stories and literature, shared by landbound societies as well as maritime ones. A writer who uses the sea as a symbol, then, does so with confidence that it calls forth certain attitudes and emotions which are very widely shared.

The power of symbols thus results partly from culture and its traditions. But by that very fact, the meaningfulness of many symbols varies from culture to culture. To a Christian, the cross conveys more than it does to a Buddhist. On the other hand, the yin–yang symbol means much more to a Buddhist than to a Christian. Furthermore, to us the power of symbols, especially those which have wide literary use, also depends in part on how much and how carefully we have read. One of the best ways to become a skilled reader, one who responds immediately to symbolic language, is to read as widely and as much as possible.

To be sure, an emphasis on symbols can be carried to extremes. If a passage describes a sunset, a storm, or a walk along a mountain path, we should read it first in those terms alone, allowing the symbolism to emerge gradually. Stephen Crane's "The Open Boat," which is based on a true experience, begins by describing how dangerous the sea was to the men in the tiny boat. Only when he weaves a complex web of associations between the sea and nature's indifference to the struggles of individual people do we recognize that the sea is used symbolically. The tendency of some close readers to search for symbols everywhere reduces the reading process to a game of hide-and-seek or to puzzle solving. Reading too much into a passage is just as dangerous as reading too little into it.

As we noted earlier, metaphors can be either traditional and shared or private. We all have our own collections of objects or ideas which have especially powerful associations for us, because of our individual experiences. And many writers have seized on particular objects in their own experience and used them as recurrent symbols of some broad idea or attitude. Shakespeare, for instance, seems to have detested the spectacle of dogs begging for sweets to be dropped from the table, and then licking and slavering over them. Time after time in his plays he uses this repellent image to symbolize hypocritical flattery, as in Hamlet's

> Why should the poor be flatter'd?
> No, let the candied tongue lick absurd pomp,
> And crook the pregnant hinges of the knee
> Where thrift may follow fawning.

In the same way, T. S. Eliot's fondness for cats informs many of his poems. Maya Angelou recently declined to walk across the railroad tracks in her home town, explaining that those tracks held strong and very painful personal associations for her. She has, in fact, used such tracks symbolically in her writing. William Blake, W. B. Yeats, Ted Hughes, Vladimir Nabokov, and many other writers can be more fully understood if we know the particular significance and value they personally attach to certain symbols. This fact sometimes makes reading them more difficult, but in the long run, we are rewarded by the extra richness the symbols provide.

Much more common in literature, as in nonliterary writing, are symbols whose associative meaning the great majority of readers share. They are important both in general communication and in imaginative writing, because writers often allow them to bear the central meaning of a passage. Symbolism, well used, is far more effective than bald literal statement. This is true for two reasons. The first is that symbols, like other kinds of metaphor, use sense imagery to call forth emotional responses. The second is that because most symbols have figured in literature for centuries, they suggest to the well-read man or woman many passages in older writings. The use of a river as a symbol of the eternal flux of life, of the absence of permanence and stability in our human existence, goes back at least to Plato and Heraclitus, and countless writers of prose and poetry have used it since. When we read *Huckleberry Finn*, most of which takes place on the Mississippi River, we hear mental echoes of many others who have used rivers symbolically. Again, the symbolic meaning of *serpent* has at least two origins: the Bible story of the Garden of Eden and the classical myth of Medusa, who had snakes for hair and who turned those who looked into her eyes into stone. The serpent symbol thus combines two ideas: moral transformation, from innocence to sin, brought about by deceit (Satan—the serpent—and Adam and Eve); and physical transformation, of a living person into stone (Medusa). Of course, either aspect of the serpent symbol may be emphasized, depending on context. In the case of the section from Meredith's *Modern Love* (Exercise 3.4 [6], pages 163–164), each aspect may contribute equally to the total meaning.

Many symbols may have more than one significance. *Blood*, for example, denotes "the red fluid that circulates in the body." But in specific contexts *blood* can have a whole cluster of symbolic references. It may represent the essence of life ("lifeblood"). Medieval physiologists, who believed that each person had a dominant fluid which determined character, gave us the expression "It makes my blood boil." *Blood* may be shorthand for family kinship ("blood is thicker than water") or for noble ancestors ("blue blood in one's veins"). Or it may identify race or nationality ("she has Norwegian blood"). It may also symbolize individual murder ("his blood is on your hands") or wholesale slaughter ("a blood bath"). And the list is still far from complete.

Readers of imaginative literature keep alert to these pregnant symbols, which signify much more than their simple denotation. In a word or two, they can sum up a very important idea. Here is a small sample of common ones. What other associations can you add to each?

> *gold*: the symbol of wealth, or great value, of material (as opposed to spiritual) possessions; also of happiness, hope, genuineness, youth, and permanence. Robert Frost *reverses* the latter association in the following poem:

> > Nature's first green is gold,
> > Her hardest hue to hold.
> > Her early leaf's a flower;
> > But only so an hour.
> > Then leaf subsides to leaf.
> > So Eden sank to grief,
> > So dawn goes down to day.
> > Nothing gold can stay.

> *moon*: peace, serenity, chastity, romantic love; also (sometimes paradoxically), inaccessibility, loneliness, changefulness.

> > O, swear not by the moon, th' inconstant moon,
> > That monthly changes in her circled orb,
> > Lest that thy love prove likewise variable.

(Have the symbolic associations with the moon changed now that people have walked on it and brought back samples of its rocks and pictures of its "deserts"?)

star: remoteness, purity, permanence.

> We walked out late, leaning back for stars
> beneath the staked-down tent of dark,
> gawking there like foreigners
> at high, and myriad, and stark. . . .

The following stanza from the ballad "The Shooting of Dan McGrew" uses *moon*, *gold*, and *stars* all together. The stranger has just begun to play the piano and " — my God! but that man could play!"

> Were you ever out in the Great Alone, when
>   the moon was awful clear,
> And the icy mountains hemmed you in with a
>   silence you most could hear;
> With only the howl of a timber wolf, and you
>   camped there in the cold,
> A half-dead thing in a stark, dead world, clean
>   mad for the muck called gold;
> While high overhead, green, yellow and red,
>   the North Lights swept in bars—
> Then you've a hunch what the music meant
>   . . . hunger and night and the stars.

crossroads: a choice between two or more courses of action—usually a critical decision.

> Two roads diverged in a yellow wood,
> And sorry I could not travel both
> And be one traveler, long I stood
> And looked down one as far as I could
> To where it bent in the undergrowth;
>
> Then took the other, as just as fair,
> And having perhaps the better claim,
> Because it was grassy and wanted wear;
> Though as for that the passing there
> Had worn them really about the same,
>
> And both that morning equally lay
> In leaves no step had trodden black.
> Oh, I kept the first for another day!
> Yet knowing how way leads on to way,
> I doubted if I should ever come back.
>
> I shall be telling this with a sigh
> Somewhere ages and ages hence:

Two roads diverged in a wood, and I—
I took the one less traveled by,
And that has made all the difference.

ice: coldness, and therefore, often death. Also hardness, and therefore
the word can imply a personal attitude.

Some say the world will end in fire,
Some say in ice.
From what I've tasted of desire
I hold with those who favor fire.
But if it had to perish twice,
I think I know enough of hate
To say that for destruction ice
Is also great
And would suffice.

The use of symbols like these adds much to the emotional tone of any piece of writing. Sometimes they reinforce an impression which is first produced by other means. At other times they create an ironic contrast, as when a writer who has just described the horrible devastation of a bombed city shifts the reader's attention to a child's face and thus emphasizes, by contrast, the evil of the bombing.

Although the general significance of a symbol may be fixed, its precise connotation varies with the tone of the passage in which it occurs. Thus symbolism and tone—the part and the whole—interact. Take for example three symbols of death, the words *sleep*, *grave*, and *worm*. Each word implies a different attitude toward death. *Sleep* is almost wholly positive in its attitudes. It connotes relief from physical and mental pain, welcome oblivion. *Grave* has less of the warmth and comfort that *sleep* suggests. It implies, above all, silence, lack of motion, coldness. *Worm* is the least pleasant of the symbols, with its grisly suggestion of the body's decay after death.

But note how, in the following passages, the precise feeling we adopt toward death is affected both by the selection of a symbol and by the context. Context always modifies to some extent the connotation of a symbol.

From too much love of living,
From hope and fear set free,
We thank with brief thanksgiving
Whatever gods may be
That no life lives for ever;
That dead men rise up never;
That even the weariest river
Winds somewhere safe to sea.

Then star nor sun shall waken,
Nor any change of light:

> Nor sound of waters shaken,
> Nor any sound or sight:
> Nor wintry leaves nor vernal,
> Nor days nor things diurnal;
> Only the sleep eternal
> In an eternal night.

Here the poet—Algernon Swinburne—regards death as a narcotic sleep. He welcomes death, not because it promises anything good, but because at least it will blot out all the disappointed hopes, frustrations, and uncertainties of life. The meaning of sleep, then, is colored by the lines that lead up to it.

> Our revels now are ended. These our actors,
> As I foretold you, were all spirits, and
> Are melted into air, into thin air;
> And, like the baseless fabric of this vision,
> The cloud-capp'd towers, the gorgeous palaces,
> The solemn temples, the great globe itself,
> Yea, all which it inherit, shall dissolve
> And, like this insubstantial pageant faded,
> Leave not a rack behind. We are such stuff
> As dreams are made on, and our little life
> Is rounded with a sleep.

To Shakespeare, in these lines, the sleep of death promises nothing more than it promises to Swinburne. But death is not just a release from life; it is a natural culmination of an existence which is itself unsubstantial and illusory. The meaning of *sleep* in the last line is compounded of the meanings of many words that preceded it, all to the same effect—*spirits, melted, thin air, baseless, vision, cloud-capp'd, dissolve, insubstantial, faded, rack* (cloud fragment), *dreams*. Death and life are two parts of a perfectly harmonious whole.

> To die—to sleep—
> No more; and by a sleep to say we end
> The heartache, and the thousand natural shocks
> That flesh is heir to. 'Tis a consummation
> Devoutly to be wish'd. To die—to sleep.
> To sleep—perchance to dream: ay, there's the rub!
> For in that sleep of death what dreams may come
> When we have shuffled off this mortal coil,
> Must give us pause. There's the respect
> That makes calamity of so long life.

Here Shakespeare uses the same basic idea that Swinburne sets forth. But he finds in the symbol of sleep elements that Swinburne did not consider. Mention of dreams as a part of sleep in effect nullifies the usual meaning of the symbol.

Compare the total effect of this passage with the preceding one, which also speaks of dreams. What is the difference?

Although we may not often associate old age, sleep, and death with love, W. B. Yeats uses sleep both literally and symbolically in a lyrical love poem:

> When you are old and grey and full of sleep,
> And nodding by the fire, take down this book,
> And slowly read, and dream of the soft look
> Your eyes had once and of their shadows deep;
>
> How many loved your moments of glad grace,
> And loved your beauty with love false or true.
> But one man loved the pilgrim soul in you,
> And loved the sorrows of your changing face;
>
> And bending down beside the glowing bars,
> Murmur, a little sadly, how love fled
> And paced upon the mountains overhead
> And hid his face amid a crowd of stars.

Thus we see that symbols offer great flexibility. They are shaped by a writer to enhance a particular purpose.

(Exercises: pages 167-169)

ALLUSIONS

Readers who know the story of the fall of Troy (Ilium) recognize Marlowe's lines

> Was this the face that launched a thousand ships,
> And burnt the topless towers of Ilium?

as a reference to Helen of Troy, the beautiful woman over whom the battle was waged. Likewise, those familiar with the *Star Wars Saga* or with the television series *Dallas* will recognize someone referred to as a "Darth Vader" or a "J. R. Ewing" as a villain. In the same way, a reference to "another Hiroshima" suggests the destruction of that city by the first atomic bomb deployed in warfare. These are examples of allusions, references to a place, person, literary passage, or event (mythical or historical) which stands for a certain idea. Successfully used, allusions carry much meaning in a few words.

Our ability to recognize and understand allusions in writing depends on the background knowledge we have at our command. The more familiar we are with history, literature, the arts and sciences, and cultural traditions, the better prepared we are to receive the full message of a piece of writing. The only way to cultivate such familiarity is to read and read and read — and then to remember. We can, of course, identify some allusions by going to reference books such as

Brewer's Dictionary of Phrase and Fable or to one of the Oxford *Companions* to subjects like English and American literature, art, music, or classical literature. But only a few conscientious souls will go to the trouble of constantly interrupting their reading to look things up. The best way to handle allusions is to be prepared for them when they come.

We can illustrate the importance of allusions by looking at an essay by Wallace Stegner called "Turtle at Home." The essay gives an intimate report of the life of a pet turtle, Achilles, who survived many close encounters with trucks but was crushed (metaphorically) by the force of Love in the person of another turtle. Unless we know the story of Homer's Achilles, one of the epic heroes of the *Iliad*, we miss the appropriateness of the turtle's name. The essay contains this paragraph:

> But strawberries were his real fleshpots. They left him giddy, speeded up his reactions, put him almost in a frenzy of bliss. I shall cherish to my last hour the picture of Achilles munching large Marshall strawberries with the juice running down his rhythmic jaws and his whole face beatific. He was Greek, he was Dionysiac, he was young Keats bursting Joy's grape against his palate fine, he was a Rabelaisian monk with his robe tucked up, glutting himself with pagan pleasures. What reflections of a like charm could one get from the sight of a dog wolfing his carnivorous meals, or a cat washing her face after meat with a fussy, old-maid, New England nasty-neatness?

Here a whole series of allusions helps build the humor of the passage. Remember that Stegner is describing the "sinful" appetite of a pet turtle. "His real fleshpots": the dictionary may define *fleshpot*, but it may omit the historical association with the fleshpots of Egypt and their place in biblical story (Exodus 16:3). "He was Greek, he was Dionysiac": an allusion to the festivals of ancient Greece in which eating, drinking, and other sensuous pleasures were indulged to a point of frenzy. (Dionysius was the god of wine.) "He was young Keats ...": here we recall Keats's "Ode on Melancholy":

> Ay, in the very temple of Delight
>   Veil'd Melancholy has her sovran shrine,
>   Though seen of none save him whose strenuous tongue
>   Can burst Joy's grape against his palate fine.

"He was a Rabelaisian monk ...": an allusion to Friar John, that celebrated figure in Rabelais who took a great delight in the pleasures of the flesh.

Thus we have, in a single paragraph, a series of four allusions, drawn from the Old Testament, the history of ancient Greece, early nineteenth-century English literature, and French Renaissance literature. All of them connote indulgence in the joys of eating and drinking. Mr. Stegner might have said, in sentences without metaphor or allusion, that his pet turtle Achilles was wild about strawberries. But the allusive paragraph is much more vivid and more humorous—if the reader recognizes the allusions! Each allusion summons up a whole complex of associations: the story that lay behind the fleshpots of Egypt, the nature of the Dionysian revels, the young Keats enamored of sensuous pleasures, Rabelais's descriptions of the sensual monk. In effect, therefore, Achilles's strawberry debauch is compared to the great eating and drinking orgies of human history.

But all this of a *turtle!* What can the gargantuan (to what does this word allude?) appetites of a pleasure-loving monk have in common with the small strawberry consumption of a turtle? Nothing—except the gusto. And that is the point. Stegner has carefully chosen his allusions for a particular purpose. First, they translate his turtle's sensuality into a series of human equivalents, and thus induce readers to regard Achilles in human terms. Second, the allusions to heroes and great revels seem so out of place when applied to a pet turtle that they have a humorous effect. Thus the connotative quality of the allusions shapes the reader's attitude toward Achilles and his passion for strawberries.

This explanation has probably seemed laborious. So it has been. But the fact that we have labored to explain the function of a few allusions in a contemporary essay has its own point. Allusions, like metaphors and symbols, are most effective when they are comprehended at once. Skilled readers do not have to stop to wonder what each allusion means. Acquaintance with literature, history, and cultural tradition enables them to react spontaneously.

Understanding allusions, as well as using them judiciously in our own writing, helps bring memorable ideas of the past to illuminate what we think and say today, for the three major sources of allusions are mythology (including folk tales), literature (including the Bible), and history.

Today we may have difficulty realizing how important a part mythology played in the imaginations of writers and readers down through the ages. The gods and goddesses of Olympus, the heroes of ancient legends, were as familiar to the people who created the literature of the Western world as popular movie stars are to us. Their names—Juno, Prometheus, Vulcan, Jupiter, Neptune, Diana—evoke rich recollections of the wondrous stories in which these figures participated. (Which of the gods have featured prominently in the names associated with the U. S. space program?) One way to learn more about mythology is to read the poems of Ovid (notably the *Metamorphoses*), of which there are many translations. Ovid's works contain many of the myths and legends of ancient Greece and Rome. Another way is to browse in such collections of mythology as Edith Hamilton's or in one of the large encyclopedias of classical mythology such as the *Larousse*. Hamilton provides a discussion of the relationship of the gods and goddesses, the histories of the royal families of the ancient world, and a concise summary of the Trojan wars. Fraser's *The Golden Bough* also provides a wealth of information about mythology. In addition, reading the works of such English authors as Spenser, Shakespeare, and Milton in editions which provide notes on the allusions will help to acquaint you with major events in mythology.

A knowledge of classical literature also helps readers to recognize allusions in everyday reading. References to events and people in Homer's *Iliad* and *Odyssey* often occur even in routine journalism. We may, for instance, read of a political figure or highly paid professional athlete who is "sulking in his tent" because he did not get what he wanted. The meaning is more clear if we recall the episode of Achilles (the warrior, not the turtle!) sulking in his tent because he has captured a beautiful woman whom his general would not let him keep. Or if someone's prophecies of doom have earned her the name of a Cassandra, it is useful to know just who Cassandra was, and to do that we must know something of Greek tragedy. (Can you identify this allusion?)

Naturally, allusions to more recent literature occur today more often than do classical allusions. Stegner, in the essay about the turtle, speaks of Achilles, after "he" has been discovered to be a "she," as "that Rosalind in boy's clothing." He expects readers to recognize the allusion to the beautiful heroine of As You Like It who is disguised as a boy, and to enjoy the implied contrast. And he concludes the essay with "Amor vincit omnia" (love conquers all). Here the skilled reader recognizes an allusion to the motto engraved on a brooch worn by the Prioress in Chaucer's Canterbury Tales. That brooch suggests another humorous contrast: the supposedly pious nun's love of personal adornment. In another reference to Shakespeare, a recent writer says that his computer's "source" (a clearing house and data base for home computer users) is an "Ariel, which ranges unbounded over the U.S., Canada, and Europe, springing from any telephone jack when summoned." The allusion is to the fairy spirit who is Prospero's servant in The Tempest. Joan Didion titled a recent collection of essays Slouching Towards Bethlehem, a double allusion to the Bible and to W. B. Yeats's poem "The Second Coming," which ends with the lines "And what rough beast, its hour come round at last, Slouches toward Bethlehem to be born?"

In such a way, literary allusions help create the precise effects of any piece of writing. In the case of references to literature, we must know just what part the characters or events play in the poem or drama or novel in which they appear. We then apply this information to the new piece of writing. If a person is called an "Uncle Tom" we recall the character in Harriet Beecher Stowe's novel who seemed willing to be subservient to his "masters." Because of his extremely servile manner, a present-day reference to an "Uncle Tom" suggests scorn or derision. If a writer refers to a "Scarlett O'Hara," what does the allusion suggest? Another familiar allusion from literature is the figure of Don Quixote, from which the adjective quixotic is derived. To those who have read Cervantes's story, the would-be hero suggests misguided idealism and foolish gallantry. When we find an action or project described as quixotic, we immediately imagine the original Don Quixote fighting windmills and battling wineskins instead of human opponents, and the implied similarity affects our attitude toward the present action. The phrase "Catch-22" alludes to Joseph Heller's war novel of that title. The major character in the novel persistently tries to get discharged from the service, but a "Catch-22" always prevents his release. Can you think of any synonyms for "Catch-22"? Does it mean the same thing as dilemma or double bind? Or does the allusion in this case serve to describe a particular situation for which no exact word exists? What other characters or places from recent literature can you think of that are now used as allusions?

Quotations provide another type of allusion. When we recognize such phrases and recall their original context, our reading is almost always enriched. A writer comparing his old-fashioned neighborhood gas station to a modern self-serve station used them both as an extended metaphor for changes in values. He entitled the essay "They Also Wait Who Stand and Serve Themselves," thus twisting the wording of the original to which it alludes: John Milton's "they also serve who only stand and wait." Milton, whose blindness kept him from taking a more active role in religious affairs, asserts in this sonnet that passive service to God is service nevertheless. The essayist uses the allusion to Milton to make an ironic contrast between Milton's religious "service" and the modern "service" station, which offers very little service of any kind. After telling of his first encounter with a self-serve pump, the author describes how he had to "stand and wait" while the attendant ignored him: "I reached up to knock again, but noticed that my glove had left a greasy smear on the window. Ever my mother's son, I reflexively reached into my pocket for my handkerchief and was about to wipe the grease away when it hit me: at last the oil industry had me where it wanted me — standing in the rain and washing its windshield." In this essay, consumers are seen as also in passive service — but service to the big oil companies rather than to Milton's God.

A third major source of allusions is history. The term *Pyrrhic victory* — one entailing so great a cost that the victory is actually futile — derives from the name of a king of Epirus who "won" such a battle against the Romans. A *Waterloo* (as in "to meet one's Waterloo") suggests a decisive, perhaps final defeat. It alludes to what happened to Napoleon at Waterloo in 1815. *Fifth column* refers to the activity of rebel sympathizers during the 1936 civil war in Spain. Today, it suggests underground support for the enemy within the borders of a country at war. *Watergate* refers to the building in Washington, D. C., where the Democratic Party headquarters were burglarized. The ensuing scandal led to the resignation of President Richard Nixon. Today, the term *Watergate* connotes abuse of official powers and subsequent attempts at cover-up. A reference to the *Plains of Abraham* or the *Bay of Pigs* might be understandable from the context, but those unfamiliar with North American history might miss the power of those particular allusions.

Popular music, film, and television have been the sources of a great many allusions, and those forms of art themselves allude to others. The contemporary folk singer Don McLean's "Vincent" alludes both to the life of Vincent Van Gogh and to his famous painting "A Starry Night." (Other popular songs also carry literary allusions. Can you name some?) A film about the Vietnam war, *Apocalypse Now*, alludes both to the apocalypse of the Bible and to Joseph Conrad's *Heart of Darkness*. Even everyday life gives us useful allusions: we all recognize the source of a "Big Mac Attack" or a reference to the "golden arches." The journalist Hunter Thompson alludes both to literature and to popular culture in the following sentence: "Our Barbie doll president, with his Barbie doll wife and his box full of Barbie doll children is also America's answer to the monstrous Mr. Hyde."

Many writers, in fact, draw allusions from a number of varied sources, and part of the fun of critical reading is watching those allusions at work. In an article on Marshall McLuhan, Tom Wolfe includes a satiric description of literary academic life. After describing McLuhan as "delphic" (what is referred to?), as "the super-savant, the Freud of our times, the omniscient philosopher, the unshakable dialectician," and "the very picture of the absent-minded professor," Wolfe begins his witty digression:

McLuhan rose up from out of a world more obscure, more invisible, more unknown to the great majority of mankind than a Bantu village or the Southeast Bronx. Namely, the EngLit academic life. Tongaland and the Puerto Rican slums may at least reek, in the imagination, of bloodlust and loins oozing after sundown. EngLit academia, so far as the outside world is concerned, neither reeks nor blooms; an occasional whiff of rotting tweeds, perhaps: otherwise, a redolence of nothing. It is a world of liberal-arts scholars, graduate schools, *carrels*, and monstrous baby-sitting drills known as freshman English. It is a far more detached life than any garret life of the artists. Garret life? Artists today spend their time calling up Bloomingdale's to see if the yellow velvet Milo Laducci chairs they ordered are in yet.

English-literature scholars start out in little cubicles known as carrels, in the stacks of the university libraries, with nothing but a couple of metal Klampiton shelves of books to sustain them, sitting there making scholarly analogies—detecting signs of Rabelais in Sterne, signs of Ovid in Pound, signs of Dickens in Dostoevsky, signs of nineteenth-century flower symbolism in Melville, signs of Schlegelianism in Coleridge, signs of the Oral-narrative use of the conjunctive in Hemingway, signs, analogies, insights—always *insights*—golden *desideratum!*—hunched over in silence with only the far-off sound of Maggie, a Girl of the Stacks, a townie who puts books back on the shelves—now she is all right, a little lower-class-puffy in the nose, you understand, but . . .—only the sound of her to inject some stray, *sport* thought into this intensely isolated regimen. In effect, the graduate-school scholar settles down at an early age, when the sap is still rising, to a life of little cubicles, little money, little journals in which his insights, if he is extremely diligent, may someday be recorded.

The allusions here are to advertising, to history, to popular culture and pop art, and to literature. Can you detect the humor in Wolfe's series of "scholarly analogies" in the second paragraph? Do you recognize "Maggie, a Girl of the Stacks" as an allusion to a novel by Stephen Crane *(Maggie, a Girl of the Streets)*?

(Exercises: pages 169-172)

DEVIATIONS FROM "NORMAL" STYLE

Tastes and fashions in writing change from generation to generation. So in one sense we can hardly speak of a "normal" style, because what at one time seems "normal" subsequently ceases to be so. Nevertheless, readers today can easily detect major differences in the following passages. One uses plain, simple words and sentences; the other is elaborate and patterned and uses elevated diction.

I look at my mama and I know what she's thinking. I been with Mama so much, just me and her, I know what she's thinking all the time. Right now it's home—Auntie and them. She's thinking if they got enough wood—if she left enough there to keep them warm till we get back. She's thinking if it go'n rain and if any of them go'n have to go out in the rain. She's thinking 'bout the hog—if he go'n get out, and if Ty and Val be able to get him back in. She always worry like that when she leaves the house. She don't worry too much if she leaves me there with the smaller ones, 'cause she know I'm go'n look after them and look after Auntie and everything else. I'm the oldest and she say I'm the man.

I look at my mama and I love my mama. She's wearing that black coat and that black hat and she's looking sad. I love my mama and I want put my arm round her and tell her. But I'm not supposed to do that. She say that's weakness and that's crybaby stuff, and she don't want no crybaby round her.

*   *   *   *   *

[Man] must teach himself that the basest of all things is to be afraid; and, teaching himself that, forget it forever, leaving no room in his workshop for anything but the old verities and truths of the heart, the old universal truths lacking which any story is ephemeral and doomed—love and honor and pity and pride and compassion and sacrifice. Until he does so he labors under a curse. He writes not of love, but of lust, of defeats in which nobody loses anything of value, of victories without hope and worst of all without pity or compassion. His griefs grieve on no universal bones, leaving no scars. He writes not of the heart but of the glands.

Until he relearns these things he will write as though he stood among and watched the end of man. I decline to accept the end of man. It is easy enough to say that man is immortal simply because he will endure; that when the last ding-dong of doom has clanged and faded from the last worthless rock hanging tideless in the last red and dying evening, that even then there will still be one more sound: that of his puny inexhaustible voice still talking. I refuse to accept this. I believe that man will not merely endure: he will prevail. He is immortal, not because he alone among creatures has an inexhaustible voice, but because he has a soul, a spirit capable of compassion and sacrifice and endurance. The poet's, the writer's, duty is to write about these things. It is his privilege to help man endure by lifting his heart, by reminding him of the courage and honor and hope and pride and compassion and pity and sacrifice which have been the glory of his past. The poet's voice need not merely be the record of man, it can be one of the props, the pillars to help him endure and prevail.

We can see at first reading that the second passage, from the speech William Faulkner gave upon receiving the Nobel Prize for Literature, is formal and that it uses dignified language, repetition, and certain sentence patterns for special emphasis. The first passage, on the other hand, uses plain, simple vocabulary and sentences, and dialect. It is informal, colloquial, and characteristic of oral rather than written language. The subject of both excerpts is human endurance. Both exhibit "deviations" from normal style, the one toward the elevated, the other toward the utterly simple and plain. Both, however, strike us as effective. We understand and appreciate the effects each writer is striving for.

Sometimes, writers go too far in their deviations from normal style, and we find their prose offensive, ineffective, or even incomprehensible. We should not, of course, reject out of hand writing that fails to conform to our own personal standards of diction. To do so would be to exclude ourselves from reading and enjoying much writing, especially from the past. After all, what seems ineffective or even stupid to us may only be unfamiliar. As we accustom ourselves to reading literature from different ages, we may find ourselves altering our opinions and acquiring a taste for what once seemed strange. But what about *modern* writing that seems to use excessively ornate and elevated style and hence deviates from the "normal"? To discover what the following writer means by departing from the present norms of diction, consider all we have already said about the function of words in setting the tone of a piece of writing:

Isolt the abandoned one, fair princess of Brittany, stands forlorn on her native strand. Her wide eyes linger long on the empty horizon of the gray North Sea, where last she has seen her beloved Tristan, dropping over the rim of the world and out of sight.

The good King Howel, fond father of Isolt, stands silent on the head- land, watching. His great heart swells with compassion, and as he turns away to his castle, he knows that he will never forget this poignant picture of her loneliness. It has been etched indelibly in his memory.

And yet, as the years unfurl, he remembers much more than her dejection. In his mind's eye he sees her standing there, with white birds circling in the sunlight overhead. He sees the majestic roll of the waves on the eternal sea. He sees the fleecy clouds drifting aloft in the blue, and the blossoming heather blowing in the wind. And so the magnificence of Nature surrounding the lonely Isolt tempered the melancholy of his memory with a glow of enduring beauty.

Plainly, the author of these paragraphs wishes to stir readers' emotions, and in this attempt (to use a metaphor it is worthwhile to pause over) the writer has pulled out all the stops. He or she has laden the passage with connotative and ornate language. But, critical readers ask, what purpose does all this fancy language serve? As we read on, we find that the author is exploiting our emotions in an attempt to sell funeral services!

> Such is the comfort, the blessing, the benediction, that beauty bestows on memory. The provision of such beauty has ever been the goal of our earnest endeavours at G——Funeral Homes. To invest a beauty of memory in our every deed, sparing no conceivable effort in providing services of immaculate refinement, always has been our ideal.

The writer clearly wants to hypnotize readers into believing in the superiority of his or her employer's funeral arrangements. And such commercial motives often lie behind present-day use (or abuse) of the deliberately "poetic" or elevated tone.

Thus, although there is no such thing as a fixed style or tone that is invariably correct, we do demand that deviations from the norm be appropriate when they do occur. In the funeral parlor advertisement, the excessively elevated tone is used for exploitive purposes. It does not suit the occasion, which is only a commercial sales pitch. Use of language that is too colloquial or too filled with slang for the subject and occasion can also be inappropriate. Here is the opening of a *New York Times* editorial which satirizes what the writer feels is unwarranted acceptance of colloquial language by *Webster's Dictionary*: "A passel of double-domes at the G. and C. Merriam Company joint in Springfield, Mass., have been confabbing and yakking for twenty-seven years—which is not intended to infer that they have not been doing plenty work—and now they have finalized *Webster's Third New International Dictionary*, Unabridged, a new edition of that swell and esteemed word book." The editorialist feels that the dictionary is not the place for an easy acceptance of slang, colloquialisms, and outright misuse of words. And the writer counts on our finding the use of such slang in a *New York Times* editorial inappropriate, thus reinforcing the point.

H. L. Mencken was a past master of the use of both kinds of deviations—the elevated and the colloquial—for comic effect. His three volumes of autobiography (*Happy Days, Newspaper Days*, and *Heathen Days*) can teach readers more about expert word-handling than can volumes of commentary:

> Today the fear of cops seems to have departed teetotally from American boys, at least on the level of the bourgeoisie. I have seen innocents of eight or nine go up to one boldly, and speak to him as if he were anyone else. Some time ago the uplifters in Baltimore actually organized a school for Boy Scouts with cops as teachers, and it did a big trade until the cops themselves revolted. What happened was that those told off to instruct the Scouts in the rules of traffic, first aid, the operation of fire-alarm boxes, etiquette toward the aged and blind, the

elements of criminal law and other such branches got so much kidding from their fellows that they were covered with shame, and in the end the police commissioner let out the academy *sine die*, and restored the faculty to more he duties.

William Buckley is another writer who can yoke elevated and colloquial language in humorous ways. In "How I Came to Rock," he tells of the five hundred letters he received in response to an unflattering review of the Beatles: "To manifest truth and beauty, I picked out one letter to reply to, because I found it so wonderfully direct, and eloquent. 'Dear Mr. Buckley,' the young lady wrote from San Francisco, 'you are a ratty, lousy, stinky, crummy idiot. P.S. You are too crummy to be called a person.' After an exchange of four or five progressively amiable letters, I came upon the final effusiveness of the human spirit. It was Christmastime, and my new girlfriend sent me, by registered mail, a square inch of white cloth from . . . the sheet on which Ringo Starr had slept while at the St. James Hotel. Thus did the Lord melt the heart of the Pharaoh."

(Exercises: pages 172-173)

IRONY

Mencken's and Buckley's deadpan humor brings us naturally to another aspect of tone, one which causes more trouble to inexperienced readers than any other. We are speaking of irony, an apparently serious statement of facts or opinions in which the writer does not believe.* Irony differs, however, from hypocrisy or lying. The ironist expects readers to realize that his expressed statements are in fact directly opposed to what he believes. The hypocrite or liar, on the other hand, wants his words to be accepted at face value. He does *not* want to be found out. The difference, in brief, is between sincerity and fraud, between an indirect statement of truth and deliberate deception. In Shakespeare's *Othello*, the villain Iago is an arch-hypocrite when he tells Othello he is devoted to him at the very moment he is plotting his downfall. On the other hand, when Mark Antony, in *Julius Caesar*, calls Caesar's assassins "all honorable men," he knows that his listeners, the Roman citizens attending Caesar's funeral, will understand that although he seems to approve of the assassins' deed, he really condemns it. (This speech, so heavy with irony, also contains sarcasm, another closely related aspect of tone. *Sarcasm* refers to the way of speaking, the intention of taunting the listener. Often irony is delivered in sarcastic terms, but a sentence or speech may be sarcastic without necessarily containing irony.)

---

*The following discussion concerns only verbal irony. The term *irony* also applies to (1) a situation or turn of events the opposite of what is expected or fitting ("an ironic twist of fate") and (2) a device in fiction and drama in which the reader or spectator knows more about the true situation than do the characters. Their unawareness of the true situation gives their actions and words extra ("ironical") meaning. These are called, respectively, *irony of situation* and *dramatic irony*.

In essence, irony implies a contrast between what *is* and what, in a more nearly perfect world, *might be*. Thus the effect of irony grows out of the incongruity or tension between the writer's apparent attitude and what he or she really means. In the following passage, the early nineteenth-century American writer Washington Irving describes his "great admiration" of Europeans:

> I was anxious to see the great men of Europe; for I had read in the works of various philosophers, that all animals degenerated in America, and man among the number. A great man in Europe, thought I, must therefore be as superior to a great man of America, as a peak of the Alps to a highland of the Hudson; and in this idea I was confirmed, by observing the comparative importance and swelling magnitude of many English travellers among us, who, I was assured, were very little people in their own country. I will visit this land of wonders, thought I, and see the gigantic race from which I am degenerated.

The more Washington Irving emphasizes this "degeneration" of Americans and the "swelling magnitude" of the English, the more we are certain that he is writing ironically. In fact, Irving is poking fun at the smugness and conceit of the foreign travelers.

Art Buchwald is a contemporary writer who frequently uses irony to humorous effect. In "Fathers for Moral America," he indirectly suggests that men may not be doing much about the problem of "moral decay":

> When I visited its headquarters the other day, a spokesman for the organization told me, "The mothers have done so much to point out the decadent aspects of the United States that we felt the fathers should help out too."
> "What do you do?"
> "We have a screening room in the back where we show dirty movies every two hours. We want to alert the fathers of America to the terrible degeneration that is going on in the United States. The response has been heartwarming. Ever since we started the screenings, there hasn't been an empty seat in the house."
> "What has been the reaction?"
> "The majority of them leave shocked that things like this could be happening in this country, and many come back a second time because they can't believe it."

Probably no American writer has used irony more expertly or consistently than Mark Twain. His dry, matter-of-fact manner often was linked to highly ironic prose. In "Advice to Youth," Twain is apparently giving a commencement address:

> Being told I would be expected to talk here, I inquired what sort of a talk I ought to make. They said it should be something suitable to

youth—something didactic, instructive, or something in the nature of good advice. Very well. I have a few things in my mind which I have often longed to say for the instruction of the young; for it is in one's tender early years that such things will best take root and be most enduring and most valuable. First, then, I will say to you, my young friends—and I say it beseechingly, urgingly—

Always obey your parents, when they are present. This is the best policy in the long run, because if you don't they will make you. Most parents think they know better than you do, and you can generally make more by humoring that superstition than you can by acting on your own better judgment. . . .

Now as to the matter of lying. You want to be very careful about lying; otherwise you are nearly sure to get caught. Once caught, you can never again be, in the eyes of the good and the pure, what you were before. Many a young person has injured himself permanently through a single clumsy and illfinished lie, the result of carelessness born of incomplete training. Some authorities hold that the young ought not to lie at all. That, of course, is putting it rather stronger than necessary; still, while I cannot go quite so far as that, I do maintain, and I believe I am right, that the young ought to be temperate in the use of this great art until practice and experience shall give them that confidence, elegance, and precision which alone can make the accomplishment graceful and profitable. Patience, diligence, pains-taking attention to detail—these are the requirements; these, in time, will make the student perfect; upon these, and upon these only, may he rely as the sure foundation for future eminence. Think what tedious years of study, thought, practice, experience, went to the equipment of that peerless old master who was able to impose upon the whole world the lofty and sounding maxim that "truth is mighty and will pre-vail"—the most majestic compound fracture of fact which any of woman born has yet achieved. For the history of our race, and each individual's experience, are sown thick with evidence that a truth is not hard to kill and that a lie told well is immortal. . . . A final word: begin your practice of this gracious and beautiful art early—begin now. If I had begun earlier, I could have learned how. . . .

But I have said enough. I hope you will treasure up the instructions which I have given you, and make them a guide to your feet and a light to your understanding. Build your character thoughtfully and painstakingly upon these precepts, and by and by, when you have got it built, you will be surprised and gratified to see how nicely and sharply it resembles everybody else's.

The effect of irony on readers comes from the pose the writer adopts. On the surface, ironists may seem detached, objective, neutral. They apparently have no emotional involvement; they stand apart from their subjects and dryly, reasona-bly comment on them. Sometimes readers may be shocked by this apparent lack of feeling — until they realize that beneath the impassive mask lies deep concern. Or ironists may seem to be genuinely concerned, anxious to do good. But their announced goals are not the actual ones. In either case, by intensifying readers' awareness (when they detect the ironic tone), ironists hope to enhance the impact of the message, whether humorous or serious.

The most famous example of sustained irony in English literature is "A Modest Proposal" by Jonathan Swift. In it, Swift describes the economic and social advantages the Irish could gain by tapping a new food supply — their own children. With all the seriousness and objectivity of a professional economist, Swift lists the benefits: parents with lots of children would get more money; public charity would be less necessary; new, delicious dishes could be invented. He then goes on to answer all objections that could be raised against the plan. Horrified by this cold-blooded urging of cannibalism, readers must finally conclude that Swift could not possibly mean what he says. He must be joking. Only then do they realize that Swift, far from joking, is writing in the bitterest vein of irony. "A Modest Proposal" is really a statement about the terrible poverty which existed in eighteenth-century Ireland. At every point in his essay, Swift denounces the barbaric political and economic practices which resulted in the desperate plight of the Irish.

Poets too may use irony to criticize evils. Here is a very simple example, a poem entitled "The Latest Decalogue" (which means — ?):

> Thou shalt have one God only; who
> Would be at the expense of two?
> No graven images may be
> Worshipped, except the currency:
> Swear not at all; for thy curse
> Thine enemy is none the worse:
> At church on Sunday to attend
> Will serve to keep the world thy friend:
> Honour thy parents; that is, all
> From whom advancement may befall;
> Thou shalt not kill; but need'st not strive
> Officiously to keep alive:
> Do not adultery commit;
> Advantage rarely comes of it:
> Thou shalt not steal; an empty feat,
> When it's so lucrative to cheat:
> Bear not false witness; let the lie
> Have time on its own wings to fly:
> Thou shalt not covet, but tradition
> Approves all forms of competition.

In this sardonic poem, Arthur Hugh Clough expresses some profound social criticism. If you can explain, on the basis of these lines, how the poet feels about the morality of his age, you have made a long step toward understanding how irony functions.

The following poem, a more complex example of irony, makes some pointed suggestions about women, abduction, and "conversation pieces." Be prepared to read this poem more than once, and to puzzle over who might have been "seized like that/And taken away."

Conversation Piece

It occurs to me, perversely, perhaps, but unmistakably,
That it would be so nice to be seized like that
And taken away.
Why?
I'm not sure why, but it occurs to me
That it would be so nice to have a change of problems,
And such a relief to be in the right for once
In the face of the interrogators, who are everywhere, anyway.

Solitary confinement sounds nice, too.
I like that word used in the reports, "incommunicado."
Why?
Well, why are you asking? I'm only saying it occurs to me
That one might be able to make a spiritual
Retreat out of it, such as I've never managed
To achieve in the atmosphere of monasteries and convents.
Unworldliness is such a distraction, you see.

Of course, the idea of being seized is
A prehistoric female urge, probably, rising
Up from the Cave, which must have been exciting.
And perhaps one would hope for a charming interrogator.

Yes, I do agree, I wouldn't like it really.
It's only just an idea. Yes, I know you don't follow.
Because, in fact, I'm not leading anywhere. Only talking,
That's all. I think I'd put up a fight, actually,
If taken away off the street. And it occurs to me that maybe
I would like a fight, but not really.
Neither would they, perhaps.

Why?
I don't know. Why are you asking questions
Like this and trying to put me in the wrong?
I've exhausted the idea, anyhow, with all this talking.

(Exercises: pages 173-177)

UNDERSTATEMENT AND OVERSTATEMENT

Two further devices of tone, often related to irony, are understatement and over-statement. The Canadian humorist Stephen Leacock introduces us to both these terms as he takes an ironic look at a review of his work — and at his own writing:

> Until two weeks ago I might have taken my pen in hand to write about humour with the confident air of an acknowledged professional. But that time is past. Such claim as I had has been taken from me. In fact I stand unmasked. An English reviewer writing in a literary journal, the very name of which is enough to put contradiction to sleep, has said of my writing, "What is there, after all, in Professor Leacock's humour but a rather ingenious mixture of hyperbole and meiosis?"
>
> The man was right. How he stumbled upon this trade secret I do not know. But I am willing to admit, since the truth is out, that it has long been my custom in preparing an article of a humorous nature to go down to the cellar and mix up half a gallon of meiosis with a pint of hyperbole. If I want to give the article a decidedly literary character, I find it well to put in about half a pint of paresis. The whole thing is amazingly simple.*

Both overstatement and understatement achieve their effect, as irony does, from the recognized gap between statement and fact. But ideas understated or overstated are not necessarily (though they may be) ironical in intention. Both are related to tone because they too are means by which a writer can influence readers' feelings. With understatement, the writer's apparent emotional response to the subject is much milder than would normally be expected. The writer seems to underreact, to regard things more coolly than seems normal. With over-statement, a writer's response seems stronger, more extravagant, than the facts evidently warrant.

Understatement often requires the reader to turn up the volume, so to speak. When, after a diver in a swimming competition gets a perfect score, the announcer remarks that it was "a pretty fair performance," we automatically understand that the speaker means that remark as high praise. Understatement often takes the form of denying the opposite of what is meant (the rhetorical figure *litotes*): The announcer who says "not bad" after a perfect dive actually means that the dive is far from bad.†

Hyperbole means "overstatement"; *meiosis,* "understatement." *Paresis,* which Leacock says adds "a decidedly literary character," means "partial paralysis."

†A reminiscence by the novelist Victoria Lincoln serves as a classic example of understatement. When she was a child in Fall River, Massachusetts, Miss Lincoln lived near Lizzie Borden, who in 1892 had been accused of murdering her father and stepmother. ("Lizzie Borden took an ax/And gave her mother forty whacks;/When she saw what she had done,/She gave her father forty-one.") Although she was acquitted, her neighbors continued to treat her with a certain reserve. Victoria Lincoln's mother explained: "Well, dear, she was very unkind to her father and mother."

Writers often use understatement to increase emphasis. In "The Open Boat," Stephen Crane describes the ordeal of four men who escaped a sinking ship and then endured days and nights of continuous battle with a stormy and vicious sea. Faced with death, one of the men remarks, merely, that if he drowns, "it would be a shame." Another example of understatement occurs in Joseph Conrad's *Heart of Darkness*. The narrator, Marlow, has risked his life to rescue a sick man named Kurtz, who is stationed in the upper Congo. Marlow finds, to his horror, that Kurtz has joined in cannibalism and has "decorated" his property with the heads of some of his victims. Marlow says,

> I am not disclosing any trade secrets. In fact, the manager said after-wards that Mr. Kurtz's methods had ruined the district. I have no opin-ion on that point, but I want you clearly to understand that there was nothing exactly profitable in these heads being there. They only showed that Mr. Kurtz lacked restraint in the gratification of his various lusts, that there was something wanting in him—some small matter which, when the pressing need arose, could not be found under his magnificent eloquence. Whether he knew of this deficiency himself I can't say.

When Marlow thus understates Kurtz's depravity, he only increases its enormity in our minds. (Irony, as well, is apparent in this passage: Marlow is really very shocked by what he learns. He makes his true feelings all the more evident through indirection.)

Novelists are not the only writers who use understatement, of course. When James Watson and Francis Crick published their first article on the structure of DNA, they felt that they had done nothing less than discover the secret of life. Yet they closed their article with a vast understatement, using it purposely to gain emphasis: "It has not escaped our notice that the specific pairing we have postulated immediately suggests a possible copying mechanism for the genetic material." Thirty years later, when we see the profound developments that have followed their discovery, we can appreciate this understatement even more.

If understatement asks us to turn up the volume, overstatement requires us to tone down our response. When we read that a guitarist's rendition of "Mala-gueña" sent the audience into fits of rapture, the obvious exaggeration tells us that this was a very good performance. And when D. H. Lawrence says in an essay on "Fenimore Cooper's Leatherstocking Novels,"

> Two monsters loomed on Cooper's horizon.
>   Mrs. Cooper   My Work
>   My Work   My Wife
>   My Wife   My Work
>   The Dear Children
>   My Work!!!
>
> There you have the essential keyboard of Cooper's soul.

we understand that the exaggeration is meant merely to emphasize Cooper's devotion to his "monsters."

Writers often use overstatement for humorous effects. Here is a columnist using exaggeration to make fun of fast-food restaurants and their food:

Napoleon Bonaparte, where are you when your country needs you? France has been invaded by fast foods. Worse, the enemy has become more deeply entrenched. It may be only a matter of time till the Arc de Triomphe doubles as a McDonald's. The nation that successfully drove out the English (whose war crime was suet pudding) and the Germans (their atrocity, Prussian pumpernickel) is surrendering to *le restaurant rapide*.

France is hoist by her own French fries.

The latest report from the front lists 1,300 sidewalk cafés as casualties last year. . . . The small cafés are putting up a gallant rearguard action, thanks to their liquor licenses. But the working wife and the shortened lunch hour have combined to assure the victory of Cordon Blah. . . .

What a travesty of the truth are those TV commercials in which we watch a family falling over themselves to reach the fast-food restaurant before they drown in their own drool! They act demented. They show what would have been the berserk behavior of Pavlov's dogs had they been conditioned to bring their dinner home in a bucket, or to wolf down the contents of a small, styrofoam casket.

Future anthropologists will study those TV convulsions and know why twentieth-century man went round the bend: we went finger-lickin' bonkers. . . .

With the possible exception of the Chinese (who are also in peril of coca-colonization) the French have done the most to make dining in a restaurant the apotheosis of living to eat instead of eating to live. What the English have done for the art of self-government, the chefs of France have done for the gourmet.

The traditional French café owners are hoping that the Big Mac attack is merely another battle of the bulge, that the people will rally behind the Michelin guide and award *le restaurant rapide* a pair of crossed plastic spoons. And those of us whose bottoms have shared with Hemingway's a Left Bank café chair pray that somewhere on the island of Corsica a stocky corporality is putting his hand on his stomach in a pledge to free France from fast food.

Tom Wolfe is another contemporary writer who characteristically uses overstatement, and his humor often accompanies a serious message. In "Pornoviolence," Wolfe exaggerates to make a telling point against a newspaper that is itself given to grossly overstating the case:

> *"Keeps His Mom-in-Law in Chains,* meet *Kills Son and Feeds Corpse to Pigs."* "Pleased to meet you," . . .

In all these years of journalism I have covered more conventions than I care to remember. Podiatrists, theosophists, Professional Budget Finance dentists, oyster farmers, mathematicians, truckers, dry cleaners, stamp collectors, Esperantists, nudists and newspaper editors—I have seen them all, together, in vast assemblies, sloughing through the wall-to-wall of a thousand hotel lobbies (the nudists excepted) in their shimmering gray-metal suits and pajama-striped shirts with white Plasti-Coat name cards on their chests, and I have sat through their speeches and seminars (the nudists included) and attentively endured ear baths such as you wouldn't believe. And yet none has ever been quite like a convention of the stringers for *The National Enquirer.*

The *Enquirer* is a weekly newspaper that is probably known by sight to millions more than know it by name. No one who ever came face-to-face with *The Enquirer* on a newsstand in its wildest days is likely to have forgotten the sight: a tabloid with great inky shocks of type all over the front page saying something on the order of *Gouges Out Wife's Eyes to Make Her Ugly, Dad Hurls Hot Grease in Daughter's Face, Wife Commits Suicide After 2 Years of Poisoning Fail to Kill Husband.* . . .

You may want to check recent issues of the *Enquirer* yourself to see in what ways Wolfe has exaggerated the titles of its characteristic stories.

Understatement works well with irony and, in addition, has the advantage of making the writer appear objective or detached from the subject and therefore a more credible witness. Overstatement is so common a habit that its power often is diminished by sheer familiarity. Recall how prone we are to use exaggerated language as part of our everyday speech (see page 67). In skilled hands, however, overstatement can often evoke a powerful emotional response.

(Exercises: pages 177-181)

SENTIMENTALITY

As our illustrations have shown, all the preceding devices—irony, understatement, and overstatement—are frequently used for humorous effect. Now we turn to the subject of sentimentality. Although it ordinarily does not involve humor, sentimentality can also be funny—though unintentionally so.

Many situations in life are highly emotional: innocent childhood viewed by an adult, young love, betrayal, married happiness, unfulfilled ambition, the conflict between ideals and circumstances, pathetic accidents, poverty, old age, death. Such situations form the basic materials of literature. Indeed, they include most of the important things in life, things that are particularly hard to write about. In attempting to convey such emotions, many fall back on sentimentality or — even worse — mawkishness.

Sentimentality can be defined as shallow and exaggerated emotion. It urges us as readers to feel some emotion without providing sufficient justification for it. Furthermore, sentimentality usually depends heavily on clichés, images and phrases which are emotionally dehydrated, having been used so often that they have lost their power to affect us. And so the effect of sentimentality, to critical readers, is the opposite of what is intended.

We can illustrate the nature of sentimentality by quoting two accounts dealing with the same material but differing radically in point of view. In the early 1940s, a social worker wrote a case report from which the following excerpts come (all proper names have been changed). The tone, whatever else it may be, is not sentimental:

> The unfinished frame summer-kitchen addition to the dilapidated farmhouse Mrs. Denby occupies on the outskirts of Birchdale is a mute reminder of the ambition Mr. Denby had entertained to remodel the property and make it more habitable: an ambition interrupted last autumn by his fatal three-month illness. He left his family in sorry straits. There are five children, the youngest only fourteen months old. They must live on their Mothers' Assistance Fund grant of $155 a month. Mrs. Denby's house is kept clean, but, with the exception of a shining new electric refrigerator in one corner of the kitchen, it is poorly furnished.
>
> One of Mrs. Denby's elder sons was badly burnt in an accident some years ago and missed a year and a half of school. His sister, Elizabeth, is now living with Mr. Denby's relatives nearby, an arrangement which Mrs. Denby is willing to tolerate at least temporarily, although she has no truck with her numerous "in-laws."
>
> Mr. Denby, the oldest of fifteen children, left school to go to work. He held various jobs, but none for long. He was a notoriously poor provider, Mrs. Denby says, but despite this shortcoming her life with him was serene.
>
> Their son George is said by his teachers to be retarded in his school work. He has not had an intelligence test, but his native ability seems possibly lower than average. He will have some difficulty in keeping up with his age group.

Soon after the social worker's visit, the Denby house burned down. One of the city newspapers ran the following story:

Widow Sobs as Flames Destroy All

A 38-year-old widow, mother of five children, poked aimlessly through the fire-blackened ruins of her little home at Center Road and Delaney Street yesterday and wept bitter tears of utter hopelessness.

"What are we to do?" Mrs. Hannah S. Denby sobbed. "The fire took everything except the clothes on our backs. It even burned my pictures of my husband . . . and he died only six months ago."

And for Mrs. Denby, the loss of that picture seemed even harder to bear than the destruction of all but a few pieces of their furniture in the blaze which broke out Sunday afternoon shortly after the family had returned from church.

For her tow-headed five-year-old daughter, Beth, the fire had meant another heart-rending loss, for her only doll and her doll coach were consumed by the flames.

And for 17-year-old Frank, now the man of the family, for 11-year-old James and seven-year-old George, the fire meant the end of the happiness they had just started to recapture in family life since the death of their father.

Only 16-month-old Robert was unaware of the feeling of family tragedy. He cooed gaily in his mother's arms.

For the time being the widow and her children have found a home with her sister. "But she is very ill," Mrs. Denby said, "and it is hardly fair for us to stay there. I wish I knew what we could do, where we could turn. Perhaps the good Lord will find a way. . . ."

Compare the two accounts, and you will have a good notion of the elements of sentimentality: details which maintain a certain impression, whether wholly or partly false; clichéd symbols (the little girl and the burned doll); and trite language ("bitter tears of utter hopelessness"). Do you think the writer of the newspaper account was sincerely moved by the Denbys' plight?

What is sentimental to one person may not be sentimental to another. Readers who respond to any subject or allusion that has something to do with babies or the first stirrings of true love, for example, will not discriminate between the sentimental and the genuinely emotional. To such readers, the subject counts much more than the treatment or the motives behind that treatment. But more mature readers will automatically reject appeals which apply a pressure pump to their tear ducts.

Of course, some ages are more inclined to be sentimental than others. From the late eighteenth century to the late nineteenth, outpourings of sentimentality were perfectly compatible with public taste. Many records tell of grown, dignified people—famous writers, hard-boiled politicians, grave judges—unashamedly crying over highly emotional passages in fiction. The long scene of little Nell's death, in Dickens's *The Old Curiosity Shop*, was as widely admired in the nineteenth century as it is ridiculed now. Oscar Wilde seemed close to the truth when he remarked, "One must have a heart of stone to read the death of little Nell without laughing." Equally praised at that time, and equally ridiculed now, is the description of little Paul Dombey's death in Dickens's *Dombey and Son*. Notice, among other elements of sentimentality, the use of our old friend the river-and-sea symbol. Here, the symbol becomes a cliché:

> "Now lay me down," he said, "and, Floy, come close to me, and let me see you!"
>
> Sister and brother wound their arms around each other, and the golden light came streaming in, and fell upon them, locked together.
>
> "How fast the river runs, between its green banks and the rushes, Floy! But it's so very near the sea. I hear the waves! They always said so!"
>
> Presently he told her that the motion of the boat upon the stream was lulling him to rest. How green the banks were now, how bright the flowers growing on them, and how tall the rushes! Now the boat was out at sea, but gliding smoothly on. And now there was a shore before him. Who stood on the bank!—
>
> He put his hands together, as he had been used to do at his prayers. He did not remove his arms to do it; but they saw him fold them so, behind her neck.
>
> "Mama is like you, Floy. I know her by the face! But tell them that the print upon the stairs at school is not divine enough. The light about the head is shining on me as I go!"
>
> The golden ripple on the wall came back again, and nothing else stirred in the room. The old, old fashion! The fashion that came in with our first garments, and will last unchanged until our race has run its course, and the wide firmament is rolled up like a scroll. The old, old fashion—Death!
>
> Oh thank God, all who see it, for that older fashion yet, of Immortality! And look upon us, angels of young children, with regards not quite estranged, when the swift river bears us to the ocean!

We do not wish to depreciate all expressions of emotion. In our day, people tend to cultivate what they think of as a tough-minded attitude, which implies that all emotion or sentiment is embarrassing. Our distrust of sentiment is doubtless as excessive as the Victorians' love for wallowing in sentimentality. But if we did not experience and acknowledge emotion, we would not be human. Without emotion, life would be unspeakably empty, and the arts, including literature, could not exist. The point is simply that sentiment is very different from sentimentality. In reading, as in living, we must distinguish between the two. Writing which expresses sentiment in clichéd and exaggerated terms, which deliberately and coarsely exploits our emotions, is far inferior to writing which expresses that same sentiment with directness and restraint.

(Exercises: pages 177-181)

RESTRAINT

Restraint does not necessarily mean the absence of emotion. Rather, it implies the careful matching of feeling to subject, manner to matter, style to substance. Indeed, the restrained style at its best shows us a writer whose intellect and emotions are well balanced. The following paragraph is the introduction to the astronomer Carl Sagan's short essay on Albert Einstein. To Sagan, Einstein was a great hero whose life and work had influenced him deeply. If Sagan had succumbed to sentimentality, imagine how this passage might have read.

> Albert Einstein was born in Ulm, Germany, in 1879, just a century ago. He is one of the small group of people in any epoch who remake the world through a special gift, a talent for perceiving old things in new ways, for posing deep challenges to conventional wisdom. For many decades he was . . . an honored figure, the only scientist the average person could readily name. In part because of his scientific accomplishments, at least dimly grasped by the public; in part because of his courageous positions on social issues; and in part because of his benign personality, Einstein was admired and revered throughout the world. For scientifically inclined children of immigrant parents, or those growing up in the Depression, like me, the reverence accorded Einstein demonstrated that there were such people as scientists, that a scientific career might not be totally beyond hope. One major function he involuntarily served was as a scientific role model. Without Einstein, many of the young people who became scientists after 1920 might never have heard of the existence of the scientific enterprise. The logic behind Einstein's Special Theory of Relativity could have been developed a century earlier, but, although there were some premonitory insights by others, relativity had to wait for Einstein. Yet fundamentally the physics of special relativity is very simple, and many of the essential results can be derived from high school algebra and pondering a boat paddling upstream and downstream. Einstein's life was rich in genius and irony, a passion for the issues of his time, insights into education, the connection between science and politics, and was a demonstration that individuals can, after all, change the world.

Sagan manages in this paragraph to evoke his feelings of deep respect for Einstein without using gushy, sentimental effects. But Sagan is, after all, essentially writing a biographical essay about someone else. We might expect a writer describing a much more personal experience, such as the breakup of a marriage, to have more difficulty controlling emotional language. But note how restrained the tone is in the following passage:

> The articles in the women's magazines did nothing to help explain the deterioration of my marriage. We had no infidelity; my husband was

a good provider and I was a good cook. He encouraged me to resume my dance classes and I listened to him practice the saxophone without interruption. He came directly home from work each afternoon and in the evening after my son was asleep I found as much enjoyment in our marital bed as he.

The form was there, but the spirit had disappeared.

A bizarre sensation pervades a relationship of pretense. No truth seems true. A simple morning's greeting and response appear loaded with innuendo and fraught with implications.

"How are you?" Does he/she really care?

"Fine." I'm not really. I'm miserable, but I'll never tell you.

Each nicety becomes more sterile and each withdrawal more permanent.

Bacon and coffee odors mingled with the aseptic aroma of Lifebuoy soap. Wisps of escaping gas, which were as real a part of a fifty-year-old San Francisco house as the fourteen-foot high ceilings and the cantankerous plumbing, solidified my reality. Those were natural morning mists. The sense that order was departing my life was refuted by the daily routine. My family would awaken. I would shower and head for the kitchen to begin making breakfast. Tosh would shower while Clyde dressed, collected his crayons and lunch pail for school. We would all sit at breakfast together. I would force unwanted pleasantries into my face. (My mother had taught me: "If you have only one smile in you, give it to the people you love. Don't be surly at home, then go out in the street and start grinning 'Good morning' at total strangers.")

Tosh was usually quiet and amiable. Clyde gabbled about his dreams, which had to do with Roy Rogers as Jesus and Br'er Rabbit as God. We would finish breakfast in a glow of family life and they would leave me with kisses, off to their separate excitements.

One new morning Tosh screamed from the bathroom, "Where in the hell are the goddamn dry towels?" The outburst caught me as unexpectedly as an uppercut. . . .

I went to the bathroom and handed him the thickest towel we owned.

As this passage demonstrates, restraint can create emotional effects which no amount of tearful sentimentality could possibly match.

We may sum up many of the points made in this chapter by reading and analyzing a poem. Almost any good lyric poem, such as this one by A. E. Housman, can test critical reading skills:

> On moonlit heath and lonesome bank
> The sheep beside me graze;
> And yon the gallows used to clank
> Fast by the four cross ways.

A careless shepherd once would keep   5
   The flocks by moonlight there,
And high amongst the glimmering sheep
   The dead man stood on air.

They hang us now in Shrewsbury jail;
   The whistles blow forlorn,   10
And trains all night groan on the rail
   To men that die at morn.

There sleeps in Shrewsbury jail to-night,
   Or wakes, as may betide,
A better lad, if things went right,   15
   Than most that sleep outside.

And naked to the hangman's noose
   The morning clocks will ring
A neck God made for other use
   Than strangling in a string.   20

And sharp the link of life will snap,
   And dead on air will stand
Heels that held up as straight a chap
   As treads upon the land.

So here I'll watch the night and wait   25
   To see the morning shine,
When he will hear the stroke of eight
   And not the stroke of nine;

And wish my friend as sound a sleep
   As lads' I did not know,   30
That shepherded the moonlit sheep
   A hundred years ago.

To begin with, we must take full advantage of any hints the poet offers outside the poem itself. In this case, Housman added a note to the poem, saying, "Hanging in chains was called keeping sheep by moonlight." This brief sentence really sums up the irony, or bitter contrast, underlying the whole poem. Watching sheep by moonlight (a most peaceful and harmless job in a most tranquil setting) is contrasted with the gruesome practice of hanging convicted criminals *in chains* (an especially severe punishment). The interplay of these two completely different associations gives the poem its dominant tone.

    The first two stanzas bring out the basic contrast of the poem. Consider the implications of *moonlit heath, sheep,* and *graze* compared to *gallows* and *clank* (what is the effect of the sound of that word?). Also compare *careless* (carefree), *shepherd, flocks, moonlight,* and *glimmering sheep* with *the dead man stood on air.* The language is simple, but the clashing associations of those two groups of words give us a key to the intense emotions behind them. What image does *the dead man stood on air* suggest? What effect does it have on the reader?

With mention of Shrewsbury jail, the whistles blowing, and the trains groaning all night, a new note enters. This time, the contrast is between the stillness of the old country setting at the crossroads and the new conditions under which criminals are executed. Does the speaker approve or disapprove of the new system? How can you tell?

The fourth stanza makes the precise situation clear. The speaker, the sheepherder, is thinking of a particular person awaiting execution in Shrewsbury jail. What is the attitude implied in the use of *us* in line 9, of *lad* in line 15, of *chap* in line 23, and of *lads'* in line 30? How do the lines "A better lad, if things went right,/Than most that sleep outside" clarify that attitude?

The fifth stanza contains a pun (*ring*—the bells of the clocks will "ring" and the noose will "ring" the man's neck; perhaps also, the criminal's neck will be *wrung*). Is a pun usually found in a poem about someone about to be hanged? Is it a humorous pun? The word *string* in the last line of the stanza is important not only to the rhyme scheme. What is the difference in implication between *rope* and *string*? How does the effect of *string* harmonize with the tone of the whole?

The sixth stanza recalls the earlier image of the criminal "standing on air." The earlier reference was to the gallows at the crossroads; here it is to the modern gallows in the jailyard. But the effect of hanging is the same in both cases.

Suddenly, at the beginning of the seventh stanza, we shift back to the original setting—the moonlit countryside, with the sheep peacefully grazing beside the speaker. He now presents the idea of death as the difference between hearing the stroke of eight o'clock and not hearing the stroke of nine. Of all the ways Housman might have evoked the fact of death, why do you think he chose that one?

Finally, the speaker alludes to the men who were hanged long years ago and thus "kept sheep by moonlight." And we realize with a shock that he too is "keeping sheep by moonlight." In other words, the ultimate effect of the poem centers in the double meaning of that phrase. If we can apply the phrase with equal accuracy to both the speaker and the condemned man, as the speaker suggests, what is the speaker implying?

One other note: both the rhythm and the colloquial diction of this poem are incongruous to the subject. Instead of having a measured, slow beat, this poem fairly skips along. The short line is aided by the simple rhyme scheme (a-b-a-b). The stanza, in fact, sounds almost like a children's kindergarten song.

The poem can seem, therefore, a more or less flippant treatment of a serious subject. Some sort of humor does accompany the image of the dead man standing on air, the double pun on *ring*, the familiar *lad* and *chap*, and the offhand way death is pictured in the seventh stanza. But careful readers will realize that the humor is of a peculiar and significant kind. It is humor without the faintest suggestion of a smile. On the contrary, it is grim and bitter. And the lightness suggested by the colloquial diction and the musical rhythm, by deviating from what we would expect, adds to its power.

The effect of Housman's poem lies in the incongruity between what is said and what is implied for attentive readers to discover. The flippancy, the offhand manner, the sing-song quality, point not to any callousness on the part of the speaker. Rather, they cover up very deep and bitter feelings. The truth about the speaker's emotions lies almost completely in the implications and connotations, rather than the external meaning, of what he says. The half-humorous tone makes the actual subject of the poem — the execution — all the more terrible.

Creating a tone suitable to a given occasion is one of the unfailing marks of a good writer. In the following passage, the novelist Thomas Wolfe writes of the ordinary circumstance of three men riding a train from North Carolina to New York. Read the passage carefully, identify the tone, and consider how suitable it is to the particular occasion.

So here they are now, three atoms on the huge breast of the indifferent earth, three youths out of a little town walled far away within the great rim of the silent mountains, already a distant, lonely dot upon the immense and sleeping visage of the continent. Here they are—three youths bound for the first time towards their image of the distant and enchanted city, sure that even though so many of their comrades had found there only dust and bitterness, the shining victory will be theirs. Here they are hurled onward in the great projectile of the train across the lonely visage of the everlasting earth. Here they are—three nameless grains of life among the manswarm ciphers of the earth, three faces of the million faces, three drops in the unceasing flood—and each of them a flame, a light, a glory, sure that his destiny is written in the blazing stars, his life shone over by the fortunate watches of the moon, his fame nourished and sustained by the huge earth, whose single darling charge he is, on whose immortal stillness he is flung onward in the night, his glorious fate set in the very brain and forehead of the fabulous, the unceasing city, of whose million-footed life he will tomorrow be a part.

Therefore they stand upon the rocking platform of the train, wild and dark and jubilant from the fierce liquor they have drunk, but more wild and dark and jubilant from the fury swelling in their hearts, the mad fury pounding in their veins, the savage, exultant and unutterable fury working like a madness in the adyts [secret places] of their soul. And the great wheels smash and pound beneath their feet, the great wheels pound and smash and give rhyme to madness, a tongue to hunger and desire, a certitude to all the savage, drunken, and exultant fury that keeps mounting, rising, swelling in them all the time!

Hundreds of such passages occur in Wolfe's novels, which are often criticized as overly extravagant in style. As one of his critics wrote,

all the experiences in *Of Time and the River* [where the quoted passage occurs] were on the same level and had the same value. When

Mr. Gant died (of enough cancer to have exterminated an army corps), the reader accepted the accompanying frenzy as proper to the death of a man's father—which is one of the most important events in anyone's life. But when the same frenzy accompanied nearly every- thing else in the book—a ride on a railroad train, a literary tea-fight, a midnight lunch in the kitchen, a quarrel between friends, a walk at night, the rejection of a play, an automobile trip, a seduction that mis- fired, the discovery of Eugene's true love—one could only decide that something was terribly wrong. If the death of a father comes out even with a ham-on-rye, then the art of fiction is cockeyed.

—Not merely the art of fiction, we may add, but the whole art of writing, in whatever form. Nothing exhausts a writer's credit with readers more quickly than striking false notes—failing, that is, to match tone to content and situation.

Do you think the critic is justified in his criticism of Wolfe? Can you use the passage quoted from Wolfe's novel to argue that the tone is appropriate? Or would you need to read a longer passage, or perhaps the entire novel, in order to decide?

Discrimination of tone marks both effective writers and skilled readers. Such readers are always alert to special effects and what they reveal about a writer's purpose. They may or may not be legitimate, and it is the reader's business to decide which they are. On the one hand, a writer who deviates as Housman does from the usual patterns of discourse, using irony, understatement, or overstate- ment, may be signaling readers to "read between the lines" for the indirect but true message. But such deviations may signal readers that they are in danger of being put upon—of being unfairly manipulated by language. Readers must, of course, make adequate allowance for intentional special effects. It would be unjust, for example, to dismiss Wolfe as a mere impostor suffering from verbal diarrhea. Wolfe had a feverish vision of the world, a Faustian lust for experience, a huge impotent rage against human limitations, which he employed his style to convey. His failure to distinguish between the momentous and the trivial, of which his critics sometimes complained, was true of Wolfe's own temperament. Whether or not Wolfe's prose persuades us to sympathize with his exaggerated manner, we do not question his sincerity. In any event, as critical readers we must decide whether we wish to respond to the tone a writer has evoked or to react against it; and we must be able to offer good reasons for our decision. The right to accept or reject is one reward earned by the reader who remains conscious of the action and influence of tone.

(Exercises: pages 177–181)

EXERCISES ▬▬▬▬▬▬▬

METAPHORICAL LANGUAGE

3.1 **(a)** From any source—today's newspaper, a current magazine, an over-heard conversation, a book—make a list of about a dozen metaphors. Take each one apart to see what makes it tick. (Note the metaphor right there.) What does the metaphor literally mean? What element of similarity makes it useful in the context in which you found it? Try making the same state-ment without using any metaphor: is your version any less vivid? Finally, how many of the metaphors in your list would you regard as hackneyed or clichéd? Do they really serve their purpose as analogies, or are they worn so smooth that their power to suggest comparison is largely lost?

(b) Choose one of the metaphors that you analyzed and write a brief description of the process you went through in discovering and tracing its underlying complexity, meaning, and usefulness (or lack of usefulness).

3.2 Here are a number of definitions of slang by past and present writers. How do the connotations of the metaphor used by each writer define the writer's own attitude toward slang?

1. Slang is language that takes off its coat, spits on its hands, and gets to work.
2. Slang is a dressing-room in which language, having an evil deed to prepare, puts on a disguise.
3. Slang is the speech of him who robs the literary garbage carts on their way to the dumps.
4. Slang is only the rude luxuriance of the uncared-for soil, knowing not the hand of the gardener.
5. The language of the street is always strong. . . . Cut these words and they would bleed; they are vascular and alive; they walk and run.
6. Slang is the wholesome fermentation or eructation of those pro-cesses eternally active in language, by which the froth and specks are thrown up, mostly to pass away, though occasionally to settle and permanently crystallize.
7. Slang: words with their shoes off.

3.3 Examine each of the following quotations with these questions in mind: (1) Is the metaphor which illuminates the idea vivid and fresh? (2) Is it appropriate to the subject discussed? (3) Does it offer clues to the writer's attitude or to the attitude the writer wishes readers to have? If so, what are those clues?

1. Her smile was silent as the smile on corpses three hours old.
2. [A visitor's impression of New York's East Side] The architecture seemed to sweat humanity at every window and door.
3. What we want
   is never simple.
   We move among the things
   we thought we wanted:
   a face, a room, an open book
   and these things bear our names—
   now they want us.
   But what we want appears
   in dreams, wearing disguises.
   We fall past,
   holding out our arms
   and in the morning
   our arms ache.
   We don't remember the dream,
   but the dream remembers us.
   It is there all day
   as an animal is there
   under the table,
   as the stars are there
   even in the full sun.
4. Inside this pencil
   Crouch words that have never been written
   Never been spoken
   Never been taught

   They're hiding

   They're awake in there
   Dark in the dark
   Hearing us
   But they won't come out
   Not for love, not for time, not for fire
   Even when the dark has worn away
   They'll still be there
   Hiding in the air
   Multitudes in days to come may walk through them
   Breathe them
   Be none the wiser

   What script can it be
   That they won't unroll
   In what language
   Would I recognize it

Would I be able to follow it
To make out the real names
Of everything

Maybe there aren't
Many
It could be that there is only one word
And it's all we need
It's here in this pencil
Every pencil in the world is like this

5. Broad on both bows, at the distance of some two or three miles,
and forming a great semicircle, embracing one-half of the level
horizon, a continuous chain of whale-jets were up-playing and
sparkling in the noon-day air. Unlike the straight perpendicular
twin jets of the Right Whale, which, dividing at top, fall over in
two branches, like the cleft drooping boughs of a willow, the single forward-slanting spout of the Sperm Whale presents a thick
curled bush of white mist, continually rising and falling away to
leeward.

   Seen from the *Pequod*'s deck, then, as she would rise on a
high hill of the sea, this host of vapory spouts, individually curl-
ing up into the air, and beheld through a blending atmosphere
of bluish haze, showed like the thousand cheerful chimneys of
some dense metropolis, descried on a balmy autumnal morning,
by some horseman on a height.

   As marching armies approaching an unfriendly defile in the
mountains, accelerate their march, all eagerness to place that
perilous passage in their rear, and once more expand in comparative security upon the plain; even so did this vast fleet of
whales now seem hurrying forward through the straits; gradually
contracting the wings of their semicircle, and swimming on, in
one solid, but still crescentic centre.

6. An Aged Man is but a paltry thing,
   A tattered coat upon a stick, unless
   Soul clap its hands and sing and louder sing
   For every tatter in its mortal dress.

7. The source of this book [*An Imagined World: A Story of Scientific Discovery*] is not to be found in a single spring but in many
rivers of experience. . . . Even by the middle of 1978 I could
sense that the river of thought and work on iron and the immune
system and cancer was about to fan into a delta. From that point
there were bound to be several streams of simultaneous activity—some were already flowing strongly—and they would continue to widen, converge, separate, and deepen.

8. That time of year thou mayst in me behold
   When yellow leaves, or none, or few, do hang
   Upon those boughs which shake against the cold,
   Bare ruined choirs, where late the sweet birds sang.
   In me thou seest the twilight of such day
   As after sunset fadeth in the west,
   Which by and by black night doth take away,
   Death's second self, that seals up all the rest.
   In me, thou seest the glowing of such fire
   That on the ashes of his youth doth lie,
   As the deathbed whereon it must expire,
   Consumed with that which it was nourished by.
      This thou perceivest, which makes thy love more strong,
      To love that well which thou must leave ere long.

9. The President's economic proposals are like rearranging the deck chairs on the *Titanic*.

10. And so it goes, alas, alas, in all his other volumes—a cent's worth of information wrapped in a bale of polysyllables. In "The Higher Learning in America" the thing perhaps reached its damndest and worst. It is as if the practise of that incredibly obscure and malodorous style were a relentless disease, a sort of progressive intellectual diabetes, a leprosy of the horse sense. Words were flung up on words until all recollection that there must be a meaning in them, a ground and excuse for them, was lost. One wanders in a labyrinth of nouns, adjectives, verbs, pronouns, adverbs, prepositions, conjunctions and participles, most of them swollen and nearly all of them unable to walk. It is impossible to imagine worse English, within the limits of intelligible grammar. It is clumsy, affected, opaque, bombastic, windy, empty. It is without grace or distinction and it is often without the most elementary order. The learned professor gets himself enmeshed in his gnarled sentences like a bull trapped by barbed wire, and his efforts to extricate himself are quite as furious and quite as spectacular. He heaves, he leaps, he writhes; at times he seems to be at the point of yelling for the police. It is a picture to bemuse the vulgar and to give the judicious grief.

11. When you came, you were like red wine and honey,
    And the taste of you burnt my mouth with its sweetness.
    Now you are like morning bread,
    Smooth and pleasant.
    I hardly taste you at all for I know your savour,
    But I am completely nourished.

12. Now the course comes to a close. The work with this group has been a particularly pleasant association between the fountain of my voice and a garden of ears—some open, others closed, many

very receptive, a few merely ornamental, but all of them human and divine.

3.4 In the light of what we have said about the consistency of metaphor, comment on the effect of each of the following passages. In addition, judge the accuracy of the analogies implied in the metaphors.

1. Every writer acts as a landlord to an unforgiving editor who squats in some upper story of his head and sends rejection slips to nearly all the writer's phrases. I have sent my editor on a long vacation. I hope he's happy. In the meantime, I'm free to write reams of unpublishable sentences.

2. The defendant, in presenting his alibi, chose the alley he was going to bowl on—and the jury wouldn't swallow it.

3. It surprised him to realize how fond he had been of his teeth. His tongue, a fat sleek seal, used to flop and slide so happily among the familiar rocks, checking the contours of a battered but still secure kingdom, plunging from cave to cove, climbing this jab, nuzzling that notch, finding a shred of sweet seaweed in the same old cleft; but now not a landmark remained, and all there existed was a great dark wound, a terra incognita of gums which dread and disgust forbade one to investigate. And when the plates were thrust in, it was like a poor fossil skull being fitted with the grinning jaws of a perfect stranger.

4. The narrative itself is heavy as lead; unrelieved by any highlighting, it just flows on and on.

5. The cosmos is all that is or ever was or ever will be. . . . The surface of the Earth is the shore of the cosmic ocean. From it we have learned most of what we know. Recently, we have waded a little out to sea, enough to dampen our toes or, at most, wet our ankles. The water seems inviting. The ocean calls. Some part of our being knows this is from where we came. We long to return. These aspirations are not, I think, irreverent, although they may trouble whatever gods may be.

6. By this he knew she wept with waking eyes:
    That, at his hand's light quiver by her head,
    The strange low sobs that shook their common bed
    Were called into her with a sharp surprise,
    And strangled mute, like little gaping snakes,
    Dreadfully venomous to him. She lay
    Stone-still, and the long darkness flowed away
    With muffled pulses. Then, as midnight makes
    Her giant heart of Memory and Tears
    Drink the pale drug of silence, and so beat

Sleep's heavy measure, they from head to feet
Were moveless, looking through their dead black years,
By vain regret scrawled over the blank wall.
Like sculptured effigies they might be seen
Upon their marriage-tomb, the sword between;
Each wishing for the sword that severs all.

7. Miss Willauer's pleasant soprano had the power to act as a fulcrum for the ensemble as she carried the top part. And at the other end, Mr. Pease held his own with distinction. But Mr. DaCosta, whom I know to be a fine artist, had an off day and the quintette did not jell, even though Miss Hupp and Messrs. Nagy and McCurdy pulled on their oars. But then this is often the case with opera in concert form. With the whole personnel squeezed onto the platform the soloists have little elbow room for their voices.

8. What happens to a dream deferred?

Does it dry up
Like a raisin in the sun?
Or fester like a sore—
And then run?
Does it stink like rotten meat?
Or crust and sugar over—
Like a syrupy sweet?

Maybe it just sags
Like a heavy load.

Or does it explode?

9. A dread disease overtakes many American novelists in middle age, and it usually attacks the best ones. It is believed that it was originally introduced from Mississippi, but its origins are obscure. The symptoms include logorrhoea, distension of the material, with elephantiasis of the form, followed by delusions of philosophic grandeur. The action of the syntax is impaired, and pornography is sometimes present. The prognosis is poor, successive books showing the same symptoms in intensified form, occasionally accompanied by the Nobel Prize. The reader is often infected, the disease in its primary stages resembling *encephalitis lethargica*, with yawns, inability to retain interest, and general apathy.

10. The study of time's relation to living systems, or chronobiology, has become a regular boom town on the frontiers of science during the past decade or so, and a great deal of information has been unearthed about the mysterious rhythms that govern us.

3.5 Personification is one form of metaphorical language: it attributes human characteristics to inanimate objects or to abstractions. What, if anything, do the following passages gain by giving their respective subjects human traits?

1. [Bach's Brandenburg Concerto Number 2] Full band leads off with theme one which sturdily pronounces the key of F major. Full band, that is, with the exception of the trumpet, whose assertive nature craves a variant of its own. Without any preparation the violin slips in the second theme but the intruder is quickly drawn back into the ranks which insist on theme one; but before they can finish it, up jumps the oboe with theme two. Once more the majority is about to win when the flute takes a turn with theme two. Full band makes a further trial and the trumpet, determined that theme two shall have its due importance, engages with the flute for an accompaniment.

2. There are masked words droning and skulking about us . . . just now,—(there never were so many, owing to the spread of a shallow, blotching, blundering, infectious "information," or rather deformation, everywhere, and to the teaching of catechisms and phrases at schools instead of human meanings)—there are masked words abroad, I say, which nobody understands, but which everybody uses, and most people will also fight for, live for, or even die for, fancying they mean this or that, or the other, of things dear to them: for such words wear chameleon cloaks— "ground lion" cloaks, of the colour of the ground of any man's fancy: on that ground they lie in wait, and rend him with a spring from it. There never were creatures of prey so mischievous, never diplomatists so cunning, never poisoners so deadly, as these masked words; they are the unjust stewards of all men's ideas: whatever fancy or favourite instinct a man most cherishes, he gives to his favourite masked word to take care of for him; the word at last comes to have an infinite power over him—you cannot get at him but by its ministry.

3. Words are queer things, possessed of queer properties, of which perhaps the queerest of all is their faculty of taking on a life of their own, independent of their creator, like the monster of Frankenstein. Man made words; but words, once made, live by their own force, assume new meanings and strange attributes, and may end by enslaving or even destroying their maker. Now there is a peculiarly subtle danger in words of a metaphorical kind. There is a curious fascination about them; they seem to come to one packed with meaning, and yet to reveal that meaning at a glance. And some metaphors are, indeed, glorious winged creatures, in whose keeping the spirit of man can pass in a flash beyond "the flaming

bounds of space and time"; they are the very substance of the noblest of man's achievements—Poetry. But there is another species of metaphor, very different from the metaphor of the poet— a serpentine, insidious thing, or—for it seems natural to use a metaphor to describe a metaphor just as one sets a thief to catch a thief—a trap . . .: under the guise of brevity and vigor it, in fact, confuses, in order to insinuate suggestions which would have been rejected in any other shape.

3.6 Find an example of political discourse (an elected official's speech or press release, for example) and examine it for metaphors. Decide how those metaphors help determine the reader's or listener's attitude toward the subject and toward the writer or speaker. Decide also whether or not the metaphors form a "trap" like the one described in passage 3 above, and give the reasons that led you to that decision. Use the information you have gathered as evidence for an essay on the "traps metaphors can set for us."

3.7 Decide how appropriate and effective the metaphors in the following quotations are:

1. No man is an island, entire of itself; every man is a piece of the continent, a part of the main. If a clod be washed away by the sea, Europe is the less, as well as if a manor of thy friend's or thine own were; any man's death diminishes me, because I am involved in mankind, and therefore never send to know for whom the bell tolls; it tolls for thee.

2. A word is not a crystal, transparent and unchanged; it is the skin of a living thought, and may vary greatly in color and content according to the circumstances and the time in which it is used.

3. What I like in a good author is not what he says, but what he whispers.

4. Adjectives are sirens; they betray all whom their music beguiles. Enslave them and you are the master of the poetic art.

5. No language after it has faded into diction, none that cannot suck up the feeding juices secreted for it in the rich mother-earth of common folk, can bring forth a sound and lusty book. True vigor and heartiness of phrase do not pass from page to page, but from man to man, where the brain is kindled and the lips supplied by downright living interests and by passion in its very throe. Language is the soil of thought, and our own especially is a rich leaf-mould, the slow deposit of ages. . . . There is death in the dictionary; and, where language is too strictly limited by convention, the ground for expression to grow in is limited also; and we get a potted literature, Chinese dwarfs instead of healthy trees.

6. The crowning event of the weekend, just hours before the town turns back into a pumpkin, is the awards banquet.
7. But what makes each of the expressions [clichés] in itself so sorry? Not merely the fact that it is a cold potato, a stereotype (any word in the dictionary enjoys the same status), but the further fact that the expression has a certain special character, even if tame and drab. It attempts to stand up and make a little joke, and the joke is out of place.
8. Why should I let the toad work
   Squat on my life?
   Can't I use my wit as a pitchfork
   And drive the brute off?

   Six days of the week it soils
   With its sickening poison—
   Just for paying a few bills!
   That's out of all proportion.

SYMBOLS

3.8 Here are several passages in which the idea of death is represented by one or another of the symbols we discussed in the text—sleep, grave, worms. By weighing the tone of the whole passage, including the connotations of other metaphors, decide what attitude each passage intends you to adopt toward death.

1. I dreamt I was all bones;
   The dead slept in my sleeve;
   Sweet Jesus tossed me back:
   I wore the sun with ease. . . .

   Can the bones breathe? This grave has an ear.
   It's still enough for the knock of a worm.
   I feel more than a fish.
   Ghost, come closer. . . .

   Wherefore, O birds and small fish, surround me.
   Lave me, ultimate waters.
   The dark showed me a face.
   My ghosts are all gay.
   The light becomes me.
2. A slumber did my spirit seal;
   I had no human fears:
   She seemed a thing that could not feel
   The touch of earthly years.

No motion has she now, no force:
  She neither hears nor sees;
Rolled round in earth's diurnal course,
  With rocks, and stones, and trees.

3. Is not short pain well borne, that brings lone ease,
   And lays the soul to sleep in quiet grave?
   Sleep after toil, port after stormy seas,
   Ease after war, death after life does greatly please.

4. I must go down to the seas again, to the vagrant gypsy life,
   To the gull's way and the whale's way where the wind's like a
     whetted knife;
   And all I ask is a merry yarn from a laughing fellow-rover,
   And quiet sleep and a sweet dream when the long trick's over.

5. The lips of time leech to the fountain head;
   Love drips and gathers, but the fallen blood
   Shall calm her sores.

   And I am dumb to tell a weather's wind
   How time has ticked a heaven round the stars.
   And I am dumb to tell the lover's tomb
   How at my sheet goes the same crooked worm.

6. From rest and sleep, which but thy pictures be
   Much pleasure, then from thee, much more must flow,
   And soonest our best men with thee do go,
   Rest of their bones and souls' delivery.
   Thou art slave to Fate, Chance, kings, and desperate men,
   And dost with poison, war, and sickness dwell,
   And poppy, or charms can make us sleep as well,
   And better than thy stroke; why swell'st thou then?
   One short sleep past, we wake eternally,
   And death shall be no more; death, thou shalt die.

7. Your worm is your only emperor for diet. We fat all creatures else
   to fat us, and we fat ourselves for maggots. Your fat king and your
   lean beggar is but variable service, two dishes, but to one table;
   that's the end. . . . A man may fish with the worm that hath eat of
   a king, and eat of the fish that hath fed of that worm . . . [and thus]
   a king may go a progress through the guts of a beggar.

8. ROMEO [*to Mercutio, who is badly wounded*]: Courage, man; the
   hurt cannot be much.
   MERCUTIO: No, 'tis not so deep as a well, nor so wide as a church-
   door, but 'tis enough, 'twill serve. Ask for me tomorrow, and
   you shall find me a grave man.

3.9 **(a)** What is the usual meaning of the following symbols? Since symbols
usually call forth a complex response, try to account for as many aspects of

your response as you can. Compare yours with those of other members of the class. Why do these responses sometimes appear contradictory or irreconcilable?

sunset, spring, fall, tide, wheat, mud, rushing water, snow, sword, eagle, lion, wolf, beaver, bread, circle, white, red, lily, blood, mirror, rose, garden

(b) Choose a symbol to which your response differs from that of others. Then write a short explanation of how the symbol came to have those special, personal associations for you.

(c) Animal fables operate on the principle of symbolism: they teach human virtues and vices by embodying those traits in animals with which they are commonly associated (whether rightly or wrongly). Tales of Reynard the Fox point up the use of cunning and deceit, for example. Make a list of animals, both real and mythical, which embody certain characteristics or ideals. (The fables of Aesop provide much material, and a dictionary of mythology will also help.) Then try your hand at writing a contemporary "Aesop's fable," using one of the originals as a model.

ALLUSIONS

3.10 (a) What are the meaning and effect of the mythological allusions in the following quotations? (You can look up the allusions in the *Oxford Classical Dictionary* or a similar reference work.)

1. So excellent a king; that was, to this,
    Hyperion to a satyr; so loving to my mother
    That he might not beteem the winds of heaven
    Visit her face too roughly . . .
        Frailty, thy name is woman!—
    A little month, or e'er those shoes were old
    With which she followed my poor father's body,
    Like Niobe, all tears—why she, even she—
    O God! a beast, that wants discourse of reason,
    Would have mourned longer—married with mine uncle,
    My father's brother, but no more like my father
    Than I to Hercules . . .
2. The world is too much with us; late and soon,
    Getting and spending, we lay waste our powers:
    Little we see in Nature that is ours;
    We have given our hearts away, a sordid boon!
    The Sea that bares her bosom to the moon;
    The winds that will be howling at all hours,

And are up-gathered now like sleeping flowers;
For this, for everything, we are out of tune;
It moves us not.—Great God! I'd rather be
A Pagan suckled in a creed outworn;
So might I, standing on this pleasant lea,
Have glimpses that would make me less forlorn;
Have sight of Proteus rising from the sea;
Or hear Old Triton blow his wreathèd horn.

(b) What is the connotative or symbolic meaning suggested by the following names from classical myth or ancient literature? Can you think of phrases or contexts in which they might appear today?

Venus, Narcissus, Atlas, Mars, Pan, Apollo, the Lotus Eaters, Cyclops, Mercury, Hydra, Gorgon, the Golden Fleece, Argonauts, Prometheus, Neptune, Endymion, Scylla and Charybdis, Eros, the Sirens

3.11 Explain the allusions in the following samples of modern conversation and writing. If necessary, consult the dictionaries of mythology previously mentioned, the *Oxford Companion to English* (or *American* or *Classical*) *Literature*, a good encyclopedia, or a dictionary of quotations.

1. If such plants could be bred, we might imagine them being seeded on the vast expanse of the Martian polar ice caps, taking root, spreading, blackening the ice caps, absorbing sunlight, heating the ice, and releasing the ancient Martian atmosphere from its long captivity. We might even imagine a kind of Martian Johnny Appleseed, robot or human, roaming the frozen polar wastes in an endeavor that benefits only the generations of humans to come.

2. Today's poets don't dwell in ivory towers or live on Parnassus; instead, most of them dwell in split levels and live on college and university payrolls.

3. After the wholesale raids over the weekend by city and state law enforcement agencies, local authorities expressed shock. "The goings-on they uncovered," said the district attorney, "make Sodom and Gomorrah pale in comparison."

4. A new broom sweeps clean, they say, and as vice-president of that outfit she'll have plenty of sweeping to do. It'll be like cleaning out the Augean stables.

5. Many historians regard the Norris-La Guardia Act of 1933 as the Magna Carta of labor.

6. She could be described as our local Lois Lane, always on the trail of a Super Man and a Super Story.

7. Like a real life, modern day Minerva, Jane Goodall has helped

us to understand and protect those animals we share the world with.

8. The hockey coach reminds me of Sisyphus. Nine times every season he rolls that miserable team up the hill, and nine times every season the team tumbles down and he gets flattened by the sports writers.

9. The columnist, after having been blinded by acid-throwing hoodlums, went on, Ahab-like, in quest of corruption in labor unions.

10. Eliot himself was described by one critic as being a Prufrock who would dare to eat a peach—if he could find a socially acceptable way to peel it.

11. Today's black writers are making Herculean efforts to create a literature that will reach and reflect common black folks.

12. After the flood, when the waters that covered the earth had receded, Raven walked upon the beach, disconsolate and alone, his mind a Wurlitzer of memories and old movies.

13. Midnight arrives, and we find ourselves on Granville Island, seeking the theatrical moment at the Arts Club Theatre, where The Rocky Horror Show is about to be presented Live on Stage.

   The show is a few minutes late starting, and the place is a zoo. Down near the front, a yahoo and his yahette, encouraged by their cohorts, take it in turns to bellow the name of a missing friend at full pitch. Across the theatre, another yahoo echoes the bellows. The brute noises chase each other round the theatre's fine acoustics like angry buffalo.

3.12 The following adjectives are sometimes used to describe people, situations, or events. What are they intended to mean when they are so applied?

   Faustian, Swiftian, Mephistophelean, Machiavellian, puckish, Falstaffian, Churchillian, Rabelaisian, Kafkaesque, Byronic, Panglossian, Orwellian, Hobbitlike, Einsteinian, Darwinian, Chaplinesque, Hitchcockian, Cleopatralike

3.13 Suppose you encounter each of the following words or phrases in a contemporary magazine article or book. What is the original source of the allusion? In what sort of modern context would it be found? What sort of event or person or situation might be described? What attitude (if any) is implied? (For example, an allusion to the lion and the lamb lying down together [but see Isaiah 11:6] might today be found in a discussion about reconciling two hostile groups.)

   the handwriting on the wall; kill the fatted calf; the New Frontier; Oedipus complex; Pandora's box; a Rhett Butler; a Trojan horse; a stoic attitude; a pound of flesh; Big Brother; Lilliputian; Camelot;

scorched earth policy; a Pearl Harbor; a Mona Lisa smile; a loaf of bread, a jug of wine; water, water everywhere, and not a drop to drink; a Holden Caulfield; a Florence Nightingale; a rolling stone gathers no moss; a Walter Mitty; Auschwitz

Look through current magazines or newspapers and find some examples of allusions used in context. Then try to explain the exact meaning the allusion carries. Is anything lost in your "translation"?

DEVIATIONS FROM "NORMAL" STYLE

3.14 How does the language of each of the following passages deviate from general norms of present-day diction? How does that difference affect your attitude toward what is said? How effective do you find the deviations?

1. The sun had already sunk behind the mountains, whose undulating forms were thrown into dark shadow against the crimson sky. The thin crescent of the new moon floated over the eastern hills, whose deep woods glowed with the rosy glories of twilight. Over the peak of a purple mountain glittered the solitary star of evening. As the sun dropped, universal silence seemed to pervade the whole face of nature. The voice of the birds was stilled; the breeze, which had refreshed them during the day, died away, as if its office were now completed; and none of the dark sounds and sights of hideous Night yet dared to triumph over the death of Day. Unseen were the circling wings of the fell bat; unheard the screech of the waking owl; silent the drowsy hum of the shade-born beetle! What heart has not acknowledged the influence of this hour, the sweet and soothing hour of twilight! the hour of love, the hour of adoration, the hour of rest! when we think of those we love, only to regret that we have not loved more dearly; when we remember our enemies only to forgive them!

2. The legend of Junior Johnson! In this legend, here is a country boy, Junior Johnson, who learns to drive by running whiskey for his father, Johnson, Senior, one of the biggest copper-still operators of all time, up in Ingle Hollow, near North Wilkesboro, in northwestern North Carolina, and grows up to be a famous stock car racing driver, rich, grossing $100,000 in 1963, for example, respected, solid, idolized in his hometown and throughout the rural South. ... It was Junior Johnson, specifically ... who was famous for the "bootleg turn" or "about-face," in which, if the Alcohol Tax agents had a roadblock up for you or were too close behind, you threw the car up into second gear, cocked the wheel, stepped on the accelerator and made the car's rear end skid

around in a complete 180-degree arc, a complete about-face, and tore on back up the road exactly the way you came from. God! The Alcohol Tax agents used to burn over Junior Johnson. . . . Finally, one night they had Junior trapped on the road up toward the bridge around Millersville, there's no way out of there, they had the barricades up and they could hear this souped-up car roaring around the bend, and here it comes—but suddenly they can hear a siren and see a red light flashing in the grille, so they think it's another agent, and boy, they run like ants and pull those barrels and boards and sawhorses out of the way, and then— Ggghhzzzzzzzzhhhhhhggggggzzzzzzzzeeeeeong!—gawdam! there he goes again, it was him, Junior Johnson! with a gawdam agent's sireen and a red light in his grille!

3. Day and night cannot dwell together. The Red Man has ever fled the approach of the White Man, as the morning mist flees before the morning sun. . . . Then we will dwell apart in peace. For the words of the Great White Chief seem to be the words of nature speaking to my people out of dense darkness.

It matters little where we pass the remnant of our days. They will not be many. A few more moons; a few more winters—and not one of the descendants of the mighty hosts that once moved over this broad land or lived in happy homes, protected by the Great Spirit, will remain to mourn over the graves of a people once more powerful and hopeful than yours. But why should I mourn at the untimely fate of my people? Tribe follows tribe. And nation follows nation, like the waves of the sea. It is the order of nature, and regret is useless. Your time of decay may be distant. But it will surely come, for even the White Man whose God walked and talked with him as friend with friend, cannot be exempt from the common destiny. We may be brothers after all. We will see.

IRONY

3.15 (a) How much irony is there in each of the following selections? How does what the writers say differ from what the ironic tone suggests?

1. To bear other people's afflictions, everyone has courage enough and to spare.

2. [From an article by an astronomer, addressed chiefly to scientists and entitled "The Principles of Poor Writing"] Write hurriedly, preferably when tired. Have no plans; write down items as they occur to you. The article will thus be spontaneous and poor. Hand in your manuscript the moment it is finished. Rereading a few days

later might lead to revision—which seldom, if ever, makes the writing worse. If you submit your manuscript to colleagues (a bad practice), pay no attention to their criticisms or comments. Later resist firmly any editorial suggestions. Be strong and infallible; don't let anyone break down your personality. The critic may be trying to help you or he may have an ulterior motive, but the chance of his causing improvement in your writing is so great that you must be on guard.

3. After the Senate got finished with its work on the gun-control bill, I received a telephone call from my friend Bromley Hurts, who told me he had a business proposition to discuss with me. I met him for lunch at a pistol range in Maryland.

"I think I've got a fantastic idea," he said. "I want to start a new business called Hurts Rent-a-Gun."

"What on earth for?" I asked.

"There are a lot of people in this country who only use a handgun once or twice a year, and they don't want to go to all the expense of buying one. So we'll rent them a gun for a day or two. . . ."

"You could set up rent-a-gun counters at gas stations," I said excitedly.

"And we could have stores in town where someone could rent a gun to settle a bet," Hurts said.

"A lot of people would want to rent a gun for a domestic quarrel," I said. . . .

"Don't forget about kids who want to play Russian roulette. They could pool their allowances and rent a gun for a couple of hours," I said.

"Our market surveys indicate," Hurts said, "that there are also a lot of kids who claim their parents don't listen to them. If they could rent a gun, they feel they could arrive at an understanding with their folks in no time. . . ."

4. Love, *n.* A temporary insanity curable by marriage or by removal of the patient from the influences under which he incurred the disorder. This disease, like *caries* and many other ailments, is prevalent only among civilized races living under artificial conditions; barbarous nations breathing pure air and eating simple food enjoy immunity from its ravages. It is sometimes fatal, but more frequently to the physician than to the patient.

5. If you can't prove what you want to prove, demonstrate something else and pretend that they are the same thing. In the daze that follows the collision of statistics with the human mind, hardly anybody will notice the difference. The semiattached figure is a device guaranteed to stand you in good stead. It always has.

You can't prove that your nostrum [remedy] cures colds, but you can publish (in large type) a sworn laboratory report that half an ounce of the stuff killed 31,108 germs in a test tube in eleven seconds. While you are about it, make sure that the laboratory is reputable or has an impressive name. Reproduce the report in full. Photograph a doctor-type model in white clothes and put his picture alongside.

6. It is in the function of directing the participants through this maze of gadgetry that the funeral director has assigned to himself the relatively new role of "grief therapist." He has relieved the family of every detail, he has revamped the corpse to look like a living doll, he has arranged for it to nap for a few days in a slumber room, he has put on a well-oiled performance in which the concept of *death* has played no part whatsoever. . . . He has done everything in his power to make the funeral a real pleasure for everybody concerned. He and his team have given their all to score an upset victory over death.

7. **The Unknown Citizen**

(To JS/07/M/378 This Marble Monument Is Erected by the State)
He was found by the Bureau of Statistics to be
One against whom there was no official complaint,
And all the reports on his conduct agree
That, in the modern sense of an old-fashioned word, he was a
  saint,
For in everything he did he served the Greater Community.
Except for the War till the day he retired
He worked in a factory and never got fired,
But satisfied his employers, Fudge Motors Inc.
Yet he wasn't a scab or odd in his views,
For his Union reports that he paid his dues,
(Our report on his Union shows it was sound)
And our Social Psychology workers found
That he was popular with his mates and liked a drink.
The Press are convinced that he bought a paper every day
And that his reactions to advertisements were normal in every
  way.
Policies taken out in his name prove that he was fully insured,
And his Health-card shows he was once in hospital but left it
  cured.
Both Producers Research and High-Grade Living declare
He was fully sensible to the advantages of the Instalment Plan
And had everything necessary to the Modern Man,
A phonograph, a radio, a car, and a frigidaire.
Our researchers into Public Opinion are content
That he held the proper opinions for the time of year;
When there was peace, he was for peace; when there was war, he
  went.

He was married and added five children to the population,
Which our Eugenist says was the right number for a parent of his
generation,
And our teachers report that he never interfered with their
education.
Was he free? Was he happy? The question is absurd:
Had anything been wrong, we should certainly have heard.

8. Dear Editor: Some suggested rules for participation in the great
forum which is the campus paper's editorial page: 1. Be extremely
sarcastic about the ideas expressed in the letter you are attacking
and of the writer's intelligence. 2. To lend credence to your own
words and to show that you are eminently qualified to belittle your
opponent, use plenty of multi-syllable words and stock foreign-
language phrases. 3. Extrapolate your opponent's views and show
grotesque and exaggerated consequences. 4. If the topic is political, create analogies between your opponent's beliefs and Hitler's policies and Orwell's *1984* (no matter what band of the political spectrum his ideas cover). 5. Appear to be highly objective
but state only "facts" which you have subtly interpreted. 6. If the
topic is campus politics and you are serious, remember—all evidence indicates this is an impossible situation.

9.

The Pool Players
Seven at the Golden Shovel.

We real cool. We
Left school. We

Lurk late. We
Strike straight. We

Sing sin. We
Thin gin. We

Jazz June. We
Die soon.

3.16 Try your hand at writing a paragraph or two in an ironical vein, using the
excerpts in the preceding exercise as possible models. First, write what you have
to say as directly as you can. Then, try to convert the direct statement into an
ironic one. Here are some possible topics for ironic treatment:

1. A letter to the campus newspaper, on the food in the campus
cafeterias, the high cost of tuition, the quality of teachers, or the
quality of students.
2. How to get better grades in a certain course.
3. How to prepare for a particular career.

4. A letter to high-school students on how to prepare for college life.
5. How to get tickets to a specific rock concert.
6. Hollywood's secret formula for making great horror films.
7. How to conquer rush-hour traffic.
8. How to get along with your parents or your spouse.
9. Conservation of natural resources is a waste of money.
10. How to read critically.
11. How to write an advertisement for a new car, household cleaning product, or cosmetic.
12. How to tell good punk rock from bad punk rock.
13. How to win at computer games.
14. How to master the computer.

UNDERSTATEMENT AND OVERSTATEMENT; SENTIMENTALITY; RESTRAINT

3.17 Here are several passages marked by either understatement or overstatement. In what specific ways does each writer use style to exaggerate or unduly minimize the reality of the situation? What seems to be the purpose in doing so? As far as you, the critical reader, are concerned, is the style effective? (Note that examples 1 and 2 deal with the same theme. Compare the two passages for their use of understatement and/or overstatement.)

1. Music, I regret to say, affects me merely as an arbitrary succession of more or less irritating noises. Under certain emotional circumstances I can stand the spasms of a rich violin, but the concert piano and all wind instruments bore me in small doses and flay me in larger ones.
2. I am constitutionally susceptible of noises. A carpenter's hammer, in a warm, summer noon, will fret me into more than midsummer madness. But those unconnected, unset sounds are nothing to the measured malice of music. The ear is passive to those single strokes; willingly enduring stripes while it hath no task to con. To music it cannot be passive. It will strive—mine at least will—spite of its inaptitude, to thrid the maze; like an unskilled eye painfully poring upon hieroglyphics. I have sat through an Italian Opera, till, for sheer pain, and inexplicable anguish, I have rushed out into the noisiest places of the crowded streets, to solace myself with sounds, which I was not obliged to follow, and get rid of the distracting torment of endless, fruitless, barren attention!
3. I believe my consumption has grown worse. Also my asthma. The wheezing comes and goes, and I get dizzy more and more frequently. I have taken to violent choking and fainting. My room is

damp and I have perpetual chills and palpitations of the heart. I noticed, too, that I am out of napkins. Will it never stop?

4. I saw a woman flayed alive today, and you have no idea how it altered her appearance for the worse.

5. Advancing more and more into the shadow of this mournful place, its dark depressing influence stole upon their spirits, and filled them with dismal gloom. On every side, and as far as the eye could see into the heavy distance, tall chimneys, crowding on each other and presenting that endless repetition of the same dull, ugly form, which is the horror of oppressive dreams, poured out their plague of smoke, obscured the light, and made foul the melancholy air. On mounds of ashes by the wayside, sheltered only by a few rough boards or rotten pent-house roofs, strange engines spun and writhed like tortured creatures; clanking their iron chains, shrieking in the rapid whirl from time to time as though in torment unendurable, and making the ground tremble with their agonies. Dismantled houses here and there appeared, tottering to the earth, propped up by fragments of others that had fallen down, unroofed, windowless, blackened, desolate, but yet inhabited. Men, women, children, wan in their looks and ragged in attire, tended the engines, fed their tributary fires, begged upon the road, or scowled half-naked from the doorless houses. Then came more of the wrathful monsters, whose like they almost seemed to be in their wildness and untamed air, screeching and turning round and round again; and still, before, behind, and to the right and left, was the same interminable perspective of brick towers never ceasing in their black vomit, blasting all things living or inanimate, shutting out the face of day, and closing in on all these horrors with a dense dark cloud.

6. Decades ago A. Y. Jackson painted Nellie Lake, using oil on canvas to preserve its beauty. The lake in turn provided Jackson with the trout on which he lived.

   Both the artist and the lake are now dead.

   Jackson died after a long and respected career. Nellie Lake died in its youth. The fish that once thrived in its waters have perished—victims of acidification from rain and snow.

   Nellie Lake is only one of the . . . lakes that have died because of acid rain. If immediate action is not taken, as many as 48,500 more may die in the next 20 years.

   Acid rain stunts trees. Damages crops. And affects your health and that of your children.

   You can do something about it. The technology to control acid rain is available. But it will only be implemented if governments and the public demand prompt action.

3.18 Try to distinguish sentiment from sentimentality in the following passages. Point to specific words and phrases which helped you make your decision.

1.   **"Then the Dragon Came ..."**

Nobody tells a story like Daddy. The everyday world fades away as his words lead you into a new and shining land.

And what if the Dragon is a bit scary? You need only climb into Daddy's arms to be safe and secure again before it's time to sleep.

To make those we love safe and secure is the very core of home-making. It is a privilege known only in a country such as ours, where men and women are free to work for it.

And taking care of our own is also the way we best take care of our country. For the strength of America is simply the strength of one secure home touching that of another.

If you've tried to save and failed, chances are it was because you didn't have a plan. Well, here's a savings system that really works—the Payroll Savings Plan for investing in U.S. Savings Bonds.

2.   They stood side by side on the granite step in the soaring bright-ness. In front of them were the seaweedy rocks of the cove and the spruces and the pointed firs and the dark bay and islands and the line of the ocean heaving with light. The waves breathed in the cove. "Husband," she said. "Wife," he said. The words made them bashful. They clung together against their bashfulness. "Today we begin," he said, "to make ..." "This wilderness our home," she said. The risen sun over the ocean shone in their faces.

3.   I had been listening and silently rebutting each sentence with my eyes closed; then there was a hush, which in an audience warns that something unplanned is happening. I looked up and saw Henry Reed, the conservative, the proper, the A student, turn his back to the audience and turn to us (the proud graduating class of 1940) and sing, nearly speaking,

> "Lift ev'ry voice and sing
> Till earth and heaven ring
> Ring with the harmonies of Liberty ..."

It was the poem written by James Weldon Johnson. It was the music composed by J. Rosamond Johnson. It was the Negro national anthem. Out of habit we were singing it. . . . And now I heard, really for the first time:

"We have come over a way that with tears
    has been watered,
We have come, treading our path through
    the blood of the slaughtered."

While echoes of the song shivered in the air, Henry Reed bowed his head, said "Thank you," and returned to his place in the line. The tears that slipped down many faces were not wiped away in shame.

We were on top again. As always, again. We survived. The depths had been icy and dark, but now a bright sun spoke to our souls. I was no longer simply a member of the proud graduating class of 1940; I was a proud member of the wonderful, beautiful Negro race.

Oh, Black known and unknown poets, how often have your auctioned pains sustained us? Who will compute the lonely nights made less lonely by your songs, or the empty pots made less tragic by your tales?

If we were a people much given to revealing secrets, we might raise monuments and sacrifice to the memories of our poets, but slavery cured us of that weakness. It may be enough, however, to have it said that we survive in exact relationship to the dedication of our poets (include preachers, musicians and blues singers).

4. **Politics**

How can I, that girl standing there,
My attention fix
On Roman or on Russian
Or on Spanish politics?
Yet here's a travelled man that knows
What he talks about,
And there's a politician
That has read and thought,
And maybe what they say is true
Of war and war's alarms,
But O that I were young again
And held her in my arms!

5. Sweet is the hour that brings us home,
    Where all will spring to meet us;
Where hands are striving, as we come,
    To be the first to greet us.
When the world hath spent its frowns and wrath,
    And care been sorely pressing:
Tis sweet to turn from our roving path,
    And find a fireside blessing.

Oh, joyfully dear is the homeward track,
If we are but sure of a welcome back.

6. Best Athlete: Muhammad Ali. The story of Ali's career was ultimately a tragedy, and there were tears in the eyes of many strong
   men when Larry Holmes pounded away the last of Ali's illusions
   beneath a huge canopy raised over the ring in the car park of
   Caesar's Palace in Las Vegas. I wrote at the time and I still believe
   it, Ali's defeat diminished us all. He was the bravest, wittiest, pret-
   tiest athlete I ever saw.

REVIEW

3.19 **(a)** As we have seen, critical readers must often draw conclusions that are
not made explicit in a text. To draw these conclusions, readers "read
between the lines," inferring an additional conclusion from the information
given. In the following excerpt from the introduction to the transcript of a
famous murder trial, the editor obviously has some knowledge or opinions
which he is not free to express directly. Analyze the paragraph, sentence
by sentence, for the various ways in which the writer manages to suggest
what he cannot say. What, in a single blunt sentence, is the conclusion or
inference the writer leads us to make about Sir James Stephen?

As a judge Sir James Stephen was considered to be at his best in a
Criminal Court; of nice legal subtleties and fine distinctions, his mind
was apt to be impatient. It is impossible for the historian of the Maybrick case to ignore the statement, frequently made, that at the time
of her trial the judge's mind was suffering from the early attacks of an
insidious disease which, two years later, compelled Sir James to retire
from the bench. The judge had had a slight stroke of paralysis at Derby
in 1885, and been obliged to give up work for a time. Whether on his
return to work his mind had entirely recovered its former vigour, or
was suffering a gradual loss of strength, is a matter that need not be
discussed. But those familiar with the judge's powers during his earlier
years on the bench may well doubt, in reading the report of Mrs. Maybrick's trial, whether those powers were as conspicuous and effective
in the trial of her case as they would have been had it taken place
some few years before. Of the judge's scrupulous anxiety to be fair,
just, and considerate toward the prisoner no impartial reader can
doubt.

(b) Here is another passage which expects the careful reader to draw a
conclusion not stated explicitly in the text. In this case, the title of the
article, "Psychology Constructs the Female, or, The Fantasy Life of the Male
Psychologist," provides us with the clue we need in order to make the infer-

ence the author leads us to. Read the passage and then try to state, in one sentence, what the author is indirectly implying about male psychologists.

It is an implicit assumption that the area of psychology which concerns itself with personality has the onerous but necessary task of describing the limits of human possibility. Thus when we are about to consider the liberation of women, we naturally look to psychology to tell us what "true" liberation would mean: what would give women the freedom to fulfill their own intrinsic natures. Psychologists have set about describing the true natures of women with a certainty and a sense of . . . infallibility rarely found in the secular world. Bruno Bettelheim, of the University of Chicago, tells us that

> We must start with the realization that, as much as women want to be good scientists or engineers, they want first and foremost to be womanly companions of men and mothers.

Eric Erikson of Harvard University, upon noting that young women often ask whether they can "have an identity before they know whom they will marry, and for whom they will make a home," explains somewhat elegiacally that

> Much of a young woman's identity is already defined in her kind of attractiveness and in the selectivity of her search for the man (or men) by whom she wishes to be sought. . . .

. . . These views from men who are assumed to be experts reflect, in a surprisingly transparent way, the cultural consensus. They not only assert that a woman is defined by her ability to attract men, they see no alternative definitions. They think that the definition of a woman in terms of a man is the way it should be; and they back it up with psychosexual incantation and biological ritual curses. . . .

3.20 In this chapter, we studied A. E. Housman's poem on an impending execution to determine the attitude we are led to adopt toward the hanging of a young man. Here are six more excerpts from prose and poetry which deal with the same general theme of execution. Analyze the tone of each passage, and try to determine what the author's attitude is to the subject. Then decide how the tone of each one influences your response.

1. As the clock began to strike, an immense sway and movement swept over the whole of that vast dense crowd. They were all uncovered directly, and a great murmur arose, more awful, bizarre, and indescribable than any sound I had ever heard before. Women and children began to shriek horridly. I don't know whether it was the bell I heard; but a dreadful, quick, feverish kind of jangling noise mingled with the noise of the people, and lasted for about two minutes. The scaffold stood before us, tenantless and black; the black chain was hanging down ready

from the beam. Nobody came. "He has been respited," someone said; another said, "He has killed himself in prison."

Just then, from under the black prison door, a pale, quiet head peered out. It was shockingly bright and distinct; it rose up directly and a man in black appeared on the scaffold, and was silently followed by about four more dark figures. The first was a tall grave man: we all knew who the second man was. "*That's he—that's he!*" you heard the people say, as the devoted man came up.

I have seen a cast of the head since, but, indeed, should never have known it. Courvoisier bore his punishment like a man, and walked very firmly. He was dressed in a new black suit, as it seemed: his shirt was open. His arms were tied in front of him. He opened his hands in a helpless kind of way, and clasped them once or twice together. He turned his head here and there, and looked about him for an instant with a wild, imploring look. His mouth was contracted into a sort of pitiful smile. He went and placed himself at once under the beam, with his face to St. Sepulchre's. The tall, grave man in black twisted round swiftly in the other direction, and, drawing from his pocket a nightcap, pulled it tight over the patient's head and face. I am not ashamed to say that I could look no more, but shut my eyes as the last dreadful act was going on, which sent this wretched guilty soul into the presence of God.

When they had nearly reached the top of the great West Hill the clocks in the town struck eight. Each gave a start at the notes, and walking onward yet a few steps, they reached the first milestone standing whitely on the green margin of the grass, and backed by the down, which here was open to the road. They entered upon the turf, and, impelled by a force that seemed to overrule their will, suddenly stood still, turned, and waited in paralyzed suspense beside the stone.

The prospect from this summit was almost unlimited. In the valley beneath lay the city they had just left, its more prominent buildings showing as in an isometric drawing— among them the broad cathedral tower, with its Norman windows and immense length of aisle and nave, the spires of St. Thomas's, the pinnacled tower of the College, and, more to the right, the tower and gables of the ancient hospice, where to this day the pilgrim may receive his dole of bread and ale. Behind the city swept the rotund upland of St. Catherine's Hill; further off, landscape beyond landscape, till the horizon was lost in the radiance of the sun hanging above it.

Against these far stretches of country rose, in front of the other city edifices, a large red-brick building, with level grey roofs, and rows of short barred windows bespeaking captivity, the whole contrasting greatly by its formalism with the quaint irregularities of the Gothic erections. It was somewhat disguised from the road in passing it by yews and evergreen oaks, but it was visible enough up here. The wicket from which the pair had lately emerged was in the wall of this structure. From the middle of the building an ugly flat-topped octagonal tower ascended against the east horizon, and viewed from this spot, on its shady side and against the light, it seemed the one blot on the city's beauty. Yet it was with this blot, and not with the beauty, that the two gazers were concerned.

Upon the cornice of the tower a tall staff was fixed. Their eyes were riveted on it. A few minutes after the hour had struck something moved slowly up the staff, and extended itself upon the breeze. It was a black flag.

"Justice" was done, and the President of the Immortals, in Aeschylean phrase, had ended his sport with Tess. And the d'Urberville knights and dames slept on in their tombs unknowing. The two speechless gazers bent themselves down to the earth, as if in prayer, and remained thus a long time, absolutely motionless: the flag continued to wave silently. As soon as they had strength they arose, joined hands again, and went on.

3. They hanged Sam Cardinella at six o'clock in the morning in the corridor of the county jail. The corridor was high and narrow with tiers of cells on either side. All the cells were occupied. The men had been brought in for the hanging. Five men sentenced to be hanged were in the five top cells. Three of the men to be hanged were negroes. They were very frightened. One of the white men sat on his cot with his head in his hands. The other lay flat on his cot with a blanket wrapped around his head.

4. "What are the bugles blowin' for?" said Files-on-Parade.*
"To turn you out, to turn you out," the Color-Sergeant said.
"What makes you look so white, so white?" said Files-on-Parade.
"I'm dreadin' what I've got to watch," the Color-Sergeant said.
> For they're hangin' Danny Deever, you can hear the Dead March play,
> The Regiment's in 'ollow square—they're hangin' him today;
> They've taken all his buttons off an' cut his stripes away,
> An' they're hangin' Danny Deever in the mornin'. . . .

"'Is cot was right-'and cot to mine," said Files-on-Parade.
"'E's sleepin' out an' far tonight," the Color-Sergeant said.
"I've drunk 'is beer a score o' times," said Files-on-Parade.

---

*Files-on-Parade is a private soldier.

"'E's drinkin' bitter beer alone," the Color-Sergeant said.
  They are hangin' Danny Deever, you must mark 'im to 'is
    place,
  For 'e shot a comrade sleepin'—you must look 'im in the face;
  Nine 'undred of 'is county an' the Regiment's disgrace,
  While they're hangin' Danny Deever in the mornin'.

"What's that so black agin the sun?" said Files-on-Parade.
"It's Danny fightin' 'ard for life," the Color-Sergeant said.
"What's that that whimpers over'ead?" said Files-on-Parade.
"It's Danny's soul that's passin' now," the Color-Sergeant said.
  For they're done with Danny Deever, you can 'ear the quick-
    step play,
  The regiment's in column, an' they're marchin' us away;
  Ho! the young recruits are shakin', an' they'll want their beer
    today,
  After hangin' Danny Deever in the mornin'.

5. Anne Boleyn had now reached the zenith of her hopes. A weak, giddy woman of no stability of character, her success turned her head and caused her to behave with insolence and impropriety. ... On the first of May following the king suddenly broke up a tournament at Greenwich, leaving the company in bewilderment and consternation. The cause was soon known. Inquiries had been made on reports of the queen's ill-conduct, and several of her reputed lovers had been arrested. On the 2nd Anne herself was committed to the Tower on a charge of adultery with various persons, including her own brother, Lord Rochford. . . . The same day (the 17th) all her reputed lovers were executed; and on the 19th she herself suffered death on Tower Green, her head being struck off with a sword by the executioner of Calais brought to England for the purpose. She had regarded the prospect of death with courage and almost with levity, laughing heartily as she put her hands about her "little neck" and recalled the skill of the executioner. "I have seen many men" (wrote Sir William Kingston, governor of the Tower) "and also women executed, and all they have been in great sorrow, and to my knowledge this lady has much joy and pleasure in death." On the following day Henry was betrothed to Jane Seymour.

6. On [the Provost-marshal's] returning with the Sheriff . . . the door was open, and they were confronted with the tall majestic figure of Mary Stuart standing there before them in splendor. The plain gray dress had been exchanged for a robe of black satin; her jacket was of black satin also, looped and slashed and trimmed with velvet. Her false hair was arranged studiously with a coif, and over her head and falling down over her back was a white veil of

delicate lawn. A crucifix of gold hung from her neck. In her hand she held a crucifix of ivory, and a number of jeweled Paternosters were attached to her girdle. . . .

She laid her crucifix on her chair. The chief executioner took it as a perquisite, but was ordered instantly to lay it down. The lawn veil was lifted carefully off, not to disturb the hair, and was hung upon the rail. The black robe was next removed. Below it was a petticoat of crimson velvet. The black jacket followed, and under the jacket was a bodice of crimson satin. One of her ladies handed her a pair of crimson sleeves, with which she hastily covered her arms; and thus she stood on the black scaffold with the black figures all around her, blood-red from head to foot.

Her reasons for adopting so extraordinary a costume must be left to conjecture. It is only certain that it must have been carefully studied, and that the pictorial effect must have been appalling. . . .

On her knees she repeated the Psalm, *In te, Domine, confido,* "In thee, O Lord, have I put my trust." . . . When the psalm was finished she felt for the block, and laying down her head muttered: "In manus, Domine tua, commendo animam meam." ("Into thy Hands, O Lord, I commend my spirit.") The hard wood seemed to hurt her, for she placed her hands under her neck. The executioners gently removed them, lest they should deaden the blow, and then one of them holding her slightly, the other raised the axe and struck. The scene had been too trying even for the practiced headsman of the Tower. His arm wandered. The blow fell on the knot of the handkerchief, and scarcely broke the skin. She neither spoke nor moved. He struck again, this time effectively. The head hung by a shred of skin, which he divided without withdrawing the axe; and at once a metamorphosis was witnessed, strange as was ever wrought by the wand of fabled enchanter. The coil fell off and the false plaits. The labored illusion vanished. The lady who had knelt before the block was in the maturity of grace and loveliness. The executioner, when he raised the head, as usual, to show it to the crowd, exposed the withered features of a grizzled, wrinkled old woman.

3.21 We can exercise our response to tone by looking at the opening paragraphs of short stories and novels. The opening, after all, "sets the scene" for our responses and often establishes some important element of the work to come. Each of the following passages introduces a well-known novel. After a careful reading, what can you infer from the tone concerning the point of view, theme, and style of the whole book? Try to distinguish between what you learn from outright statement of fact (analogous to denotation) and what you find implied in the tone itself (analogous to connotation).

1. It is a truth universally acknowledged, that a single man in possession of a good fortune must be in want of a wife.

    However little known the feelings or views of such a man may
be on his first entering a neighbourhood, this truth is so well fixed
in the minds of the surrounding families, that he is considered as
the rightful property of some one or other of their daughters.

    "My dear Mr. Bennet," said his lady to him one day, "have you
heard that Netherfield Park is let at last?"

    Mr. Bennet replied that he had not.

    "But it is," returned she; "for Mrs. Long has just been here, and
she told me all about it."

    Mr. Bennet made no answer.

    "Do not you want to know who has taken it?" cried his wife
impatiently.

    "You want to tell me, and I have no objection to hearing it."

    This was invitation enough.

    "Why, my dear, you must know, Mrs. Long says that Netherfield
is taken by a young man of large fortune from the north of
England; that he came down on Monday in a chaise and four to
see the place, and was so much delighted with it, that he agreed
with Mr. Morris immediately; that he is to take possession before
Michaelmas, and some of his servants are to be in the house by
the end of next week."

    "What is his name?"

    "Bingley."

    "Is he married or single?"

    "Oh! single, my dear, to be sure! A single man of large fortune;
four or five thousand a year. What a fine thing for our girls!"

2. My lifelong involvement with Mrs. Dempster began at 5:58
o'clock p.m. on 27 December 1908, at which time I was ten years
and seven months old.

    I am able to date the occasion with complete certainty because
that afternoon I had been sledding with my lifelong friend and
enemy Percy Boyd Staunton, and we had quarreled, because his
fine new Christmas sled would not go as fast as my old one. Snow
was never heavy in our part of the world, but this Christmas it had
been plentiful enough almost to cover the tallest spears of dried
grass in the fields; in such snow his sled with its tall runners and
foolish steering apparatus was clumsy and apt to stick, whereas my
low-slung old affair would almost have slid on grass without snow.

    The afternoon had been humiliating for him, and when Percy
was humiliated he was vindictive. His parents were rich, his
clothes were fine, and his mittens were of skin and came from a
store in the city, whereas mine were knitted by my mother; it was

manifestly wrong, therefore, that his splendid sled should not go faster than mine, and when such injustice showed itself Percy became cranky. He slighted my sled, scoffed at my mittens, and at last came right out and said that his father was better than my father. Instead of hitting him, which might have started a fight that could have ended in a draw or even a defeat for me, I said, all right, then, I would go home and he could have the field to himself. This was crafty of me, for I knew it was getting on for supper-time, and one of our home rules was that nobody, under any circumstances, was to be late for a meal. So I was keeping the home rule, while at the same time leaving Percy to himself.

As I walked back to the village he followed me, shouting fresh insults. When I walked, he taunted, I staggered like an old cow; my woollen cap was absurd beyond belief; my backside was immense and wobbled when I walked; and more of the same sort, for his invention was not lively. I said nothing, because I knew that this spited him more than any retort, and that every time he shouted at me he lost face.

Our village was so small that you came on it at once; it lacked the dignity of outskirts. I darted up our street, putting on speed, for I had looked ostentatiously at my new Christmas dollar watch (Percy had a watch but was not let wear it because it was too good) and saw that it was 5:57; just time to get indoors, wash my hands in the noisy, splashy way my parents seemed to like, and be in my place at six, my head bent for grace. Percy was by this time hopping mad, and I knew I had spoiled his supper and probably his whole evening. Then the unforeseen took over.

3. A squat building of only thirty-four stories. Over the main entrance the words, CENTRAL LONDON HATCHERY AND CONDITIONING CENTRE, and, in a shield, the World State's motto, COMMUNITY, IDENTITY, STABILITY.

The enormous room on the ground floor faced towards the north. Cold for all the summer beyond the panes, for all the tropical heat of the room itself, a harsh thin light glared through the windows, hungrily seeking some draped lay figure, some pallid shape of academic goose-flesh, but finding only the glass and nickel and bleakly shining porcelain of a laboratory. Wintriness responded to wintriness. The overalls of the workers were white, their hands gloved with a pale corpse-coloured rubber. The light was frozen, dead, a ghost. Only from the yellow barrels of the microscopes did it borrow a certain rich and living substance, lying along the polished tubes like butter, streak after luscious streak in long recession down the work-tables.

"And this," said the Director opening the door, "is the Fertilizing Room."

4. It was the afternoon of my eighty-first birthday, and I was in bed with my catamite when Ali announced that the archbishop had come to see me.

"Very good, Ali," I quavered in Spanish through the closed door of the master bedroom. "Take him into the bar. Give him a drink."

"*Hay dos. Su capellán también.*"

"Very good, Ali. Give his chaplain a drink also."

I retired twelve years ago from the profession of novelist. Nevertheless you will be constrained to consider, if you know my work at all and take the trouble now to reread that first sentence, that I have lost none of my old cunning in the contrivance of what is known as *an arresting opening.* But there is really nothing of contrivance about it. Actuality sometimes plays into the hands of art. That I was eighty-one I could hardly doubt: congratulatory cables had been rubbing it in all through the forenoon. Geoffrey, who was already pulling on his overtight summer slacks, was, I suppose, my Ganymede or male lover as well as my secretary. The Spanish word *arzobispo* certainly means archbishop. The time was something after four o'clock on a Maltese June day—the twenty-third, to be exact and to spare the truly interested the trouble of consulting *Who's Who.*

3.22 Try your hand at writing an effective opening paragraph or paragraphs for a short story, using one of the following situations. Or set up a situation of your own or one devised by you and other classmates. The opening should be about 150–200 words long. Your aim is to give necessary information, set the tone of the whole story, and capture your readers' interest. (Write the entire story if you want!) The situations may be changed in any way—they merely offer you a means of getting started—and of course you will want to add appropriate details. Before beginning, decide which element (scene, situation, atmosphere, character) you wish to stress, and build your opening around that center.

1. A hot summer day in the city; downtown street scene. Kids sitting on steps. Baseball in the street. Suddenly a policeman runs onto the street, his gun drawn.
2. An average, middle-class home; living room; family watching television. Contentment. Suddenly the telephone rings.
3. Cool jazz on a hot day. Crowds. Some people listen; some throw Frisbees; some dance. Then the moment they had all been waiting for:
4. Inside a church on a rainy evening. A dim figure (man or woman) enters furtively.
5. The last two miles of a long day's hike. A hard climb up a hill. Loose stones. Thirsty and tired. The camp just one mile ahead.

6. A quiet hospital corridor at midnight; a sudden commotion outside Room 429.

7. The tough, three-hour exam draws to a close. The unsuspecting instructor, who has been outside drinking coffee, suddenly returns.

8. Brand new Jaguar. Electric red. Your first tank of gas. You drive into the station and watch the attendant lumber toward you, rubbing his filthy hands.

9. Unemployed people standing in the cold. Trash can fires for heat. Rum and cheap beer. Anger. Boredom. Then a fight breaks out.

10. A dance contest. Two couples in the finals. Big prizes and a television appearance for the winners. Then . . .

3.23 The following poem, "To His Coy Mistress," illustrates the way in which tone can shift dramatically within the course of relatively few lines. (1) How would you describe the attitude of the speaker to his "coy mistress" as the poem begins? (Look up *coy* and *mistress* to make sure you understand what these words meant when the poem was written, in the latter part of the seventeenth century.) What devices of diction and allusion does the speaker use to communicate this attitude? (2) Exactly where does the shift in tone occur? What is the tone from then on? (3) Does the change in tone mean that the speaker's attitude toward his beloved suddenly changes? Or can we say, on the other hand, that his underlying feeling is consistent throughout the poem? (4) Study carefully the figures of speech to see how each contributes to the effectiveness of tone.

```
Had we but world enough, and time,
This coyness, lady, were no crime.
We would sit down, and think which way
To walk, and pass our long love's day.
Thou by the Indian Ganges' side                          5
Shouldst rubies find: I by the tide
Of Humber would complain. I would        [complain: sing of love]
Love you ten years before the flood,
And you should, if you please, refuse
Till the conversion of the Jews.                        10
My vegetable love should grow              [vegetable: plantlike]
Vaster than empires and more slow;
An hundred years should go to praise
Thine eyes, and on thy forehead gaze;
Two hundred to adore each breast,                       15
But thirty thousand to the rest;
An age at least to every part,
And the last age should show your heart.
For, lady, you deserve this state;              [state: honor]
```

Nor would I love at lower rate.   20
But at my back I always hear
Time's wingèd chariot hurrying near;
And yonder all before us lie
Deserts of vast eternity.
Thy beauty shall no more be found,   25
Nor, in thy marble vault, shall sound
My echoing song; then worms shall try
That long preserved virginity,
And your quaint honor turn to dust,   [*quaint*: proud]
And into ashes all my lust: 30
The grave's a fine and private place,
But none, I think, do there embrace.
Now therefore, while the youthful hue
Sits on thy skin like morning dew,
And while thy willing soul transpires   35
At every pore with instant fires,
Now let us sport us while we may,
And now, like amorous birds of prey,
Rather at once our time devour
Than languish in his slow-chapped power.   [*slow-chapped*: slowly
Let us roll all our strength and all   devouring]
Our sweetness up into one ball,
And tear our pleasures with rough strife
Through the iron gates of life:
Thus, though we cannot make our sun   45
Stand still, yet we will make him run.

3.24 Tone is closely related to mood. Often a writer is successful in affecting our mood by creating an "atmosphere" — describing the setting in rich detail so that we can feel we are actually there. How effective are the following passages in creating mood? How would you characterize the tone of each?

1. In the gathering darkness of a cold winter evening on 9 November 1965, just before sixteen minutes and eleven seconds past five o'clock, a small metal cup inside a black rectangular box began slowly to revolve. As it turned, a spindle set in its centre and carrying a tiny arm also rotated, gradually moving the arm closer and closer to a metal contact. Only a handful of people knew of the exact location of the cup, and none of them knew that it had been triggered. At precisely eleven seconds past the minute the two tiny metal projections made contact, and in doing so set in motion a sequence of events that would lead, within twelve minutes, to chaos. During that time life within 80,000 square miles of one of the richest, most highly industrialized, most densely pop-

ulated areas in the Western world would come to a virtual stand-still. Over thirty million people would be affected for periods of from three minutes to thirteen hours. As a result some of them would die. For all of them, life would never be quite the same again. [The 1965 Northeast coast blackout had just begun.]

2.   **Living in Sin**

She had thought the studio would keep itself;
no dust upon the furniture of love.
Half heresy, to wish the taps less vocal,
the panes relieved of grime. A plate of pears,
a piano with a Persian shawl, a cat
stalking the picturesque amusing mouse
had risen at his urging.
Not that at five each separate stair would writhe
under the milkman's tramp; that morning light
so coldly would delineate the scraps
of last night's cheese and three sepulchral bottles;
that on the kitchen shelf among the saucers
a pair of beetle-eyes would fix her own—
envoy from some village in the moldings . . .
Meanwhile, he, with a yawn,
sounded a dozen notes upon the keyboard,
declared it out of tune, shrugged at the mirror,
rubbed at his beard, went out for cigarettes;
while she, jeered by the minor demons,
pulled back the sheets and made the bed and found
a towel to dust the table-top,
and let the coffee-pot boil over on the stove.
By evening she was back in love again,
though not so wholly but throughout the night
she woke sometimes to feel the daylight coming
like a relentless milkman up the stairs.

3.   One Christmas was so much like another, in those years, around the sea-town corner now and out of all sound except the distant speaking of the voices I sometimes hear a moment before sleep, that I can never remember whether it snowed for six days and six nights when I was twelve or whether it snowed for twelve days and twelve nights when I was six; or whether the ice broke and the skating grocer vanished like a snowman through a white trap-door on that same Christmas Day that the mince-pies finished Uncle Arnold and we tobogganed down the seaward hill, all the after-noon, on the best tea-tray, and Mrs. Griffiths complained, and we threw a snowball at her niece, and my hands burned so, with the

heat and the cold, when I held them in front of the fire, that I cried for twenty minutes and then had some jelly.

3.25 How would you characterize the tone of each of the following passages? What means (diction, metaphor, allusion, overstatement, restraint, and so on) does the writer use to create that tone?

1. I have been, all my life, what is known as a conservationist. I am not at all sure that this has done myself or anyone else any good, but I am quite sure that no intelligent man, least of all a country-man, has any alternative. It seems clear beyond possibility of argument that any given generation of men can have only a lease, not ownership, of the earth; and one essential term of the lease is that the earth be handed on to the next generation with unimpaired potentialities. This is the conservationist's concern.

2. For forty-seven years they had been married. How deep back the stubborn, gnarled roots of the quarrel reached, no one could say—but only now, when tending to the needs of others no longer shackled them together, the roots swelled up visibly, split the earth between them, and the tearing shook even the children, long since grown.

   Why now, why now? wailed Hannah.

   As if when we grew up weren't enough, said Paul.

   Poor Ma. Poor Dad. It hurts so for both of them, said Vivi. They never had very much; at least in old age they should be happy.

   Knock their heads together, insisted Sammy; tell 'em: you're too old for this kind of thing; no reason not to get along now.

   Lennie wrote to Clara: They've lived over so much together; what could possibly tear them apart?

3. In Cincinnati, everyone knows that a four-way is chili on spaghetti with cheese and onions added. I never saw any numbers on menus in Cincinnati, but it is accepted that a customer can walk into any chili parlor—an Empress or a Skyline or any of the independent neighborhood parlors—and say "One three-way" and be assured of getting chili on spaghetti with cheese. Cincinnati eaters take it for granted that the basic way to serve chili is on spaghetti, just as they take it for granted that the other ways to serve it go up to the five-way (chili, spaghetti, onions, cheese, and beans) and that the people who do the serving are Greeks. When the Kiradjieff family, which introduced authentic Cincinnati chili at the Empress in 1922, was sued several years ago by a manager who alleged that he had been fired unfairly, one of his claims amounted to the contention that anyone fired under suspicious circumstances from a chili parlor with the Empress's

prestige was all through in the Greek community. There are probably people in Cincinnati who reach maturity without realizing that Mexicans eat anything called chili, in the same way that there are probably young men from Nevada who have to be drafted and sent to an out-of-state Army camp before they realize that all laundromats are not equipped with slot machines.

4. **For My Daughter's Best Friend, the Night Before Moving**

They lie tangled like lovers
who dream they will never part
Hand in hand, they swim to the moon
Sisters in a legend,
wearing each other's face
There will be nightmares
later, when she wakes
on a strange bed
crying for something
she almost recognizes
The feeling of flight
A shape
A doll, maybe, left
under the cellar steps
Ignorant of departures
in a corner of the cave
Up to its polished thighs
in rusty water quietly staring
out of one blind eye
Already headed
for the perfection of the lost

5. In the great meteor shower of August, the Perseid, I wait all day for the shooting stars I miss. They're out there showering down, committing hara-kiri in a flame of fatal attraction, and hissing perhaps at last into the ocean. But at dawn what looks like a blue dome clamps down over me like a lid on a pot. The stars and planets could smash and I'd never know. Only a piece of ashen moon occasionally climbs up or down the inside of the dome, and our local star without surcease explodes on our heads. We have really only that one light, one source for all power, and yet we must turn away from it by universal decree. Nobody here on the planet seems aware of this strange, powerful taboo, that we all walk about carefully averting our faces, this way and that, lest our eyes be blasted forever.

6. [Newton's] prodigious intellectual powers persisted unabated. In 1696, the Swiss mathematician Johann Bernoulli challenged his

colleagues to solve an unresolved issue called the brachistochrone problem, specifying the curve connecting two points dis-
placed from each other laterally, along which a body, acted only
upon by gravity, would fall in the shortest time. Bernoulli originally specified a deadline of six months, but extended it to a year
and a half at the request of Leibniz, one of the leading scholars
of the time, and the man who had, independently of Newton,
invented the differential and integral calculus. The challenge
was delivered to Newton at four P.M. on January 29, 1697.
Before leaving for work the next morning, he had invented an
entire new branch of mathematics called the calculus of varia-
tions, used it to solve the brachistochrone problem and sent off
the solution, which was published, at Newton's request, anony-
mously. But the brilliance and originality of the work betrayed
the identity of its author. When Bernoulli saw the solution, he
commented, "We recognize the lion by his claw." Newton was
then in his fifty-fifth year.

7.   **Death of a Young Son by Drowning**

He, who navigated with success
the dangerous river of his own birth
once more set forth

on a voyage of discovery
into the land I floated on
but could not touch to claim.

His feet slid on the bank,
the currents took him;
he swirled with ice and trees in the swollen water

and plunged into distant regions,
his head a bathysphere;
through his eyes' thin glass bubbles

he looked out, reckless adventurer
on a landscape stranger than Uranus
we have all been to and some remember.

There was an accident; the air locked,
he was hung in the river like a heart.
They retrieved the swamped body,

cairn of my plans and future charts,
with poles and hooks
from among the nudging logs.

It was spring, the sun kept shining, the new grass
lept to solidity;
my hands glistened with details.

After the long trip I was tired of waves.
My foot hit rock. The dreamed sails
collapsed, ragged.

 I planted him in this country
 like a flag.

8. I remember being totally unable to recite the Pledge of Alle-
giance until I was seven years old. Why? At seven years old I
was certainly not a card-carrying Communist, and no one had
told me not to recite "with liberty and justice for all." In fact, my
father thought I should recite it for safety's sake. But I knew that
he believed it no more than I, and that his recital of the pledge
had done nothing to contribute to his safety, to say nothing of
the tormented safety of his children.

How did I know that? How does any child know that? I knew
it from watching my father's face, my father's hours, days, and
nights. I knew it from scrubbing the floor of the tenements in
which we lived, knew it from the eviction notices, knew it from
the bitter winters when the landlords gave us no heat, knew it
from my mother's face when a new child was born, knew it by
contrasting the kitchens in which my mother was employed with
our kitchen, knew it from the kind of desperate miasma in which
you grow up learning that you have been born to be despised.
Forever.

It remains impossible to describe the Byzantine labyrinth black
people find themselves in when they attempt to save their children. A high school diploma, which had almost no meaning in
my day, nevertheless suggested that you had been to school. But
today it operates merely as a credential for jobs . . . that demand
virtually nothing in the way of education. And the attendance
certificate merely states that you have been through school without having managed to learn anything.

The educational system of this country is, in short, designed to
destroy the black child.

9.   **When I Was a Little Girl**

When I was a little girl
We used to walk together
Tim, my brother who wore glasses,
And I, holding hands
Tightly as we crossed the bridge

And he'd murmur, "you pray now"
—being a clergyman's son—
Until the big white boys
Had kicked on past.
Later we'd climb the bluffs
Overhanging the ghost town
And pick the small white lilies
And fling them like bombers
Over Slocan.

10. When whirlpools appear in the onward run of time and history seems to swirl around a snag, as in the curious matter of the Succession of Karhide, then pictures come in handy: snapshots, which may be taken up and matched to compare the parent to the child, the young king to the old, and which may also be rearranged and shuffled till the years run straight. For despite the tricks played by instantaneous interstellar travel, time (as the Plenipotentiary Axt remarked) does not reverse itself; nor is death mocked.

   Thus, although the best-known picture is that dark image of a young king standing above an old king who lies dead in a corridor lit only by mirror-reflections of a burning city, set it aside a while. Look first at the young king, a nation's pride, as bright and fortunate a soul as ever lived to the age of twenty-two; but when this picture was taken the young king had her back against a wall. She was filthy, she was trembling, and her face was blank and mad, for she had lost that minimal confidence in the world which is called sanity.

11.   **Poetry of Departures**

Sometimes you hear, fifth-hand,
As epitaph:
He chucked up everything
And just cleared off,
And always the voice will sound
Certain you approve
This audacious, purifying,
Elemental move.

And they are right, I think.
We all hate home
And having to be there:
I detest my room,
Its specially-chosen junk,
The good books, the good bed,

And my life, in perfect order:
So to hear it said

He walked out on the whole crowd
Leaves me flushed and stirred,
Like *Then she undid her dress*
Or *Take that you bastard*;
Surely I can, if he did?
And that helps me stay
Sober and industrious.
But I'd go today,

Yes, swagger the nut-strewn roads,
Crouch in the fo'c'sle
Stubbly with goodness, if
It weren't so artificial,
Such a deliberate step backwards
To create an object:
Books; china; a life
Reprehensibly perfect.

SENTENCES AND PARAGRAPHS: THE SIGNIFICANCE OF FORM

The sentence is the basic unit of written communication. Individual words, as we have seen in the chapters on diction, have meanings in and of themselves. But a sentence expresses the *relationships* among the ideas represented by separate words. The words in a sentence thus act on each other and in turn create a whole that is larger than the sum of its parts. The form of a sentence can be as simple as the one-word sentence "Run!" Or it can be stretched to its limits, as it is in the long, race-car-finish sentence of Tom Wolfe's on page 173 or the detail-filled sentence of Vladimir Nabokov's on page 43. The effectiveness of such sentence form depends partly on readers' intuitive knowledge of English sentences, that knowledge which tells them that "Over under too manned outer" is not intelligible English but that "Over the door hung a welcome sign" is. This intuitive knowledge involves *syntax*, the word-order arrangement in sentences. And in written English, a subject and a predicate constitute the basic unit of syntax. Additional information is added to this basic unit through coordination and subordination, as in the following sentence from Bertrand Russell:

Subject	Predicate	
I	was interested in my fellow prisoners;	*(basic unit)*
	who seemed in no way morally inferior to the rest of the population,	*(subordinate clause)*
	though they were on the whole slightly below the usual level of intelligence.	*(subordinate clause)*

The subject (*I*) and the verb phrase *(was interested)* lead readers to expect more information that will tell what Russell is interested in (and so the prepositional phrase *in my fellow prisoners* follows). Readers would also naturally expect that additions to this basic unit (in this case the main clause *I was interested in my fellow prisoners*) would tell something about those fellow prisoners, as is the case with the two succeeding subordinate clauses. (The glossary at the end of the book contains brief definitions of such terms as *subject, predicate, phrase,* and *clause.* But if those and other grammatical terms such as *modification* are puzzling or unfamiliar to you, consult a grammar handbook.)

On similar basic subject-predicate units, all sentences, even the most elaborate and complex, are built. What appears to be a very simple unit leads, through skillful addition, to the infinite variety of English sentences.

SENTENCE LENGTH: THE IMPORTANCE OF VARIETY

Sentence length is one important means through which writers avoid monotony. Of course, sentence length depends partly on the complexity of the idea to be expressed. A simple, unqualified statement requires only a very short sentence; the statement of an idea that is more subtle, or set forth in more detail, requires a longer one. In addition, sentence length is related to the needs and capacities of particular audiences. In ordinary magazine writing (the *Reader's Digest, Cosmopolitan, Time*), the average sentence length ranges between eighteen and twenty-five words. In ordinary newspapers it is lower; in more academic or technical magazines and journals it usually is considerably higher.

Fashions in sentence length change, however. Although very long or very short sentences have never been overwhelmingly predominant in writing, past generations liked long sentences more than we do. When we read Shakespeare or Milton or Scott or Melville, we are struck by their frequent use of what seem to us to be extremely long sentences. Milton's poems contain sentences running to thirty or more lines of verse, and prose writers sometimes produced sentences two or three hundred words long. In the past century, the tendency in writing designed for large general audiences has been toward shorter, easier-to-grasp-at-one-glance sentences. The spread of literacy, the development of inexpensive books, magazines, and newspapers, and the increase in the tempo of living all combined to make the shorter sentence desirable and necessary. Since as a rule the millions who formed a popular market for reading matter had only a few years of schooling, everything they read had to be in simple English, the vocabulary confined to everyday words, and the sentences brief and uncomplicated. In time, this tendency toward simple expression spread from large-circulation magazines and newspapers into many fields of writing, so that today books and periodicals designed for a relatively small, well-educated audience often are written in shorter sentences as well. Finally, the accelerated pace of living has become virtually a symbol of modern civilization. And the long sentence cannot be read and comprehended by those in a hurry. Thus reading matter must be suited to the needs of those who manage to read only in the odd moments of their lives, between business and social duties, household chores, and television programs. All of these factors have contributed to the modern tendency toward shorter sentences.

But such generalizing about sentence length is dangerous for several reasons. The type of writing and the writer's purpose will naturally suggest certain lengths. A children's story, for instance, requires short sentences, whereas a discussion of the complex causes of the Second World War demands longer ones. More importantly, good writers for an adult audience in any field avoid uniform sentence length and instead use sentence variety to keep readers interested. You can test this principle by choosing two or three pages from a piece of writing you admire and marking off each sentence. Note how sentence length varies, and consider how much that variety adds to the overall effect of the passage.

We can illustrate the importance of varying sentence lengths by focusing on two extremes: the very short and the very long sentence. Brief, uncomplicated sentences characterize children's writing, as well as prose written for children:

One early morning, Papa Rabbit was up on the roof repairing the shingles. Pretty soon he heard his small daughter, Bettina, calling him to breakfast.

"I don't have time to eat breakfast this morning," Papa Rabbit called down. "My list of jobs is very long this weekend."

"But today is *FATHER'S DAY,* Papa!" cried Bettina. "Mama has made waffles for breakfast. And Pinky, Joe, and I have presents for you!"

* * * * *

It was just before hunting season. The fire was burning low. A group of Indians and trappers were seated around the glowing coals. A French trapper had just finished a story of French Canada.

"I've told you a story of how our people came in big canoes," he said. "It is your turn, my Indian friends, to tell us a story of your people. I have heard about the terrible dragons that lived long ago. What has become of these dragons? Can you tell us?"

The free use of coordination to join main clauses is also typical of children's writing, as we can see in the following sentence written by a third-grader: "It was by birthday and my mother baked a cake and we all ate the cake and we had ice cream and I got presents and then it wasn't my birthday any more." This sentence is thirty-three words long, but note that it actually contains six subject-and predicate units (or main clauses), all connected with *and* (a coordinating conjunction).

It was my birthday

>   and

my mother baked a cake

>   and

we all ate the cake

>   and

we had ice cream

>   and

I got presents

>   and

then it wasn't my birthday any more.

When we read prose characterized predominantly by simple vocabulary, short sentences, and coordination, we assume that it was probably written by or for children. An adult who habitually writes in this way either has an immature style or is deliberately creating some special effect. In the case of immature style, stringing sentences together with *and* in the manner of a toy train of cars implies that all the items are of equal importance. Such dependence on coordination can obscure the true relationships among items, which in more mature writing are indicated by the careful use of subordination. The effect is of simple all-on-one-level enumeration, as in the third-grader's sentence about a birthday. In the case of special effects, however, the writer deliberately uses the short, simple clauses or fragments of sentences for emphasis or to evoke a certain atmosphere. Certainly this is the case with advertisements, whose copy consists of very short sentences and often of fragments:

> Great news! White Chunked Chicken from Valley Fresh. Finest quality! Tuna was never this good! Here's the starter for those very special meals. The most select white meat you can buy in the big, economical 12½ ounce can. Casseroles! Salads! Chicken and Noodles—the All-American favorite! They all earn special raves with Chunked Chicken. New from Valley Fresh!

From the reader's point of view, the danger in a writer's use of brief, sharp sentences is that it can make the ideas appear much more important and unqualified than they really are. Anyone can write such sentences, but not everyone has something to say that deserves the prominence and emphasis they provide. For many readers, the short sentence carries connotations of wisdom, because of its association with adages or "old sayings": "spare the rod and spoil the child"; "never put off until tomorrow what you can do today"; "a penny saved is a penny earned." So writers who wish to convince their readers often use forms of language which people associate with proverbs and axioms.

> Our nation has always taken the middle road. Its motto is, Nothing to excess. On the one hand, it spurns the advice of the Cassandras that change means disaster. On the other hand, it rejects the proposals of those who would create Utopia overnight. Nothing is more profoundly characteristic of Americans than their reverence for the golden mean. It follows, then, that progressivism is the true American philosophy. Neither conservative nor radical, it believes in gradual, well-considered, above all sound evolution.

In essence, we have here an example of what we will discuss in the next chapter (pages 291–293): the transfer device, or borrowing of prestige. Here the prestige is obtained not so much from the words themselves as from the manner of the sentences—short, dignified, reminiscent of the style of popular philosophers. Such sentences can lull our critical powers and lead us to accept a message unthinkingly.

Nevertheless, the short sentence and the fragment are often used for legitimate special effects. What, for example, would a crime thriller be without the terse, clipped sentences that lead up to a crisis or describe a tense episode? The very absence of elaboration, the concentration on a few bare, simple facts, adds suspense and excitement to the narrative. Again, particularly among writers who have been influenced by Ernest Hemingway, conspicuously brief, laconic sentences made up of short, common words suggest the direct, uncomplicated reactions and thoughts of characters:

> I touched the gun butt inside my coat and walked forward. There was more room between the brush and the end of the white barrier than there had seemed to be from the car. Someone had hacked the brush away and there were car marks in the dirt. Probably kids going down there to neck on warm nights. I went on past the barrier. The road dropped and curved. Below was darkness and a vague far off sea-sound. And the lights of cars on the highway. I went on. The road ended in a shallow bowl entirely surrounded by brush. It was empty. There seemed to be no way into it but the way I had come. I stood there in the silence and listened.

Short sentences and fragments can also be used to call special attention to a thought. In an essay on Nathaniel Hawthorne, D. H. Lawrence uses a fragment in this way: "There you have a nice little bunch of idealists, transcendentalists, Brook farmers, and disintegrated gentry. All going slightly rotten." The connotations of *bunch* and *disintegrated* in the first sentence are made more emphatic by the fragment which ends with *rotten*.

James Joyce is most often associated with long, labyrinthine sentences. But note in the following passage his powerful use of short sentences, fragments, and repetition:

> He began to confess his sins; masses missed, prayers not said, lies.
> —Anything else, my child?
> Sins of anger, envy of others, gluttony, vanity, disobedience.
> —Anything else, my child?
> Sloth.
> —Anything else, my child?
> There was no help: He murmured:
> —I . . . committed sins of impurity, father.
> The priest did not turn his head.
> —With yourself, my child?
> —And . . . with others.
> —With women, my child?
> —Yes, father.
> —Were they married women, my child?
> He did not know. His sins trickled from his lips, one by one, trickled in shameful drops from his soul festering and oozing like a sore, a squalid stream of vice. His last sins oozed forth, sluggish, filthy. There was no more to tell. He bowed his head, overcome.

In this passage, the short fragments mirror the sins that trickle, one by one, from the boy's lips.

Two additional passages will complete our demonstration of how short sentences, coordination, and even fragments can reinforce ideas and add emphasis. The first passage was written 150 years ago by Benjamin Disraeli, a future prime minister of Britain:

> Am I a Whig or a Tory? I forget. As for the Tories, I admire antiquity, particularly a ruin; even the relics of the Temple of Intolerance have a charm. I think I am a Tory. But then the Whigs give such good dinners, and are the more amusing. I think I am a Whig. But then the Tories are so moral, and morality is my forte; I must be a Tory. But the Whigs dress so much better. . . .

Note how the use of coordinate conjunctions and short sentences adds to the sense that Disraeli can't make up his mind. The staccato sentences, like Disraeli, jump back and forth from party to party.

The second passage is a brief paragraph written by a *Time* essayist:

> Of course, much that was once excellent has fallen into disrepair, or worse. The dollar, for example. New York City. American public education. Cars from Detroit. Standards of civility (which may not have been as civil in the past as we imagine). Public safety. But who said that any excellence is permanent?

The use of fragments to enumerate things that are no longer excellent attracts the reader's attention and makes the writer's point more emphatically than embedding them in a long subordinate clause would have done.

We have already noted that the presence of long sentences should not deter one from reading older literature. In modern writing for a general audience, they are relatively infrequent. Very long sentences which occur in an author's manuscript, in fact, are often broken up by the editor, before the manuscript goes to the printer. They do, however, occur in some kinds of specialized writing, such as legal documents or governmental correspondence and records. As we saw in Chapter 2, such long sentences are sometimes necessary and effective. But often, they are not. A satirical commentary on sprawling, formless sentences that run on and on—as well as on the kind of writing we discussed on pages 64–84—is found in the following excerpt from an irreverent government publication:

> The present movement toward simplification of language and directness of statement in government writing and the elimination of jargon and unnecessary wordiness as well as the use of short, direct statements instead of long sentences which are difficult to understand because the reader is apt to get lost before he arrives, if he ever does, at the meaning intended by the writer, is a valuable attempt to achieve economy and intelligibility, for many pamphlets, instruction sheets, ordinary memoranda and assorted missives circulated through the War Department fail of their primary purpose through befogging their contents by use of pseudo-official phraseology which only the initiated can hope to understand and of which even they cannot be certain without reference either to the key works needed for translating them or to their own garbled and confused memories of dealing, usually without much success and always after a long period of time and travail, with similar kinds of wording in similar situations, so, though don't be too hopeful, for someone with unusual gifts and energy in applying them will manage triumphantly to misunderstand you no matter what you say or how you say it, try saying what you have to say as simply and as briefly as you can, and then after you've said it, stop saying it and don't say it any more.

But just as short sentences, fragments, and excessive coordination can be effective in the hands of a skillful writer, so can very long sentences. Note how in the following example Dylan Thomas uses a long sentence to reinforce the central image of a snowball getting bigger and bigger as it rolls downhill:

> All the Christmases roll down the hill towards the Welsh-speaking sea, like a snowball growing whiter and bigger and rounder, like a cold and headlong moon bundling down the sky that was our street; and they stop at the rim of the ice-edged, fish-freezing waves, and I plunge my hands in the snow and bring out whatever I can find; holly or robins or pudding, squabbles and carols and oranges and tin whistles,

and the fire in the front room, and bang go the crackers, and holy, holy, holy, ring the bells, and the glass bells shaking on the tree, and Mother Goose, and Struwelpeter—oh! the baby-burning flames and the clacking scissorman!—Billy Bunter and Black Beauty, Little Women and boys who have three helpings, Alice and Mrs. Potter's badgers, penknives, teddy-bears—named after a Mr. Theodore Bear, their inventor, or father, who died recently in the United States— mouth-organs, tin-soldiers, and blancmange, and Aunt Bessie playing "Pop Goes the Weasel" and "Nuts in May" and "Oranges and Lemons" on the untuned piano in the parlor all through the thimble-hiding musical-chairing blindman's-buffing party at the end of the never-to-be-forgotten day at the end of the unremembered year.

If we return once more to Tom Wolfe's long sentence (page 173), we find that it is technically a "run-on" sentence: it joins main clauses without using conjunctions (*and, but,* and so on) or appropriate punctuation (the semicolon). Just like fragments, however, run-on sentences can be used very effectively by a skilled writer. We will examine more long sentences in our discussion of sentence patterns. For now, we reiterate the main point of our discussion: skillful variation of sentence length adds much to the liveliness of prose.

(Exercises: pages 235–240)

SENTENCE ARRANGEMENT: THE IMPORTANCE OF PATTERNS

The precise order in which elements of a sentence are arranged helps determine how clearly and emphatically a writer's ideas are communicated to readers. Why is this so? What happens in the reader's mind as it meets sentences of various types? What makes a passage "hard" or "easy" to read? What clues to the author's skill and intention can readers infer from the choice of one kind of sentence rather than another?

We still do not have the answers to many questions about how people read. We do know that fluent readers read not word by word but in "meaning chunks"—tight little clusters of ideas represented by a short sequence of words—and that difficulties arise when ambiguous wording or punctuation mismatches the ideas into clusters that do not convey the intended meaning. This sentence, taken from a newspaper advertisement, illustrates the point:

OUR SPECIAL GUARANTEE HELPS CAR BUYERS WITH FLAWS

Although the writer no doubt intended readers to associate "our special guarantee helps" with "flaws," many readers would instead link "car buyers" with "flaws" and hence have to reread the sentence to make sense of it.

We also know that native speakers of English expect sentences to contain both a subject and a predicate, and often a complement—in that order. In fact, the sequence of subject-verb-object is so common that our minds early adopt it as a habit. Almost by instinct, when we read or listen, we expect the same order. It is related to a basic principle of readable prose: subjects and verbs, and verbs and their objects, are easier to read if they are kept fairly close together.

> The movie, in spite of its elegant special effects, unique musical score, and evidence of masterful directing, lost, during the first four weeks, its chance to capture the imagination of viewers.

We can understand this sentence, of course, but note how much easier to read the revised version is:

> In spite of its elegant special effects, unique musical score, and evidence of masterful directing, the movie lost its chance to capture the imagination of viewers during the first four weeks.

Finally, we know that readers tend to remember the endings and beginnings of sentences much more easily than they do the middle parts. Sentence patterns that put the syntactic focus on the endings and the beginnings fall into two different but equally effective types: the periodic and the cumulative.

The Periodic Sentence

The end of a sentence, which is usually the easiest part for readers to remember and which usually has the greatest impact, is the syntactic focus of *periodic sentences*. Such sentences delay or postpone completing the main clause until the very end. This kind of sentence, like the one you are reading right now, which forces you to hold the subject in mind until the very end, keeps syntactic tension high. In the hands of skilled writers, periodic sentences can (1) keep readers alert for what is to come and (2) make the main idea, when it finally does appear, all the more impressive. As a student of prose techniques puts it, "The virtue of a periodic sentence is that it keeps a number of related matters suspended in midair while we gradually master the relations, and then deposits the whole safely on the ground after the relations have been apprehended and the suspense gratified."

Remember what we have said about the importance of sentence endings as you compare these two sentences:

> The dancer somehow suggested a Chinese princess, with her jet-black hair, her singularly high cheekbones, her slanting eyes, her hands with their long, tapered fingers.
>
> With her jet-black hair, her singularly high cheekbones, her slanting eyes, her hands with their long, tapered fingers, the dancer somehow suggested a Chinese princess.

Nothing is wrong with the first sentence: it covers all the details, systematically and clearly. But if the writer wishes above all to impress readers with the fact that the dancer resembled a Chinese princess, that clause would have been better kept for last. In the first sentence, the image of the Chinese princess is immediately pushed into the background by the details of the dancer's appearance. The item on which the mind dwells, when it completes the sentence, is the fact that she had long, tapered fingers—which may not be the most significant of all the details. This emphasis shifts in the second version, which presents a series of details that merge and are effectively summarized by the core of the sentence—the subject, verb, and object.

The following sentences all follow basically the same scheme:

> Even as the eagle rested, looking out across the valley floor, a war was being waged within the tree itself.

> When Enrico Fermi, an Italian immigrant to the United States, and his colleagues triggered the world's first atomic pile in Chicago in 1941, science opened Pandora's box.

> Essentially, in sorting out the relationship between men and machines, what one wants to know is the answer to one question: can computers think?

> Although in many ways Trevino's achievements are not sufficiently appreciated, this June, at forty, thirteen years after he came out of nowhere and announced himself so memorably at Baltusrol, he returned to that course as a man who has gained for himself a secure position in golf history.

In these sentences the main clause is completely delayed. A second common means of maintaining interest throughout the sentence is to begin the main clause and then postpone its completion by inserting modifiers or other interrupting material.

> The supplicant, far from rebelling or even disagreeing with the forces that have caused him to suffer, readily backs them up and finally tries to become an honorary oppressor himself.

> A few minutes after noon the police, who had been awaiting the arrival of reinforcements from several other precincts, rushed into the barricaded house.

> The nations of the world, because another world war would be unthinkable annihilation, have no alternative but to find some means of coexisting.

This particular adaptation of the periodic sentence is often punctuated with dashes, and often the dashes enclose an entire sentence rather than a clause or phrase: "Maria, as one who grew up in haunting poverty—her grandmother's two-room shack had no running water or electricity—knows what job security and fair wages can mean to people." An informal survey we made of writing in several well-written magazines turned up a larger number of such sentences than of formal periodic sentences. Perhaps writers use the "interrupted" sentence to suggest the immediacy of speech; after all, we often interrupt our sentences while speaking to insert full-sentence thoughts. The use of dashes also suggests informality, another feature of speech. Here are some additional examples of "interrupted" sentences:

> Over the next year, up to 78 percent of the students enrolled in colleges—or roughly a quarter of the student population at any given time—may suffer symptoms of depression.
>
> Jim Sanders and his family—there were his wife, June, two boys, one girl, and a runt of a dog—came to work in the factory.
>
> Modern houseboats being what they are—sinfully luxurious is what they are—it ought to be enough to run them lazily around back rivers and bayous.

Such sentences may defeat their purpose if the interruption between subject and predicate is too long. The intervening matter may completely erase the subject of the main clause from one's mind: "A fresh approach to the problem, free of partisan bias, motivated by a realization of the disaster that would result from neglect or unintelligent handling of the complex factors involved, utilizing the information amassed by the experts who have been studying the question for many months—" (at this point the reader suddenly realizes that the subject of the sentence is lost and must go back to the beginning) "is needed." And the end, when it comes, is so brief and so flat that the reader may feel cheated by such a small reward.

The Cumulative Sentence

Although sentences using various degrees of periodicity can be very effective in challenging and interesting readers, they do not constitute the most frequently used pattern in modern English. Rather, the *cumulative sentence*, which adds details after the main clause, is the more dominant:

> The main clause, which may or may not have a sentence modifier before it, advances the discussion; but the additions move backwards, as in this clause, to modify the statement of the main clause or more often to explicate it or exemplify it, so that the sentence has a flowing and ebbing movement, advancing to a new position and then pausing to consolidate it, leaping and lingering as the popular ballad does.

This example shows how the cumulative sentence differs from the periodic: the main clause appears near the beginning rather than partially or wholly at the end. If you look back to the Joyce passage quoted on page 204, you will see that the sentence beginning "His sins trickled" is a cumulative one. In the following examples, note how the main clause comes first and then "accumulates" details.

> I watched this human ocean, of which I was an unwilling droplet, rolling past, its individual faces like whitecaps passing on a night of a storm, fixed, merciless, indifferent; man in the mass marching like the machinery of which he is already a replaceable part, toward desks, computers, missiles, and machines, marching like waves toward his own death with a conscious ruthlessness no watery shore could ever duplicate.

*   *   *   *   *

> He could sail for hours, searching the blanched grasses below him with his telescopic eyes, gaining height against the wind, descending in mile-long, gently declining swoops when he curved and rode back, never beating a wing.

Because they present the main clause at or near the beginning of the sentence, cumulative sentences don't require readers to hold the subject in suspense, waiting for the main verb or main clause at the end of the sentence. In one sense, then, cumulative sentences may be easier to read than periodic sentences. As our examples indicate, however, they are not simple, and as in the sentence describing the bird in flight, they often position the most important piece of information at the end. Like all sentence patterns, however, the cumulative sentence can be used either effectively or ineffectively: "The cumulative sentence in unskilled hands is unsteady, allowing a writer to ramble on, adding modifier after modifier, until the reader is almost overwhelmed, because the writer's central idea is lost." Here is another such ineffective sentence: "Professor Baker said that 'we can learn a great deal from primitive cultures,' although this was not by any means the only point that was made in the lecture which she gave yesterday at noon, in Hughes Hall." Here the idea the sentence was intended to convey is concentrated in the first clause. The succeeding subordinate clauses, explicating or explaining it in some important way, merely distract attention from it. And that can be the effect of many cumulative sentences, particularly when used by the inexpert writer.

Using exclusively periodic or cumulative sentences, of course, would be desperately monotonous. And so the best writers mingle sentences—short and long, periodic and cumulative—though never forgetting that the most important ideas naturally deserve the most prominent positions.

The placement of important ideas calls our attention to the matter of *climax*. The principle underlying most climactic sentences is that of suspense; it depends on the fact that the reader's attention is held by the progression of ideas, the implicit questions being (1) what will prove to be most important in the writer's

estimation? and (2) when will the idea be complete? Herman Melville's long periodic sentence on the whiteness of Moby-Dick provides a good illustration of the
principle of climax:

> Though in many natural objects, whiteness refiningly enhances
> beauty, as in imparting some special virtue of its own, as in marbles,
> japonicas, and pearls; and though various nations have in some way
> recognized a certain royal pre-eminence in this hue; even the bar-
> baric, grand old kings of Pegu placing the title "Lord of the White
> Elephants" above all their other magniloquent ascriptions of domin-
> ion; and the modern kings of Siam unfurling the same snow-white
> quadruped in the royal standard; and the Hanoverian flag bearing the
> one figure of a snow-white charger; and the great Austrian Empire,
> Caesarian heir to overlording Rome, having for the imperial color the
> same imperial hue; and though this pre-eminence in it applies to the
> human race itself, giving the white man ideal mastership over every
> dusky tribe; and though, besides all this, whiteness has been made
> significant of gladness, for among the Romans a white stone marked a
> joyful day; and though in other mortal sympathies and symbolizings,
> this same hue is made the emblem of many touching, noble things—
> the innocence of brides, the benignity of age; though among the Red
> Men of America the giving of the white belt of wampum was the deep-
> est pledge of honor; though in many climes, whiteness typifies the maj-
> esty of Justice in the ermine of the Judge, and contributes to the daily
> state of kings and queens drawn by milk-white steeds; though even in
> the higher mysteries of the most august religions it has been made the
> symbol of the divine spotlessness and power; by the Persian fire wor-
> shippers, the white forked flame being held the holiest on the altar;
> and in the Greek mythologies, Great Jove himself being made incar-
> nate in the snow-white bull; and though to the noble Iroquois, the mid-
> winter sacrifice of the sacred White Dog was by far the holiest festival
> of their theology, that spotless, faithful creature being held the purest
> envoy they could send to the Great Spirit with the annual tidings of
> their own fidelity; and though directly from the Latin word for white,
> all Christian priests derive the name of one part of their sacred ves-
> ture, the alb or tunic, worn beneath the cassock; and though among
> the holy pomps of the Romish faith, white is specially employed in the
> celebration of the Passion of our Lord; though in the Vision of St. John,
> white robes are given to the redeemed, and the four-and-twenty el-
> ders stand clothed in white before the great white throne; and the
> Holy One that sitteth there white like wool; yet for all these accumu-
> lated associations, with whatever is sweet, and honorable, and sub-
> lime, there yet lurks an elusive something in the innermost of this hue,
> which strikes more of panic to the soul than that redness which
> affrights in blood.

This is indeed a long and difficult sentence, and Melville uses it to overwhelm the reader with curiosity: twelve long subordinate clauses opening with *though* lead readers to expect a contrast. And when that contrast finally comes, in the climax of the sentence, it is more vivid for all its associations with the foregoing clauses: in spite of the associations of the color white with goodness and purity, the idea of whiteness "strikes more panic to the soul" than even the color of blood.

Cumulative sentences can also build to strong climaxes, as in Charles Lamb's sentence describing a fearsome schoolmaster:

> Nothing was more common than to see him make a head-long entry into the schoolroom, from his inner recess, or library, and with turbulent eye, singling out a lad, roar out, "Od's my life, Sirrah," (his favorite adjuration) "I have a great mind to whip you,"—then, with as sudden a retracting impulse, fling back into his lair—and, after a cooling lapse of some minutes (during which all but the culprit had totally forgotten the context) drive headlong out again, piecing out his imperfect sense, as if it had been some Devil's litany, with the expletory yell—"and I WILL, too."

Lamb's sentence begins with a main clause, but follows it with a number of additional clauses and phrases which build on the base, leading up to the final "And I WILL, too." Robertson Davies uses climax in this cumulative sentence: "Then the cheers were loud, and the children hopped and scampered round the foot of the flagpole, shouting, 'Hang the Kaiser!' with growing hysteria, some of them much too small to know what hanging was, or what a Kaiser might be, but I cannot call them innocent, for they were being as vicious as their age and experience allowed."

The principle of climax for surprise may also be used for humor, sometimes humor with a barb. Thus Lytton Strachey writes, "Johnson's esthetic judgments are almost invariably subtle, or solid, or bold; they have always some good quality to recommend them—except one: they are never right." In this sentence, Strachey deliberately leads the reader to believe that he thinks highly of Dr. Johnson's criticism; then, in the last six words, he negates all he said before. Strachey's point is that subtle, solid, and bold views are irrelevant when the views are always *wrong*. (Whether Strachey himself is correct in thus condemning Johnson is another question.) In the same way, Lord Byron often both shocks and delights his readers, and implies his own cynical view of human pretensions, in the unexpected climaxes of many stanzas of his poems. In his comic masterpiece, *Don Juan*, he describes the courtship of the chaste Julia by Don Juan:

> And Julia's voice was lost, except in sighs,
>   Until too late for useful conversation;
> The tears were gushing from her gentle eyes,

> I wish, indeed, they had not had occasion;
> But who, alas! can love, and then be wise?
> Not that remorse did not oppose temptation;
> A little still she strove, and much repented,
> And whispering "I will ne'er consent"—consented.

If the general context of a passage is serious, readers naturally expect serious ideas. Hence, any sudden shift to the trivial, incongruous, or ridiculous, which is called *anticlimax*, is bound to arrest attention, like jarring discord after sweet harmony. Anticlimax occurs also when the excitement is not matched by the result, or the anticipation by the event, as when a five-inch firecracker sputters out with a damp *pffffft*. "There he goes!" shouts the radio announcer at the football game. "One tackler bowled over—he evades another, and another—he gets fine interference—he's LOOSE! Look at him run!" And then, after the tumult has died down and the official has spotted the ball, it turns out that the ball carrier, having done most of his running laterally, has gained only two yards, net.

Sometimes a writer or speaker creates this effect without intending to do so, as when an evangelist ends an impassioned sermon with these words: "And as our prayers ascend to heaven and God blesses us, we find he is well pleased with our good works, our acts of kindness and love—and with the money you folks are sending in week by week to keep this program of true gospel witness on the air, so keep that money rolling in! Don't forget the post office box number. . . ." Any unintentional anticlimax of this sort suggests that the writer or speaker lacks a sure sense of relative values. The unconscious implication here is that the preacher thinks money is of greater importance in the eyes of the Lord than acts of kindness and love. On the other hand, the deliberate use of anticlimax may be a sign of wit, of a mind which instinctively sees the ridiculous side by side with the serious. The eighteenth-century poet Alexander Pope often used anticlimax to create such dramatic effects. In his mock-epic poem "The Rape of the Lock," Pope emphasizes the triviality of much of society by describing the unspeakable, major tragedy of his young heroine's life: a lover cuts off one ringlet of her hair! The following passage occurs in *Peri Bathos*, Pope's witty satire on "The Art of Sinking in Poetry." Here he is heaping "praise" on the actors and directors of theaters of his day:

> Here, therefore, . . . let me return our sincere and humble Thanks to the Most August Mr. *Barton Booth*, the Most Serene Mr. *Robert Wilks*, and the Most Undaunted Mr. *Colley Cibber*; of whom, let it be known when the People of this Age shall be Ancestors, and to all the Succession of our Successors, that to this present day they continue to Outdo even their own Out-doings: And when the inevitable Hand of Sweeping Time shall have brushed off all the Works of To-day, may this Testimony of a Co-temporary Critick to their fame, be extended as far as—*To-morrow!*

Lord Byron was as adept at using anticlimax as climax in his poetry. In *Don Juan*, the hero is forced to leave Spain and Julia, his love. As the ship pulls away, Juan reads and rereads Julia's last letter, and declares his unceasing love:

> And oh! if e'er I should forget, I swear—
>   But that's impossible, and cannot be—
> Sooner shall this blue ocean melt to air,
>   Sooner shall earth resolve itself to sea,
> Than I resign thine image, oh, my fair!
>   Or think of anything, excepting thee;
> A mind diseased no remedy can physic—
> (Here the ship gave a lurch, and he grew seasick.)

Here Byron sustains a high serious note which is effectively undercut by the stroke of humor at the end.

We have illustrated anticlimax in passages involving fairly long sentences, because often writers need to build up to the fall, as Pope does when he leads readers to expect that his elaborate praise will last forever, only to find that he intends it to extend only until tomorrow. Anticlimax can occur, however, in even a single short sentence, as in this one from a student paper: "He was a tall, dark, and handsome creep."

Special Patterns of Arrangement

We noted previously (page 207) that readers generally expect sentences to follow the order of subject-verb-object. Writers can play on this expectation, producing long periodic sentences that delay completion of the familiar pattern or cumulative sentences that build on its framework. Another pattern writers use to jolt readers accustomed to the subject-verb-object order is *inversion:* "The car sped on. [subject-verb] Jack's foot pressed the accelerator almost to the floor. [subject-verb-object] Then suddenly the foot lifted and jammed down the brake pedal instead. [subject-verb-object] Looming ahead, its black mass lying inert directly across the concrete highway, was an overturned truck." (Surprise! Modifiers, verb, *then* subject.) Here the established pattern suddenly is broken. The author has reversed his sentence order and, in so doing, created a dramatic effect to which we, as readers, respond.

Inversion, then, is most often used to add emphasis, as in the following sentences:

> Down he plunged, to the very base of the cliff.

> The emotional isolation, the preoccupation with God and themselves, the struggles for freedom, which seem to have possessed many of my friends at the same age, I know almost nothing of.

> In the dim interior of the hut crouched a withered old woman.

Good looking he was not; wealthy he was not; but brilliant—he was.

Into this gray lake plopped the thought, I know that man, don't I?

Although it can be effective in small doses, inversion can easily lose its power if overused. A well-known parody of the style used by writers for *Time* magazine in the 1930s and 1940s begins, "Backward run the sentences, until reels the mind." In addition, inverted word order or sentence patterns can make a writer sound affected or pompous. Max Shulman plays on this effect when he has the speaker in "Love Is a Fallacy" introduce himself by saying, "Cool was I, and logical. Keen, calculating, perspicacious, acute, and astute—I was all of these." Inversion, however, depends for its effectiveness on being used infrequently.

Ellipsis, or deletion, gives writers another means of surprising readers by leaving out elements normally expected in a sentence, as in "Gotta go. No time to talk. Later." Writers can use such extreme forms of ellipsis to give an impression of abrupt movement or of hurriedness. Such is the case in Charles Dickens's *Pickwick Papers*, in which one character, Alfred Jingle, is known by his elliptical speech patterns:

Ah! you should keep dogs—fine animals—sagacious creatures—dog of my own once—Pointer—surprising instinct—out shooting one day—entering inclosure—whistled—dog stopped—whistled again—Ponto—no go: stock still—called him—Ponto, Ponto—wouldn't move—dog transfixed—staring at a board—looked up, saw an inscription—"Gamekeeper has orders to shoot all dogs found in this inclosure"—wouldn't pass it—wonderful dog—valuable dog that—very.

But we also find ellipsis used for emphasis in everyday writing. Here is a letter sent by one irate customer—to a computer:

To: Deep Well Oil Company
From: Credit Card #4960-110338

For God's sake. In February—you were wrong. March—wrong. April—wrong. May—wrong. Still wrong. It's $35. Not $135. Have you blown a fuse? Pleaseseepreviouscorrespondence. Five service station tickets: $7.50 + $8.00 + $4.25 + $10.25 + $5.00 = $35.00. Repeat. $35.00. Repeat. $35.00. I am praying for you and your circuits, but not a penny more business with Deep Well until you correct error.

Like the other sentence patterns we have examined, effective use of ellipsis depends on readers' intuitive sense of English syntax and on their ability to fill in the gaps. Used extensively, ellipsis and extreme forms of deletion can quickly become tiresome.

Still another important pattern in English is *parallelism*, which depends on readers' sense of rhythm for its effectiveness. At its simplest, parallelism uses words or phrases of the same grammatical type in a series, as in

I liked—loved—adored her every move.

Politics, religion, and sex: three subjects guaranteed to cause controversy.

He ran through the brush, across the beach, and into the sea.

We have already seen an example of parallelism in Melville's long periodic sentence (page 211). In that sentence, the series of parallel subordinate clauses helps build up to the climax. Here is another example of a long periodic sentence built on parallel clauses, this time from Martin Luther King's "Letter from a Birmingham Jail":

Perhaps it is easy for those who have never felt the stinging darts of segregation to say, "Wait." But when you have seen vicious mobs lynch your mothers and fathers at will and drown your sisters and brothers at whim; when you have seen hate-filled policemen curse, kick, and even kill your black brothers and sisters; when you see the vast majority of your twenty million Negro brothers smothering in an airtight cage of poverty in the midst of an affluent society; . . . when you have to concoct an answer for a five-year-old son who is asking: "Daddy, why do white people treat colored people so mean?"; when you take a cross-country drive and find it necessary to sleep night after night in the uncomfortable corners of your automobile because no motel will accept you; when you are humiliated day in and day out by nagging signs reading "white" and "colored"; when your first name becomes "nigger," your middle name becomes "boy" (however old you are) and your last name becomes "John," and your wife and mother are never given the respected title "Mrs."; when you are harried by day and haunted by night by the fact that you are a Negro, living constantly at tiptoe stance, never quite knowing what to expect next, and are plagued with inner fears and outer resentments; when you are forever fighting a degenerating sense of "nobodiness"—then you will understand why we find it difficult to wait.

Both King's and Melville's sentences blend repetition with parallelism and periodic structure to create strong emphasis. Repetition is, in fact, often effectively linked with parallelism and antithesis (next page).

One clear and simple form of parallelism is the balanced sentence, in which the structure of one half of the sentence mirrors the other:

Those who kill people are murderers; those who kill animals are sportsmen.

Mankind must put an end to war—or war will put an end to mankind.

Not only are they just, they are rational.

Because of its powerful rhythmic qualities, the parallel structure (including the balanced sentence) gives a sense of neatness, of orderliness. Therefore, a writer who sets up a parallel or balanced structure, causing readers to expect its continuation, and then breaks the pattern, can surprise them and stir their interest. Such is the case in a sentence from John Steinbeck's "Sweet Thursday," which gains emphasis by breaking the expected parallel pattern: "Here was himself, young, good-looking, snappy dresser, and making dough."

A forest of identical trees growing in perfectly symmetrical rows might satisfy a rage for order, but on the whole it would make a monotonous landscape. Just so with an unrelieved series of parallel structures. A writer for the *New Yorker* got a warning against the overuse of parallelism and balance when his editor wrote beside one perfectly balanced sentence: "If you tapped this sentence at one end, it would never stop rocking."

Antithesis is the sentence pattern that embodies the concept of contrast, of difference, of negation:

To learn what one can know is important, but to learn what one cannot know is essential to one's well-being.

It is a sin to believe evil of others, but it is not a mistake.

We observe today not a victory of party but a celebration of freedom—symbolizing an end as well as a beginning—signifying renewal as well as change.

The congregation didn't think much of the new preacher, and what the new preacher thought of the congregation she didn't wish to say.

[My classmate] Hicks had no imagination; I had a double supply. . . . No vision could start a rapture in him and he was constipated as to language anyway; but if I saw a vision I emptied the dictionary on it and lost the remnant of my mind into the bargain.

As these examples indicate, the use of antithesis can add emphasis to a sentence. This device was used very effectively in John F. Kennedy's 1961 inaugural address, from which the third preceding example is taken. Antithesis, in fact, is one of the major patterns in this famous speech, and it is partly the reason why it is so quotable.

All the patterns we have examined can add emphasis to prose when shrewdly employed in the right situation. And all depend on the reader's expectations regarding the basic rhythm and structures of English sentences. But overusing any one of these patterns leads to ineffective prose, and so the best writers carefully vary sentence patterns, just as they do sentence length.

(Exercises: pages 240–248)

SENTENCE RHYTHM: THE IMPORTANCE OF SOUND

We have already seen rhythm operating in parallel and balanced structures as well as in periodic and cumulative sentences. The human voice (and the mind when reading silently) puts most stress on those sentence elements whose meaning is most important. Nouns and verbs receive the most emphasis, modifying words (adjectives and adverbs) less, connectives (prepositions and conjunctions) least. However, if a modifier or a connective word plays an unusually vital role in the idea that the sentence contains, it receives more stress than it ordinarily would: "I was going to order the *small* pizza, but my stomach insisted on the *jumbo* one instead." "I'm going to take advantage of this sale and buy the blue suit *and* the gray suit."

Prose, as well as poetry, has all degrees of stress. Any attempt to mark off each syllable as being unstressed, lightly stressed, or heavily stressed, is at best an approximation. Reading a passage normally, the voice rises and falls, emphasizes and modulates, in ways far too subtle for precise analysis or notation. Yet we often speak of "bad rhythm" and "good rhythm" in sentences, and we respond automatically to the musical qualities of rhythmic prose. If we cannot measure such rhythm, except by the roughest of standards, how can we distinguish between the bad and the good?

With all their knowledge, music critics still must depend on a practiced ear for a final verdict on the quality of the music they hear. In exactly the same way, readers who would judge the rhythm of a passage or writers who want to polish the rhythm of their own prose must first teach their ears to be sensitive. Elaborate treatises on English prose rhythm have been written, but they offer little quick, practical advice. All that is possible in a short space is to make several very broad observations on an extremely complex subject.

In the first place, unless it is written by an expert craftsman, an overlong sentence is apt to be unrhythmical. Compare, in this respect, the sentences on pages 205 and 206; the latter has a graceful yet dignified rhythm, whereas the former has little rhythm at all. If you have studied a musical instrument, you know that the heart of rhythm lies in (1) accent — the grouping of notes (words) into pleasing accentual patterns, and (2) phrasing — the clever distribution of rests (punctuation: commas, semicolons, colons, dashes, periods). The most important of these rests are the long ones, which most often correspond to the breaks between sentences. During these tiny intermissions, readers have a chance to pause and let what they have just read sink in. If those all-important full stops are long delayed, the reader may become tired and lose the continuity of the thought. In addition, greater or lesser pauses, provided by punctuation and stress, must be inserted to set off the units within a sentence. Such a vague phrase as "greater or lesser pauses" is not very helpful, because we have not defined our terms. But degree varies from sentence to sentence, idea to idea, writer to writer. Everyone probably would agree, however, that most long sentences written without any full stops (provided by colons, semicolons, or dashes) are unrhythmical. On the other hand, a sentence excessively interrupted by punctuation is no better. We can suggest what we mean by two examples:

The period of reappraisal of Western policy inaugurated by the repudiation of the European Defense Community in the French Assembly presents one of those rare moments in which private persons can enter into the discussion of delicate matters of high policy without fear of bringing into question existing decisions or of embarrassing their own Government in its undertakings.

Sentences just as long as this, and as innocent of punctuation, appear all around us in everyday life. Yet the eye cannot comprehend in a single sweep, nor the voice utter in a single breath, a sentence as unbroken as this.

On the other hand:

Society, through every fibre, was rent asunder: all things, it was then becoming visible, but could not then be understood, were moving onwards, with an impulse received ages before, yet now first with a decisive rapidity, towards that great chaotic gulf, where, whether in the shape of French Revolutions, Reform Bills, or what shape soever, bloody or bloodless, the descent and engulfment assume, we now see them weltering and boiling.

In this sentence there are too many pauses. The fault lies primarily in the author's insistence on qualifying phrases and clauses. Putting aside the first independent clause (down to the colon), we see that the remainder of the basic sentence is "all things . . . were moving onwards . . . towards the great chaotic gulf, where . . . we now see them weltering and boiling." All the rest is a sort of spasmodic parenthesis. Not only is the mind led, with justifiable reluctance, through a tortuous labyrinth of subordinate ideas; the sentence has too many jerky stops and starts. Most importantly, those stops and starts are not called for by the subject matter and hence are ineffective.

In the second place, prose lacks something which verse possesses: namely, meter. Underlying most verse is a regular rhythmic pattern, made up of a constantly recurring combination of accented and unaccented syllables. Prose, however, possesses no such pattern. Indeed, one of the earmarks of ineffective prose is a tendency to suggest the regular rhythms of verse. English prose rhythms have their own charms, but absolute regularity is not one of them. You will recall that one of our counts against unnecessarily difficult language in Chapter 2 was that a long string of prepositional phrases, for example, gives an unpleasant recurring beat to the same sentence. "The description of the construction of the portion of the road between Mifford Center and the county line is incorrect in nature, inasmuch as the road is actually rough in character." Read that aloud (which you should do whenever testing for rhythmic quality) and you will understand what we mean. An extreme example of an unpleasant, overregular beat is this sentence: "And so no force, however great, can strain a cord, however fine, into a horizontal line that shall be absolutely straight." It is true that many gifted writers produce prose which comes close to the borderline of verse. Some passages from John Steinbeck's *The Grapes of Wrath*, for instance, have been put directly into poetic form. But as a general rule, writers are well advised to avoid the use of regular poetic rhythm patterns in prose.

A third general characteristic of good sentence rhythm only superficially conflicts with the second. Although using poetic meter in prose is usually undesirable, some regular patterns (such as parallelism, examined previously) can often prove pleasing to the ear. A sentence that sounds like a record with a deep scratch across its surface (click, click, click, click) is disagreeable. But one whose larger elements match, like the three arches of a cathedral, gives pleasure. The matching of phrase against phrase, clause against clause, as we noted in our discussion of parallelism and antithesis, lends an unmistakable rhythmic eloquence to prose. That, indeed, is one of the principal beauties of the King James Bible:

> Though I speak with the tongues of men and of angels, and have not charity, I am become as sounding brass, or a tinkling cymbal.
> And though I have the gift of prophecy and understand all mysteries and knowledge . . . and have not charity, I am nothing. . . .
> Charity suffereth long, and is kind; charity envieth not; charity vaunteth not itself, is not puffed up. . . .
> Rejoiceth not in iniquity, but rejoiceth in the truth;
> Beareth all things, believeth all things, hopeth all things, endureth all things.
> Charity never faileth.
>
> [I Corinthians, 13:1–8]

In this passage, expert use of parallelism, repetition, and both coordinate and subordinate clauses creates a moving and dignified rhythm.

Two other devices that help build sentence rhythm are alliteration and onomatopoeia. *Alliteration** refers to the repetition of sounds in syllables or words placed closely together. Dylan Thomas's stories, essays, and poems are full of skillfully used alliteration, which helps readers to hear the rhythm of the passage:

> I was staying at the time with my uncle and his wife. Although she was my aunt, I never thought of her as anything but the wife of my uncle, partly because he was so big and trumpeting and red-hairy and used to fill every inch of the hot little house like an old buffalo squeezed into an airing cupboard, and partly because she was so small and silk and quick and made no noise at all as she whisked about on padded paws, dusting the china dogs, feeding the buffalo, setting the mousetraps that never caught her; and once she sneaked out of the room, to squeak in a nook or nibble in the hayloft, you forgot she had ever been there.

---

*Alliteration technically refers to repetition of consonant sounds (as in the cow kicked the bucket), while *assonance* refers to repetition of vowel sounds (as in how now brown cow). We will use the term *alliteration* to cover both consonant and vowel repetition.

Here the subtle use of alliteration adds to the rhythm of the sentences and helps create the image of the aunt. What is that image, and what sounds does Thomas repeat in building it?

In Chapter 1, we presented some examples of *onomatopoeia* (page 7), though we did not use that term to describe them. The following sentences, which describe a basketball game, use onomatopoeia — words whose sounds suggest their sense — to good effect:

> The young men, leaping, extend their arms and race through puddles of amber light, their bodies glistening. In a lull, though it rarely occurs, you can hear the squeal of tennis shoes against the floor. Then the yelling begins again, and then continues; fathers, mothers, neighbors joining in to form a single pulsing ululation. . . . Only the ball moves serenely through this dazzling din.

This passage has a number of notable rhythmic elements, including the pattern of sentence 1 which itself "leaps" and "extends"; the use of images which combine sense impressions (as in *puddles of amber light*); and alliteration (note particularly the *r* and *l* sounds). In addition, the effects of onomatopoeia created by *squeak, ululation,* and *din* add to the rhythmic movement of the passage. Note too that the connotations of the onomatopoeic words are as important as their sounds in building the effect of the whole passage, so that sound and sense converge. Read the following sentences aloud, noting their use of onomatopoeia:

> Underfoot crunches the oldest of city dirt, last crystallization of all the city had denied, threatened, lied to its children.
>
> The old men snored and wheezed in many rhythms, like a sinister chorus.
>
> The strident hisses of the kettle announced tea time at last.
>
> "When I grow up there ain't nothin' ever gonna hurt me. Not ever," Stevie used to tell me, doubling up his grimy fists until his knuckles whitened, and snarling like a small, trapped animal, a fox or a feral cat maybe, as he squeezed back the tears at the corners of the eyes that looked ridiculously huge in his peaked ten-year-old's face.

Of course, we don't often have time to read aloud, or even to read silently with special attention to harmony and sound. But when we can read this way, we are treated to one of the true beauties of prose. Read the following excerpts aloud, and then note the way that varying sentence length, sentence patterns, and the use of rhythmic effects such as alliteration, onomatopoeia, and repetition help create the tone. The narrator of the first excerpt is working at a cash register in a supermarket when three girls wearing "nothing but bathing suits" come in:

> She must have felt in the corner of her eye me and over my shoulder Stokesie in the second slot watching, but she didn't tip. Not this queen.

She kept her eyes moving across the racks, and stopped, and turned so slow it made my stomach rub the inside of my apron, and buzzed to the other two, who kind of huddled against her for relief, and then they all three of them went up the cat-and-dog-food-breakfast-cereal-macaroni-rice-raisins-seasonings-spreads-spaghetti-soft-drinks-crackers-and-cookies aisle. From the third slot I look straight up this aisle to the meat counter, and I watched them all the way. The fat one with the tan sort of fumbled with the cookies, but on second thought she put the package back. The sheep pushing their carts down the aisle—the girls were walking against the usual traffic (not that we have one-way signs or anything)—were pretty hilarious. You could see them, when Queenie's white shoulders dawned on them, kind of jerk, or hop, or hiccup, but their eyes snapped back to their own baskets and on they pushed. I bet you could set off dynamite in an A&P and the people would by and large keep reaching and checking oatmeal off their lists and muttering "Let me see, there was a third thing, began with A, asparagus, no, ah, yes, applesauce!" or whatever it is they do mutter. But there was no doubt, this jiggled them.

*　*　*　*　*

It was on the afternoon of the day of Christmas Eve, and I was in Mrs. Prothero's garden, waiting for cats, with her son Jim. It was snowing. It was always snowing at Christmas. December, in my memory, is white as Lapland, though there were no reindeers. But there were cats. Patient, cold and callous, our hands wrapped in socks, we waited to snowball the cats. Sleek and long as jaguars and horrible-whiskered, spitting and snarling, they would slink and slide over the white garden walls, and the lynx-eyed hunters, Jim and I, fur-capped and moccasined trappers from Hudson Bay, off Mumbles Road, would hurl our deadly snowballs at the green of their eyes. The wise cats never appeared.

Awareness of rhythm and arrangement inevitably increases the reader's pleasure, heightening an emotional experience whose other principal element is the connotative power of the words themselves. In fact, readers come to associate certain rhythmic effects with certain intentions on the part of writer or speaker. Rhythm, in other words, has its own connotative value. And just as word connotations may affect emotion rather than reason, so too may the connotations of rhythm. Advertisers and headline writers in particular make constant use of alliteration and other rhythmic devices, as slogans such as "No-Nonsense Diet," "New Nice 'n Easy by Clairol," "Wet N' Wild," and "Go for the Gusto"—or an irritating headline such as BIG BARK BEETLE BATTLE BEHIND SCHEDULE—suggest. Consider the rhythmic qualities of the following sentences:

If, perchance, you have seen a copy of the first issue of *Gentry* in the home of a discerning friend, then you know why we say that only those of an unusual turn of mind can fully appreciate this quarterly magazine. *Gentry* is edited for the rather rare individual whose mind is ever open to new ideas, new forms; for the individual who respects the best of the thinking and art which has endured over the years; who feels that there is much much more to living than merely making a living; and therefore works constantly to gain more from his hourly association with people, objects, and ideas.

Among your friends there may be one, possibly three or four such people; and since you wish to present them with a Christmas gift of an especial nature, which is attuned to their high level of thinking, we suggest a year's subscription to *Gentry* (4 issues) as a suitable gift. Here, for example, is a brief description of just a few out of the long list of editorial features which will appear in the next issue of *Gentry*; you can judge from them how intrigued and enthralled your discerning friends will be when they receive this fine magazine.

We will not pause to analyze the implications of the diction, although you should do so on your own, in order to review what we discussed in Chapters 1 and 2. Here we are concerned only with rhythm. Contrast the preceding paragraphs with this version:

Have you seen the first issue of *Gentry*? Maybe your most cultured, intelligent friend has a copy. Look at it—then you'll know why *Gentry* is for a very special kind of person. The person who keeps up with things. The person who reads a lot, is well-educated, and is interested in the old and the new. The person who wants to live, not just make a living. The person who's always alert to learn more about life, art, philosophy.

People like that are pretty scarce. You may know one, two, three—hardly more. Naturally, they deserve the most unusual kind of Christmas present you can find. Why not a year's subscription to *Gentry*? Look at this brief list of some of the features in the next issue. Just think how happy those friends of yours will be to receive *Gentry*—as a gift from you.

Our question here is, which advertisement would persuade most readers to pay a relatively high price for a magazine subscription? (Despite the Christmas-gift angle of this advertisement, the writer naturally wanted readers to subscribe for themselves as well as for friends.) Quite probably the version that sounds more cultured, more "high-class," would be the more impressive: it seems more elegant. It suggests that here is something precious and rare, something that can be appreciated only by the discriminating few, not by the mob. If it costs seven dollars a copy, it is worth it; high quality never comes cheap. In brief, the writer tries to imply this message through a conspicuously dignified rhythm, along with well-chosen connotative words. Together, they convey the idea of a magazine appealing to the cultured few — a select group to which you, as the reader of the advertisement, are assumed to belong.

> Who can say at what point the revelations come? A man falls in love
> . . . or suddenly sees the growing character of his son . . . or knows the
> quick pride of being needed, although no longer young. Each has his
> discoveries . . . a series, making up the sharp core of life. From birth
> and being . . . through youth, maturity, and lengthening years . . .
> each follows his own way, and hopes to find it good. We believe that
> this is as it should be . . . we believe, too, that we can help you plan to
> make your way a little easier, whatever it may be. (Security Mutual Life
> Insurance Company, Binghamton, New York)

Here too the key to the advertisement's effectiveness is the carefully wrought rhythm of the sentences. Many of the devices of the prose-poet-turned-advertising-writer are here, such as the parallel clauses (*A man falls in love . . . or sees . . . or knows; each follows . . . and hopes; we believe . . . we believe*), the repetition of sound to give the effect of alliteration or internal rhyme (*suddenly sees; son/young; discoveries/series; birth and being; should be/may be*), and the selection of words weighted with certain connotations (*falls in love; quick pride of being needed; sharp core of life; youth, maturity, and lengthening years; find it good*). Only the signature, and perhaps a hint in the last sentence, identifies the passage as a commercial appeal. Up to that point, it appears to be an extract from a book of meditations. And that is just what the writer desires. Readers are put into a meditative frame of mind. They are asked to meditate, that is, on whether they have enough insurance.

Throughout this chapter, we have stressed the fact that average sentence lengths, dominant sentence patterns, and regular rhythmic devices are important in two main ways. If the regular structures are used, they bring pleasure to readers by meeting their expectations. But writers who break regular structures and deviate from normal patterns also bring readers pleasure through a sudden twist or surprise, causing them to revise their opinions of, and their reactions to, the ideas being presented. Many important writers have stretched the limits of rhythmic language which we have been emphasizing in these pages. Writers like Virginia Woolf, James Joyce, John Dos Passos, William Faulkner, and Thomas Pynchon, to name only a very few, have often deliberately abandoned or violated the usual conventions of punctuation and the other devices by which written units are marked off and rhythms established. Earlier we noted the use of ellipsis and sentence fragments by Dickens in representing the speech of his character, Mr. Jingle. In this century, writers have used similar devices to represent the "stream of consciousness" — the uncontrolled, casual, fragmentary thoughts and moods that course continuously through the human mind. But such thoughts and moods have nothing of the neat packaged quality which written sentence and paragraph organization implies. Thus these writers suggest the chaotic nature of consciousness by a chaotic style.

James Joyce, for example, sometimes represents the movement of his hero Leopold Bloom's thought by mere fragments of discourse, rather than by complete sentences. He uses a free-associational mixture of sense impressions, reveries, memories, and the other miscellaneous musings of the mind. Thus he suggests the disorderliness, the incompleteness, indeed the half-inarticulate quality of our ordinary mental processes:

He crossed to the bright side, avoiding the loose cellarflap of number seventy-five. The sun was nearing the steeple of George's church. Be a warm day I fancy. Specially in these black clothes feel it more. Black conducts, reflects (refracts is it?), the heat. But I couldn't go in that light suit. Make a picnic of it. His eyelids sank quietly often as he walked in happy warmth. Boland's breadvan delivering with trays of our daily but she prefers yesterday's loaves turnovers crisp crowns hot. Makes you feel young. Somewhere in the east: early morning: set off at dawn, travel round in front of the sun, steal a day's march on him. Keep it up for ever never grow a day older technically. Walk along the strand, strange land, come to a city gate, sentry there, old ranker too, old Tweedy's big moustaches leaning on a long kind of a spear. Wander through awned streets. Turbaned faces going by. Dark caves of carpet shops, big man, Turko the terrible, seated crosslegged smoking a coiled pipe.

Another modern technique which attempts to represent the uncontrolled sequence of thoughts is that of running ideas together without any punctuation whatsoever. This device emphasizes not the fragmentariness of consciousness but its unbroken continuity. The most famous example of this device is the report of Mrs. Bloom's extravagant wandering thoughts in the last section of *Ulysses*—forty-five closely printed pages without a single punctuation mark.

The novelist may also wish to suggest the prevailing atmosphere of a character's mind. In this excerpt from Faulkner's *The Sound and the Fury*, the "run-on" monotonous rhythm conveys the drab hopelessness of the mood weighing down a woman's mind:

what have I done to have been given children like these Benjamin was punishment enough and now for her to have no more regard for me her own mother I've suffered for her dreamed and planned and sacrificed I went down into the valley yet never since she opened her eyes has she given me one unselfish thought at times I look at her I wonder if she can be my child except Jason he has never given me one moment's sorrow since I first held him in my arms I knew then that he was to be my joy and my salvation I thought that Benjamin was punishment enough for any sins I have committed I thought he was punishment for putting aside my pride and marrying a man who held himself above me I don't complain I loved him above all of them because of it because my duty though Jason pulling at my heart all the while but I see now that I have not suffered enough I see now that I must pay for your sins as well as mine what have you done what sins have your high and mighty people visited upon me but you'll take up for them you always have found excuses for your own blood

Montage is another device used to good effect by modern writers. The "Camera Eye" sequences in Dos Passos's *U.S.A.* trilogy provide a series of sharp sense impressions intimately mingled with a character's inner mood and thought. In the human mind, in its relaxed state, simultaneous thoughts and impressions are not tidily separated. Note the use of montage in the following passages, one from Dos Passos's *The Big Money,* the other from Sheila Watson's *The Double Hook:*

walk the streets and walk the streets inquiring of Coca Cola signs Lucky Strike ads pricetags in storewindows scraps of overheard conversations stray tatters of newsprint yesterday's headlines sticking out of ashcans

for a set of figures a formula of action an address you don't quite know you've forgotten the number the street may be in Brooklyn a train leaving for somewhere a steamboat whistle stabbing your ears a job chalked up in front of an agency

to do to make there are more lives than walking desperate the streets hurry underdog do   make

a speech urging action in the crowded hall after handclapping the pats and smiles of others on the platform the scrape of chairs the expectant hush the few coughs during the first stuttering attempt to talk straight tough going the snatch for a slogan they are listening and then the easy climb slogan by slogan to applause

*   *   *   *   *

In the folds of the hills
under Coyote's eyes
lived
the old lady, mother of William
of James and of Greta

lived James and Greta
lived William and Ara his wife
lived the Widow Wagner
the Widow's girl Lenchen
the Widow's boy
lived Felix Prosper and Angel
lived Theophil
and Kip

until one morning in July

Greta was at the stove. Turning hotcakes. Reaching for the coffee beans. Grinding away James's voice.

James was at the top of the stairs. His hand half-raised. His voice in the rafters.

James walking away. The old lady falling. There under the jaw of the roof. In the vault of the bed loft. Into the shadow of death. Pushed by James's will. By James's hand. By James's word: This is my day. You'll not fish today.

Still the old lady fished. If the reeds had dried up and the banks folded and crumbled down she would have fished still. If God had come into the valley, come holding out the long finger of salvation, moaning in the darkness, thundering down the gap at the lake head, skimming across the water, drying up the blue signature like blotting-paper, asking where, asking why, defying an answer, she would have thrown her line against the rebuke; she would have caught a piece of mud and looked it over; she would have drawn a line with the barb when the fire of righteousness baked the bottom.

Skillful stretching of, and deviation from, the normal or expected patterns and rhythms of discourse are important means by which modern writers attain psychological realism and depth. Prose styles that challenge or break our expectations require much more concentration than those which use a "normal" or a "regular" style. We are asked to read between the lines, to stretch our minds and imaginations to make the necessary associations so that we may experience the full effect of a passage. But for any reading that is really important to us, reading we want to enjoy and savor, the extra effort expended is well worth while.

(Exercises: pages 248-252)

PARAGRAPH FORM

What we have said thus far about the way sentence form relates to readers' intuitive knowledge and expectations applies also to paragraphs. Such knowledge on the part of readers allows writers to meet, to strain against, or to break the expected paragraph form, as they create the larger form of the whole essay, story, or novel. What effect, for instance, does Sheila Watson's failure in part to use conventional paragraph form in *The Double Hook* have on us?

Like the sentences we examined in the last section, paragraphs which seem to break all the rules can be extremely effective. In skilled hands, the paragraph is not a fixed form or a mold into which ideas are poured. Rather, it is a flexible rhetorical tool which may be used by the individual writer in many differing ways. For these reasons, it is difficult if not impossible to define "the" paragraph. We will not attempt such an all-purpose definition here. Instead, we will present some general principles relating to the kinds of expository paragraphs most often encountered in college studies and then examine several such paragraphs in action.

One fundamental thing to remember about the paragraph is that it is written; paragraphing doesn't exist in speech. In writing, it functions as a special mark of punctuation. It allows the reader a healthy pause, it establishes patterns of emphasis, and it can signal relationships.

Although paragraphs are hard to define and come in almost every conceivable shape and size, most good expository paragraphs share certain characteristics. In the first place, such a paragraph forms a unit which includes a topic and development of that topic. The "development" may expand a definition, offer examples and analogies, break down a main point into subheads; but in some way or other it comments on the topic. Handbooks of composition usually lay much stress on the so-called topic sentence — the sentence that contains the essence of what the paragraph is about. Sometimes a lucidly organized paragraph contains no such topic sentence, but one can be inferred from the relationships among sentences. Sometimes, also, one topic sentence may serve more than one paragraph, if the material to be developed would result in an overlong and overloaded single paragraph.

In the second place, a good expository paragraph must take readers somewhere, and take them by a fairly direct route. No piece of expository writing is worth much if it does not move along, conducting readers to some new region of information or argument. Moreover, readers must be given new ideas systematically, not haphazardly. They must be able to follow the writer's train of thought without being sidetracked by digressions, omitted links of development, or other violations of continuity — unless their presence can be wholly justified by the writer's purpose.

You are probably already very familiar with the basic form of expository paragraphs, although you may not be conscious of this fact. To prove the point for yourself, read the following passages, from which we have removed all paragraph markers. Then indicate the places where you think new paragraphs should begin.

[1]Few Americans stay put for a lifetime. [2]We move from town to city to suburb, from high school to college in a different state, from a job in one region to a better job somewhere else, from the home where we raise our children to the home where we plan to live in retirement. [3]With each move we are forever making new friends, who become part of our new life at that time. [4]For many of us the summer is a special time for forming new friendships. [5]Today millions of Americans vacation abroad, and they go not only to see new sights but also—in those places where they do not feel too strange—with the hope of meeting new people. [6]No one really expects a vacation trip to produce a close friend. [7]But surely the beginning of a friendship is possible? [8]Surely in every country people value friendship? [9]They do. [10]The difficulty when strangers from two countries meet is not a lack of appreciation of friendship, but different expectations about what constitutes friend-

ship and how it comes into being. [11]In those European countries that Americans are most likely to visit, friendship is quite sharply distinguished from other, more casual relations, and is differently related to family life. [12]For a Frenchman, a German, or an Englishman friendship is usually more particularized and carries a heavier burden of commitment. [13]But as we use the word, "friend" can be applied to a wide range of relationships—to someone one has known for a few weeks in a new place, to a close business associate, to a childhood playmate, to a man or woman, to a trusted confidant. [14]There are real differences among these relations for Americans—a friendship may be superficial, casual, situational or deep and enduring. [15]But to a European, who sees only our surface behavior, the differences are not clear.

You probably paragraphed the passage in much the same way the authors did. (To check, refer to this passage in the Sources of Quotations, page 346.) You could do so because you have developed a general sense of expository paragraph structure.

The analysis of paragraph structure can offer clues to the orderliness of a writer's mind. If the organization of a paragraph is clear, if the sentences are arranged in a logical pattern with each leading directly into the next, we assume the writer has good control over the material and a clear sense of purpose. Only inexperienced writers usually are conscious of the process by which they organize their materials. To practiced writers, organizing and paragraph structuring are tacit, seemingly automatic acts. An analysis of two paragraphs from a readable and informative book on the city of Washington, D.C., during the Civil War can illustrate how sound expository paragraphs are built.

[1]The most famous of all hotels, however, was Willard's at Fourteenth Street. [2]Formerly a small and unsuccessful hostelry, its failure had been ascribed to the fact that it was too far uptown. [3]Its reputation had been made under the efficient management of the Willard brothers, who hailed from Vermont; and, enlarged and redecorated, Willard's had become the great meeting place of Washington. [4]Much of the business of Government was said to be done in its passages and its bar. [5]From eight to eleven in the morning—for Washingtonians were not early risers—a procession of celebrities might be observed passing to the breakfast table. [6]The huge breakfast, which included such items as fried oysters, steak and onions, *blanc mange* and *paté de foie gras,* was succeeded by a gargantuan midday dinner; by another dinner at five o'clock; by a robust tea at seven-thirty; and finally by supper at nine. [7]Englishmen, themselves no inconsiderable feeders, were appalled by the meals that the American guests, ladies as well as gentlemen, were able to consume.

[8]The British visitors hated Willard's. [9]Its very architecture offended them. [10]Accustomed to snug inns with private parlors, they could find

no decent seclusion in this rambling, uncomfortable barracks. [11]American hotel life was gregarious, and a peaceful withdrawal from an atmosphere of "heat, noise, dust, smoke, expectoration" was the last thing that the natives appeared to be seeking. [12]After breakfast, as after dinner, the guests hastened to mingle in the public rooms. [13]At Willard's, the parlor furniture was occupied by the same sallow determined men, the same dressy ladies and the same screaming, precocious children that travelers observed elsewhere in the United States.

Sentence 1 announces the topic of Willard's Hotel. (In the preceding paragraph other Washington hotels of the era had been described. Willard's, however, seems to call for special treatment, and the new paragraph promises to explain why.)

Sentences 2 and 3 develop the topic by telling something of the hotel's past. Sentence 2, by referring to Willard's earlier failure, emphasizes by contrast the idea of sentence 3, its present success and fame.

Sentence 4 then expands on the closing note of sentence 3 — "the great meeting place of Washington."

Sentences 5, 6, and 7 continue to develop this idea but move the reader's attention from "its passages and its bar" (sentence 4) to the dining room. In sentence 5, a shift in the order of treatment, from spatial to chronological, is anticipated by showing that in the morning the traffic in the passages led to the breakfast table; and in sentence 6 we move from breakfast through the other meals of the day. The sentence looks backward in that it suggests that Willard's guests thus had five occasions a day for getting together ("the great meeting place of Washington"), and forward in that it prepares for sentence 7, the visiting Englishmen's reaction to the Americans' huge appetites.

The second paragraph turns from what the guests ate to what they saw and who they were and retains the view of the "British visitors." These visitors firmly connect the new paragraph with the last sentence of the preceding one, and the use of *hated* defines the specific attitude toward Willard's that will dominate the paragraph. Sentence 9 makes explicit the change of topic from the meals to the hotel's physical setting and clientele. Sentence 10 makes concrete the general observation of sentence 9 and uses contrast to highlight Willard's lack of snugness and privacy. Sentence 11 restates the matter in a positive way; *gregarious* and *peaceful withdrawal* relate to the *snug, private,* and *seclusion* of the previous sentence. In addition, although the British visitors do not appear in this sentence, the use of *natives* implies that we are still seeing the hotel through their eyes. Sentence 12 restresses the idea of gregariousness and provides another link with the preceding paragraph in its reference to meals. Sentence 13, finally, sums up the atmosphere of the hotel by describing the guests — men, women, and children — as seen by foreign travelers. It makes clear, however, that the clientele of Willard's was not unique. For better or worse, it was representative of the American people of the time.

Thus the two paragraphs have contributed their share to the purpose of the whole book, which is to give readers a detailed view of Washington and its inhabitants during the Civil War. The paragraphs have consistently emphasized certain aspects of the scene: the crowds, their noise and bustle, their gregariousness, and their hearty vulgarity. And the steady point of view within each paragraph sustains consistency of impression. In the first paragraph, Willard's is seen through the eyes of the historian. But in the second paragraph, for the sake of presenting the material from a special angle, the writer puts on the glasses of the visiting Englishmen. She keeps the glasses on for the length of the paragraph and thus retains the all-important unity of impression.

The orderly progression of thought is assisted by the little links which, although usually so unobtrusive as to escape notice, do much to speed readers on their smooth way. Note how many such connecting devices are used in the paragraphs quoted:

Sentence 1: *however* announces a change of topic, or at least of subtopic.

Sentence 2: *hostelry* and *its* refer to Willard's in 1.

Sentences 3 and 4: *its* and *Willard's* keep the subject steadily in view.

Sentence 5: *procession* and *passing* pick up the idea of *passages* in 4.

Sentence 6: *breakfast* in turn links with *breakfast table* at the end of 5.

Sentence 7: *meals* recapitulates the *breakfast, tea, dinner,* and *supper* of 6.

Sentences 8, 9, and 10: the subject of the preceding paragraph (*Willard's* in 8, *its* in 9, and *this . . . barracks* in 10) and the point of view introduced at its end (the *British visitors* in 8, *them* in 9, and *they* in 10) are systematically sustained.

Sentence 11: the *natives* neatly shifts attention from the hotel itself back to the guests of sentence 7, as seen by the *British visitors* of the last three sentences.

Sentence 12: now the *natives* are *guests* again.

Sentence 13: the two groups of people dealt with in the paragraph are brought together: the *guests* as *men . . . ladies . . .* and *children* and the *British visitors* as *travelers.*

These important links help create coherence in the paragraphs. In the second paragraph about the Willard Hotel, for instance, readers can easily infer the British attitude toward Americans, though it is not directly stated. The greater the number of inferences readers must draw to make sense of a passage, the more that passage is considered difficult. If the number of inferences required to make sense of a passage is too great, readers see that passage as incoherent. As an example of this principle, read the following short passage, *one sentence at a time,* pausing after each sentence to form a mental picture of the event and draw conclusions about it:

He plunked the $5.00 down at the window.
She tried to give him $2.50 back, but he wouldn't take it.
So when they got inside, she insisted on buying the popcorn.

A psychologist asked groups of people to respond to this passage, one sentence at a time. He found that interpretations of the "scene" varied widely — until the last sentence was presented. Then the passage became "coherent" for most people: they could infer that the couple is attending a movie and trying to settle who pays for what. Thus readers add significantly to coherence, for nowhere in the passage is *movie* mentioned. This example illustrates how coherence is related both to particular linking words in a passage and to the inferences readers draw from those words. An inexperienced reader needs every transition and linkage marked, whereas more skilled readers can follow an argument with less aid from explicit signposts. But the very lack of such direction-pointers (used inconspicuously in the best writing) demands that the writer couple sentence with sentence, paragraph with paragraph, with such firm logic that readers have no difficulty in following along.

Keep these principles of good expository paragraph construction in mind as you read the preface to Rachel Carson's *Silent Spring:*

There was once a town in the heart of America where all life seemed to live in harmony with its surroundings. The town lay in the midst of a checkerboard of prosperous farms, with fields of grain and hillsides of orchards where, in spring, white clouds of bloom drifted above the green fields. In autumn, oak and maple and birch set up a blaze of color that flamed and flickered across a backdrop of pines. Then foxes barked in the hills and deer silently crossed the fields, half hidden in the mists of the fall mornings.

Along the roads, laurel, viburnum and alder, great ferns and wild-flowers delighted the traveler's eye through much of the year. Even in winter the roadsides were places of beauty, where countless birds came to feed on the berries and on the seed heads of the dried weeds rising above the snow. The countryside was, in fact, famous for the abundance and variety of its bird life, and when the flood of migrants was pouring through in spring and fall people traveled from great distances to observe them. Others came to fish the streams, which flowed clear and cold out of the hills and contained shady pools where trout lay. So it had been from the days many years ago when the first settlers raised their houses, sank their wells, and built their barns.

Then a strange blight crept over the area and everything began to change. Some evil spell had settled on the community: mysterious maladies swept the flocks of chickens; the cattle and sheep sickened and died. Everywhere was a shadow of death. The farmers spoke of much illness among their families. In the town the doctors had become more and more puzzled by new kinds of sickness appearing among their patients. There had been several sudden and unexplained deaths, not only among adults but even among children, who would be stricken suddenly while at play and die within a few hours.

There was a strange stillness. The birds, for example—where had they gone? Many people spoke of them, puzzled and disturbed. The feeding stations in the backyards were deserted. The few birds seen anywhere were moribund; they trembled violently and could not fly. It was a spring without voices. On the mornings that had once throbbed with the dawn chorus of robins, catbirds, doves, jays, wrens, and scores of other bird voices there was now no sound; only silence lay over the fields and woods and marsh.

On the farms the hens brooded, but no chicks hatched. The farmers complained that they were unable to raise any pigs—the litters were small and the young survived only a few days. The apple trees were coming into bloom but no bees droned among the blossoms, so there was no pollination and there would be no fruit.

The roadsides, once so attractive, were now lined with browned and withered vegetation as though swept by fire. These, too, were silent, deserted by all living things. Even the streams were now lifeless. Anglers no longer visited them, for all the fish had died.

In the gutters under the eaves and between the shingles of the roofs, a white granular powder still showed a few patches; some weeks before it had fallen like snow upon the roofs and the lawns, the fields and the streams.

No witchcraft, no enemy action had silenced the rebirth of new life in this stricken world. The people had done it themselves.

This town does not actually exist, but it might easily have a thousand counterparts in America or elsewhere in the world. I know of no community that has experienced all the misfortunes I described. Yet every one of these disasters has actually happened somewhere, and many real communities have already suffered a substantial number of them. A grim specter has crept upon us almost unnoticed, and this imagined tragedy may easily become a stark reality we all shall know.

What has already silenced the voices of spring in countless towns in America? This book is an attempt to explain.

In this preface, Rachel Carson uses normal expository paragraph structure in crafting a passage that is both easy to read and moving. If the paragraphing were removed, most readers would divide the passage more or less as Carson did. One paragraph, however, breaks ordinary expectations—for special emphasis. Which?

"Ordinary" paragraph form, of course, exists only as a concept to be used, stretched, or broken by expert writers. We have already examined the long, unpunctuated passage from Faulkner (pages 225–226) and mentioned the huge, unpunctuated "paragraph" with which *Ulysses* ends. Very short, staccato paragraphs can also create special emphasis. Here is Carl Sandburg's description of the people's reaction to the first news of Abraham Lincoln's death:

Men tried to talk about it and the words failed and they came back to silence.

To say nothing was best.

Lincoln was dead.

Was there anything more to say?

Yes, they would go through the motions of grief and they would take part in a national funeral and a ceremony of humiliation and abasement and tears.

But words were no help.

Lincoln was dead.

Nothing more than that could be said.

He was gone.

He would never speak again to the American people.

A great friend of man had suddenly vanished.

Nothing could be done about it.

Death is terribly final.

Here Sandburg evidently wished to suggest the dazed state of the people, the incoherence brought on by shock, and the essentially uncommunicable nature of grief. The tiny sentences—hardly more than fragmentary phrases—illustrate the first statement, that "Men tried to talk about it and the words failed." Such few ideas as are expressed are utterly commonplace; when they are stunned into silence, people are capable of only the most obvious thoughts ("He was gone. He would never speak again to the American people."). And the stunned mind thinks the same thoughts over and over: "Lincoln was dead ... Lincoln was dead." The bereaved people of 1865, Sandburg suggests, were too filled with emotion to speak. When they did manage a few words, the phrases they uttered were like sobs. And the phrases Sandburg *writes* are like sobs. (Why, by the way, did he not combine the thirteen sentences into a single paragraph?)

In *Silences,* Tillie Olsen uses a similar technique to suggest the fears that haunt many women:

Fear. How could it be otherwise, as one is also woman.

The centuries past. The other determining difference—not biology—for woman. Constrictions, coercions, penalties for being female. Enforced. Sometimes physically enforced.

Reprisals, coercions, penalties for not remaining in what was, is, deemed suitable in her sex.

The writer-woman is not excepted, because she writes.

Fear—the need to please, to be safe—in the literary realm too. Founded fear. Power is still in the hands of men. Power of validation, publication, approval, reputation, coercion, penalties.

"The womanhood emotion." Fear to hurt.

"Liberty is the right not to lie."

"What are rights without means?"

In the passage from which this excerpt is taken, Olsen is meditating on Virginia Woolf and on how difficult it is to be a writer ("Difficult for any male not born into a class that breeds such confidence. Almost impossible for a girl, a woman."). Her staccato sentences and short, fragmentary paragraphs represent the threats, the thrusts and jabs, which a woman writer's confidence must endure.

Thus writers can stretch the limits of paragraph form, fulfilling, straining against, or breaking the topic/development-of-topic model so familiar to readers of expository prose. But writers must also respond to limits imposed by the medium of publication. Newspapers or magazines that use narrow columns call for shorter paragraphs, and books or journals with big, one-column pages call for longer ones.

In spite of what might seem like restrictions on paragraph form, our examples have demonstrated that the English paragraph is enormously flexible. Students in one of our advanced composition classes recently surveyed a broad range of writing, from textbooks to essays by experimental writers such as Donald Barthelme and Hunter S. Thompson. They found that in textbooks paragraphs most often follow the topic/development-of-topic model, proceeding logically, through comparison and contrast, enumeration, examples, or causal relationships. But the experimental essayists followed no such model, using the paragraph in individual ways to create particular rhythms, emphases, or atmospheres.

These informal findings make a good deal of sense. Textbook writers are trying to present information as clearly as possible. Because their student readers are expending much energy attending to that information, textbook writers use all the means at their disposal to reduce the mental "load" students have to carry while reading their texts. Such a purpose demands that the writers dispense student readers from inferring transitional links and reading between the lines for unstated conclusions and watching for subtle shifts in expected sentence or paragraph form. Experimental essayists are not bound by these considerations. Thus they are free to be more playful, using the rhetorical power of the paragraph to surprise readers. We appreciate, perhaps even delight in, the unorthodox use of paragraphing in such prose. But we also very much appreciate the care taken by those who use the expository paragraph in a straightforward, logical way.

Not all writers are able to set forth the sequence of their thoughts as plainly as it exists in their own minds. Clear thinking does not inevitably mean clear writing, and people of very sharp intellect may make a sorry muddle of their ideas when they try to put them on paper. But the converse is always true. Well-organized writing is a sure sign of a well-organized mind.

(Exercises: pages 252–258)

EXERCISES ══════════

SENTENCE LENGTH

4.1 In each of the following excerpts, the author, a practiced writer addressing an adult audience, adopts the prose style (spoken or written) of a child. What are the characteristics of this style as each author interprets it, and what is the purpose in using it?

1. You don't know about me, without you have read a book by the name of "The Adventures of Tom Sawyer," but that ain't no matter. That book was made by Mr. Mark Twain, and he told the truth, mainly. There was things which he stretched, but mainly he told the truth. That is nothing. I never seen anybody but lied, one time or another, without it was Aunt Polly, or the widow, or maybe Mary. Aunt Polly—Tom's Aunt Polly—she is—and Mary, and the Widow Douglas, is all told about in that book—which is mostly a true book; with some stretchers, as I said before.

2. Once upon a time and a very good time it was there was a moocow coming down along the road and this moocow that was coming down along the road met a nicens little boy named baby tuckoo. . . .

   His father told him that story: his father looked at him through a glass: he had a hairy face.

   He was baby tuckoo. The moocow came down the road where Betty Byrne lived: she sold lemon platt.

   > O, the wild rose blossoms
   > On the little green place.

   He sang that song. That was his song.

3. It is some kind of special day. "Where's Sissie?" Ma says. Her face gets sharp, she is frightened. When I run around her chair she laughs and hugs me. She is pretty when she laughs. Her hair is long and pretty.

   We are sitting at the best table of all, out near the water. The sun is warm and the air smells nice. Daddy is coming back from the building with some glasses of beer, held in his arms. He makes a grunting noise when he sits down.

   "Is the lake deep?" I ask them.

   They don't hear me, they're talking. A woman and a man are sitting with us. The man marched in the parade we saw just a while ago; he is a volunteer fireman and is wearing a uniform. Now his shirt is pulled open because it is hot. I can see the dark curly hair way up his throat; it looks hot and prickly.

4.2 **(a)** Since this book is intended for readers who are attending college, its sentences should come fairly close to the norms described on page 200. To check this, count the words in a sufficient number of sentences to permit a sound generalization and then find the arithmetical mean (see page 280 for a definition). If the average sentence turns out to be longer than you expected, can you attribute it to any special intention on the part of the authors? (At the same time, in anticipation of later exercises in which the topic of paragraph length is discussed, determine the average number of sentences contained in a sample of paragraphs from this book.)

(b) In the same manner, study the sentences and paragraphs in each of the following, and estimate how well adapted they are for the intended audience and for the authors' assumed purposes:

A copy of *Newsweek; Reader's Digest;* the *New York Review of Books; Better Homes and Gardens; Critical Inquiry;* the *Atlantic Monthly;* a true-romance, western, or detective magazine.

4.3 The following sentences were written between 1775 and 1875. What changes would have to be made if they were to be printed in a contemporary magazine? Decide on such a magazine and then try your hand at rewriting one or more of the passages in modern prose for the magazine you have chosen. You may find it desirable or necessary to make more than one sentence.

1. I made a study of the ancient and indispensable art of breadmaking, consulting such authorities as offered, going back to the primitive days and first invention of the unleavened kind, when from the wildness of nuts and meats men first reached the mildness and refinement of this diet, and travelling gradually down in my studies through that accidental souring of the dough which, it is supposed, taught the leavening process, and through the various fermentations thereafter, till I came to "good, sweet, wholesome bread," the staff of life.

2. It has been observed in all ages, that the advantages of nature or of fortune have contributed very little to the promotion of happiness; and that those whom the splendour of their rank, or the extent of their capacity, have placed upon the summits of human life, have not often given any just occasion to envy in those who look up to them from a lower station: whether it be that apparent superiority incites great designs, and great designs are naturally liable to fatal mis-carriages; or that the general lot of mankind is misery, and the misfortunes of those whose eminence drew upon them an universal attention, have been more carefully recorded, because they were more generally observed, and have in reality been only more conspicuous than those of others not more frequent, or more severe.

3. Her mighty lakes, like oceans of liquid silver; her mountains, with their bright aerial tints; her valleys, teeming with wild fertility; her tremendous cataracts, thundering in their solitudes; her boundless plains, waving with spontaneous verdure; her broad deep rivers, rolling in solemn silence to the ocean; her trackless forests, where vegetation puts forth all its magnificence; her skies, kindling with the magic of summer clouds and glorious sunshine;— no, never need an American look beyond his own country for the sublime and beautiful of natural scenery.

4. The man who had been a servant, who had wanted bread, who knew the horrors of the midnight street, who had slept in dens, who had been befriended by rough men and rougher women, who saw the goodness of humanity under its coarsest outside, and who above all never tried to shut these things out from his memory, but accepted them as the most interesting, the most touching, the most real of all his experiences, might well be expected to penetrate to the root of the matter, and to protest to the few who usurp literature and policy with their ideas, aspirations, interests, that it is not they but the many, whose existence stirs the heart and fills the eye with the great prime elements of the human lot.

4.4 Now that you have rewritten one of those sentences in modern prose, try to imitate its structure, keeping as close as possible to the original but using your own subject matter. Here is a sample imitation of the first sentence in the preceding exercise:

I decided I would learn all I could about bicycling, reading such books as existed, learning about its history from the earliest bicycles to the invention of the ten-speed, and focusing in my research on the special skills and strategies of current racers who, most believe, have thoroughly developed the art of bicycling, including a few not so legal "tricks of the trade," until most can now go many times faster than the first cyclists, their progenitors.

Note that we have tried to match clause for clause, phrase for phrase. You might begin this exercise by dividing the sentence you want to imitate into such units and writing each unit on a separate line, so that the structure becomes more clear, as in the following example. Put the main clause and any coordinate clauses at the left margin: they are "level 1" parts of the sentence. Indent subordinate clauses and phrases, designating them as "level 2, 3, or 4" parts of the sentence:

(1) I made a study of the ancient and indispensable art of breadmaking,
(2) consulting such authorities as offered,
(2) going back to the primitive days and first invention of the unleavened kind,
   (3) when from the wildness of nuts and meats men first reached the mildness and refinement of this diet,
(2) and travelling gradually down in my studies
   (3) through that accidental souring of the dough
      (4) which, it is supposed, taught the leavening process,
   (3) and through the various fermentations thereafter,
   (3) till I came to "good, sweet, wholesome bread,"
      (4) the staff of life.

4.5 Each of the following passages is from the work of a celebrated novelist. One writer is distinguished for the use of short, staccato sentences and clauses; the other, for elaborate sentences. Define as precisely as you can the effect of each of these passages. Then try to describe the mental operations of the character whose point of view the author is portraying. How does the form of the sentences help reveal the nature of each character's response to experience?

1. The sun came through the open window and shone through the beer bottles on the table. The bottles were half full. There was a little froth on the beer in the bottles, not much because it was very cold. It collared up when you poured it into the tall glasses. I looked out of the open window at the white road. The trees beside the road were dusty. Beyond was a green field and a stream. There were trees along the stream and a mill with a water wheel. Through the open side of the mill I saw a long log and a saw in it rising and falling. No one seemed to be tending it. There were four crows walking in the green field. One crow sat in a tree watching. Outside on the porch the cook got off his chair and passed into the hall that led back into the kitchen. Inside, the sunlight shone through the empty glasses on the table. John was leaning forward with his head on his arms.

2. From a little after two o'clock until almost sundown of the long still hot weary dead September afternoon they sat in what Miss Coldfield still called the office because her father had called it that—a dim hot airless room with the blinds all closed and fastened for forty-three summers because when she was a girl someone had believed that light and moving air carried heat and that dark was always cooler, and which (as the sun shone fuller and fuller on that side of the house) became latticed with yellow slashes full of dust motes which Quentin thought of as being flecks of the dead old dried paint itself blown inward from the scaling blinds as wind might have blown them. There was a wisteria vine blooming for the second time that summer on a wooden trellis before one window, into which sparrows came now and then in random gusts, making a dry vivid gusty sound before going away: and opposite Quentin, Miss Coldfield in the eternal black which she had worn for forty-three years now, whether for sister, father, or nothusband none knew, sitting so bolt upright in the straight hard chair that was so tall for her that her legs hung straight and rigid as if she had iron shinbones and ankles, clear of the floor with that air of impotent yet indomitable frustration would appear, as though by outraged recapitulation evoked, quite inattentive and harmless, out of the biding and dreamy and victorious dust.

4.6 The following anecdote appeared in a leaflet enclosed with a telephone bill. For the purpose its author had in mind—to create good will for the company—

it is expertly written. Your job: rewrite the story in a less breathless and more serious fashion, with more complex sentence structures. Before you begin, decide on a possible place of publication, such as the magazine section of your local newspaper or the *Reader's Digest* as a personal experience feature. You need not retain the one-paragraph form of the original.

Here's a question with which most of us are familiar: "Who pays the bill?" Well, the answer to this was a life-saver in one case at least. A little girl in suburban Chicago couldn't seem to find anything to swallow but silver polish. This wasn't too healthful. Father rushed her to Resurrection Hospital and was informed an hour later that she wasn't staging much of a come-back. Father had lived with telephones all his life. It came natural for him to reach. He reached twice, once for the silver polish with the label on it and once for the telephone. He got a voice and read the label to it. Then there were other voices. A telephone in the offices of the manufacturer in New York began to ring but no one answered—closed for the weekend. No emergency numbers were listed, but the telephone girls were thinking all along the line and someone asked, "Who pays the bill?" "WHO PAYS THE BILL?" routed out of bed an accountant for the telephone company in New York. He raced to the office where records showed a name. Eleven calls in the five boroughs finally located an executive. Seconds later the polish formula and antidote were being dictated to the doctors. The child recovered, probably to grow up to be the mother of someone who sometimes will do something that will send Mother flying to the telephone.

4.7 Choose an issue of a current magazine and examine the advertisements for sentence length. What conclusions can you draw about the use of short sentences and fragments in advertising copy? Do such sentences appear in certain types of ads but not in others? Then examine several articles in the same magazine for sentence length. How do those lengths compare to the ones used in ads?

4.8 Try your hand at writing a sentence that is at least 200 words long. Should you want a model to study or to imitate, you can use the long sentence from *Moby-Dick* on page 211, or the one by Martin Luther King on page 216. Or find a long sentence which you admire and use it as a model. The criteria for success in this exercise: punctuation must be appropriate, and all phrases and clauses must really add to the effect of the sentence: no padding!

SENTENCE ARRANGEMENT

4.9 Keeping in mind the general principles discussed on pages 206–214, improve the following sentences. In each case, explain your rationale for revision.

1. The first age of television, which ended just a few years ago, and which was dominated by three networks, united us in boredom and passivity because, after all, it offered little, if any, choices.
2. R. F. Delderfield's novel *To Serve Them All My Days*, which was published in 1972 by Simon and Schuster—you might want to check it out before the public television dramatization begins—is superlong, complex, and all about things like British education and class differences and similar ideas, at least that's what I think.
3. The River Café, which is underneath the Brooklyn Bridge, on Water Street, in Brooklyn, provides a view, from somewhere near the Statue of Liberty to near the Empire State Building, that is, as the ships sail past and the moon rises, sweeping, majestic, and haunting.
4. So, when family life in Oak Park in that spring of 1909, conspired against the freedom to which I had come to feel every soul entitled and I had no choice would I keep my self-respect, but go out, a voluntary exile, into the uncharted and unknown deprived of legal protection to get my back against the wall and live, if I could, an unconventional life—then I turned to the hill in the Valley as my Grandfather before me had turned to America—as a hope and haven—forgetful for the first time of being my grandfather's "Isaiah."

4.10 This group of sentences illustrates the various principles of arrangement discussed in the text. In each instance, decide what point the author probably wished to emphasize and whether he or she was successful in doing so. If not, rewrite the sentence so that the emphasis is achieved.

1. One of the things that the general public perpetually fails to understand about the life of a creative writer is that he is hard at work when he appears to be loafing, for sitting about and staring into space in pursuit of an idea or a good way of expressing it is just as much a part of the writing process as pecking away furiously at a typewriter, and indeed takes up much more of an author's days—and nights.
2. There are some who can live without wild things, and some who cannot. These essays are the delights and dilemmas of one who cannot.
3. That the American theatre today lacks original talent both in playwrights and performers is a frequently heard complaint, even if, in the opinion of some (among whom I include myself), this situation is over-emphasized, considering the number of really first-rate new plays which have appeared briefly on the stage and then disappeared because of the indifference of the critics and the

public, who seem to fail to recognize new talent when it does show up.

4. There are few more obvious, natural, apparent, ostensible, plain, intelligent, literal, and downright objects on this earth than a boiled potato.

5. The history of *Sister Carrie* is a case of uxorious publishers. The first edition of 1900 was already in print when the wife of the publisher read it and refused to allow her husband to have anything to do with it, it is reported.

6. There were no foreclosures of mortgages, no protested notes, no notes payable, no debts of honor in Typee; no unreasonable tailors and shoemakers, perversely bent on being paid; no duns of any description; no assault and battery attorneys, to foment discord, backing their clients up to a quarrel, and then knocking their heads together; no poor relations, everlastingly occupying the spare bed-chamber, and diminishing the elbow-room at the family table; no destitute widows with their children starving on the cold charities of the world; no beggars; no debtors' prisons; no proud and hard-hearted nabobs in Typee; or to sum up all in one word—no Money!

7. About half way between West Egg and New York the motor road hastily joins the railroad and runs beside it for a quarter of a mile, so as to shrink from a certain desolate area of land. This is a valley of ashes—a fantastic farm where ashes grow like wheat into ridges and hills and grotesque gardens; where ashes take the form of houses and chimneys and rising smoke and, finally, with a transcendent effort, of men who move dimly and already crumbling through the powdery air. Occasionally a line of grey cars crawls along an invisible track, gives out a ghastly creak, and comes to rest, and immediately the ash-grey men swarm up with leaden spades and stir up an impenetrable cloud, which screens their obscure operations from your sight.

4.11 Following are five packages of raw data. The contents of each package are to be sorted, rearranged, and developed into a series of sentences to form a coherent paragraph. All the facts are relevant and therefore must be used. You must decide, however, which are more important than others, and what various relations these bear one to another. You may wish to write two, three, or four sentences, depending on your estimate of the way the material should be organized, the particular emphasis and sentence patterns you want to create, and the audience you intend the paragraphs for.

1. Prominent in civic affairs. Term as common pleas judge will run three years. Born 1948. Sworn enemy of gambling interests. Unexpected appointment. Part-time teacher at university law

school. Member of firm of Coke, Blackstone, Howe, and Hummel. Governor a Democrat, she a Republican. Had been county prosecuting attorney for four years. Mother of three children.

2. New group. Combination rock and rhythm and blues. Members from West Coast. Hit single, "Daring." Superb drummer. Woman plays electric violin. Singer also plays keyboards and flute. New sound. New audience.

3. Good example of postimpressionist art. Restoration now completed; took six months. Model for the leading female figure said to be artist's mistress. Three other paintings too badly burned to be restored. Artist named Rougon Macquart. Color values suggest those of Van Gogh. Artist was twenty-three when picture was painted. Acquired by museum in 1941. Place of honor in Gallery XIII during current show. "Café on Montparnasse" is the title.

4. Stub of ticket to Dempsey-Tunney fight, 1926. Curious assortment. Miniature by unknown artist; little girl in maybe late eighteenth-century dress, his great-great-grandmother? Indian arrowheads. Finding it an accident. Junk and valuables. Unpublished diary of trip to Paris peace conference in 1919 as Wilson's adviser. Hidden drawer in desk. Proper Bostonian. Intricate Chinese puzzle carved in ivory. Little red book, addresses of New York speakeasies.

5. Exposure meter. Camera itself about five years old. Real bargain. German made. Carrying case somewhat battered. Sol's camera shop. Good lens, reconditioned shutter mechanism. Also extra filters, telescopic lens. Down by the City Hall. Wanted $100 for the outfit. Took $75.

4.12 Now choose one of the preceding packages of data, rescramble the information, and write another paragraph — this time for a different audience and with a different emphasis. How does the change in audience and purpose affect the sentence patterns and the sentence lengths you choose? How does the new paragraph differ from the original version?

4.13 Rewrite the following periodic and cumulative sentences so that (1) the first group opens with the main clause rather than delaying it until the end, and (2) the second group postpones part or all of the main clause until the end. Compare each pair of versions and determine the strengths and weaknesses of each sentence.

Periodic Sentences

1. Early one morning, under the arc of a lamp, carefully, silently, in smock and leather gloves, old Doctor Manza grafted a cat's head onto a chicken's trunk.

244 SENTENCES AND PARAGRAPHS: THE SIGNIFICANCE OF FORM

2. Here, amid the throngs, the buses, the dodging taxicabs, the clanging streetcars; here, among the gaudy billboards and the glaring colors of the night-time spectacular; here, in this public and popular spot—fenced in by glass and brick, stone and asphalt, cement and steel—is a world so divorced from that of the open fields and woods that it seems impossible that the two should ever meet.

3. Commissioned by the Italian magazine *L'Europeo* and syndicated nearly everywhere, Oriana Fallaci's interviews are scathing, scolding, and sometimes outrageous.

4. As a forcing ground for self-delusion, self-importance, greed, plagiarism, hypocrisy, vanity, hindsight, malice, treachery, impatience, superstition, sycophancy and fatty degeneration of the moral fibre, the cinema has few equals.

5. Crossing a bare common, in snow puddles, at twilight, under a clouded sky, without having in my thoughts any occurrence of special good fortune, I have enjoyed a perfect exhilaration.

6. Looking back in the big windows, over the bags of peat moss and aluminum lawn furniture stacked on the pavement, I could see Lengel in my place in the slot, checking the sheep through.

Cumulative Sentences

1. Four steps past the turnstiles everybody is already backed up haunch to paunch for the climb up the ramp and the stairs to the surface, a great funnel of flesh, wool, felt, leather, rubber and steaming alumicrom, with the blood squeezing through everybody's old sclerotic arteries in hopped-up spurts from too much coffee and the effort of surfacing from the subway at the rush hour.

2. I was born in 1927, the only child of middle-class parents, both English, and themselves born in the grotesquely elongated shadow, which they never rose sufficiently above history to leave, of that monstrous dwarf Queen Victoria.

3. Censorship can, and often does, lead into absurdity, though not often slapstick absurdity like the New Jersey legislature achieved in the 1960's when it enacted a subsequently vetoed antiobscenity bill so explicit that it was deemed too dirty to be read in the legislative chambers without clearing out the public first.

4. Between [my parents], as the evening progressed, I strutted, and trotted, and strutted again, from sun fleck to sun fleck, along the middle of a path, which I easily identify today with an alley of ornamental oaklings in the park of our country estate, Vyra, in the former Province of St. Petersburg, Russia.

5. He went to speak to Mrs. Bean, tiny among the pillows, her small toothless mouth open like an ''O,'' her skin stretched so thin and

white over her bones, her huge eye-sockets and eyes in a fixed, infant-like stare, and her sparse white hair short and straggling over her brow.

6. A book—like any piece of writing—is conceived, it gestates, and its delivery is frequently overdue, accompanied by severe labor pains and followed by post partum depression.

4.14 In the following passage from D. H. Lawrence's "Herman Melville's *Moby-Dick*," the author uses ellipsis and sentence fragments. Rewrite the passage, using complete sentences throughout. Then compare the two versions. What effects do the ellipsis and fragments used by Lawrence create?

> Doom.
> Doom! Doom! Doom! Something seems to whisper it in the very dark trees of America. Doom!
> Doom of what?
> Doom of our white day. We are doomed, doomed. And the doom is in America. The doom of our white day.
> Ah, well, if my day is doomed, and I am doomed with my day, it is something greater than I which dooms me, so I accept my doom as a sign of the greatness which is more than I am.
> Melville knew. He knew his race was doomed. His white soul, doomed. His great white epoch, doomed. Himself, doomed. The idealist, doomed. The spirit, doomed.

4.15 Comment on the word order in each of the following sentences. Does the use of inversion or the particular placement of modifying elements alter the effect of the sentence? Compose a few descriptive or narrative sentences of your own in "normal" word order. Then rewrite them in rearranged form, on the model of the sentences printed here. How, if at all, have you altered their effect?

1. In a hole in the ground there lived a hobbit.
2. Fat as a pig he was, and his face was the color of cottage cheese.
3. On a stool in the corner, a bloodied towel around his neck, sat the dejected loser.
4. Tall, powerful, barefoot, graceful, soundless, Missouri Fever was like a supple black cat as she paraded serenely about the kitchen, the casual flow of her walk beautifully sensuous and haughty.

4.16 Rewrite each of the following groups of sentences to make one sentence, using parallel structure, as in this example:

> The worried weather announcer warned viewers.
> He warned them to prepare for everything.
> They should prepare for hurricane-force winds.

They should prepare for rains that could blind them.
They should prepare for flooding.
They should even prepare for losing their homes.

Combined sentence: The worried weather announcer warned viewers to prepare for everything: hurricane-force winds, blinding rains, floods, even the loss of their homes.

1. (a) Two dangers can come from not owning a farm.
   (b) Thinking breakfast comes from the grocery is one danger.
   (c) Also, some people could think that heat comes from a furnace.
2. (a) People can be categorized.
   (b) Some happen to be born lucky.
   (c) Some others, however, make their own luck.
3. (a) Long ago, freight was carried by horses and mules.
   (b) Later, trains took over the job.
   (c) Now most freight is carried by trucks.
4. (a) When he was good he was very, very good.
   (b) Then his words flowed freely as birdsong.
   (c) But other times he was bad.
   (d) He was a bombastic wizard.
   (e) He then poured forth jingo and transcendental eyewash.

4.17 Follow the same instructions for this exercise, but this time use antithesis as the principle for combining the groups of short sentences.

1. (a) Earning an A in a course is easy to imagine.
   (b) It's difficult to actually get the grade, however.
2. (a) A soothing voice is a blessing.
   (b) A bane, on the other hand, describes the harsh voice.
3. (a) Winning and a drink of salt water have something in common.
   (b) They can't quench your thirst.
4. (a) The story is memorable.
   (b) It mixes horror and beauty.
   (c) It describes the terrible.
   (d) It makes the terrible terrifying to read.

4.18 Comment on the use of rhythmic effects, diction, sentence length, and pattern in each of the following advertisements:

1.   **Oh What a Steal!**

   Is Tercel a Steal? Consider the evidence. A front-wheel-drive Corolla Tercel 2-Door Sedan for just $4998! So much car for the price, it's hard to believe.

Take mileage. Tercel is rated at 48 EPA Estimated Highway MPG, 36 EPA Estimated MPG. Remember: Compare this estimate to the EPA "Estimated MPG" of other small cars. You may get different mileage, depending on how fast you drive, weather conditions and trip length. Actual highway mileage will probably be less than the EPA "Highway Estimate."

More evidence of Toyota quality—a standard 1.5 liter engine, for quick getaways. 4-speed transmission. Rack-and-pinion steering. Hardly your average "economy" car.

Now look inside. You'll find reclining hi-back front bucket seats, and power assisted flo-thru ventilation. Downright rich for a car in its class.

The Corolla Tercel. A steal? Actually, it's completely legal. It's a simple case of value in the first degree!

2.   **JAGUAR XJ-S. Elegance Is Only Half the Story.**

Behold the optimal performance car: the Jaguar XJ-S. An uncommon blending of pure luxury, aerodynamic design and advanced engineering elevates the XJ-S to a singular level among the world's few fine cars.

Beneath its clean, wind-defiant shape, the XJ-S is endowed with a refined 5.3 litre, V-12 engine. Jaguar engineering coupled with the remarkable May head has created a high-performance engine unrivalled for dependably smooth power, high torque and economy.

The secret lies in the innovative design of the combustion chamber. Its shape promotes an extremely strong swirl to compact the fuel-air mixture at the point of ignition. The burn is rapid and efficient, enabling the engine to run on a leaner mixture, with higher compression, while using regular unleaded fuel. In terms of response and performance, the result is electrifying.

The heritage of Jaguar racing champions lives in the XJ-S. Skilled craftsmen meticulously machine and hand-work critical components to meet the most exacting tolerances. The result is a dimension of dependability and performance beyond the scope of ordinary cars. Power-assisted rack and pinion steering is extraordinarily precise. Fully independent suspension on all four wheels transmits a sure and positive feel for the road. Four wheel power disc brakes respond instantly to your command. Even the tires are specially designed to meet stringent Jaguar standards. Pirelli P5 215/70VR15 tires mounted on precision balanced Bugatti-type alloy wheels, take charge of the road, to further enhance handling and stability. You're in complete control, as the XJ-S responds to your every driving skill.

Within, luxury excels as never before. Lustrous elm burl veneer enriches the dashboard and door panels. Rich, supple leather graces the entire seating compartment. A new, four speaker stereophonic AM/FM radio has a signal scanning tuner and cassette player to deliver concert-hall sound—without drift or fade. What's more, every XJ-S is equipped with cruise control, power windows and door locks, climate control, plus a host of other features and appointments that you would only expect from Jaguar.

Our confidence in the quality and dependability of Jaguar has resulted in the finest warranty in our long history. See your authorized Jaguar dealer for the complete story on the remarkable XJ-S sports coupe or the XJ6 and the XJ12 Vanden Plus Sedans.

SENTENCE RHYTHM

4.19 Comment on the rhythm of the following passages. Try to identify the part that repetition and special sentence patterns such as parallelism, alliteration, and onomatopoeia play in creating the overall rhythm—or lack of rhythm.

1. Here you shall find emphasized true hospitality and history so intertwined that upon departure, all ideas you have encountered shall have become blended into a decision that Washington surely has been emerging as a typical expression of American civilization which has surmounted all problems as they appeared and here we have proven a wholesome, sturdy pioneer philosophy which has strengthened your belief in your mission in coming to the Capitol City to give your measure of effort for the stabilization and survival of sound government which "under God" shall operate upon the premise "that the value of history lies in the perspective it gives us as we take up the problems of the present" with a common faith in "liberty and justice for all."

2. What treaty that the whites have kept has the red man broken? Not one. What treaty that the white men ever made with us have they kept? Not one. When I was a boy the Sioux owned the world; the sun rose and set on their land; they sent ten thousand men to battle. Where are the warriors today? Who slew them? Where are our lands? Who owns them? What white man can say I ever stole his land or a penny of his money? Yet they say I am a thief. What white woman, however lonely, was ever captive or insulted by me? Yet they say I am a bad Indian. What white man has ever seen me drunk? Who has ever come to me hungry and unfed? Who has ever seen me beat my wives or abuse my children? What law have I broken? Is it wrong for me to love my own? Is it wicked for

me because my skin is red? Because I am a Sioux; because I was born where my father lived; because I would die for my people and my country.

3. Dickens shows lamentable taste in his treatment of the Smallweed family, not especially palatable at best, almost revolting in the scenes in which, for the sake, I am afraid, of comic relief, he has old Smallweed, a paralytic, amuse himself by repeatedly crowning his senile consort, who crouches in the chimney corner across from him, with a cushion or two.

4. The confusion of the present times is great, the multitude of voices counselling differing things bewildering, the number of existing works capable of attracting a young writer's attention and of becoming his models, immense: what he wants is a hand to guide him through the confusion, a voice to prescribe to him the aim which he should keep in view, and to explain to him that the value of the literary works which offer themselves to his attention is relative to their power of helping him forward on his road towards this aim.

4.20 Following are three excerpts which describe the first astronauts' walk on the moon in 1969. Examine the three passages for the ways in which sentence rhythm helps to achieve a particular tone. How do the rhythms of the three passages vary?

1. Man stepped out onto the moon tonight for the first time in his two-million-year history.

   "That's one small step for man," declared pioneer astronaut Neil Armstrong at 10:56 EDT, "one giant leap for mankind."

   Just after that historic moment in man's quest for his origins, Armstrong walked on the dead satellite and found the surface very powdery, littered with fine grains of black dust.

   A few minutes later, Edwin (Buzz) Aldrin joined Armstrong on the lunar surface and in less than an hour they put on a show that will long be remembered by the worldwide television audience.

   The two men walked easily, talked easily, even ran and jumped happily, so it seemed. They picked up rocks, talked at length of what they saw, planted an American flag, saluted it, and talked by radiophone with the President in the White House, and then faced the camera and saluted Mr. Nixon.

2. As a freshman at college seeking grist for the under-graduate newspaper, I approached a famous astro-physicist, Lyman Spitzer, and asked if it was true that he intended to fly to the moon. He replied frostily, "I shouldn't know what to do if I got there."

   And indeed the scientific community went back to somnambulism, leaving the moon to science fiction, until the great pressures of our competition with the Soviet Union worked their way through to the White House and John F. Kennedy wrote a memorandum to Lyndon Baines Johnson: "Do we have a chance of beating the Soviets by putting a laboratory into space, or by a trip around the moon, or by a rocket to land on the moon, or by a rocket to go to the moon and back with a man? Is there any other space program which promises dramatic results in which we could win?"

Here in London the *Sunday Times* is quite explicit about it all. The editors regret the choice of the American flag over against the choice of, say, the flag of the United Nations to plant down on the moon but concede that "without Old Glory standing there alone the objectives set by President Kennedy when he sent America to the moon in 1961 would have been betrayed in the last stride." The gentleman is saying that America suffers from *amour propre*, which is true, which should be true.

3. Did his foot tingle in the heavy lunar overshoe? "I'm going to step off the Lem now."

Did something in him shudder at the touch of the new ground? Or did he draw a sweet strength from the balls of his feet? Nobody was necessarily going ever to know.

"That's one small step for man," said Armstrong, "one giant leap for mankind." He had joined the ranks of the forever quoted. Patrick Henry, Henry Stanley, and Admiral Dewey moved over for him. . . .

It was at this point that patriotism, the corporation, and the national taste all came to occupy the same head of a pin, for the astronauts next proceeded to set up the flag. But that operation, as always, presented its exquisite problems. There was, we remind ourselves, no atmosphere for the flag to wave in. Any flag made of cloth would droop, indeed it would dangle. Therefore a species of starched plastic flag had to be employed, a flag which could stand out, there, out to the nonexistent breeze, flat as a piece of plywood. No, that would not do either. The flag was better crinkled and curled. Waves and billows were bent into it, and a full cork-screw of a curl at the end. There it stands for posterity, photographed in the twists of a high gale on the windless moon, curled up tin flag, numb as a pickled pepper.

4.21 One of the outstanding characteristics of traditional oratory is the orator's use of elaborate structural and rhythmic patterns in sentences and paragraphs. Examine the following selections closely and describe the devices of repetition, parallelism, antithesis, alliteration, and onomatopoeia by which each speaker tries to achieve particular effects.

1. Even though large tracts of Europe and many old and famous States have fallen or may fall into the grip of the Gestapo and all the odious apparatus of Nazi rule, we shall not flag or fail. We shall go on to the end. We shall fight in France, we shall fight on the seas and oceans, we shall fight with growing confidence and growing strength in the air; we shall defend our Island, whatever the cost may be. We shall fight on the beaches, . . . we shall fight in the fields and in the streets, we shall fight in the hills; we shall never surrender; and even if, which I do not for a moment believe, this Island or a large part of it were subjugated and starving, then our Empire beyond the seas, armed and guarded by the British fleet, would carry on the struggle, until, in God's good time, the New World, with all its power and might, steps forth to the rescue and the liberation of the old.

2. Our tragedy is a general and universal physical fear so long sustained by now that we can even bear it. There are no longer problems of the spirit. There is only one question: When will I be blown up? Because of this, the young man or woman writing today has forgotten the problems of the human heart in conflict with itself which alone can make good writing because only that is worth writing about, worth the agony and the sweat.

   He must learn them again. He must teach himself that the basest of all things is to be afraid; and, teaching himself that, forget it forever, leaving no room in his workshop for anything but the old verities and truths of the heart, the old universal truths lacking which any story is ephemeral and doomed—love and honor and pity and pride and compassion and sacrifice. Until he does so, he labors under a curse. He writes not of love but of lust, of defeats in which nobody loses anything of value, of victories without hope and, worst of all, without pity or compassion. His griefs grieve on no universal bones, leaving no scars. He writes not of the heart but of the glands.

3. In the long hundred years since the white man came, I have seen my freedom disappear like the salmon going mysteriously out to sea. The white man's strange customs, which I could not understand, pressed down upon me until I could no longer breathe. . . .

   Oh, God in Heaven! Give me back the courage of the olden Chiefs. Let me wrestle with my surroundings. Let me again, as in the days of old, dominate my environment. Let me humbly accept this new culture and through it rise up and go on.

   Oh God! Like the Thunderbird of old I shall rise again out of the sea; I shall grab the instruments of the white man's success— his education, his skills, and with these new tools I shall build my race into the proudest segment of your society. Before I follow the great Chiefs who have gone before us . . . I shall see these things come to pass.

4.22 Many prose excerpts printed in the text or in exercises attached to other chapters provide good additional places to study sentence length, arrangement, and rhythm. See, for example, the passages in exercise 1.34, pages 48–49; exercise 2.8, pages 88–89; or exercise 3.21, pages 186–189.

PARAGRAPH FORM

4.23 Examine each of the following passages for the clarity with which an idea, or a set of related ideas, is developed. Does each sentence logically follow from what has preceded it? Are there any irrelevant or misplaced ideas? If you find any of the paragraphs difficult to follow, rewrite them, eliminating the sources of difficulty.

1. Our profession has no room for intemperate criticism of any kind, least of all in print. Differences of opinion there will always be, and scholarly competence not being a gift distributed equally among all practitioners, lapses of judgment and imperfections of knowledge will sometimes call for correction. Otherwise literary studies would stagnate, complacent in its intellectual lethargy and spotted with uncorrected errors. But the necessary process of debate and correction can, and should, be conducted with dignity and courtesy. Name-calling, personalities, aspersions on a man's professional ability, and similar below-the-belt tactics are not to be condoned. Controversial points can be made, effectively and adequately, without betraying the ancient association of scholarship and civility.

2. Someone who has a serious interest in eating Dungeness crabs cannot dally indefinitely on the East Coast; the Dungeness is a West Coast creature, named for a small town in Washington. Even on the West Coast, someone who wants to eat a Dungeness crab that was alive and crawling twenty minutes before the meal has his work cut out for him. On either coast of the United States, a lot of fish seem to leap out of the sea straight into a flash freezer. Even fish restaurants on harbors often seem to have chosen the spot more for the ambiance than the source of supply—the fish caught in the picturesque bay visible through the fishnet-covered windows having apparently found their way by truck to Boston, where they were frozen and sent back, without unseemly haste. For a long time, I have had the suspicion that Alaska and Florida are providing each other's storefront restaurants with bland frozen

fish, in the way that some countries with cultural-exchange agreements provide each other with overly polite high school students.

3. The inductive method has been practised ever since the beginning of the world by every human being. It is constantly practised by the most ignorant clown, by the most thoughtless schoolboy, by the very child at the breast. That method leads the clown to the conclusion that if he sows barley he shall not reap wheat. By that method the schoolboy learns that a cloudy day is the best for catching trout. The very infant, we imagine, is led by induction to expect milk from his mother or nurse, and none from his father.

4. As a student he was eager to learn, and his recitations in class, though somewhat irrelevant to the matter under discussion at the moment, were so full of wit and odd miscellaneous information that teachers welcomed his presence. Rather taller than most boys his age, he had a thick mop of brown hair which had a tendency to become uncombed under the stress of ideas, and his brown eyes and wide humorous mouth had the power of putting people under his spell before he was with them for ten minutes. He had not yet got over the adolescent tendency toward awkwardness, and his hands, a little larger than the common run of hands, often sought refuge in his pockets. It was the fashion in his day to wear trousers above the ankles, but the fact that his trousers dangled not far below his calf may have been due more to the rapid, uncheckable upward expansion of his frame than to any conscious desire to be in style. What annoyed his teachers most was his invariable habit of gazing out of the window just when they were making the most important point in their day's lecture. Quite plainly his mind was a thousand miles away, yet when it came to a showdown he always turned out to have been listening—and retaining. He was too exasperating on occasion to be a model student, but no teacher ever regretted having had the chance to teach him.

5. When I was a teenager, there were two distinct streams of popular music: one was black, and the other was white. The former could only be heard way at the end of the radio dial, while white music dominated everywhere else. A fact of life, the equivalent of blacks sitting in the back of the bus and "whites only" signs below the Mason-Dixon line. Satchmo might grin for days on "The Ed Sullivan Show" and certain historians hold forth *ad nauseam* on the black contribution to American music, but the truth was that our worlds rarely twined.

6. The magical mystery of drawing ability seems to be, in part at least, an ability to make a shift in brain state to a very different mode of seeing/perceiving. When you see in the special way in which experienced artists see, then you can draw. This is not to

say that the drawings of great artists such as Leonardo da Vinci or Rembrandt are not still wondrous because we may know something about the cerebral process that went into their creation. Indeed, scientific research makes master drawings seem even more remarkable because they seem to cause a viewer to shift to the artist's mode of perceiving. But the basic skill of drawing is also accessible to everyone who can learn to make the shift to the artist's mode and to see in the artist's way.

7. He was about the middle height, but the thinness of his body, and the length of his legs, gave him the appearance of being much taller. The green coat had been a smart dress garment in the days of swallow-tails, but had evidently in those times adorned a much shorter man than the stranger, for the soiled and faded sleeves scarcely reached to his wrists. It was buttoned closely up to his chin, at the imminent hazard of splitting the back; and an old stock, without a vestige of shirt collar, ornamented his neck. His scanty black trousers displayed here and there those shiny patches which bespeak long service, and were strapped very tightly over a pair of patched and mended shoes, as if to conceal the dirty white stockings, which were nevertheless distinctly visible. His long black hair escaped in negligent waves from beneath each side of his old pinched up hat; and glimpses of his bare wrist might be observed, between the tops of his gloves, and the cuffs of his coat sleeves. His face was thin and haggard; but an indescribable air of jaunty impudence and perfect self-possession pervaded the whole man. [The man here described is Dickens's character Mr. Jingle, whose elliptical speech patterns are illustrated on page 215.]

4.24 The following dispatch from McMurdo Station, Antarctica, was written by a student journalist for his campus paper. Note that the author uses short, simple sentences and very brief paragraphs. Using the same materials, rewrite the article, using more complex syntax and absorbing the details in longer sentences through the use of subordination, and reducing the number of paragraphs by writing longer, more carefully unified ones.

At first glance, McMurdo Station looks every bit like an Alaskan mining town built 70 years ago. But then you notice the telephone poles and the tire tracks going down the unpaved streets.

McMurdo is built on the side of a black, lava rock hill. Covering the surface of the hill is coarse, weather-beaten, sand-like lava dust.

The buildings are made of wood. To give color to the settlement, many huts have been painted. All of them are raised off the ground.

There is another difference between McMurdo and the early Alaskan mining town. There are no saloons filling the streets with honky-tonk music and drunken miners. And there are no dance-hall girls.

For the Navy enlisted personnel, there are three important buildings, the Club Erebus, the station theater, and building Number 121.

The Club Erebus is the enlisted men's club. Beer and whiskey are served.

Every "night" at 8:00, there is a movie in the station theater. Old movies and episodes from television programs are shown.

Building 121 is open only three times a week. It is the beer warehouse. For $3 you can buy a case of beer.

There is also a recreation building that contains a bowling alley and library.

There is an officers' wardroom where Navy officers, scientists, and reporters can get a drink or watch a movie.

The mess hall is open almost all day. Anyone can go there for a between-meal snack. There is always coffee, hot chocolate, orange juice and Kool-Aid ready to serve. Thirst is a common affliction in Antarctica.

For all the snow and ice, the humidity is so low it is almost automatically recorded as zero. The dryness makes you thirsty, and so does the warm air in the huts.

Also available in the mess hall is bread, peanut butter, jelly, soft ice cream, and graham crackers.

You can eat all you want, and there are four meals daily. There is an extra one that begins at 11:00 P.M. It is a breakfast for those men who work at "night."

"Night" is definitely a problem. The sun shines brightly 24 hours a day. Without a watch, you quickly lose all sense of time.

McMurdo Station, however, is unlike all other U.S. bases in Antarctica. McMurdo is built on a hill with above-ground huts. Not so at the South Pole Base and at the Byrd Base where the bases are built six to eight feet beneath the summer snow.

All in all, life in the Antarctic is comfortable and enjoyable—especially to a visitor who will be leaving soon. But for those who live and work here for an extended period of time, well, they have a different outlook on life in Antarctica.

4.25 Examine any sequence of three or four paragraphs in the text of this book. How clearly organized is each paragraph? Are transitional points and logical relationships clearly marked? Are successive paragraphs tied together so that readers can follow the direction of the argument without difficulty? Do most of the paragraphs present a topic and then comment on that topic through various means of development (as does the model discussed on pages 229–231)?

4.26 Examine the following paragraph for the use of the topic/development-of-topic model. Where is the topic presented? In what ways does the author comment on and develop it? Finally, go through the paragraph, identifying all the links that help make it coherent (see pages 228–231 for an example of such an analysis).

> Why is there this intense public furor over recombinant DNA experiments? The public concern arose because two quite separate issues became confused. On the one hand, there may be an immediate danger to public health if certain kinds of recombinant DNA are grown in the laboratory and released into the environment in an irresponsible fashion. On the other hand, there are the long-range horrors, beginning with Doctor Moreau and ending with the cloning of human beings, that may come to pass as a result of misapplication of biological knowledge. The biologists who began the recombinant DNA experiments were aware of the possibility of an immediate public health danger. The molecular biologist Maxine Singer, wife of the Daniel Singer who had been the Federation of American Scientists' general counsel, published a statement calling attention to the danger, soon after the first experiments were done. In 1975 an international meeting of biologists voluntarily drew up a set of guidelines, prohibiting experiments that seemed to them irresponsible and recommending containment procedures for permissible experiments. Guidelines similar to theirs have now been accepted by biologists and governments all over the world. These guidelines have made any immediate public health hazard resulting from DNA experiments very unlikely. One cannot say that the immediate hazards are nonexistent, but they are smaller than the hazards associated with the standard procedures for handling disease germs in clinical laboratories and hospitals. So from the point of view of the public health authorities, the risks of recombinant DNA experiments are adequately controlled. Why, then, is the public still scared? The public is scared because the public sees farther into the future and is concerned with larger issues than immediate health hazards. The public knows that recombinant DNA experiments will ultimately give the biologists knowledge of the genetic design of all creatures including ourselves. The public is rightly afraid of the abuse of this knowledge. When the National Academy of Sciences organized a meeting in Washington to give all sides of the recombinant DNA debate a chance to be heard, the public appeared in the guise of a gang of young people carrying placards and chanting, "We won't be cloned." The public sees, behind the honest faces of Matthew Meselson and Maxine Singer, the sinister figures of Doctor Moreau and Daedalus.

4.27 Following are the *second* paragraphs from two articles. On the basis of the information offered in them, write a *lead* paragraph for each. (The title of the first article, to help you get started, is "Late for Class? O.K., If the Excuse Is Show Business.")

1. One sunny Tuesday, for example, a reporter found that more than a dozen students [from New York's Professional Children's School] were on Broadway, appearing in current hits or rehearsing for shows soon to open ("Evita," "Camelot," "The Little Prince"). Several dozen more were in Hollywood or on location making movies ("Pennies from Heaven," "Taps") and TV shows ("Harper Valley P.T.A.," "Search for Tomorrow," "Fame," "One Day at a Time") or at "go-sees" at various modeling agencies around town. Others were on Long Island or in the Caribbean or elsewhere making TV commercials (Kool-Aid, Cheerios, Tab, Kellogg's Corn Flakes). Others were all across America or abroad in touring companies.

2. Many people don't think of log cabins in the same way they think of ordinary modern houses. Frequently they just pick a size and build it, and then try to fit everything they want in afterwards. The problem with this approach is that you can't always fit in the things you want, or even if it all fits, it may be so inconvenient that you have to be running back and forth constantly. You might even build the cabin too big, and end up occupying only one corner of it.

4.28 The following passages were originally printed as three separate paragraphs. Analyze the passages, and then decide where you think the second and third paragraphs should begin. What are the reasons for your choice?

1. A dawn wind stirs on the great marsh. With almost imperceptible slowness it rolls a bank of fog across a wide morass. Like the white ghost of a glacier the mists advance, riding over phalanxes of tamarack, sliding across bogmeadows heavy with dew. A single silence hangs from horizon to horizon. Out of some far recess of the sky a tinkling of little bells falls soft upon the listening land. Then again silence. Now comes a baying of some sweet-throated hound, soon the clamor of a responding pack. Then a far clear blast of hunting horns, out of a sky into the fog. High horns, low horns, silence, and finally a pandemonium of trumpets, rattles, croaks, and cries that almost shakes the bog with its nearness, but without yet disclosing whence it comes. At last a glint of sun reveals the approach of a great echelon of birds. On motionless wing they emerge from the lifting mists, sweep a final arc of sky, and settle in clangorous descending spirals to their feeding grounds. A new day has begun on the crane marsh.

2. Two long blasts of the whistle, a jolting of cars, and the train slowly rumbles forward. A bell is clanging, and as big wheels start to turn, you can hear the engine working, choo-choo-choo-choo. It is a rhythm as familiar and insistent as a heartbeat. Until the early

1950s, this was the song of round-houses, switchyards, depots, and whistle-stops—a symphony of huffing and puffing and tooting and ringing from some 70,000 working steam engines. Running across the continent trailing clouds of steam and sooty smoke, or working the "short lines" to remote mines and logging camps, these locomotives linked a far-flung nation. In the last three decades these mechanical marvels have practically disappeared, their places taken by more powerful, more efficient diesel locomotives. But this summer some 20-plus railroads throughout the West still offer visitors a chance to board old-fashioned steam trains for a ride into the past. Many of the outfits listed on the following pages are within an easy day or weekend outing of most cities; others can be included in a summer vacation.

REVIEW

4.29 This exercise is designed to help you draw together what you have learned about the length, arrangement, and rhythm of sentences. Analyze each passage for such matters as the movement of thought from sentence to sentence; the relative effectiveness of short and long sentences; the use of periodic and cumulative sentences; and patterns such as parallelism, antithesis, inversion, and ellipsis.

1. She slipped into the water behind Arie [her four-year-old son] and held him against her. Now, for this time in their lives, she could still hold his body against hers, enfolding him, his slim buttocks resting against her softness, his fine hair lightly brushing her breasts. In the circle of her loosely crossed legs, in the warm small circle of the tub, they formed a perfect unity.

2. Apart from the peculiar tenets of individual thinkers, there is also in the world at large an increasing inclination to stretch unduly the powers of society over the individual, both by force of opinion and even by that of legislation: and as the tendency of all the changes taking place in the world is to strengthen society, and diminish the power of the individual, this encroachment is not one of the evils which tend spontaneously to disappear, but on the contrary, to grow more and more formidable. The disposition of mankind, whether as rulers or as fellow citizens, to impose their own opinions and inclinations as a rule of conduct on others, is so energetically supported by some of the best and by some of the worst feelings incident to human nature, that it is hardly ever kept under restraint by anything but want of power; and as the power is not declining, but growing, unless a strong barrier of moral conviction can be raised against the mischief, we must expect, in the present circumstances of the world, to see it increase.

3. But we now confront these possibilities as real choices. We *can* provide ourselves with the material basis for a truly human life and also produce enough to help other human beings achieve the same position. We can do so, moreover, while simultaneously decentralizing our economic and political institutions, so as to enable us to live at the scale, and in the kinds of relationships with ourselves and each other, appropriate to our nature.

    We can no longer take refuge, or seek escape, in the question of whether or not we can become truly human.

    We *can*.

    The question now is whether or not we *will*.

4. Science has changed the conditions of man's life. It has changed material conditions; by changing them it has altered our labor and our rest, our power, and the limits of that power, as men and as communities of men, the means and instruments as well as the substance of our learning, the terms and the forms in which decisions of right and wrong come before us. It has altered the communities in which we live and cherish, learn and act. It has brought an acute and pervasive sense of change itself into our own life's span. The ideas of science have changed the way men think of themselves and of the world.

5. Fog everywhere. Fog up the river, where it flows among green aits and meadows; fog down the river where it rolls defiled among the tiers of shipping and the waterside pollutions of a great (and dirty) city. Fog on the Essex marshes, fog on the Kentish heights. Fog creeping into the cabooses of collier-brigs, fog lying out on the yards, and hovering in the rigging of great ships; fog drooping on the gunwales of barges and small boats. Fog in the eyes and throats of ancient Greenwich pensioners, wheezing by the firesides of their wards; fog in the stem and bowl of the afternoon pipe of the wrathful skipper, down in his close cabin; fog cruelly pinching the toes and fingers of his shivering little 'prentice boy on deck. Chance people on the bridges peeping over the parapets into a nether sky of fog, with fog all round them, as if they were up in a balloon and hanging in the misty clouds.

6. From the Carolinas south, the nation was awash in red last week, that astonishing red produced only by nature and the art directors of seed catalogs. It was the red of ripe tomatoes: tomatoes ready to be canned, pickled, mashed into sauce, diced into relish, sliced along all three axes or carved into a paraboloid to enclose a ball of tuna salad. Northward toward New Jersey, the red faded to the orange of not-quite-ripeness, that tantalizing, agonizing state in which a tomato garden can languish for days before suddenly plunging into utter glut. Further north still was a region of creamy yellow and the pale green of tomatoes the size of Ping-Pong balls.

Or marbles. Or fingertips. Here, there was nothing to be done but hope that nature would take its course, encouraged by a side dressing of fertilizer, a handful of limestone as a precaution against blossom-end rot and a mulch of salt-marsh hay laid 5 to 6 inches deep and carried out to the drip line. For those who grow tomatoes, however much they may like to eat them, a tomato on the plate means one thing above all: it is a tomato forever safe from fusarium wilt.

7.   This book will not tell you how to die. Some cheer-leaders of war can always get out a pamphlet telling the best way to go through that small but necessary business at the end. . . .

No. This book will not tell you how to die. This book will tell you, though, how all men from the earliest times we know have fought and died. So when you have read it you will know that there are no worse things to be gone through than men have been through before.

When you read the account of Saint Louis the IX's Crusade you will see that no expeditionary force can ever have to go through anything as bad as those men endured. We have only to fight as well as the men who stayed and fought at Shiloh. It is not necessary that we should fight better. There can be no such thing as better.

4.30 Analyze the advertisements on pages 261 and 262 for the use of sentence length; sentence patterns; special patterns such as parallelism, antithesis, inversion, and ellipsis; and rhythmic effects, including alliteration, and onomatopoeia. Also consider the effects created through the use of pictures and other elements of visual design.

4.31 For this exercise, we have taken apart some sentences from well-known authors and written them as lists of much shorter sentences. Your job: to turn each group into the best single sentence you can. After you have written your versions of the sentences, compare them with those of your classmates. Which versions do you find most effective? What sentence patterns and other elements are responsible for that effectiveness? We will get you started by offering the first group as an example.

1.   Bethe lived in a modest house.
Bethe lived in the house a short time.
The house was on Prytania Street.
Bethe slept on a cot.
The cot was in the dining room.
Bethe rose at five o'clock.
Bethe carried the cot to the back porch.
Bethe was the first to heat the water.

Relax with a friend.

After tennis, jogging, or anytime you just want to relax, do it with a friend. Sweet 'N Low. Sprinkle some in a tall glass of iced tea for the perfect diet drink. Sweet 'N Low dissolves instantly to give you a sweet, satisfying taste—without those extra calories. And cutting calories is important when you're trying to stay in shape.

So whether you work out on the courts—or on the track—when you take a break, relax with a friend.

#1 in America for over a generation.

EARTH'S FIRST SOFT DRINK.

When the earth was new, mountains rose and valleys were carved and there was created, in what is now called France, a spring that is now called Perrier.®

All the Perrier in the world is born in that spring.

Still clear, pure and sparkling, and minus all those additives that civilization has invented. There's no sugar. No artificial sweetener. No calories. There's no caffeine, no coloring. And Perrier is recommended for salt-free diets, as well.

In modern times, when most beverages are made with water that's been disinfected, softened, oxidated or chlorinated, it's nice also to know that Perrier is naturally filtered as it rises to the surface from its deep underground source.

And so our only concession to civilization is the green Perrier bottle. Because without it, you would never get to enjoy Perrier.

Perrier. Earth's first soft drink. Not manufactured, but created by the earth when it was new.

Bethe was first to make coffee.
Bethe was first to roll breakfast rolls.
Bethe baked the breakfast rolls.
The rolls were German breakfast rolls.
Nobody liked the German breakfast rolls.

The sentences combined: Bethe for a short time lived in the modest house on Prytania Street, sleeping on a cot in the dining room, rising at five o'clock to carry it to the back porch, to be the first to heat the water, to make the coffee, to roll and bake the German breakfast rolls nobody liked.

Now, combine the next group yourself:

2. Then Bethe walked to the end of Canal Street.
    Bethe walked to the end of Canal Street to save carfare.
    Canal Street was a long distance.
    At Canal Street she carried shoe box stacks.
    She carried shoe box stacks back and forth all day.
    She carried them for a merchant.
    The merchant was German.
    The merchant ran a mean store.
    The store was for sailors.
    The sailors lived off the wharves.

For the next two groups, combine each subgroup of sentences into one single sentence. The subgroups are marked off by asterisks.

3. Dr. Reefy's office was large.
    It was large as a barn.

                        *   *   *

    A stove sat in the middle of the room.
    The stove had a round paunch.

                        *   *   *

    Sawdust was piled around its base.
    Its base was held in place by planks.
    The planks were heavy.
    The planks were nailed to the floor.

                        *   *   *

    A huge table stood.
    It stood by the door.
    It had once been a part of the furniture.
    The furniture was from Herrick's Clothing Store.

It had been used for displaying clothes.
The clothes were custom-made.

* * *

It was covered with books.
It was covered with bottles.
It was covered with surgical instruments.

4. The bride was not very pretty.
The bride was not very young.

* * *

She wore a dress of cashmere.
The cashmere was blue.
The dress had small reservations of velvet.
The reservations of velvet were here and there.
The dress had buttons.
The buttons were small.
The buttons were abounding.

* * *

She continually twisted her head.
She twisted her head to regard her sleeves.
The sleeves were puff sleeves.
They were very stiff.
They were very straight.
They were very high.

* * *

The sleeves embarrassed her.
They were the puff sleeves.

4.32 As many of the preceding passages have illustrated, the structure and rhythm of sentences and paragraphs make a major contribution to the total effect of any piece of writing. In the following examples, how do these combine with diction, metaphors, and other elements to produce the overall tone? Isolate and define the specific devices.

1. I have often noticed that after I had bestowed on the characters of my novels some treasured item of my past, it would pine away in the artificial world where I had so abruptly placed it. Although it lingered on in my mind, its personal warmth, its retrospective appeal had gone and, presently, it became more closely identified with my novel than with my former self, where it had seemed to be so safe from the intrusion of the artist. Houses have crumbled in my memory as soundlessly as they did in the mute films of yore,

and the portrait of my old French governess, whom I once lent to
a boy in one of my books, is fading fast, now that it is engulfed in
the description of a childhood entirely unrelated to my own. The
man in me revolts against the fictionist, and here is my desperate
attempt to save what is left of poor Mademoiselle.

Now You Can Own an Oriental Masterwork of the Treasured Art of Chokin.

To the Japanese, the fresh evergreen pine represents prosperity
... and the gentle wading crane is a symbol of longevity. These
images prevail on the traditional Japanese Floral Calendar from
January 1 to 15, as wishes for the new year ahead.

The symbols of nature represented in the Japanese Floral Calendar have been handed down across scores of generations, and
today the Japanese continue to feel a true reverence for the Floral
Calendar.

In the same manner, the sensitive art of Chokin has been
handed down from father to son for more than 700 years. Created
by etching solid copper and gilding it with gold and silver, the
stunning Chokin master-works first appeared on the armaments of
the mighty Samurai warriors in the late 12th century.

Unfortunately, today there are few surviving masters of the
Chokin art style. But one of these great artists, Shuho, was
retained to design and hand-engrave the "New Year's Day" art of
pine and crane exclusively for the Hamilton Collection.

EACH CHOKIN IMAGE CREATED BY HAND

The re-creation of Shuho's floral calendar images involves performing many delicate operations for each individual plate. Master craftsmen hand-gild each central image, using 24K gold, copper and silver. This central piece is then fused to a plate body of
pure, glistening white porcelain. In addition, a ⅝"-wide band of
23K gold borders the plate body, enhanced by etched symbols
from the Floral Calendar. . . .

A STRICTLY LIMITED EDITION

Because of the difficult hand work involved in the creation of
each "New Year's Day" plate, the firing period must be *strictly*
limited to ten days only. And when this edition closes, no further
plates will ever be created. Because of this, a further limit of one
plate per customer must be enforced. Each plate will be hand-
numbered, attesting to its place in the edition.

3. The flames bit him, and the hot smoke broiled his skin. His rifle

barrel grew so hot that ordinarily he could not have borne it upon his palms; but he kept on stuffing cartridges into it, and pounding them with his clanking, bending ramrod. If he aimed at some changing form through the smoke, he pulled his trigger with a fierce grunt, as if he were dealing a blow of the fist with all his strength.

When the enemy seemed falling back before him and his fellows, he went instantly forward, like a dog who, seeing his foes lagging, turns and insists upon being pursued. And when he was compelled to retire again, he did it slowly, sullenly, taking steps of wrathful despair.

Once he, in his intent hate, was almost alone, and was firing, when all those near him had ceased. He was so engrossed in his occupation that he was not aware of a lull.

He was recalled by a hoarse laugh and a sentence that came to his ears in a voice of contempt and amazement. "Yeh infernal fool, don't yeh know enough t' quit when there ain't anything t' shoot at? Good Gawd!"

He turned then and, pausing with his rifle thrown half into position, looked at the blue line of his comrades. During this moment of leisure they seemed all to be engaged in staring with astonishment at him. They had become spectators. Turning to the front again, he saw, under the lifted smoke, a deserted ground.

He looked bewildered for a moment. Then there appeared upon the glazed vacancy of his eyes a diamond point of intelligence. "Oh," he said, comprehending.

4. I had a sense of *déjà vu* when the creationists in California tried to have evolution presented in biology textbooks as a mere hypothesis. This was precisely the tactic the Inquisition adopted with Copernicus' book: they made it acceptable by making it appear hypothetical. I expect the creationists will have about as much success as the Holy Congregation of the Index did. Of course, Galileo believed the Copernican system could be defended as physically real, and not simply as a hypothetical geometric arrangement. It is an irony of history that Galileo's own methods of scientific argument were instrumental in showing that what passes for truth in science is only the likely or the probable; truth can never be final and never absolute. What makes science so fascinating is the task of pushing ever closer to the unattainable goal of complete knowledge.

It is this process that the poet Robinson Jeffers had in mind when he wrote: "The mathematicians and the physics men have their mythology; they work alongside the truth, never touching it; their equations are false but the things *work*." The mathematicians and the physicists cannot really claim truth, but they have certainly sorted out a lot of things that do not work, and they are building a wondrously coherent picture of the universe. The Copernican system is surely a part of that coherency. A universe billions of years old and evolving is also part of that coherency. Galileo made a noble effort to convey such a picture of beauty and rational coherency to his public. Scientists today would honor him by helping their own public to understand better not only the majesty and beauty of the modern scientific picture of the universe but also the process of hypothesizing and testing by which that view is achieved.

5. The sun had not yet risen. The sea was indistinguishable from the sky, except that the sea was slightly creased as if a cloth had wrinkles in it. Gradually as the sky whitened a dark line lay on the horizon dividing the sea from the sky and the grey cloth became barred with thick strokes moving, one after another, beneath the surface, following each other, pursuing each other, perpetually.

   As they neared the shore each bar rose, heaped itself, broke and swept a thin veil of white water across the sand. The wave paused, and then drew out again, sighing like a sleeper whose breath comes and goes unconsciously. Gradually the dark bar on the horizon became clear as if the sediment and an old wine-bottle had sunk and left the glass green. Behind it, too, the sky cleared as if the sediment there had sunk, or as if the arm of a woman crouched beneath the horizon had raised a lamp and flat bars of white, green, and yellow spread across the sky like the blades of a fan. Then she raised her lamp higher and the air seemed to become fibrous and to tear away from the green surface flickering and flaming in red and yellow fibres like the smoky fire that roars from a bonfire. Gradually the fibres of the burning bonfire were fused into one haze, one incandescence which lifted the weight of the woolen grey sky on top of it and turned it to a million atoms of soft blue. The surface of the sea slowly became transparent and lay rippling and sparkling until the dark stripes were almost rubbed out. Slowly the arm that held the lamp raised it higher and then higher until a broad flame became visible; an arc of fire burnt on the rim of the horizon, and all round it the sea blazed gold.

4.33 Choose one paper you have written for a college course and analyze it for sentence length, sentence patterns, sentence rhythm, and paragraph form. A thorough analysis will take several hours, so do not try to do it all at once. Begin by charting your sentence length and noting its variety. Then gather data concerning your sentence patterns, rhythmic devices such as alliteration, and paragraph forms. When you have completed your survey, use the information to write a brief evaluation of your prose style, ending with a series of specific recommendations for improving it.

PATTERNS
OF CLEAR
THINKING

In the preceding chapters we have stressed many ways in which language molds readers' responses to messages by affecting their emotions and their reason. The two phenomena are, of course, inseparable: most everyday acts of communication appeal to the entire person — heart as well as mind. We will touch on some further emotional aspects of language use when we examine informal fallacies. For the most part in these concluding pages, however, we shall concentrate on the primarily intellectual aspect of language, the way in which words reflect patterns of thought.

We have already seen abundant evidence of the flexibility of words, their capacity for holding many shades of meaning or even several separate meanings. This same characteristic of language constantly shadows our efforts to communicate reasoned ideas. Whereas the essence of sound reasoning is precision, language normally tends toward imprecision. Only in formal scientific discourse do words usually come close to achieving the exactness that strict definition of ideas and their logical relationships demands.

And so, when a process of reasoning is described or implied in words, two opposing tendencies are at work: on the one hand, the sharpness, singleness, and constancy of meaning that are requisite to scientific thought, and on the other, the ambiguity, the lack of sharp and stable definition, that resides in most language. These opposing tendencies can perhaps best be seen in legal language, which often appears to be a jungle of tangled words and phrases — which, in a given context, all appear to mean the same thing — and of almost endless qualifying clauses. Such complicated and seemingly redundant language, forbidding as it appears to most of us, is often the product of necessity. Ideally, the laws and legal documents that govern human conduct should be as clearly stated as a proposition in formal logic, free of uncertain or possibly shifting meanings and capable of uniform interpretation, no matter who does the interpreting. A legal system would be virtually useless if its provisions were subject to limitless different interpretations. To avoid this pitfall as far as possible, laws and documents are worded in such a manner as to plug up all foreseeable loopholes, minimize erroneous interpretation, and take care of all contingencies. When legal writing is complicated because it is meant to be precise and unambiguous, we accept the difficulty and simply work hard at trying to understand it. Much legal language, however, is used by bureaucrats and others simply to intimidate or to confuse. When we see complicated language used in these ways, we should examine the motives of the writer very carefully.

The jurist's attempt to use the flexible, imprecise tool of human language to pin down fine legal distinctions is only one illustration of the complex relationship between patterns of thought and language. We shall devote the major part of this chapter to examining the ways in which logical structures are reflected in everyday writing and in public argument. But first we must look briefly at the writing of scientists, who try to match thought and language as closely as possible.

SCIENTIFIC REASONING

In trying to determine truths about the universe and put them in precise, clear, unambiguous statements, scientists use patterns of reasoning we will call *scientific induction* and *scientific deduction*. Scientific induction involves the extensive gathering of verifiable and often empirical data (data which may be gathered through sensory observation), elaborate testing of hypotheses, and strictly controlled laboratory conditions. Scientific deduction is based on the classic formal *syllogism*, a rigidly organized series of three statements which offers a means of establishing definite relationships among terms. If the first two statements, or *premises*, are true, and if the rules of constructing valid syllogisms are followed, then the resulting conclusion is absolutely true. Although this form of deduction rarely if ever appears in everyday writing, we shall review its principles briefly, because syllogistic reasoning has been extremely important in Western culture and because its principles can be applied in analyzing ordinary communication.

A scientific syllogism has three and only three terms organized in a series of three statements, as in this example:

Qualifier	Subject Term	Predicate Term	
All	people	are mortal	*Major Premise*
		Middle Term	
X	is a	person.	*Minor Premise*
X	is	mortal.	*Conclusion*

Each of the individual statements that make up a syllogism always has two, and usually three, elements: a subject term, a predicate term, and a qualifier. In the statement "All people are mortal," the subject term is *people*, the predicate term is *mortal*, and the qualifier is *all*. In cases where the subject term is a name or a definite description ("Ms. Blaine is a Democrat"), however, no qualifier appears. Formal logic recognizes four classes of qualifiers: (1) the universal affirmative *(all, each, every)*; (2) the universal negative *(no, never, none)*; (3) the particular affirmative *(some, a few,* and so on); and (4) the particular negative *(not all, not every,* and so on). If a statement contains a qualifier, the qualifier must belong to one or another of these classes.

In the conclusion, the subject term must come from one premise and the predicate term from the other. The premise that contains the predicate term of the conclusion is the *major premise,* and the one that contains the subject term of the conclusion is the *minor premise.* The term that appears in both the major and minor premises is called the *middle term.*

Because the middle term can occur only in four different positions, syllogisms have four basic forms. For this brief review, however, we shall confine ourselves to the most commonly used form, the one illustrated in the preceding syllogism.

To test the truth of any statement resulting from a series of premises, we must determine whether the premises themselves are true. In scientific reasoning, this step is usually carried out through inductive data gathering* and hypothesis testing. But in addition to true premises, a scientific syllogism must have a valid form or structure. There are several ways to test scientific deduction for this validity.

Central to these ways is the concept of the "distributed middle term," which must be present if a categorical syllogism (one whose conclusion is asserted to be categorically or universally true and which includes such absolute terms as *all, always, no,* or *never*) is valid. A valid syllogism must have three terms, each being used exactly twice to refer to the same class. As we just saw, one term is found in the major premise and the conclusion; one term is found in the minor premise and the conclusion; and the third term, the middle term, is found in both premises but not in the conclusion. To validate a categorical syllogism, the middle term must be *distributed.* This means that the middle term must include or exclude all members of the class to which it refers, thus admitting no exceptions. In addition, a term which is distributed in the conclusion must have been distributed in the premise in which it occurs. In our sample syllogism, the middle term *(people)* is properly distributed *(all* allows for no exceptions), and the conclusion is valid:

A. All people (i. e., persons) are mortal.	(That is, all people have the quality of mortality.)
B. X is a person.	(X is an individual member of the "all people" category.)

---

*The process of looking for instances or individual cases where the truth of the premise is supported by observation of some fact or event.

C. *X* is mortal. (That is, *X* must have the quality of mortality that belongs to all those in the category to which *X* belongs.)

Now consider the following variation on this syllogism.

A. All people are mortal.
B. *X* is mortal.
C. *X* is a person.

In this case, the middle term, *mortal*, is not distributed in either premise. That is, we are told nothing about the entire class of mortals to which "all people" belong. Therefore, we cannot validly conclude that *X* is a person simply because *X* is mortal. Many other beings—cats, dogs, fish—also belong to the class of mortal beings.

A syllogism closely related to the model we have been examining appeared in a recent discussion in *Scientific American:*

Consider this syllogism:

A. If it is raining, the streets are wet.
B. It is raining.
C. Therefore, the streets are wet.

Now consider the converse:

A. If it is raining, the streets are wet.
B. The streets are wet.
C. Therefore, it is raining.

To students of logic this procedure of *confirming the consequent* is a well-known fallacy. After all, the streets could be wet for other reasons: the winter snow could be melting, the street-cleaning department might be out in force, or the Lippizaner horses might have been on parade.

How does . . . [such] logical analysis apply to Galileo's defense of Copernicanism?* Consider this syllogism:

A. If the planetary system is heliocentric, Venus will show phases.
B. The system is heliocentric.
C. Therefore, Venus will show phases.

---

*Galileo, the famous Renaissance scientist, argued that Copernicus was right in believing that the planets, including the earth, revolved around the sun, rather than that the planets revolved around the earth. Kepler, a contemporary of Galileo, was also a supporter of Copernicus's theory.

True enough; but this was not the form of Galileo's argument. He had exchanged the second premise and the conclusion:

A. If the planetary system is heliocentric, Venus will show phases.
B. Venus shows phases.
C. Therefore, the planetary system is heliocentric.

Clearly Galileo had committed an elementary blunder of logic, and even Kepler criticized him for it. There might well be other explanations for the observed phases of Venus. . . .

These examples have demonstrated the most common errors in scientific reasoning based on syllogisms. In addition, violating any of the following rules can render a syllogism invalid.

1. *The language must be accurate and consistent.* No matter how the major premise has been obtained—whether through logical processes or by simple assumption—the wording must be exact and clear. In addition, all terms must be defined precisely, and each definition must be adhered to throughout the syllogism. Otherwise, a slip in meaning can occur between premises and conclusion, and thus invalidate the argument. If the syllogism appears to have the requisite three terms, but the initial meaning of one of them is shifted when it reappears, a fourth term has in effect been introduced. Such a shift, called *equivocation*, violates the laws of scientific reasoning.

2. *Only two affirmative premises can produce an affirmative conclusion.* If the major premise is affirmative and the minor is negative, or if the major premise is negative and the minor is affirmative, the conclusion must be negative. In other words, a qualifier stating *not*, *never*, or *none* in one of the premises must be retained in the conclusion. Its presence in one of the premises automatically rules out any affirmative conclusion. Two negative premises can produce no conclusion at all.

3. *The conclusion of a syllogism must not be identical with a premise.* This is the fallacy known as "begging the question," in which an argument doubles back on itself, and is therefore useless. Begging the question most often occurs in a statement which says the same thing in two ways. An example occurred in the late medieval explanation of the cause of heat. Heat in objects, some thinkers reasoned, could be explained by the presence of the substance called *caloric*. That is, all hot objects contained *caloric*. But what was *caloric?* The answer was: What every hot object contained. Syllogisms based on this premise were of little use, because to say that "All hot objects contain caloric; X is hot; X contains caloric" really only says the same thing twice. The syllogism does not lead to any new information at all.

4. *The strength or scope of the conclusion can be no greater than that of the more restricted premise.* As we have seen, only when the middle term is distributed is a categorical (an all-inclusive or a no-exceptions) conclusion possible. Noncategorical syllogisms (that is, those allowing for a stated degree of exception) are

valid, but only to the extent specifically allowed for in the terms. Between an affirmative categorical statement *(all, always . . .)* and a negative categorical statement *(none, never . . .)* lie qualifiers like *almost all, a majority* (more than 50 percent), *almost half of* (less than 50 percent), *few,* and *at least one.* If one premise is an *all* statement, and the other is an *almost half* statement, the conclusion cannot contain a qualifier higher on the scale than *almost half.* If it did so, it would be making an assertion for whose breadth there is no justification in the premise.

When we first read the adventures of Sherlock Holmes, we are impressed by the uncanny accuracy of his split-second deductions. But our admiration is somewhat tempered when we realize that much of it is due to the unjustified categorical way in which the deductions are phrased. In "The Case of the Norwood Builder," for example, Holmes welcomed John Hector McFarlane to his Baker Street rooms with these words: "I assure you that, beyond the obvious facts that you are a bachelor, a solicitor [lawyer], a Freemason, and an asthmatic, I know nothing whatever about you."

"Familiar as I was with my friend's methods," writes Dr. Watson, "it was not difficult for me to follow his deductions, and to observe the untidiness of attire, the sheaf of legal papers, the watch-charm, and the breathing which had prompted them."

The implication is that Holmes reasoned in this way:

Men who dress untidily are bachelors.
This man is dressed untidily.
This man is a bachelor.

—and so with the other three deductions. On that basis, we are prone to assume that there could be no question at all that McFarlane was everything Holmes said he was. But let us phrase the syllogism more strictly to emphasize the distributed middle term:

All men who dress untidily are bachelors.
This man is dressed untidily.
This man *must be* a bachelor.

Now we have brought the vital idea of *all* (which was hidden in the syllogism as previously stated) into the open, and the weakness of the major premise is exposed. Obviously it is untrue that *all* men who dress untidily are bachelors. Therefore the conclusion—that this man must be a bachelor—is invalid. Maybe he *is* a bachelor, but the proof does not lie in that syllogism.

Actually, of course, what Holmes did, though his manner concealed the fact, was to count on the probabilities:

Most men who dress untidily are bachelors.
This man is dressed untidily.
This man probably is a bachelor.

Thus even though the odds may have been in favor of McFarlane's being a bachelor, Holmes quite possibly could have been wrong. The degree of probability in the conclusion depended, as always in such reasoning, on the degree expressed in the qualifier of the major premise.

(Exercises: pages 301–302)

RHETORICAL REASONING

The Sherlock Holmes story, however, takes us out of the realm of strict scientific reasoning and the search for absolute knowledge and moves us into *rhetorical reasoning*, the realm of probable knowledge. Aristotle remarked that where absolute knowledge or truth was available, debate was unnecessary. He went on to add, however, that with almost every issue in everyday life absolute knowledge is decidedly *not* available. Since few definite, clear-cut answers exist to the questions life presents us, we must make use of rhetorical reasoning, the form used when the best we can do is to say that *very probably* a conclusion is true. But saying that rhetorical reasoning deals with probable truth does not mean it is an inferior form of reasoning or that "anything goes" in such argument. Rather, it suggests that readers must recognize the often subtle gradations between fact and opinion, between the objective and the subjective, and that they must require good reasons for their judgments and beliefs.

Fact and Opinion: Objectivity and Subjectivity

Let us begin our discussion with an extreme example: (1) "Fast-food restaurants are disgusting." (2) "Fast-food restaurants are found throughout North America." Statement 1 obviously lies in the realm of pure opinion and subjectivity. The speaker is entitled to this particular opinion about fast-food restaurants, but trying to force that opinion on others without strong substantiation would be both irrational and a waste of time. Statement 2 is obviously a more factual and objective one. We could test it by gathering evidence to support it. Most of our opinions grow directly out of our own backgrounds, tastes, and temperaments, and hence are often highly subjective. In the broadest terms, the entire way we perceive the world around us is far from objective, because the very act of seeing involves the observer as well as the things observed. As a contemporary writer on argument says,

> As a perceiver I am not merely limited by my spatial relationship to that activity; I am limited by the experience I bring to the perception, by my intelligence, by my estimate of what I ought to perceive—in short, I am limited by myself. Any account of complicated human

behavior, for instance, is necessarily an act of self-revelation as well as a statement about what has been observed.

Nor do human beings really perceive objects. We do not perceive white balls or mothers or psychologists; we perceive contexts in which these happen to be found. . . . Human beings share a world, but it is necessarily different for each one. It is not even fixed for a single individual over any length of time.

Does this mean, then, that people can never agree on the meaning of a message, if each person inhabits "a different world"? The answer is No. In spite of the enormous variation in perceptions, there is no question that shared knowledge, traditions, and values do exist; if they did not, our personal lives, as well as the life of society, would be chaotic. This area of shared, as opposed to private, knowledge is what we generally call *objective.*

If someone were to assert that Beethoven was born in the eighteenth century, and another person maintained that he was born in the nineteenth century, the two could settle the argument by consulting historical records which they agreed would tell the truth of the matter. But a similar disagreement over whether Beethoven was a greater composer than Brahms cannot be settled so easily or definitely. The latter is a question of taste or opinion, and a meeting of minds may be impossible.

The statement about Beethoven's birth is ordinarily regarded as an objective one. So are the assertions that giraffes are found today in Africa, that oxygen has a valence of two, and that this book has certain dimensions. For these, one can adduce proof that will be acceptable to all reasonable persons. We know giraffes are found in Africa because many trustworthy explorers have brought them back from there and because we have seen them on television in their native habitat. We know that oxygen has a valence of two, for one reason because many kinds of chemical experiments have been based on that principle, and it has never failed to hold good. We know that this book has certain dimensions because a hundred people can measure it with an accurately calibrated ruler and give the same answer.

But a disagreement over Beethoven's greatness as a composer is described as subjective. So are statements such as "Beer is an unpleasant beverage" and "This is an ugly suit." Here agreement is far less likely than in the case of objective statements, partly because of the lack of generally shared definitions and standards. What is the definition of "greatness" whereby we can confidently assert that Beethoven was a "greater" composer than Brahms? What does "unpleasant" mean in reference to a drink? (People who like beer and people who don't would certainly have trouble agreeing on standards.) Although fifty people might find the suit "ugly," fifty others might respond quite differently. It depends on point of view, taste, or opinion.

Just as there is no sharp dividing line between denotation and connotation, so there is no plain division between the realm of the objective and the realm of the subjective. What is the color of the walls of a classroom? Some may call it cream, some buff, some eggshell, some off-white, some yellowish, some vanilla. There is no community of shared opinion because our common names for colors are based on more or less personal standards. Yet experts on pigments or optical physicists could say with certainty that the walls are painted one specific shade, and one alone. They could do so because they use an agreed-upon term based on a system of scientific measurements. Using a colorimeter, they can reach a conclusion which no one who accepts their standards will dispute. In other words, where no commonly accepted measure of truth exists, no shared knowledge or value, there can be no objective facts. Everything that is judged by the individual, on the basis of his or her personal standard alone, is subjective. But what is a subjective observation in one respect — as for example the cry of an excited fan that "They got the first down!" — is turned into an objective statement when the measuring chain is brought out. On the other hand, many sense impressions cannot be measured. Do any agreed-upon standards justify an advertisement's assertion that "Studies prove that freshly ground coffee *tastes better* than coffee ground weeks before you buy it"? And even what appear to be factual, objective statements may turn out to be highly subjective when closely scrutinized. Police who listen to ten eye-witness accounts often contradict one another will attest to this point.

The degree to which we must be aware of the subtle gradations between objectivity and subjectivity depends on the reason why we are reading at any given moment. If we are reading a recipe, we expect factual measurements and directions, not testimonials about how delicious it will taste. If we are reading a textbook on economics, we want facts or well worked-out theories of economic phenomena. If we are listening to a radio or television report on international developments, we are primarily interested in the facts of those occurrences.

But we may also want someone's interpretation of facts. Thus we may be interested in getting not only a straight news summary from our commentator but also his or her own viewpoint and the opinions of various people interviewed. In a lecture on history, a magazine article on contemporary music, or a book on business management, we normally do not wish the writer to stick to bare facts; we also want the writer's informed opinion on what they mean. Was the disaster of Pearl Harbor the result of a conspiracy in high governmental circles to get us into war? Is contemporary music running out of things to say and ways to say them? Can inflation be curbed? In such cases, where both objective and subjective data are involved, we must keep alert to distinguish between the fact and the interpretive comment. Both can be valuable, but for different reasons.

Most of the great imaginative writing of the world is essentially subjective. It is the account, in one form or another, of private, personal experience — of the inner feelings and moods of very sensitive men and women, of the way in which the external world impinges on their senses and spirits. A personal essay, an autobiography, a love lyric, an appreciation of the art of Shakespeare, a bit of nature writing, a philosophical meditation — each is intensely subjective. The objective facts contained in such pieces we can easily obtain from encyclopedias. But the impressions and reactions reported in them are unique to that writer. And that constitutes one of the chief values of literature: we are able to view life and people through the spirit of someone else, someone gifted both in experience and in the ability to recapture and communicate that experience to us. Although we think of imaginative writing as highly subjective, such writing tells the truth, in the sense that it is true and faithful to the writer's unique perception and interpretation of the world.

As critical readers of any kind of writing, we need to be able to sort out varying degrees of fact and opinion and to draw our own conclusions based on our analysis of them. But as we have seen, most ideas in this world are extremely hard to prove or disprove in the scientific sense. Countless volumes have been written attempting to "prove logically or scientifically" a particular religious doctrine. But few if any such proofs command the nearly universal acceptance expected in the sciences. Arguments relating to ethics, esthetics, philosophy, and politics are of this type also. They belong to the realm of probable or contingent truth. Such issues are at the very heart of our lives: Should we vote one way or the other? Should we marry? Should we have children or not? Can death and personal dignity coexist? These are questions which normally fall in the middle range between objective and subjective; they certainly fall outside the scope of scientific reasoning. Yet it would be a mistake to think we cannot reason clearly about such questions. As critical readers and thinkers we are called on to do so at almost every turn in our lives. In rhetorical reasoning, the search for good reasons — those reasons that would be accepted by most reasonable people — replaces the scientist's search for certain or absolute truth. How we establish and measure good reasons is the subject of the remainder of this chapter.

(Exercises: pages 302–306)

Rhetorical Induction

Most learning involves drawing generalizations or conclusions from particular pieces of information or instances. This process, generally referred to as *induction,* was the process we used when we first learned that a light bulb which has been burning for hours is hot; that when we step on the rubber mat at the exit to the supermarket, the door automatically opens; or that careful note-taking and thorough review usually improve grades on written examinations. It is also the process we use when we read a news report on five major economic indicators and then surmise that a recession is at hand or when we decide who our true friends are and whom we can trust.

Such generalizations, however, present at least two dangers: unconscious or deliberate exaggeration and insufficient or weighted evidence. When we generalize only from our own limited experience, we often go further than we are entitled to go. Instead of reminding ourselves of what is actually true according to our own observations ("Quite often, politicians give evasive answers to important questions"), we prefer a sweeping generalization: "All politicians give evasive answers to important questions." Like Sherlock Holmes, we take a risk when we assume that a generalization is *always* true, whereas the fact is that it is only usually or often true.

If we keep aware of this human tendency in ourselves, we shall constantly discover that the sweeping "truths" which others express every day in print or speech actually are not as all-embracing as they seem. Few generalizations related to the issues of our lives always hold true. The first test to apply to a generalization, therefore, is this: if the speaker or writer uses such a sweeping word as *all* or *always* or *never*, is that word justified? Are there no exceptions to the statement? And as is often the case, if the writer does not explicitly use *all, always, never*, and so on, are those words implied? If they are implied, we must return to the same question: is the writer justified in implying that no exceptions exist?

Even when a generalization is duly qualified, its truth still must be demonstrated. Often readers are thrown off guard by a writer's readiness to concede the possibility of exceptions, thus suggesting a careful, honest person who is unwilling to sacrifice truth for the sake of a forcible argument. Granting that such caution may be a good sign, we are still entitled to ask whether the generalization holds true even in as many cases as the writer claims. Does *usually* really mean only "some of the time"? Does *very few* really mean only "less than half"? Does *probably* or *likely* really mean only a better than fifty-fifty chance? The reader has a perfect right to demand more specific language — proportions and percentages — rather than elastic terms that often mean one thing to the writer and another to the reader.

Having considered the possibility of exaggeration for rhetorical effect, the critical reader's next job is to find out just what evidence lies behind a general statement. Take the question of whether engineering majors are better students than education majors. A college professor may say that "engineering majors most definitely are better students than education majors." What the professor means is that in his or her limited experience, engineering majors have proved better students (however "better" may be defined) than education majors. Such a judgment must be regarded as an opinion, being primarily subjective and based on too few instances. But suppose that the dean of the institution issues a report which shows that for the year just ended, the engineering students' average (on a 4.0 basis) was 2.756, whereas the education majors' average was 2.445. The student body of the college includes 967 engineering majors and 1,083 education majors. Such a report is of more value than the professor's, but its value is still limited, because the dean says only, in effect, that in *this* college the engineering majors during the past year earned somewhat higher marks than the education majors did. But higher marks don't necessarily mean "better" students, particularly if the rigors of one curriculum are not equivalent to those of the other. Furthermore, this difference in marks may not be true everywhere; the experience of a single college cannot be broadened into a generalization covering all colleges.

Suppose, however, that some ambitious researcher assembled reports from fifty institutions of every description, from small liberal arts colleges to large universities, geographically scattered all over North America. The only aim in selecting those fifty institutions was to get as wide a sampling as possible of all North American colleges which enroll both engineering and education students. The researcher emerges with a report showing that in these fifty schools, with a total of 156,980 engineering majors and 187,072 education majors, the former's average in grades for the year was some 15 percent higher than that of the education majors. Now we may still question whether those who get higher grades are necessarily "better" students (and we emphasize again that the argument is open to challenge unless that crucial term is clearly defined), but we have some justification for the general statement. It is based on a large number of examples, which are widely representative of institutions of higher learning in North America. If the researchers were to analyze the records of fifty more comparable institutions, the likelihood would be that the new results would closely approximate the first ones.

Consumer analysts and public opinion pollsters go to elaborate lengths to interview a number of persons sufficient to permit generalization, and to distribute their interviews among various sections of a country and among various income groups, occupations, and educational levels, so that they will have a reasonably accurate cross-section of "the public." Such analysts are also adept at profiling one particular age, income, or interest group to which advertisers wish to appeal. But general statements containing or implying such phrases as *tends to, majority, most, as a group* . . . should be examined no less critically than those which contain or imply the categorical *all, every, only, never,* or *always.* To assert that something is true in a large majority of instances, or even in 61 percent of those instances, requires as much carefully gathered and evaluated evidence as to say that it is always true.

Another familiar kind of dangerous generalization involves terms like *average, normal,* and *typical.* Just what is meant by "the normal college student," "the typical homeowner," or "the average rural family" — or by phrases that try to generalize about a large group by referring to an imaginary individual like "the Canadian voter" or "the British workingman"? What is meant by the "typical homeowner" who is more attracted by one kind of insurance than by another kind? Of what is he or she "typical"? How many homeowners do *not* conform to the specified pattern of behavior? Or take "the Canadian voter": we can be sure that he or she is Canadian and votes, but beyond that, any statement concerning attitudes, motivations, and habits as a voter must be heavily qualified. The pitfall here, which is exactly the same as that which lies behind the associated fallacy of the stereotype (page 7), is the assumption that the large group "represented" by an individual is homogeneous — everybody thinking and acting alike in certain respects. The truth is that the group is composed of hundreds or thousands or millions of individuals who can seldom be lumped together in a sweeping generalization.

Like *typical,* the word *average,* so constantly used in asserting the "truth" of a matter, requires precise definition before readers can evaluate the statement. It can refer to any of four things: (1) the *arithmetical mean*, which is produced by adding up all the figures in a group and dividing by the number of figures; (2) the *simple mean*, which is the halfway point between the extremes; (3) the *median*, which is the middle number in a series; and (4) the *mode*, which is the figure most common in a series. Suppose that in a group of twenty candidates, the grades on a civil service examination are 95, 92, 88, 84, 84, 84, 84, 83, 80, 76, 76, 75, 70, 69, 60, 58, 53, 50, 42, and 40. The arithmetical mean is 72.15, the simple mean is 67.5, the median is 76, and the mode is 84. The "average" of the group therefore may be 72.15, 67.5, 76, or 84, depending on how you figure — or on what you want to prove.

Since statistics are so widely offered as "good reasons" to support or to clinch an argument, it always pays to be alert not only for insufficient or weighted samplings but also for hidden qualifications. On each holiday weekend, the National Safety Council gives wide publicity to the "mounting highway death toll." The casualty figures it predicts — 400, 500, or even more — are misleading, because they silently include deaths that would have occurred, holiday or no holiday. If, say, an average (arithmetical mean) of 180 people die in automobile accidents on an ordinary weekend, then the much-publicized "Labor Day slaughter" of 550, bad though it is, is exaggerated.

Two other common errors in interpreting statistics are (1) the lack of uniformity between two or more sets offered for comparison and (2) the confusion of absolute figures with rates. Sixty years ago, for instance, each police department had its own special way of defining and classifying crime. Some departments contributed their data to a central agency whereas others did not. Consequently, figures purporting to give the totals and breakdowns for criminal activity in the 1920s were both inconsistent and incomplete. Later, however, a uniform code for classifying crimes was adopted, and most local law enforcement agencies now report their data, arranged according to this system, to a central agency. Hence a comparison of figures for the past year with those for, say, 1928, can provide only a very rough idea of the degree to which crime has increased or decreased in that period. Account must be taken, too, of factors like the tendency of certain groups not to report crimes for fear of reprisal. The presence of many such groups in some cities would make the incidence of reported crime there unrealistically low. In the same way, the figures for both rape and child abuse are widely regarded as inaccurate. Because so many variables and inconsistencies are involved, the published statistics of crime give at best only an approximate notion, and sometimes a distorted one, of the actual situation, which may be either more or less alarming than depicted in our era when crime has become a serious national issue.

Even if two sets of statistics used for comparison were based on the same system, derived from an equal number of sources, and corrected wherever possible for variables, one would have to distinguish carefully between absolute figures and rates. Simple totals, especially when used to show trends over a number of years, can be very misleading, because the totals fail to take into account increases in population. An alarmist may "prove" that morality is degenerating by pointing to the swelling number of violent crimes, year by year, but in view of the great growth of population, this rise in crime is only to be expected. However, if the number of crimes *per 100,000 population* had steeply risen, the argument would be more impressive. Often, therefore, absolute figures can be, and are, used to distort the actual state of affairs. Statistics showing ratios are, on the whole, safer indications of both trends and immediate situations. But even they can be manipulated to suit the purposes of their users.

Another form of induction involves *testing hypotheses.** When investigators set up a hypothesis, they seek to test it, in order to discover grounds for accepting it. "Supposing, for the sake of argument," they say, "that such-and-such is true, what would be the consequences of its being true?" Having made a list of the consequences, the investigators proceed to see if they exist. If they do—and if the investigators know of no other equally plausible explanation for them—then the investigators decide that the hypothesis is correct.

A few years ago, doctors in Quebec City were puzzled by the occurrence in a short period of fifty cases involving the same symptoms: nausea, shortness of breath, a cough, stomach pains, loss of weight, and a marked blue-gray coloration. These symptoms alone suggested severe vitamin deficiency. But too many cases in too short a time disproved this hypothesis, because vitamin deficiency does not ordinarily appear as a sudden epidemic. In addition, post mortems on the twenty persons who died revealed severe damage to the heart muscle and the liver, features which were inconsistent with the vitamin-deficiency hypothesis. The doctors therefore sought a clue to the mysterious disease in some element the fifty victims had in common. They eventually found it: all fifty had been lovers of beer, and they habitually drank a particular Canadian brand.

It seemed logical that the serious illness these people suffered was somehow connected with the beer, which was brewed in both Quebec City and Montreal. But Montreal had no such incidence of the mysterious disease. Evidently, then, some significant difference existed in the brewing processes. And such proved to be the case. The Quebec brewery had added a cobalt compound to its product in order to enhance the foamy head. The Montreal brewery had not. Furthermore, the compound had been added only a month before the first victims became sick. The investigators' reasonable conclusion was that the cobalt salt had caused the illness. This hypothesis held up shortly afterward, when sixty-four Omaha beer drinkers showed precisely the same combination of symptoms. Investigators soon found that a local brewery had been using the same cobalt compound. When it ceased doing so, the illness disappeared.

Nevertheless, despite this seeming proof that the salt had been directly and exclusively responsible for the disease, doctors who reported the affair were cau-

*A hypothesis is an assertion that can be tested for verification. Ideally, the hypothesis is not subject to the biases or expectations of the investigator, though such ideal circumstances are rare. Today such hypotheses are sometimes called *models*.

tious. Although cobalt certainly could cause serious illness, as it had in Quebec City and Omaha, it had not been present in the beer in sufficient quantities to kill a normal person. Yet thirty had died in Omaha in addition to the twenty in Quebec City. This fact seemed to be related to the victims' drinking habits, which in some way reduced their resistance to the chemical. With them, a normally nonlethal dose of the cobalt had been fatal. The effect was somewhat analogous to that produced by mixing barbiturates and alcohol. Either, taken by itself, might have no untoward results. But under certain conditions the combination of the two can kill.

This true story illustrates several important points of inductive reasoning:

1. An initial hypothesis (here, the diagnosis of vitamin deficiency) is progressively invalidated as inconsistent evidence accumulates (the uncommon number of cases in a short period and the unexpected results of the autopsies).

2. Converging pieces of evidence (all the victims drank a lot of beer, all drank one particular brand, and only drinkers of beer in quantity were affected) can lead to a valid conclusion (that one particular beer was somehow at fault). Note, however, that if even one of the victims had been shown not to have been a heavy beer drinker or drank another brand of beer, the conclusion would have been thrown into serious question.

3. The opposite situation — pieces of evidence which differ rather than agree with other pieces — often helps narrow the range of possibilities. Although all the victims drank the same brand of beer, it did not have the same effect on drinkers in Montreal as it did on those in Quebec City. Because they drank Quebec City-brewed beer alone, the point of origin seemed to make some critical difference.

4. By a process of elimination, a cause can often be pinpointed. When the investigators compared processes in the two breweries, they found only one significant difference: the use of cobalt salt in Quebec City. They reasonably assumed that this was the difference responsible for making Quebec City drinkers sick but leaving the Montreal drinkers unscathed. Quite possibly other incidental differences occurred in the brewing process, but if these could be shown to have no connection with the disease they could be set aside.

5. The probability that the cobalt compound was the true cause of the illness was supported by further evidence. Just as the disease had appeared following the introduction of the cobalt, so the disease disappeared as soon as the cobalt was no longer used.

6. Nevertheless, one could not simply say that the cobalt, and it alone, was to blame. So sweeping a conclusion was cast into doubt by conflicting evidence (the dose of cobalt was not large enough to kill in ordinary circumstances). Therefore the conclusion had to be a qualified one. Although the cobalt was the primary cause of the illness, a contributory cause was the victims' abnormal susceptibility to this kind of poison. Without that susceptibility, the cobalt might have had no seriously adverse effects.

Readers must remember that most events can have more than one cause. Indeed, causal relationships are usually very complex. Overlooking this fact often leads to the *post hoc ergo propter hoc* ("after this, therefore because of this") fallacy. This fallacy assumes that because *B* happened after *A*, *B* was necessarily caused by *A* and by nothing else but *A*. (Check the difference in meaning between *sub*sequent and *con*sequent.) A hypothesized single cause, as we have just seen, may be considered confirmed only if it alone can produce the effects noted. When we read that one, and only one, factor is the cause of unemployment or inflation or high crime rates or a political crisis, we can almost always be sure that the writer is oversimplifying the causal relationships.

Hypothesis testing of the kind we have been examining is a consciously deliberate act of sorting out evidence. But all readers are testing hypotheses as they read, although they are hardly ever aware of the fact. Good critical readers, in fact, have the ability not only to form hypotheses that will "make sense" of what they are reading but also to alter those hypotheses as new evidence is presented. Readers start forming hypotheses the moment they begin to read a piece of writing. To take a simple example, the title of a recent article in *Psychology Today*, "On Becoming a Dictator," leads most readers to hypothesize that the article will discuss the psychological makeup of dictators. Note how you revise that hypothesis as you read the opening of the article:

> Most people engaged in a creative enterprise, such as writing or composing music or painting, spend a fair amount of time musing on ways to increase their productivity. Either alone or with colleagues, they may ponder a variety of prods to "getting started," better ways to plan priorities, more efficient methods of revising and correcting errors, or the use of mechanical "prosthetic" tools for enhancing their output.
>
> By no means immune from this vanity, I recently began to dictate my manuscripts into a tape recorder rather than compose them on a typewriter. The transition has created at least the illusion of a tremendous increase in the speed of production, and possibly, an improvement in the quality of my work.

How soon did you alter your original hypothesis of what "dictator" referred to?

In this same way, a novel whose opening scene describes a bitterly cold and rainy winter night through which strides a solitary figure clutching a murderous weapon and uttering mumbled threats leads readers to hypothesize that a crime is about to be committed. Part of the fun of reading a classic detective story comes from hypothesizing about the mystery to be solved, trying to keep up with—or even get ahead of—the narrator, and seeing whether or not the initial hypotheses are borne out or instead are altered by further reading.

Readers, then, must not only recognize and evaluate the use of induction—of generalizations based on sufficient or insufficient numbers of instances, the careful or careless use of statistics and reports about "typical consumers," and hypotheses more or less well tested. They must also exercise the basic processes of induction, especially of generalizing and testing hypotheses, as they read. Read the following excerpt slowly, stopping to note the hypotheses you formulate about this article, including the person the article is about and its author. When you finish reading the excerpt, list the general conclusions you have drawn about the subject of the article, George Steinbrenner, and — by identifying the overall tone of the article — describe the writer's purpose. Begin by noting the implications suggested by the word *Lessons* and by the *ism* in the title, "The Lessons of Steinbrennerism." Note also how the presence of connotative language, metaphors, and allusions adds to your ability to draw conclusions and generalizations.

The story of Steinbrenner and his baseball team occasionally takes on odd, mythic dimensions, the quality of an American parable, like *The Great Gatsby*. Steinbrenner has invented an archetype for himself: Superowner, a primordial character, all barging and beefy dictatorial will, more famous than any of his players. He is a sort of celebrity despot; his enemies regard him as an oaf. But Steinbrenner is so thoroughly Steinbrenner, a kind of masterpiece of himself, that he invites a sneaking wonder of the kind we reserve sometimes for natural phenomena. He runs the team the way Don Vito Corleone ran the rackets. He dismisses managers the way Bluebeard ditched wives. Steinbrenner has gone through nine managers in the ten years he has been principal owner of the Yankees.

This year Steinbrenner is worse than usual, more restlessly peremptory. He is now on his third manager of the season. *Off with their heads!* But this maniacally impulsive policy toward personnel, including pogroms of player trading, has exacted a psychic cost. It has tended to reduce what could be the finest team in baseball (once called "the best team that money can buy") into a gang of anxious neurotics who wonder what each night's line-up card will look like. . . .

Steinbrenner has a wonderfully representative American quality. In a way, he is that old American story, energetic money let loose in the world, shooting its cuffs, buying everything off, singing "I did it my way." It is the sort of money that purchases the restaurant to make sure that the lamb chops stay on the menu, or to settle a grudge with the maitre d'. Steinbrenner's emotional, almost physical inability to leave the Yankees alone produces great psychodrama.

Throughout this article the author uses induction to lead up to generalizations about Steinbrenner. As critical readers, we can evaluate this use of the inductive process, deciding whether or not he provides sufficient evidence, enough good reasons, for his generalizations.

(Exercises: pages 306–310)

Rhetorical Deduction

We have seen that formal scientific syllogisms rarely appear, as such, in ordinary writing. Nevertheless, their presence is implied by statements or conclusions which are, in effect, the products of such structured arguments. An elementary understanding of the syllogism can help readers determine the implied premises on which the conclusion of an informal argument rests.

But the syllogism, which is best suited to scientific reasoning, is not the major tool of rhetorical deduction. Those arguments for which no certain answers exist demand a more flexible tool, the *enthymeme* (pronounced *en'-tha-meem*). Although it resembles the syllogism, the enthymeme often suppresses or omits a premise or conclusion, is concerned with questions of probability rather than certainty, and rests on a premise acceptable or *assumed* to be acceptable to both writer and reader. This premise is often the crucial consideration in analyzing a statement based on rhetorical deduction, because it silently assumes that all people agree on its truth, whereas if it were directly stated, it might turn out to be an idea that was far from commanding general agreement. A writer who states that young people are poorly educated because they know little or nothing of history assumes that readers will agree that those who are *well* educated do have a knowledge of history. But this assumption may or may not be true; it remains to be established before any conclusion drawn from it can be accepted.

The most valid enthymemes move from a genuine area of agreement to present good reasons that may lead to agreement in an area of dispute. Much analysis of rhetorical deduction thus depends on the search for an area of implied agreement. If the assumed agreement is *only* assumed, not established, the argument collapses. Take the statement "Kim shouldn't smoke because other members of the family who smoke have heart trouble." This loosely structured argument actually contains two enthymemes, with several premises omitted:

Cigarette smoking causes heart trouble.
Members of Kim's family smoke.
Members of Kim's family have heart disease.

*   *   *

Those who don't want to suffer heart trouble shouldn't smoke.
Kim doesn't want to suffer heart trouble.
Kim shouldn't smoke.

What is the matter with these deductions? First of all, is the major premise of the first enthymeme genuinely agreed upon? We are offered no evidence or reasons to believe that it is. The major premise of the second enthymeme is also questionable, because many people refuse to accept a causal connection between smoking and heart disease. In addition, we have been told nothing of possible alternative causes of heart trouble. Hence, this argument fails to stand up to our demand for genuine areas of agreement and for sufficient evidence. This example also shows the importance of searching out hidden or implied premises. Finally, it demonstrates that arguments which involve moral questions of "should" or "should not," as many rhetorical arguments do, almost always rest on unstated major premises with which the writer *assumes* the audience agrees. If the author of this argument wants to convince Kim not to smoke (or wants to convince us that Kim should not smoke), a shared area of agreement will have to be forged, and good reasons produced to lead us from that area to the desired conclusion.

Arguments that end in shouting matches or in bitter silence often fail precisely because the assumption of shared agreement is unwarranted. In fact, for emotion-laden subjects, finding that area may be the hardest thing two disputants have to do. Yet if they do not discover or establish it, the argument is usually doomed to failure.

A modern logician, Stephen Toulmin, has offered a flexible way to analyze rhetorical deductions, and we have adapted from his system the following questions, which help determine how valid such arguments may be.

1. What is the claim?
2. What are the grounds or good reasons for the claim?
3. What underlying assumption supports the grounds and claim?
4. What backup evidence supports that assumption?
5. What refutations could be brought forward against the claim?
6. What qualifiers appear in the claim?

Let us apply these questions in an analysis of the following advertisement:

The Burrowing Owl. Harmless to Man. Would You Shoot Him?

He borrows old badger and prairie dog burrows for his home, and stands on his doorstep most of the day eyeing anyone who happens by.

Though he damages no crops and causes Man no trouble, somebody thought it amusing one holiday weekend in July 1978 to shoot all the Burrowing Owls in the largest known colony of them, in Saskatchewan.

What with idle pot-shots, and poisoning the things he eats, and running over him at night, Man has reduced Canada's population of Burrowing Owls to about 2,000 pairs. In British Columbia, he has already disappeared.

Can we save him? It is just possible.

You probably know something of the work the World Wildlife Fund has done internationally. It is the world's leading independent organization for conservation. Its symbol, the Giant Panda, has become a world symbol for survival.

Through its Survival Projects the World Wildlife Fund has already helped save more than a hundred birds and mammals, thirty-three of which were on the brink of extinction. It has given more than $40 million to conservation projects around the world. It has created or supported 260 Nature Parks. . . .

You might feel that any contribution you could make would be too small for the vastness of the task.

But if only you and other readers of this ad would each send us $20, it would be a very real help. And it might possibly save the Burrowing Owl from extinction. There's a lot that can be done, but only with your help. If you'd like to send more, or less, fine. But $20 would be fine, too.

The *claim* (1) is the point or main assertion of an argument, in this case, that the burrowing owl should be saved. Most arguments offer some *grounds* (2) for a claim, just as you might offer your increased workload as grounds for your claim to a higher salary. In this argument, the authors tell us that the population of burrowing owls is reduced to 2,000 pairs and that in some places this kind of owl has completely disappeared. At this point in the argument, we are asked to accept the word of the World Wildlife Fund that these figures are accurate.

The *underlying assumption* (3) is not stated, but it can be inferred: namely, that wildlife has a right to continued existence. Here, the underlying assumption does not rest on a cause-effect relationship but on a moral justification for the claim that the burrowing owl should be saved.

Backup support (4) for an underlying assumption might be likened to the deciding factor in a law case — whatever theory, law, legal precedent, or widely held general principle serves as justification for the assumption. In the advertisement we are analyzing, what backup support would justify the assumption that wildlife has a right to continued existence? In other words, how would the advertisement writers answer those who question the assumption? In this advertisement, no such support appears. If it did, it would no doubt cite the Endangered Species Acts as legal precedents for the statement that wildlife has a right to continued existence.

Asking for possible *refutation* (5) might be called an invitation to pose the "Yes, but . . ." question. Under what conditions can the claim *not* be made? In our example, can you think of conditions which would argue *against* saving the burrowing owl? The authors of this advertisement anticipate possible refutation on two counts (there might be others) with the assertion " . . .he damages no crops and causes Man no trouble . . .". Their argument is weaker to the extent that they provide no evidence to support the assertion and hence fail to answer the expected refutation.

Qualifiers (6) are usually words such as *most, usually, certainly,* or *probably* which, as in this very sentence, indicate the degree to which the claim is made. We have already discussed some of the dangers in interpreting qualifiers, including absolute ones, on pages 272–273 and 278–279.

Now examine the schematic representation of the expanded argument.

	The burrowing owl is fast disappearing	*Grounds*
	SO	
	The burrowing owl should be saved	*Claim*
	SINCE	
(only implied)	Wildlife has a right to continued existence	*Underlying Assumption*
	BECAUSE	
	The Endangered Species Acts protect wildlife	*Backup Support*
	EXCEPT WHEN	
	That wildlife damages crops or people	*Refutation*
		Qualifiers (None)

The argument could also be schematized as a pair of enthymemes:

1. Wildlife has a right to continued   *Assumed Area*
   existence.   *of Agreement*
   The burrowing owl is a part of wildlife.
   The burrowing owl has a right to
   continued existence.
2. All threatened wildlife should be saved. *Assumed Area*
                                             of Agreement

   The burrowing owl is threatened.
   The burrowing owl should be saved.

Whenever you analyze an argument, you should look for areas of assumed agreement and determine whether the assumption is justified. Then ask the six questions listed above. If they cannot be answered satisfactorily, it is likely that the argument is confusing or even deceptive. And if answers to the questions are omitted, as the questions about underlying assumption and backup support were in the advertisement we have just analyzed, the answers may be implied or assumed.

We have not taken the time to analyze the connotative language, imagery, sentence and paragraph form, or overall tone in this short argument. We should, however, point out that here, as in almost all arguments, rhetorical deduction and induction work hand in hand. In this case, inductive listing of examples, or enumeration, leads to the suggested generalization that "The World Wildlife Fund is an effective conservation group."

(Exercises: pages 310-311)

The Question of Authority

Our analysis of this advertisement leads us to one final set of questions to be asked when analyzing arguments: (1) Who is writing or speaking? (2) What authority does the writer or speaker have? (3) What are the motives involved? These are questions concerning what Aristotle called *ethos,* the character and aims of the speaker or writer. Questions of *ethos* should hover in our minds as we read, for they will help pierce to the basic truth or falseness of any piece of writing.

Not only people who are qualified to speak with authority on a certain subject have access to our attention. Actually, much of what we hear and read on a given topic comes from persons with no special expertise in the area under discussion. Politicians are constantly expressing their views on many topics of current interest. Sometimes we listen with attention and respect because they may have made a special study of their subject. But on the other hand they may know little or nothing at all about the issue, apart from what they have read in the newspapers or heard from their colleagues or from lobbyists. Part of our responsibility as citizens is to follow the careers of public officials so that we may know whose utterances should normally be attended to and whose should be discounted, as based on nothing but opinion, prejudice, or political strategy.

Every field of information has charlatans as well as honest, reliable writers. It always pays to find out which writers belong to which category. The most reliable authorities on any subject are usually those who specialize in it and therefore know the most about it: professional historians, pathologists, literary scholars, geneticists, physical chemists, economists, engineers. Unfortunately, many genuine experts have neither the ability nor the time to write for laypeople. To cull the most essential information from their specialized books, articles, and reports, and put it into readable form, is the job of writers for a wide general audience. Their indispensable qualification is that they can write simply and interestingly about complex matters. Good popular writers have sufficient knowledge of the subject about which they are writing and sufficient scholarly sense to be able to report accurately to the audience. They may simplify their material—indeed, they have to do so—but in simplifying they guard against distortion or misinformation. Bad popular writers, on the other hand, fail to understand their subject in the first place. Nevertheless, they proceed to give readers a twisted account of it, discredited by misstatements, exaggerations, and fantasy.

"Does the author know what he or she is talking about?" is, then, a question that must remain uppermost in our minds as we read anything that gives information or argues a case. Again and again we must conclude that a writer knows no more about the subject than we do, who also read the newspapers and watch television. Such a writer is not likely to change our minds about an issue of importance.

"What is the motive?" is another important question. In many cases the motive is apparent: the writer of a magazine article on the outlook for interplanetary travel, for instance, probably wants to make money. But what of articles and books written for more complex reasons? If they deal with a controversial subject, nearly all such works are written from a particular viewpoint or bias. Few are impartial or disinterested, if only because the subjects they deal with can scarcely be talked about at all without taking sides. And as we indicated in our discussion of subjectivity and objectivity (pages 274–277), complete objectivity is all but impossible. After all, we are limited to our own perceptions of the world, though we may be as honest and true to those perceptions as possible.

Major radio and television news analysts offer a good illustration of the principle of point of view. They usually develop their discussions from a hard kernel of fact: for example, the President or Prime Minister has actually made such and such a statement. But their interpretations of this fact may differ significantly, because each naturally has a point of view, a distinctive way he or she sees the world. When we listen to or read these commentators, we must remember that each construes an event or situation in terms of what he or she judges to be right and wrong, accurate and inaccurate.

Keeping in mind the point of view and possible motives of a writer can be a great aid to critical readers. When we know that the author of a book on recent American foreign policy was for many years a high official in the Department of State, we must remember that his analysis of our foreign policy is written from a certain point of view. It may be a thoroughly able and honest book, but it may also be colored by a desire to justify the author's own position.

The more confident the manner of a writer or speaker, the more necessary it is to discover the basis for that confidence and determine whether or not it is justified. A forthright assertion that "every reasonable person will agree . . ." or "there can be no question that . . ." or "it has been proved time and time again . . ." may or may not be justified. Certainly such statements should not be accepted without careful scrutiny. An air of supreme confidence often suggests that speakers or writers "really know what they're talking about!" — but do they?

(Exercises: pages 311–312)

Informal Fallacies

If sound rhetorical thinking can be characterized as the search for good reasons, informal fallacies are often the "bad reasons" over which readers stumble. Here are a few of the most frequently encountered ones:

1. Introducing emotion in place of evidence.
2. Introducing irrelevant or unproved evidence.
3. Attacking a person instead of a principle.

4. Oversimplifying and distorting the issue or evidence.
5. Suppressing evidence.

1. We have already looked at the first kind of obstacle to clear thinking—substituting emotion for evidence—in Chapter 1. The effectiveness of name-calling and the glittering generality depends on stock responses. Just as the scientist Pavlov, in a classic experiment, conditioned dogs to increase their production of saliva every time he rang a bell, so the calculating persuader expects readers to react automatically to language that appeals to their prejudices.

2. We have also touched on the second kind of fallacy in the preceding discussion of authority. The abuse of authority is one of the *transfer devices* which exploit readers' willingness to link one idea or person with another, even though the two may not be logically connected. The familiar *testimonials* of present-day advertising provide an instance of this device. In some cases, the "authority" who testifies has some connection with the product advertised. The problem to settle here is, when we try to decide which brand of sunburn cream is best, how much weight may we reasonably attach to the enthusiastic statements of certain nurses? When we are thinking of buying a tennis racket, should we accept the say-so of a champion who, after all, is well paid for telling us that a certain make is the best? In other cases, the testifying authorities may have no formal, professional connection with the products they recommend. An actor, who may very well be a master of his particular art, praises a whiskey, a coffee, or an airline. He likes it, he says. But, we may ask, does the fact that he is a successful actor make him better qualified than any person who is not an actor to judge a whiskey, a coffee, or an airline? Competence in one field does not necessarily "transfer" to competence in another.

Furthermore, advertisers often borrow the prestige of science and medicine to enhance the reputation of their products. Many people have come to feel for the laboratory scientist and the physician an awe once reserved for bishops or statesmen. The alleged approval of such people thus carries great weight in selling something or inducing someone to believe something. Phrases such as "leading medical authorities say ..." or "independent laboratory tests show ..." are designed simply to transfer the prestige of science to a toothpaste or deodorant. Seldom are the precise "medical authorities" or "independent laboratories" named. But the mere phrases carry weight with uncritical listeners or readers. Similarly, the title "Dr." or "Professor" implies that the person quoted speaks with all the authority of which learned people are capable—when as a matter of fact doctoral degrees can be bought from mail-order colleges. Therefore, whenever a writer or speaker appeals to the prestige that surrounds the learned, the reader should demand credentials. Just *what* "medical authorities" say this? Can they be trusted? What independent laboratories made the tests—and what did the tests actually reveal? Who are the people who speak as expert educators, psychologists, or economists? Regardless of the fact that they are "doctors," do they know what they are talking about?

Another, closely related form of transfer is the borrowing of prestige from a highly respected institution (country, religion, education) or individual (world leader, philosopher, scientist) for the sake of enhancing something else. Political speakers sometimes work into their speeches quotations from the Bible or from secular "sacred writings" (such as a national constitution). Such quotations usually arouse favorable emotions in listeners, emotions which are then transferred to the speaker's policy or subject. When analyzing an appeal that uses quotations from men and women who have achieved renown in one field or another, the chief question is whether the quotation is appropriate in context. Does it have real relevance to the point at issue? It is all very well to quote George Washington or Abraham Lincoln in support of one's political stand. But circumstances have changed immensely since those statements were first uttered, and their applicability to a new situation may be dubious indeed. The implication is, "This person, who we agree was great and wise, said certain things which 'prove' the justice of my own stand. Therefore, you should believe I am right." But to have a valid argument, the writer must prove that the word of the authorities is really applicable to the present issue. If that is true, then the speaker is borrowing not so much their prestige as their wisdom—which is perfectly justifiable.

Another version of the transfer device is one which gains prestige not through quotations or testimonials of authorities but from linking one idea to another. Here is an advertisement that illustrates how this device works:

The Telephone Pole That Became a Memorial

The cottage on Lincoln Street in Portland, Oregon, is shaded by graceful trees and covered with ivy.

Many years ago, A. H. Feldman and his wife remodeled the house to fit their dreams . . . and set out slips of ivy around it. And when their son, Danny, came along, he, too, liked to watch things grow. One day, when he was only nine, he took a handful of ivy slips and planted them at the base of the telephone pole in front of the house.

Time passed . . . and the ivy grew, climbing to the top of the pole. Like the ivy, Danny grew too. He finished high school, went to college. The war came along before he finished—and Danny went overseas. And there he gave his life for his country.

Not very long ago the overhead telephone lines were being removed from the poles on Lincoln Street. The ivy-covered telephone pole in front of the Feldman home was about to be taken down. Its work was done.

But, when the telephone crew arrived, Mrs. Feldman came out to meet them. "Couldn't it be left standing?" she asked. And then she told them about her son.

So the pole, although no longer needed, wasn't touched at all. At the request of the telephone company, the Portland City Council passed a special ordinance permitting the company to leave it standing. And there it is today, mantled in ivy, a living memorial to Sergeant Danny Feldman.

What did the telephone company wish to accomplish by this ad? Readers are not urged to install a telephone, equip their homes with extra telephones, or use any of the various new services the company has developed. Nor are they told how inexpensive and efficient the telephone company thinks those services are. Instead, this is what is known as an "institutional" advertisement. Its purpose is to inspire public esteem, even affection, for the company.

How do such advertisements inspire esteem and respect? Simply by telling an anecdote, without a single word to point up the moral. In this ad, every detail is carefully chosen for its emotional appeal: the cottage ("home, sweet home" theme), the ivy (symbol of endurance through the years; often combined, as here, with the idea of the family home), the little boy (evoking all the feelings associated with childhood), the young man dying in the war (evoking patriotic sentiment). Thus at least four symbols are combined — all of them with great power to touch the emotions. Then the climax: Will the company cut down the ivy-covered pole? To many people, *company* has a connotation of hardheartedness, impersonality, coldness, which is the very impression this particular company, one of the biggest in the world, wants to erase. So the company modestly reports that it went to the trouble of getting special permission to leave this one pole standing, "mantled in ivy, a living memorial."

The writer of this advertisement has, in effect, urged readers to transfer to the telephone company the sympathies aroused by the story. The ivy-covered pole aptly symbolizes what the writer wanted to do — "mantle" the pole (symbolizing the company) with the ivy that is associated with home, childhood, and heroic death. If it is possible to make one feel sentimental about a giant corporation, an advertisement like this one — arousing certain feelings by means of one set of objects and then transferring those feelings to another object — will do it. But the story, although true enough, is after all only one incident, and a sound generalization about the character of a vast company cannot be formed from a single anecdote. The company may well be as "human" as the advertisement implies, but readers are led to that belief through an appeal to their sympathies, not their reason.

3. A third kind of fallacy involves *mudslinging*, attacking a person rather than a principle. Mudslingers make personal attacks on an opponent (formally known as *ad hominem* arguments, those "against the man"), not merely by calling names, but often by presenting what they offer as damaging evidence against the opponent's motives, character, and private life. Thus the audience's attention is diverted from the argument itself to a subject which is more likely to stir up prejudices. If, for example, in denouncing an opponent's position on reducing the national debt, a candidate refers to X's connection with certain well-known gamblers, then the candidate ceases to argue the case on its merits and casts doubt on the opponent's personal character. The object is not to hurt X's feelings but to arouse bias against that person in the hearer's mind. Critical readers or listeners must train themselves to detect and reject these irrelevant aspersions. It may be, indeed, that X has shady connections with underworld gamblers. But that may have nothing to do with the abstract right or wrong of his stand on the national debt. Issues should be discussed apart from character and motives. Both character

and motives are important, of course, since they bear on any candidate's fitness for public office and on whether we can give him or her our support. But they call for a separate discussion.

A somewhat more subtle kind of personal attack is the *innuendo*, which differs from direct accusation roughly as a hint differs from a plain statement. Innuendo is chiefly useful where no facts exist to give even a semblance of support to a direct charge. The writer or speaker therefore slyly plants seeds of doubt or suspicion in the reader's or listener's mind, as the villainous Iago does in the mind of Shakespeare's Othello. Innuendo is a trick that is safe, effective—and unfair. "They were in the office with the door locked for four hours after closing time." The statement, in itself, may be entirely true. But what counts is the implication it is meant to convey. The unfairness increases when the doubts that the innuendo raises concern matters that have nothing to do with the issue anyway. An example of the irrelevant innuendo is found in the writings of the historian Charles A. Beard. In assailing the ideas of another historian, Admiral Alfred T. Mahan, Beard called him "the son of a professor and swivel-chair tactician at West Point," who "served respectably, but without distinction, for a time in the navy" and "found an easy berth at the Naval War College." Actually, the occupation of Mahan's father has nothing to do with the validity of the son's arguments. But observe the sneer—which is meant to be transferred from father to son—in "professor" and "swivel-chair tactician." Beard's reference to Mahan's naval record is a good elementary instance of damning with faint praise. And whether or not Mahan's was "an easy berth" at the Naval War College (a matter of opinion), it too has no place in a discussion of the man's ideas or intellectual capacities.

Newspapers often use this device to imply more than they can state without risking a libel suit. In reporting the latest bit of gossip about celebrated members of the "jet set" or the "beautiful people" (what do the terms suggest about the habits and tastes of the people referred to?), a paper may mention the fact that "gorgeous movie actress A is a frequent companion of thrice-divorced playboy B" or that they "are seen constantly together at the Vegas night spots" or that they are "flitting from the Riviera to Sun Valley together." The inference suggested, however unfounded it may be, is that their relationship is not just that of good friends who happen to be in the same place at the same time. Similarly, newspapers which value sensationalism more than responsibility may describe an accused "child slayer" or "woman molester" as "dirty and bearded" (implication: he is a suspicious-looking bum). His face may, in addition, be "scarred" (implication: he is physically violent). Such literal details may be true enough. But how much have they to do with the guilt or innocence of the person in this particular case? The effect on the reader is what courts of law term "prejudicial" and therefore inadmissible. Unfortunately the law does not extend to slanted writing, however powerfully it may sway public opinion.

Another instance of the way in which emotionally loaded language can be combined with unproved evidence to stir up prejudice may be taken from the field of art. A modern critic condemned certain paintings as "a conventional rehash of cubist patterns born among the wastrels of Paris forty years ago." In so doing, the critic attacked the art through the artist. The artistic merit of paintings has nothing to do with the private lives of the people who paint them. The painters referred to may well have been wastrels. But that fact—if it is a fact—has no bearing on the point at issue. The assumed connection between the personal virtues or shortcomings of artists and the artistic value of their productions has resulted in a great deal of confused thinking about literature, music, and the other arts.

Another diversionary tactic which introduces an irrelevant issue into a debate is the *red herring*. It too may involve shifting attention from principles to personalities, but without necessarily slinging mud or calling names. Since neither relaxing at a disco nor having a taste for serious books is yet sinful or criminal, a political party slings no mud when it portrays the other party's candidate as a playboy or an intellectual. Still, such matters are largely irrelevant to the main argument, which is whether one or the other candidate will better serve the interests of the people. The red-herring device need not involve personalities at all; it may take the form simply of substituting one issue for another. If a large corporation is under fire for alleged monopolistic practices, its public relations people may start an elaborate advertising campaign to show how well the company's workers are treated. Thus, if the campaign succeeds, the bad publicity suffered because of the assertions that the company has been trying to corner the market may be counteracted by the public's approval of its allegedly fine labor policy.

4. At many places in this chapter we have touched on various kinds of *oversimplification*, though not usually identifying them as such. We have said that generalizations based on only a very few instances are dangerous, as are causal arguments that ignore alternatives (pages 278–281). And when we briefly discussed the syllogism, we warned against the error of drawing a universal or categorical conclusion *(all, always, never, none)* from a qualified premise *(most, some, few, sometimes)*. Unfortunately, most of us are eager to view questions in their simplest terms and to make our decisions on the basis of only a few of the many elements the problem may involve. The problem of minority groups in North America, for instance, is not simply one of abstract justice, as many would like to think. Rather, it involves complex and by no means easily resolvable issues of economics, sociology, politics, and psychology. Nor can one say with easy assurance, "The federal government should guarantee every farmer a decent income, even if the money comes from the pocketbooks of the citizens who are the farmer's own customers" or "It is the obligation of every educational institution to purge its faculty of all who hold radical sympathies." Perhaps each of these propositions is sound; perhaps neither is. But before either is adopted as a conviction, intelligent readers must canvass their full implications, much as we did in analyzing the argument on pages 286–288. After the implications have been explored, more evidence may be found *against* the proposition than in support of it.

Countless reductive generalizations concerning parties, races, religions, and nations, to say nothing of individuals, are the result of the deep-seated human desire to reduce complicated ideas to their simplest terms. We saw the process working when we touched on stereotypes in Chapter 1 and in our discussion of rhetorical induction in this chapter. Unfortunately, condemning with a few quick, perhaps indefensible assumptions is easier than recognizing the actual diversity in any social group. But every man and woman has an urgent obligation to analyze the basis of each judgment he or she makes: "Am I examining every aspect of the issue that needs to be examined? Do I understand the problem sufficiently to be able to make a fair decision? Or am I taking the easiest and simplest way out?"

A particularly insidious form of oversimplification is the *false dilemma*. Life, as we know, provides plenty of situations where we have only two choices. If both choices are unpleasant or unsatisfactory, they constitute a true dilemma. To be "caught on the horns of a dilemma" is therefore — to shift metaphors for the sake of two more clichés — to be caught between the devil and the deep blue sea or between a rock and a hard place. Voters who have to choose between two candidates, neither of whom they like, are in a dilemma unless they decide not to vote at all. They know that if one candidate, possibly the lesser of two evils, does win, his victory will be interpreted by press and politicians as a "mandate from the people" to proceed with a particular program, even though the people may have serious reservations about some of the things the candidate has pledged to do. On the other hand, the losing candidate's program will be said to have been "rejected by the voters" even though many people were in favor of certain proposals. To citizens aware of the actual complexity of the issues involved, a vote either way is bound to misrepresent opinion because it falsely implies blanket approval of one candidate and disapproval of the other. True dilemmas often occur, also, with private moral decisions, where the claims of conscience must be balanced against those of discretion, and in decisions about governmental policy, where, as candid observers point out, a country is often damned if it does and damned if it doesn't.

But very often, an argument assumes that only two choices exist when in truth there may be several. A false dilemma, often described as an *either-or assumption*, insists that something is either A or Z, and that B, C, ... X, and Y do not exist. But everywhere we turn in life, we know that such is not the case. Instead of two positions between which we must choose, there may be three, or half a dozen. To divide all people into two classes, the "sane" and the "insane," is to neglect the innumerable gradations of sanity. In fact, only by an arbitrary definition do doctors and jurists decide that one person is sane and another insane. The law also recognizes the existence of degrees of guilt, as in allowing any one of several different charges to be brought against a person accused of killing, in allowing a jury to accompany a verdict of guilty with a recommendation of mercy, and in giving judges wide discretion in determining the severity of sentences.

The false dilemma is often met in classroom interpretations of literature which assume, for example, that a poem can be read or interpreted in only *one* way, and that any other interpretation is therefore wrong. The dilemma: either the first interpretation is the correct reading or it isn't. Here the fallacy lies in the word *the*. The real issue is whether the first interpretation is justified, not whether it is the *only* justifiable one. Works of literature may often be read in a number of acceptable ways, on different "levels of meaning" — the symbolic, the implicitly autobiographical, the literal, and so on. One interpretation does not necessarily exclude others, although it may exclude another on the same level, where obvious contradictions are involved.

The either-or assumption is the prime weapon of intolerant people. It is the means by which one group, which flatters itself that it, and it alone, stands in the light of truth, denounces all others as children of darkness. All too familiar is the conflict represented in this dialogue:

> "We have all the right on our side (*A*). We are militantly opposed to the evil which is *Z*. Therefore you must come out in favor of *A* and help us fight this evil."
>
> "But I don't think the issue is absolutely clear-cut. There's something to be said for and against both *A* and *Z*. And isn't there at least one alternative—*M*?"
>
> "No, there isn't. You've got to make your choice between *A* and *Z*. *A* is wholly right; *Z* is wholly wrong. If you're not pro-*A*, heart and soul, then you must be pro-*Z*. If you're pro-*Z*, obviously you're on the side of evil."

This dogmatic dialogue, it need hardly be said, is imaginary. It never takes place because, by describing their position in such bald terms, the partisans of the all-good *A* would expose the weakness of their stand. Doctrinaire arrogance based on the either-or assumption is a poor substitute for the open-mindedness that leads to true conviction. Careful thinkers realize that most issues in life are not as simple as many people make them out to be.

False analogy is still another kind of oversimplification. We have already seen the analogical principle at work in metaphorical language, because every metaphor is based on an assumed resemblance between two situations, objects, or persons that are in some ways dissimilar. The "bond of similarity" between the two is the abstract idea the metaphor makes concrete. More generally, analogy is often used to clarify, simplify, and make more vivid a complex idea. Analogy transfers a statement from a single subject (to which it does apply) to another subject (to which it may or may not apply, although the assertion is that it does):

> *A* and *B* are related (that is, they have one or more qualities in common);
> *P* is true of *A*;
> So *P* must be true of *B*.

But the fact that *A* and *B* are related in one or more respects does not necessarily mean that they share the particular quality *P*. An analogy is valid only to the degree that the two subjects of comparison are related. The more dissimilar they are (the fewer the qualities they have in common), the less sound must be the conclusion drawn from the assumed likeness.

Newspaper political cartoons are often nothing more than pictorial analogies. Often such analogies serve admirably to point up, dramatically and colorfully, the crux of a problem. The analogy of a governmental agency in the role of the legendary Dutch boy, trying to stop a leak in the dike (the "national economy") while the waves of the sea ("inflation") are already spilling over the top of the dike, is plainly useful. But the danger is that the analogy will assume a nonexistent resemblance between the two objects of comparison. "Don't change horses in the middle of the stream" is a familiar cry in political campaigns when the partisans of the incumbent argue that a change in leaders during a national emergency would be dangerous to the country. Of course, a superficial similarity does exist between the two situations. Changing horses in the middle of a swift stream is dangerous, and so too may be changing leaders during national crises. But riding horseback is not much like being the head of a government, and although we can imagine only one or two reasons why one should or should not change horses, we can think of many reasons, none having anything to do with horseback riding, why one person should be elected and not another. Equally dangerous is any attempt to prove a point based on the analogy that the nations of the world are like children, and that when one nation does not have its way it goes into a corner and refuses to play the game by, for example, not paying its dues to an international agency; or that two opponents, labor and management, for example, may be likened to two prizefighters squaring off in the ring, with an arbitrator as referee. Such analogies can be very helpful, we repeat, in dramatizing a situation. But it is always dangerous to base an argument on only one, perhaps flimsy, analogy.

In one way or another, the various techniques of oversimplification distort the truth: they fail to "give the whole picture." *Taking out of context* is one other device that accomplishes the same end. A sentence or a phrase can easily mean one thing when it is quoted alone and a quite different thing when read against the background of the entire discussion to which it belongs. An extreme but familiar example of this practice is the way in which advertisements of movies, plays, and books quote fragments of apparent praise, often with exclamation points added to heighten the effect. A Broadway play called *Boeing, Boeing,* for instance, was advertised in this way:

"All around me people were SCREAMING WITH LAUGHTER!"
—McClain, *Journal American*

"'Charley's Aunt' has been crossed with 'Pajama Tops'!"
—Kerr, *Herald-Tribune*

"IAN CARMICHAEL IS AN EXCELLENT AGILE FARCEUR!"
—Chapman, *Daily News*

"EXPERT LIKABLE FARCEUR!"
—Watts, *Post*

The sentences from which these rapturous opinions were taken read, in full, as follows:

> McClain: "All around me people were screaming with laughter, and there I sat, unable to hustle up even a synthetic snicker."
>
> Kerr: "There's no concealing the fact that 'Charley's Aunt' has here been crossed with 'Pajama Tops' or the further fact that adapter Beverley Cross has accomplished this match without adding a single funny line to the sound of all those whiplashed doors."
>
> Chapman: "Carmichael is an excellent, agile farceur, and I hope he comes back from London in something better."
>
> Watts: "Ian Carmichael, who is an expert and likable farceur, strives gallantly as the debonair friend ... but [he is] laboring in a vacuum."

Probably no public figure whose statements are quoted in the newspapers or on the radio has ever escaped the chagrin that comes from seeing prominence given to one or two paragraphs of a speech which, thus isolated, completely distort the argument. Listening to a speech or reading an advance copy, reporters may quickly select a passage or two which they think will make the best story and headline and, if the speech is a controversial one, will fit in best with their paper's policy. The sentences thus selected for quotation may be relatively unimportant, an incidental part of the speaker's argument. Thus, when wrenched from context, they may completely misrepresent the speaker's true theme. Critical readers will never base an important decision on the fragmentary press report of someone's public utterance. They will withhold judgment until they can read the full text.

Although in everyday usage quotations alone are usually said to be "taken out of context," the meaning of events themselves is often exaggerated and otherwise distorted when they are separated from their background. (In its wider sense, *context* means "the whole background or situation against which an occurrence is viewed.") This is one of the chief shortcomings of daily journalism, in both the print and electronic media. The content of news columns and broadcasts is determined, for one thing, by physical limitations—space in the case of newspapers and newsmagazines, time in that of radio and television. Various other considerations isolate the event from the context which is necessary to understand its true importance—or lack of importance. One such consideration is the need for a "news angle"—something a copy editor can put a dramatic headline over. No matter if the "angle" seizes on some trivial occurrence or insignificant side issue. The "story" is the thing. In an international conference, a brief "clash" of tempers between two diplomats will provide fine headlines for the daily papers. The "clash" may be over in two minutes and someone else may make a speech of top importance an hour later. The momentary flaring of tempers nevertheless remains the news of the day.

Because newspapers and news programs are preoccupied with unusual or dramatic events, and television, by its very nature, favors stories with a "picture angle," much important news goes unreported. What usually determines the course of events goes on quietly, in the unpublicized routine of the United Nations, in the various offices of governments, in the headquarters of great corporations and laboratories and research libraries. Wherever policy is being determined, wherever knowledge is being applied to the solution of contemporary problems — there the future is truly being shaped. But until these proceedings result in a public statement or provoke a sharp controversy, as a rule they go unreported. What we read in the newspapers or hear on news broadcasts is — to risk another cliché — only the tip of the iceberg of news beneath the surface. An editor of the *New York Times* has written, "No week passes without someone prominent in politics, industry, labor, or civic affairs complaining to me, always in virtually identical terms: 'Whenever I read a story about something in which I really know what's going on, I'm astonished at how little of what's important gets into the papers — and how often even that little is wrong.'"

5. From oversimplification and distortion of truth, it is but a step to the outright suppression of truth. A common name for this device is *card stacking* or *stacking the deck*, which means playing up evidence favorable to one's cause and concealing evidence that weakens one's position. News reporting can again furnish an illustration. Virtually all newspapers are biased in one way or another, because they must take stands and represent some point of view. Although many make an honest, though never wholly successful, attempt to present a balanced account of the news, others deliberately give prominence to news that supports their own editorial position, especially in respect to politics. In the same way, they play down or simply fail to print news that is more favorable to the other side.

Similarly with political parties themselves, and with advertisers. A local administration, running for reelection, may devote all its propaganda to boasting how it made good a campaign promise not to raise taxes by instituting an "economy program." It will fail to mention, however, the way in which services have deteriorated as a result of the "slashed budget." This same practice is evident in virtually every advertisement one reads. The attractive points of a product are dwelt on unceasingly; the less attractive ones, never. A car may be fashionably designed and easy riding; it may have fast pickup in traffic; it may have a wealth of gadgets. These facts will be proclaimed from every newspaper, magazine, and television screen. But that the car eats up gasoline and oil, has a poorly made engine block, and costs $1,500 more than other cars in the same class — these facts are carefully suppressed. But as you will no doubt agree, they are well worth knowing about.

(Exercises: pages 312–319)

This book would be of little use if it led you merely to substitute habitual disbelief for uncritical belief. Believing nothing is probably just as easy as believing everything. Practiced readers will find no dearth of things to believe in, to give their full assent to. But a healthy skepticism, a quiet determination to discover an author's real intent, notwithstanding the obstacles presented by the bad reasons of fallacious argument or by loaded language, is the mark of genuinely critical readers. They cannot passively accept what is offered them in the guise of truth. Their role is always an active, searching one.

If we prefer the gold of truth to the baser metal of error or distortion, we have no choice but to work to discover it. Discovering truth and meaning on the printed page is a real art, which involves above all what Emerson calls "invention": the total engagement and exercise of the creatively critical intelligence. The foregoing chapters have suggested some of the ways in which the skills necessary to "invention" can be cultivated. Both the mental energy that quest requires and the rewards it offers are well expressed by Emerson in sentences which can fitly serve as this book's last word:

> One must be an inventor to read well. As the proverb says, "He that would bring home the wealth of the Indies, must carry out the wealth of the Indies." There is then creative reading as well as creative writing. When the mind is braced by labor and invention, the page of whatever book we read becomes luminous with manifold allusion. Every sentence is doubly significant, and the sense of our author is as broad as the world.

EXERCISES

SCIENTIFIC REASONING

5.1 Here are several syllogisms with one statement missing. From the information given in the other two statements, reconstruct the missing one. Does each full syllogism as constructed meet the tests for validity discussed on pages 270-274?

1. Major premise — All members of Congress are U. S. citizens.

   Minor premise — Mr. Benton is a member of Congress.

   Conclusion

2. Major premise

   Minor premise — Captain Turner is a pilot.

   Conclusion — Captain Turner does not have defective eyesight.

3. Major premise — All families threatened by the floodwaters were safely evacuated.

   Minor premise

   Conclusion — Our uncle and his family were safely evacuated.

4. Major premise   All Quakers refuse to take oaths.
    Minor premise
    Conclusion   Most of the witnesses in this case
                             will refuse to take oaths.

5. Major premise   All the rivers on the western
                             side of this watershed flow
                             into the Gulf of Mexico.
    Minor premise   Two-thirds of the rivers I'm talk-
                             ing about are on the western
                             side of this watershed.
    Conclusion

6. Major premise
    Minor premise   Whales are mammals.
    Conclusion   Whales bear their young live.

5.2 **(a)** One of the best-known recent investigations that have combined the major techniques of scientific induction and deduction has been the attempt to establish whether or not cigarette smoking causes cancer. In the course of their inquiry, scientists analyzed masses of public health statistics to find the degree of correlation between heavy smoking and the occurrence of cancer. They also conducted many thousands of experiments. Many questions arose, such as, Is it smoking that accounts for the increase in the rate of lung and other cancers, or is it the noxious elements poured into the air by automobile exhausts and industrial plants, or is it a combination of factors? If chemicals from cigarette smoke definitely can induce skin cancer in laboratory animals, can it therefore be said that the same chemicals produce lung cancer in human beings? Can smoking by others, in a confined space, harm nonsmokers over a period of time? Now that some of these questions have been answered, it is instructive to look back and examine the various ways in which the answers were reached. Using library aids such as the *Readers' Guide*, find a representative selection of the many articles printed on the topic beginning, say, in 1953. On the basis of this material write a brief description of the uses scientific investigators made of induction and deduction.

(b) Another important medical question relates to the contribution which excessive cholesterol in the diet may make to heart disease. Look up recent articles on the subject and report how inductive and deductive reasoning are being employed to settle this question.

RHETORICAL REASONING

Fact and Opinion; Objectivity and Subjectivity

5.3 Although no absolute distinction between fact and opinion exists, it is possible to distinguish between those statements which may be verified through some relatively objective means (checking historical records or performing an experiment) and those which require personal or subjective confirmation. Analyze the following statements to determine which might best be called facts and which opinions. Which seem to reflect a middle range between fact and opinion?

1. The United Nations was founded in 1945.
2. Children from single-parent homes tend to have problems in school.
3. Italians make the best ice cream.
4. The Pacific Northwest is one of the few places in North America where farming and industrial development have not destroyed the ecosystem.
5. Killer whales usually feed on sea lions and seals.
6. The capital of the United States is Washington, D. C.
7. The large number of people migrating to the Sunbelt has created serious strains in these states' social welfare systems.
8. Canada and the United States have always had a good relationship.
9. The *Rocky Horror Show* was the best movie of the 1970s.
10. A college degree no longer guarantees a good job.
11. In North America, middle-class people bear the largest tax burden.
12. The earth revolves around the sun.

5.4 To illustrate the difference between subjective and objective reports of the same sight or event, choose a subject and write two separate accounts of it (two or three paragraphs each). As far as you are able, confine one account to facts on which most, if not all, people would agree (in the case of a symphony, for example, the key, the tempo, the orchestration, the succession of themes and movements). In the other paper, concentrate on your personal impressions (for instance, on the pictures, emotions, or other sensory impressions a passage in the symphony suggests). In practice, is it ordinarily possible to write either with absolute objectivity or utter subjectivity? The effect of this exercise will be heightened if everybody in the class takes the same topic and the results are then compared. Some possible subjects:

A laboratory experiment in chemistry or physics.
A rock or jazz concert.
The nature of a certain short poem (for example, one of those printed in this book).
A room you know well.
An especially novel or eye-catching window display.
A certain movie or art exhibit.
A much-heralded television show.
The aftermath of a recent dramatic happening on campus (subsequent

events, effect on student morale and on the institution as a whole, and so on).

A museum exhibit.

A particular antique shop.

5.5 **(a)** The following essay is from "My Turn," a regular feature of *Newsweek* magazine. Analyze it, paying particular attention to the author's handling of objective and subjective evidence. Does her reliance on personal experience limit the effectiveness of her argument? Why or why not? How does the kind of evidence she uses influence the scope and specificity of her argument? How persuasive do you think this essay would be to a general readership, such as *Newsweek* attracts?

My Unprodigal Sons*

Carolyn Lewis

My two sons live lives starkly different from my own. They make their homes in small rural places, and theirs are the lives of voluntary simplicity.

They have chosen work that gives service to others, requires no harm in the name of greater good. They share a singular lack of interest in accruing possessions. Their clothes would make Brooks Brothers shudder, and they drive automobiles that are both ancient and uncomely.

They till the earth around their modest houses to grow vegetables, trees and flowers. They are entertained by shared festivities with neighbors, wives and children. They have records for music, books for learning, and each lives close enough to the sea to enjoy the esthetic pleasures of blue vistas and open sky.

This curious phenomenon—of ambitious, competitive, urban parents spawning gentle, unambitious, country offspring—is not unique to my own experience. I observe it all around me and listen with amusement to the puzzled comments of middle-aged parents faced with this unexpected generational shift.

"We gave him everything, and he chooses to weave blankets in Maine," they say accusingly. Or, "We invested in Andover and Harvard, and he cuts trees in Oregon." The refrain is sorrowful, even embarrassed, as though our children have somehow turned against us by choosing to live in ways different from our own.

But I confess that every time I return to the big city after visiting my children, I am haunted by a psychic malaise. I go through my days comparing this with that, and more and more the *that* is looking better.

What my sons have is a world that is small enough to be readily understood, where those responsible wear a human face. When I talk about the big city where I live, in the only terms that can grasp its enormity—about groups and studies, trends and polls—my sons smile sweetly and speak of the people who live around the corner, have specific names and definitive problems. Theirs are flesh-and-blood realities instead of my pale, theoretical formulations. They remind me that the collective humanity I measure and label is far less interesting and vital than the individual who, mercifully, in the end will defy categorization.

When I ask him how he likes living in a town of 500 people three hours away from the nearest large city, my son Peter says: "Just fine. You see, I know who I am here."

That statement resonates in my brain. It's true; he has a definable space to call his own. He has warming relationships with family and neighbors. He has what E. F. Schumacher would call "good work."

On the other hand, he certainly cannot be labeled rich. His income is hardly the kind that makes the GNP go into a tailspin. When the sophisticated instruments of measurement are applied to his life—husband, wife, two children (family of four earning so much)—they mark him low income.

I, by comparison, living in my overpriced city apartment, walking to work past putrid sacks of street garbage, paying usurious taxes to local and state governments I generally abhor, I am rated middle class. This causes me to wonder, do the measurements make sense? Are we measuring only that which is easily measured—the numbers on the money chart—and ignoring values more central to the good life?

For my sons there is of course the rural bounty of fresh-grown vegetables, line-caught fish and the shared riches of neighbors' orchards and gardens. There is the unpaid baby-sitter for whose children my daughter-in-law baby-sits in return, and neighbors who barter their skills and labor. But more than that, how do you measure serenity? Sense of self? The feeling that, in order to get ahead, you don't have to trample on somebody else's skull?

I don't want to idealize life in small places. There are times when the outside world intrudes brutally, as when the cost of gasoline goes up or developers cast their eyes on untouched farmland. There are cruelties, there is bigotry, there are all the many vices and meannesses in small places that exist in large cities. Furthermore, it is harder to ignore them when they cannot be banished psychologically to another part of town or excused as the vagaries of alien groups—when they have to be acknowledged as "part of us."

Nor do I want to belittle the opportunities for small decencies in cities—the eruptions of one-stranger-to-another caring that always surprise and delight. But these are, sadly, more exceptions than rules and are often overwhelmed by the awful corruptions and dangers that surround us.

In this society, where material riches and a certain notoriety are considered admirable achievements, it takes some courage to say, no thanks, not for me. The urban pleasures and delights—restaurants, museums, theater, crowds in the streets—continue to have an urgent seductiveness for many young people. For parents like myself, who strove to offer our children these opportunities and riches, it is hard to be reconciled to those same children spurning the offer and choosing otherwise.

Plainly, what my sons want and need is something different—something smaller, simpler and more manageable. They march to a different drummer, searching for an ethic that recognizes limits, that scorns overbearing competition and what it does to human relations, and that says simply and gently, enough is enough.

Is my sons' solution to the complexity and seeming intractability of modern problems the answer for everyone? Of course not. Some of us have to stay in the cities, do what we can, fight when it is necessary, compete in order to survive. Maybe if we are diligent, we can make things a little better where we are.

But to choose small places, modest ambitions and values that are tolerant and loving is surely an admirable alternative. It may in the end be the only alternative we have to an urban culture in which we have created so much ugliness, and where we seem to inflict so much pain on each other through neglect, selfishness and failure of will.

(b) Try your hand at writing a "My Turn" essay, using the preceding as a guide to length and general form. Address a topic of public significance, but, as the author of "My Unprodigal Sons" does, use your own personal experience as evidence for your assertions. *After* you have written your essay, analyze your use of evidence, listing all the counterarguments that could be brought against it and sorting out levels of subjectivity and objectivity.

Rhetorical Induction

5.6 The following statements are based on some form of rhetorical induction. Examine each statement, with particular attention to these points: (1) Are all terms satisfactorily defined? (2) If the statement is based on an accumulation of evidence, how much evidence, and what kind, would justify the generalization? (3) If the statement is a hypothesis, could enough evidence be collected to prove or disprove it? (4) If it is a causal assertion, does it take into account the possibility of more than one cause?

1. The bathtub is the most dangerous place in the house.
2. If you answer all the questions on a true-false test "true," you're

bound to score at least 50 percent. I went into the exam not knowing a thing; I used the system and came out with a 70.

3. Pregnant women should not be required to work at video display terminals because of the threat of birth defects.

4. Last year the grade distribution in this course was 6 A's, 10 B's, 15 C's, 10 D's, and 8 E's. College students are getting worse every year.

5. Now I know that what I suspected is true. There are termites in my garage. I've seen the characteristic mud tunnels they build.

6. The tomb of Tutankhamen bears a curse. It has brought bad luck to all those who had a hand in discovering it.

7. Racial prejudice is much more pronounced in adolescents and adults than it is in young children.

8. American propaganda efforts, such as the Voice of America and Radio Free Europe, have been failures.

9. Excessive speed and drinking are responsible for most fatal automobile accidents.

10. Politicians are not necessarily dishonest, but they all look out primarily for themselves.

11. I will never shop at that grocery store again, because I once bought a piece of meat there that was spoiled.

12. The danger of pesticides to farm workers has been greatly exaggerated, because there are many, many farm workers who suffer no ill effects at all.

13. If only a few people who were obviously crackpots reported seeing strange objects in the sky, you could say there weren't any such things. But when the reports mount into the hundreds, there is a strong probability that flying saucers, or whatever you want to call them, exist.

14. The present generation of young men and women is stronger and more capable of physical feats than previous ones. Look at all the athletic records that are being broken.

15. I'm going to read that new adventure novel; it's been on the bestseller list for months!

16. The steady decline of interest in debating and in campus literary magazines shows that the modern college student simply isn't interested in serious intellectual activity.

17. This airport obviously is unsafe. There have been three crashes here in as many years.

18. The results of the recent election prove that most people want their government to follow a conservative philosophy.

19. It is sure to rain today, since my hair has lost all its curliness.

20. Good guys finish last.

5.7 Select several assertions from the following list and, in a paragraph devoted to each, explain what kind of evidence you would require to be convinced that the assertion was true. Consider also the difficulties and pitfalls involved in gathering and assessing such evidence.

1. "Scientific" predictions of election returns on television before the polls close can affect the outcome of an election, because they influence the decisions of last-minute voters.
2. In a national election, late voters on the West Coast are affected by the fact that they have already learned the earlier results from the East Coast.
3. If a rich person gets picked up for drunken driving, the police quietly forget about it. If a poor person gets picked up, they throw the book at him. So much for justice and "equality."
4. The use of hard drugs seriously impairs reasoning ability.
5. Smoking marijuana is no more injurious to the health than drinking a cocktail, and therefore it should not be punishable by law.
6. City slums breed crime.
7. Violence shown on television is a major cause of violent crime, especially among the young.
8. Censorship of books and movies should be restored, because it has been proved that dirty books and movies often are behind today's widespread immorality and crime.
9. The best way to bring on a rainstorm is to wash your car.
10. Acid rain represents a major threat to North America's lakes and forests.
11. The increase of suburban shopping centers has seriously affected the business of downtown stores.
12. It is rank superstition for anyone to believe that we can communicate with the dead.
13. The popularity of television has sharply reduced the time people devote to reading books.
14. Frequent and excessive playing of video games causes antisocial tendencies in youngsters.
15. Solar energy is the most efficient means of heating homes in the West.
16. The four people who have most influenced the thinking of mankind in the past century have been Darwin, Marx, Freud, and Einstein.
17. The tendency toward cancer runs in certain families.
18. Some families are just plain unlucky; they suffer one serious illness after another.

5.8 **(a)** Citing official figures from several areas, which show that men are responsible for twice as many fatal automobile accidents as women, someone has concluded that female drivers are twice as safe as male drivers. What factors has the investigator probably failed to take into account?

(b) In the nineteenth century, statistics on the literacy rate in England were based on the number of men and women who were able to write their names at the time they were married. In 1861, the percentage of bridegrooms who could do so was 69.3; of brides, 54.8. In 1900, the percentages were 97.2 and 96.8 respectively. Can we conclude, therefore, that by 1900 almost everybody in England could read and write?

(c) The ten newest houses built in a certain subdivision sold for these prices: $120,000 (two); $95,000; $84,000; $70,000 (two); $65,000; $60,000; $48,000 (two). What is the "average" price?

(d) What questions should you insist on having answered before you will accept the following statement? "It is simply not true that athletes in this college are poorer students than nonathletes. Official figures in the registrar's office show that the athletes' average is slightly above that of the student body as a whole."

(e) What are the errors here? "According to the government's index (based on the prices of rent, clothing, food, and a number of other expenses), the cost of living rose 5 percent in the past year. Therefore, our family spent 5 percent more on food in the past year."

(f) What considerations should be taken into account when evaluating the following arguments? (1) "Automobile insurance rates should be higher for all teenage drivers." (2) "Statistics prove that raising the legal drinking age reduces highway accidents." (3) "The 55 mile per hour speed limit has been responsible for lower accident rates."

5.9 Choose one of the following statements and make notes regarding any personal experience you have had that supports or refutes it. Then, using library resources, gather as much additional evidence as possible. Use this information and your notes on personal experiences to write a short essay arguing either for or against the statement.

1. Training in English composition in the secondary schools is inadequate for students who go on to college.
2. The weather has a definite influence on people's mental states.
3. The North American labor movement is corrupt.
4. Students who wait a few years before going on to college get more out of their education than those who go to college immediately after high school.
5. The practice of having piped-in music in places like banks, offices, and restaurants makes employees more efficient and content and also has a good effect on customers.
6. Capital punishment deters crime.
7. Old adages like "Red sky in morning, sailor's warning; red sky

at night, sailor's delight" have a considerable body of scientific truth in them.

8. Interstate highways are much safer than other roads.
9. You can't believe half of what you read in the newspapers, but you can believe more when you see it on television.
10. The day of the conscientious craftsman is over. Everything you buy nowadays is poorly built.
11. Airplanes are the safest means of transportation.

5.10 Using the *Readers' Guide* and other library resources, trace the history of Legionnaire's Disease. Identify the methods of hypothesis testing used (see pages 281-283) by the various investigators in learning about this disease.

Rhetorical Deduction

5.11 The following statements depend for their effectiveness on enthymemes, the basic tool of rhetorical deduction. Identify the enthymeme or enthymemes implicit in these assertions, and note any assumed areas of shared agreement. Are these enthymemes valid, or are they, as sometimes happens, used to conceal the lack of clear reasoning?

1. The large increase in church membership in recent years shows that people are becoming more religious.
2. Students should be required to write in all of their college classes, not just in English classes.
3. Organizations like the United Nations must do everything in their power to encourage those nations whose food supply is inadequate to limit their birthrates.
4. Until we find a solution to the problem of waste disposal, we must prohibit further nuclear development.
5. Students nowadays care nothing about social problems; there hasn't been a demonstration or rally on this campus for ten years.
6. Vegetarians are crazy. Meat has got to be good for you. People have been eating it for thousands of years.
7. I don't deny that I copied most of the essay from a magazine article. What's the matter with that? Everybody does it.
8. If television programs are mostly insults to mature intelligence, don't blame the networks or the advertisers. They are simply giving the great American public what it wants. Look at the program ratings in the audience surveys.
9. Books containing dirty language should be banned from school libraries.
10. When airlines are able to offer group and excursion fares much cheaper than regular fares, it is clear that the regular fares are too high and the airlines are making excessive profits.

5.12 Using the questions discussed on pages 286-288, analyze the logic of the following advertisement:

The Bad News That Showed How Good CNN News Really Is.

When Air Florida Flight 90 crashed in the Potomac, CNN (Cable News Network) covered the story continuously from first report right through the night. Unlike the other networks that just interrupted regularly scheduled programs with short reports.

During the frantic early moments, CNN was the first and only TV network to accurately report that it really WAS Flight 90 that crashed.

CNN was also the only TV network to provide live coverage of the many attempts to recover the plane. Because CNN is the only TV network that can take the time to give stories the depth they deserve.

When President Reagan was shot, CNN was once again the only TV network to stay with it from first report to Hinckley's actual jailing.

No wonder so many of the nation's wire services and newspapers stay tuned to CNN 24 hours a day.

See for yourself why millions of Americans who need to know the news the minute it happens, know they can always find it on CNN. Cable's most important network. Turn to CNN on your system. Or if you don't have it, contact your cable operator to get it.

The Question of Authority

5.13 (a) From the current *Reader's Digest*, select five or six articles which seem to you to call for specialized knowledge of certain topics—aviation, science, diplomacy, and so on. Then, consulting reliable reference works, such as *Who's Who in America, American Men of Science,* or *Living Authors,* try to determine how well qualified was the author of each article.

(b) Try the same experiment with the current issue of *Scientific American*. Note that every issue of *Scientific American* includes a section titled "The Authors." How well do the short biographical sketches of each author in this section establish the credibility of both the authors and the magazine?

(c) The following persons (most living, several recently deceased) are well known as popularizers in various fields. Try to find out from an expert in each field—the most learned professor you know, for example—how each popularizer is regarded by the experts, and why.

Carl Sagan (astronomy), Margaret Mead (anthropology), Marshall McLuhan (media), David Attenborough (natural history), James Michener (American history), Rachel Carson (marine biology), Lewis Thomas (biology), Loren Eiseley (science), Will and Ariel Durant (history and philosophy), Daniel Lang (nuclear research and space science), (Lord) Kenneth Clark (art history).

5.14 How much attention should be paid to the pronouncements of the following writers on the stated subjects? Why?

1. A sports expert, writing in the September 14 issue of a magazine, on which will be "the nation's ten top teams" in the coming football season.
2. A probation officer, with thirty years' experience, on the causes of juvenile delinquency.
3. A retired air force general, on the proper course the Department of State should follow in dealing with current international problems.
4. A beautiful and well-known fashion model, on the moisturizer that is best for your complexion.
5. The president of the National Association of Manufacturers, on a proposed law to curb union activity in politics.
6. The president of the United Automobile Workers, on the same subject.
7. A young, single father, in a short article in a parents' magazine, on ways to keep children entertained during rainy spells.
8. The author of the standard biography of Robert E. Lee, reviewing a newly published book on the life of Lee.
9. A Harvard economist, on the long-range prospects of a uranium mine stock you are thinking of buying.
10. Three friends of yours, on whether or not you should elect a certain course next year.

5.15 Examine the use of authority in the advertisement on the opposite page. Is the authority legitimately and effectively used? What is the claim being made? What grounds, underlying assumption(s), and backup support lie behind that claim? Go to the library and, using the sources mentioned in exercise 5.13(a), find out as much as you can about the qualifications of these experts.

Informal Fallacies

5.16 Comment on the advertisements on pages 314 and 315 as examples of the "transfer" device.

5.17 Make a collection of current advertisements that borrow the prestige of science to help sell products like hand lotion, toothpaste, or deodorant. Try to determine just what the scientific terms they use really mean ("homogenized lanolin"; "vitamin-fortified emollient").

5.18 Examine the use of the "transfer" device in the "Unsinkable Mr. Brown" advertisement quoted on pages 61–62.

5.19 Look up Mark Antony's funeral oration in Shakespeare's *Julius Caesar* (Act III, Scene 2) and analyze the various ways in which Mark Antony arouses the emotions of his listeners. How does this speech differ from a calm appeal to reason? What informal fallacies, if any, can you detect in the speech?

5.20 (a) From current areas of discussion (political, social, economic, ethical), choose and dissect some good cases of oversimplification and the false dilemma. (Example: the United States, in formulating and applying its future foreign policy, must choose between a return to strict isolationism and total global commitment.)

(b) Study samples of true-false or multiple-choice examinations used in one of your college courses. Are they constructed so that all possible correct answers are provided for, or do they fail to recognize one or more legitimate alternatives? If the latter, specify what alternatives are omitted.

5.21 In the following passage, a contemporary writer draws a startling analogy between Little League baseball and the sweatshop horrors of the nineteenth century. What attributes do the two have in common? How valid is the analogy as part of the author's criticism of organized juvenile baseball?

> The corporations . . . have now entered into this arena too, to organize the next stage of growing up. This is the meaning, surely, of the publicity that has been trumped up for the Little League, the baseball teams of subteen-agers sponsored and underwritten by various business firms. . . . The high-pressure advertising has been violently denounced by the older sportswriters as giving kids an unsportsmanlike taste for publicity. As a school of rule-making, responsibility, and impersonality, the Little League certainly cannot compare with the free games of the street, but we saw that these have been passing away. Economically, however, the function of the Little League is clear-cut: it is child labor, analogous to ten-year-olds picking hemp in the factory a century ago: it keeps idle hands out of mischief; it is not profitable as production, but it provides valuable training in attitudes and work habits.

5.22 (a) Make a collection of current newspaper cartoons as examples of possibly false or misleading analogies. What is the basis of the implied resemblance between the two situations? What does the cartoonist imply by selecting that particular analogy? How far can the analogy be logically extended?

(b) In the *Reader's Digest* or a similar magazine, find an article such as "How City X Licked Its Air Pollution Problem," the implication being that other cities might profitably follow the same procedure. How far can the implied analogy usefully be carried? What differences between the two entities involved in the comparison might invalidate the analogy?

(c) Make a collection of advertisements which use implied analogy and evaluate the reasoning each one contains.

(d) Gather a number of examples of informal analogy used in everyday situations. (For instance: a friend argues that you should major in science, because she did so and enjoyed every science course she took.) How sound are these everyday analogies? How far can each one be logically extended? Even if the analogies involve flawed reasoning, could the conclusions they urge still be essentially right?

5.23 (a) The advertisements for books in the weekly book sections of large metropolitan newspapers, the *New York Review of Books,* and some magazines such as the *New Yorker* or the *Atlantic* often quote enthusiastic comments from newspaper or magazine reviews. Copy a handful of such quotations from recent advertisements and, using the *Book Review Digest,* look up the reviews from which they were taken. Were the critics really as happy about the books as the brief fragments quoted in the advertisements suggest they were?

(b) Compare the full text of a recent speech with the excerpts quoted in a newspaper or magazine article. How adequately and fairly do the quotations represent the speaker's argument? Does he or she have any cause to complain, as speakers often do, that the reporter has distorted the views presented in the speech? (For this exercise, remember that the *New York Times* usually prints complete texts of important speeches and public documents, and that speeches in Congress are printed in full in the *Congressional Record.* If reportage in your campus paper is being examined, the speaker's manuscript or a tape recording of the remarks might be obtained. Or, better yet, attend the meeting yourself, taking adequate notes, and compare what you heard with the subsequent printed report.)

5.24 (a) If you have recently been involved in an event covered by newspapers, compare your own firsthand knowledge of that event with the account which was printed. In what respects, if any, was the event misrepresented or distorted? Were any important details not mentioned? Were any unimportant details given exaggerated treatment? How can you account for these discrepancies between the actual event and the newspaper report?

(b) As a cooperative class exercise, select a current news story of political significance and compare the treatment it has received, or is receiving, in several newspapers, among them a local paper, a respected national newspaper such as the *Wall Street Journal*, and two newspapers with opposing political biases (one conservative, one liberal, for instance). In what ways, if any, are the various accounts "slanted"? How do they differ in selection and emphasis of details? What reasons can you suggest for these differences? Compare the treatment of the same story in one or two newsmagazines. Do these magazines give any broader perspective on the events and the personalities involved? Does their treatment reflect editorial bias or a policy of dramatizing news? How close to the actual truth of the matter do you think such a study has brought you?

(c) Compare a story that is reported in an American newsmagazine (such as *Time* or *Newsweek*) with the same story as reported in a British newsmagazine (such as the British edition of *Time*) or in a Canadian newsmagazine (such as *Maclean's* or a Canadian edition of *Time*). How do the accounts differ in selection of details, in emphasis, and in interpretation?

5.25 Make a collection of current "institutional" advertisements, from either television or magazines, which stress the endearing, "human," altruistic, socially responsible qualities the company is alleged to possess. (The telephone company advertisement quoted on page 292 has such a purpose.) What other, perhaps less admirable, characteristics of the company are left unmentioned or converted into positive virtues? What techniques are used to make the company seem "human"?

5.26 Comment on the reasoning displayed in each of the following statements, identifying the particular fallacy or fallacies involved:

1. [Reply by an advertising copywriter when asked whether or not he had any pangs of conscience at writing advertisements for cigarettes] "Writing cigarette copy doesn't bother me one bit! Why should it? Should an automobile copywriter worry about writing copy for automobiles just because thousands of people die in car accidents every year? Is it wrong to write liquor ads just because there are alcoholics?"
2. The local barbers' union today announced that the price of haircuts was raised from $5.00 to $7.50. In explanation of the rise, the head of the union pointed out that this is the only large city in the area in which haircuts have not previously cost $7.50.
3. [From the newsletter of Phi Beta Kappa, noting that a grandmother had won high honors on graduating from the School of General Studies at Columbia University] "The adult mind," said Dean Louis M. Hacker, of the School of General Studies, "is as good as the youthful mind, if not better. It's time we stopped

underestimating the potential mental growth of our adult men and women." The grandmother's record proves his point.

4. Certainly I don't want to cast any aspersions on his integrity as a bank cashier. I have no reason for believing he isn't 100 percent honest. I'm merely saying that he seems to have a pretty keen interest in horses. I've seen him at the races several times in the last couple of months.

5.   All Nature is but Art, unknown to thee;
       All Chance, Direction, which thou canst not see;
       All Discord, Harmony not understood;
       All partial Evil, universal Good:
       And, spite of Pride, in erring Reason's spite,
       One truth is clear, WHATEVER IS, IS RIGHT.

These famous lines, from Alexander Pope's "Essay on Man," admirably illustrate not only the fatuous optimism of the poet himself, willfully closing his eyes to the evil rampant in the world, but also the complacency of the whole age in which he lived. Pope and his fellow men in the first half of the eighteenth century deliberately lived in a fool's paradise, deluding themselves by the simple process of refusing to look reality in the face.

6. There's no question that the home computer we looked at is the best value for the money. Nothing else we've seen can compare to it. Still, I don't think we should buy it. I don't like the high-pressure methods the salesman used, and the big words he used scared me anyway.

7. Make this simple test to *prove* to yourself that Nurp is the best antacid remedy on the market! Drop a single handy tablet in water! See how quickly it dissolves! It gets to work faster in your stomach! Give it a trial this very day!

8. This theory about a new cure for heart disease has been put forward by a woman known for her radical politics. We shouldn't pay any attention to her.

9. Computer games can't possibly harm children, since they occupy their attention and keep them out of trouble outdoors.

10. [Advertisement] People either ask for *Beefeater* or they ask for gin.

11. Better dead than Red.

12. Guns don't kill; people do.

REVIEW

5.27 Make a collection of letters to the editor in the local newspapers or a newsmagazine and analyze them closely for examples of the various types of reasoning and errors in reasoning discussed in this chapter.

5.28 Choose a controversial international, national, or local issue that is being widely discussed at the moment, preferably one on which you already have formed a strong opinion. Collect all the arguments you can for the side you do *not* agree with and try to rebut them, one by one, by the use of the tools of reasoning with which this chapter has provided you. Can you refute all the arguments to your own satisfaction, or has your difficulty in answering some of them caused you to reconsider your own position? If your instructor directs, use the materials you have gathered to write an essay analyzing and refuting the major points made by the opposite side on the issue.

5.29 Using the questions discussed on pages 286–288, analyze the argument put forward in the following letter to the editor. Note assumed area(s) of agreement, implied premises, the claim made, and the support offered for the claim.

Cuts Hurt

As a student at Linn-Benton Community College, my future is in your hands next Tuesday, Sept. 21. Even if the levy passes, LBCC will have to operate on fewer dollars than the college had last year when students were already encountering problems getting the classes they needed.

As a continuing full-time student last spring, I was only able to get one of the five classes I had planned to take, because the other classes were full. No new sections could be added, no matter how great the student need, because the college lacked the funds. Taking sequenced courses out of sequence is not the best way to get an education.

The Sept. 21 levy will cost the average homeowner an extra $10 for the entire year. Its failure could cost me and many other LBCC students our future.

5.30 The following communication was addressed to the faculty senate of a large university by a campus "note service." (Occasional grammatical and other lapses have been retained.) Closely examine the reasoning in this communication, especially for suppressed premises and invalid conclusions.

Primarily a student comes to your university for educational purposes. It is the partial responsibility of the university to give that student all possible aid in acquiring as much knowledge as possible in any course that the student chooses. For his own benefit, the student buys textbooks, books of references, and takes notes in class. Now it is evident that no two sets of notes are identical because, the student might have omitted an important fact, missed the substance of the lecture, or jotted down an erroneous statement.

We of the Acme Note Service hire students with high point average who take notes in class, check them for accuracy and clarity. These are duplicated and sold to students in the class. These notes are easy to read, complete, accurate and will enable the student to compare his or her notes with ours.

If perchance our notes might contain an error or something misleading, the student buying our notes questions it and our notetaker makes it a point to enter the correct information in the next day's notes.

The aim of a professor is to give every possible aid to a student in obtaining as much knowledge in a particular course, whether the latter acquires it from a textbook, reference books or lecture notes. We feel that if a student can compare his or her notes with ours, that student will be able to derive more from the course in regards to retention of the material and thought stimulation.

On such a basis it has been found that students derive a greater benefit from the lecture material to which they are exposed. This fact has been borne out at universities such as The University of California at Berkeley, Princeton, Harvard, Penn, Columbia and others.

An administrative viewpoint has been expressed that it would be dangerous to sell notes to undergraduate students. That this viewpoint is without foundation is borne out by favorable results at other universities in which such note services are in operation. We have surveyed the students who buy our notes and find that almost in all cases their grades are up compared to the previous quarter.

We have been told that some of the faculty oppose the fact that we commercialize this service. Need we only point out that the university itself is a commercialized institution as is the sale of the textbooks, reference books, and other student aids. Furthermore, we do not compel anyone to buy our notes. They may do so if they want to and if they feel it will help them at all in their schoolwork here.

It has been mentioned that a person using another's notes is cheating. In response to this we pose the following questions: Is it considered cheating when two students study together? Is it cheating when a student hires a tutor? We are of the impression that one cheats when a student turns in for grading some one elses work. However we feel all will agree that using textbooks, reference books and other sources of material such as edited notes does not constitute cheating.

5.31 Neither of the advertisements on pages 322 and 323 is trying to sell a product directly, yet each has a definite point to make. Analyze these ads. What is their purpose? How is that purpose carried out? Is the implied intent the same as the explicit intent? What informal fallacies, if any, do these ads reveal? How valid is their use of evidence? How effective do you find them?

5.32 Choose a controversial industry or business and write an advertisement designed to deflect or reduce public criticism. Also write a short explanation of the strategies you used in the ad, including rhetorical induction and deduction, appeals to emotion, appeals to authority, and subjective and objective evidence. As preparation, you might look through current magazines for advertisements for a major industry or an agency thereof, such as the Tobacco Institute. Examine the advertisements used by the group to determine the strategies used.

5.33 Not all arguments are of the straightforward "I'm in favor of gun control and here are three reasons why" variety. Many evaluations and analyses contain implied, rather than stated, arguments. Critical readers examine such arguments with the same care as they do editorials or political campaign speeches. Here is a book review which contains several implied arguments. Analyze it, paying close attention to suppressed premises, implied judgments, and assumed areas of agreement. In addition, examine the use of connotative language and other elements of diction which help to determine the tone. What are the strategies the author employs to make his point? How fair is this argument?

Deafening Roar

ANGEL OF LIGHT
by Joyce Carol Oates
Dutton; 434 pages; $15.50

There has always been something off-putting about the fiction of Joyce Carol Oates, even when, as in her short stories, it is at its most controlled and least melodramatic. What sets the teeth on edge is not the appalling prolificacy that has driven her to turn out thirteen novels, eleven collections of stories, three books of criticism and five volumes of poetry in less than two decades while maintaining a full university schedule. It is not the author's bloodthirstiness—her plots are more sanguinary even than real life in the 20th century—or the unvarying over-burden of emotions that lies on all of her characters and all of her situations.

The sense of monstrousness that arises from her work seems to have its source in an unbridgeable gap between the highly rational and ordered intelligence of the writer, and the chaos and hysteria of nearly everything she writes about. Thus, perhaps, her chronic melodrama, her pumping of more emotion into situations than they have been built to withstand.

The latest model from the Oates fiction factory, *Angel of Light,* is an anthology of the author's excesses. The flaccid, irritating soap opera is jerry-built around the hatreds of a wealthy family in Washington, D. C. A senior bureaucrat, Maurice Halleck, head of the "Commission for the Ministry of Justice," has died, apparently by suicide, after seeming to confess to bribe taking. Halleck's two nearly grown children, drug-frazzled Kirsten and lard-witted Owen, vow to wreak vengeance on their gorgeous mother Isabel, and their father's best friend from boyhood, whom they take to be the killers. Here, as elsewhere, the author has far more energy than her characters, who sag into torpor when she busies herself with other scenes and lurch groggily back into motion when she summons them again.

Terrorists enter the situation, although not explosively enough or early enough to save the book. The reader is trapped for lengthy incoherent chapters in the minds of Owen and his sister, specimens who would have a psychiatrist looking at his watch well before the end of each 50-minute hour. The only breaks come in equally long and profitless flashbacks to the boyhood of Maurice Halleck. The writing here is of the "It was a dark and stormy night" variety that Snoopy, the *Peanuts* dog, concocts whenever he tries to write his own novel. Halleck and his friend take a canoe trip, and he is nearly drowned in "the deafening roar" of the wild Loughrea. This is a Celtic place name, used for a Canadian river. But it sounds almost exactly like logorrhea, and in this sibylline choice, abused readers will take malicious pleasure.

5.34 Go to the library and, using the *Book Review Digest*, look up other reviews of this novel. Choose three reviews and analyze the different approaches of the authors in each one. How do they vary in use of subjectivity and objectivity, selection of details, uses of enthymemes, and other strategies of reasoning? What claim or claims, either implied or directly stated, does each contain? What elements of diction are used to support the claim? Although you may not have read the novel in question, which of the reviews do you judge to be most fair, and why? Is it the review you also think is most persuasive?

5.35 Comment on the reasoning reflected in each of the following exhibits. If your instructor directs, write an essay analyzing the reasoning in one of them.

1.

Franklin Roosevelt

"If I were starting life over again, I am inclined to think that I would go into the advertising business in preference to almost any other. This is because advertising has come to cover the whole range of human needs and also because it combines real imagination with a deep study of human psychology. Because it brings to the greatest number of people actual knowledge concerning useful things, it is essentially a form of education. . . . It has risen with ever-growing rapidity to the dignity of an art. It is constantly paving new paths. . . . The general raising of the standards of modern civilization among all groups of people during the past half century would have been impossible without the spreading of the knowledge of higher standards by means of advertising."

Isn't it strange to find people in this country today who, in the name of everything Franklin D. Roosevelt stood for, criticize advertising and seek to restrict it? Well-meaning people who say that it is unfair competition for a big company to spend more on advertising than a small company. Ignoring the fact that it is advertising that helps small companies grow big. . . . companies like Polaroid, Xerox, Sony and dozens more who have taken on the giants in the marketplace and won their niche.

These people think we should restrict the amount of advertising a company can do—just to be fair. But, of course, big companies spend more on research and development than little companies, too. And that's even more unfair because it helps develop new products that little companies don't have. So, perhaps, we should restrict research and development.

It's too bad somebody didn't think of this 40 years ago. Then we'd all still have iceboxes. And you wouldn't have to worry about getting all that frozen food home from the supermarket before it thaws. In your late Model "T."

2. ### Let's Junk the Term "Junk Mail"

First, what is "junk mail"?

Mail you didn't send for? Then you'll have to include Federal Income Tax forms, bills, draft notices, etc.

Mail that doesn't pay first-class rates?

Then what about the *Congressional Record,* letters from the White House, and the Bible?

Mail that offers things for sale? Then half of America's largest and most respected corporations are in the junk business, and the millions spent on mail order merchandise last year were wasted.

Actually, "junk mail" is just a catch-phrase for critics who don't understand the importance of this 2.5-billion-dollar marketplace in the nation's economy.

One way to help junk the term "junk mail" is with education.

Another way is to make your mailings so good they're hard to throw away.

And that's easy to do. We make more than 30 Oxford papers created especially to help a good product look good, and a good mailing turn into a good puller.

And isn't it amazing? Nobody ever called a direct mail piece "junk mail" when they were acting on it.*

GLOSSARY

Abstract A term applied to words or phrases that refer to general ideas or qualities not perceivable to the five senses. (Antonym: CONCRETE.) *Conservatism, courage, decency, love, power,* and *truth* are examples of abstract terms. Not all terms are equally abstract, however. The word *automobile,* for instance, is less general than *vehicle* or *mode of transportation* but more general and abstract than the concrete and specific *1984 red Honda Civic.* See **Concrete.**

Ad hominem argument Literally an argument "against the man." Such arguments usually attack the character or person of an opponent rather than the issues at hand (see pages 293–294).

Alliteration The repetition of sounds, especially to create emphasis or rhythm (see pages 220–222). Example: Wavering in the winter wind.

Allusion A reference to a generally well-known person, place, event, or work; often drawn from history, literature, or mythology (see pages 132–137). Example: "She finally met her Waterloo" alludes to the defeat of Napoleon during the Battle of Waterloo.

Analogy A comparison based on similar features of two dissimilar things (see pages 112–113). The following sentence uses an analogy to dramatize the growth of the computer industry: "If the aircraft industry had evolved as spectacularly as the computer industry over the past twenty-five years, a Boeing 767 would cost $500 today, and it would circle the globe in twenty minutes on five gallons of fuel." For **False Analogy**, see pages 297–298.

Anticlimax A sudden, unexpected shift from the impressive or significant to the ludicrous or insignificant (see pages 213–214). Example: "For God, for country, and for Jefferson High."

Antithesis The juxtaposition of contrasting ideas, usually in parallel structures (see page 217). Example: "He for God only; she for God in him."

Antonym A word that has a meaning opposite that of another word. *Light* and *dark* are antonyms.

Circumlocution An indirect, roundabout, or evasive expression which cloaks a disagreeable idea. Closely related in meaning to **Euphemism** (see pages 73–76).

Clause A group of words containing a subject and a verb that can change tenses. Types of clauses:

1. *Main* or *Independent Clause:* A group of words containing a subject and a verb that can change tenses; it can take the form of a grammatically complete sentence. In this book, we refer to the main clause as the basic unit of syntax, one that contains a

    subject   predicate

    subject and a predicate. Example: "The tall woman/dashed out the door."

2. *Coordinate Clauses:* Main clauses joined by one of the coordinating conjunctions or by a semicolon. Examples: "He came; he saw; he conquered." "I got up early, and I ate breakfast, and then I went to school." Excessive use of coordinate clauses is typical of the writing of children or of prose written for children.

3. *Subordinate Clause:* A group of words which contains a subject and a verb that can change tenses, but which cannot take the form of a grammatically complete sentence. Subordinate clauses function as nouns, adjectives, or adverbs. Examples: "*What he said last night* means little today" (noun clause as subject). "They earned high marks *because they wrote exceptionally good answers on the examination*" (adverb clause modifying verb). "The rare map *that I ordered* had already been sold" (adjective clause, modifying subject).

Cliché   An expression that has become dull and trite through frequent repetition (see pages 68–73). Although clichés are often used in speech, they should be used sparingly in writing. Overuse of clichés suggests to readers that the writer is writing "automatically" and perhaps thoughtlessly.

Climax   Words, phrases, or clauses arranged in order of increasing importance (see page 210). Example: "I think we have reached a point of great decision, not just for our nation, not only for all humanity, but for life on earth."

Coherence   The quality of prose which indicates clear connections among the parts— the logical and orderly progression of ideas—and thus helps readers comprehend the ideas presented (see pages 228–233). Coherence is often achieved through the use of temporal or spatial cues *(first, next, finally; here, around the corner);* repetition of a key word or its synonym; and/or logical connectives *(in contrast, as a result, in addition, furthermore).*

Concrete   A term applied to words or phrases that refer to specific things we can perceive through our senses: *pepperoni pizza, orca whale, fire,* and *goaltender* are all concrete terms. (Antonym: ABSTRACT.) No clear-cut line, however, exists between abstract and concrete; rather, most words fall somewhere on a continuum between the two, as for example:

Concrete	Less concrete, more abstract	Abstract
1852 maple rope ... old wooden bed ... bed ... bedroom furnishing ... furniture bed in grandmother's room		

Connotation   Suggested or associated meanings, feelings, and attitudes surrounding a word or phrase (see pages 2–10). In our culture, words like *freedom* generally carry strong positive connotations, whereas words like *death* or *disease* carry negative ones.

Context   The words, phrases, and sentences which come before and after a particular word or phrase and help to fix its meaning (see pages 27–31 and 298–300). If a passage is quoted *out of context,* it often is susceptible to misinterpretation. In its broadest sense, *context* refers to the entire situation in which any event occurs.

Coordinate clause   See **Clause.**

Cumulative sentence   One which places the main clause at or near the beginning and adds modifiers after the main clause. Compare **Periodic sentence** (and see pages 209–214.) Example: "Their trim boots prattled as they stood on the steps of the colonnade, talking quietly and gaily, glancing at the clouds, holding their umbrellas at cunning angles against the last few raindrops, closing them again, holding their skirts demurely." In this example, the main clause *(Their trim boots prattled)* is followed by a subordinate clause *(as they stood on the steps of the colonnade)* and then by a parallel series of participial phrases beginning with *talking, glancing, holding, closing,* and *holding.*

Deduction A process of inferential reasoning in which the truth of the conclusion depends on the truth of the premises on which that conclusion rests (see pages 269–274 and 285–289). Compare **Induction.**

Denotation The explicit definition of a word or phrase, as identified by the dictionary. *Thin* and *skinny,* for instance, have very nearly the same denotative meaning, though they carry different connotations. Compare **Literal language.**

Diction A general term covering the choice and use of words (see pages 50–52). Diction may be technical (*Araucaria araucana* instead of *monkey puzzle tree*), informal *(give me a call if there's anything I can do),* formal *(please contact me at your earliest convenience if I can be of further assistance),* colloquial *(prices are high as a cat's back these days),* and so on. Each kind of diction may be appropriate for a particular occasion, depending on the writer's purpose, the nature of the subject, and the audience.

Ellipsis The omission of a word or words which can be readily inferred from the context (see page 215). Example: "At twenty years of age, the will reigns; at thirty, the wit; and at forty, the judgment."

Enthymeme A loosely structured argument that is the basic tool of rhetorical deduction (see page 285 for a full definition and examples).

Euphemism An inoffensive term substituted for one that is thought to be in some way offensive (see pages 73–76). Example: *slumber room* instead of *mortuary.*

Expository paragraph The term *exposition* means a setting forth of meaning or intent (see pages 227–233). The term *expository paragraph* is used to refer to those paragraphs in most straightforward, nonliterary prose which express the author's meaning. Such paragraphs generally include a statement of topic, and they develop that topic through the use of definition, comparison and contrast, classification, cause and effect, or examples.

False dilemma A form of oversimplification which assumes that only two choices or solutions exist when additional ones may be available (see pages 296–298).

Figures of speech and **figurative language** Expressions in which words are used not in their literal sense but to create an image or special effect. *A heart of stone* literally means a heart-shaped object made from stone or rock. The figurative use of *heart of stone,* however, refers to personal qualities: "hardheartedness" or "coldness" (which are themselves figures). Specific figures are listed separately in this glossary.

Fragment A group of words lacking either a subject or a verb that can change tenses (or both) but which functions as a sentence. Example: "Movies this summer have been a waste of time and money. *Although I've seen one or two good ones.*" Fragments are characteristic of spoken language and are widely used in advertising and certain other kinds of writing. See pages 203–204 for examples of fragments effectively used.

Hyperbole or **overstatement** The use of exaggeration to achieve emphasis (see pages 147–149 and below, under **Understatement**). Example: "I could sleep forever!"

Image A vivid descriptive word or phrase which evokes a picture or appeals to the other senses — touch, sound, smell, or taste (see pages 6–8). Examples: *pale, corpse-colored plastic; tobacco-plug eyes; peaches and cream complexion.* **Imagery** is the collective form of the word. Compare **Metaphor, Simile,** and **Figurative language.**

Induction An inferential reasoning process that builds conclusions from particular data (see pages 277–285). All nondeductive reasoning strategies are inductive: argument from analogy, argument from statistical data, argument from examples, and so on. Compare **Deduction.**

Inference A conclusion or generalization drawn from evidence, whether implicitly or explicitly provided. For example, if we read that construction starts are up in the housing industry and that mortgage rates are dropping rapidly, we draw the inference that more people are buying houses.

Innuendo An indirect implication or hint, usually uncomplimentary (see page 294). Example: "A charwoman reported seeing the young prince leaving the actress's flat at five o'clock in the morning."

Inversion A change in the usual word order (see pages 214–215). Example: "Around the corner ran two mangy cats" (which in normal order would be "Two mangy cats ran around the corner.").

Irony The use of language to convey a meaning opposite to the literal meaning of the words (see pages 141–145). Example: "What a feast!" referring to a piece of stale pizza and a bottle of tepid soft drink that has lost its fizz. See **Understatement.**

Literal language The strict, dictionary meaning of a word or phrase. The phrase "waiting for my ship to come in" literally means the speaker is expecting a ship's arrival. The figurative meaning of this phrase, on the other hand, is "expecting or hoping for a piece of luck." Compare **Figurative language** and **Denotation.**

Main clause See **Clause.**

Metaphor An implicit comparison (see pages 112–123). Example: "the evening of life" is a metaphor comparing old age to the end of the day. Compare **Simile.**

Modifier A word, phrase, or clause that describes or limits another part of a sentence. In the sentence "The butterscotch brownies disappeared," *butterscotch* is the modifier of *brownies.* In the sentence "She stared into the water," *into the water* is the modifier of *stared.* And in "After you leave, I will pack," *after you leave* is the modifier of *will pack.* Some modifiers, called *free modifiers,* are not tied to one position in a sentence but can be moved to several places. For example, note the free modifier in the following sentences:

Carrying a basket of apples, the grocer entered the store.
The grocer, *carrying a basket of apples,* entered the store.
The grocer entered the store, *carrying a basket of apples.*

Free modifiers allow writers great flexibility in building the exact rhythm and emphasis they want. You will find a number of examples of free modifiers in the discussion of cumulative sentences on pages 209–210.

Montage The effect created by a rapid sequence of short scenes, images, or ideas which together form one overall impression. In art, a montage is created by superimposing or closely arranging many pictures or designs. In literature, a montage is created, for example, by joining brief snippets of conversation, parts of advertisements, and images, all of which merge to make up one impression. See pages 226–227 for examples of montage in literature.

Object A grammatical term referring to the recipient of an action. Examples: "Marty threw *the ball*" (direct object); "Marty threw *me* the ball" (indirect object); "Marty threw the ball *to me*" (object of preposition).

Onomatopoeia The characteristic of words whose sound echoes the meaning (see pages 221–222). Examples: *buzz, crack, cuckoo.*

Oversimplification An informal fallacy characterized by ignoring the complexities of an issue and hence distorting it by presenting it in too simple a form. There are several major types of oversimplification, for which see pages 295–298.

Overstatement See **Hyperbole.**

Oxymoron The juxtaposition for particular emphasis of two words which are usually contradictory. Examples: *exquisite pain; cruel kindness; waking sleep; quiet frenzy.*

Paradox An apparently contradictory statement that, on closer inspection, is at least partially true. Examples: "He is guilty of being innocent." "The truly wise person, according to Socrates, is one who recognizes his ignorance." "Freedom is but a just measure of restraint." "The end is always a beginning."

Parallelism A series of words, phrases, or clauses with similar or identical grammatical structures (see pages 216–217). Example: "She tried to make the law *clear, precise,* and *fair."* See **Repetition.**

Parody An imitation which mimics the style of a writer by overemphasizing or distorting characteristics, often for comic effect. The *New Yorker* piece excerpted on pages 38–39 is a parody of advertisements that attempt to sell "collectible" items, for an example of which see page 265.

Periodic sentence: One that delays all or most of the main clause until the end (see pages 207–209). Compare **Cumulative sentence.** Example: "When a writer begins to be successful, when he begins to soar, outwardly but especially inwardly, then, to save him from infatuation, he needs to be pelted with bitter apples."

Personification Attributing human qualities or abilities to animals, inanimate objects, or abstractions. Examples: "Death, be not proud." "The stars winked and laughed at her."

Phrase A group of words that functions as a single part of speech but does not contain both a subject and a verb that can change tense. The major types of phrases, which are useful in building a powerful cumulative sentence, are these:

1. *Participial Phrase:* a present or past participle (*-ing* or *-ed* form of the verb, as in *proving* or *proved*) with its object and/or modifiers; it functions as an adjective. Examples: "*Sweeping everything before it,* the swollen river flooded its banks" (present participial phrase). "*Swept along helplessly,* the small craft began to sink" (past participial phrase).

2. *Infinitive Phrase:* the *to* form of the verb *(to act, to go, to see)* plus its subject, object, and modifiers; it can function as a noun, adjective, or adverb. Examples: "*To hear Pavarotti* is a great pleasure" (infinitive phrase used as noun). "Pavarotti's is a voice *to remember forever"* (infinitive phrase used as adjective). "Pavarotti gave the recital *to raise money for charity"* (infinitive phrase used as adverb).

3. *Gerund Phrase:* an *-ing* form of the verb plus its object, subject, or modifiers; it functions as a noun. Examples: "*Swimming against the current* is not always easy" (gerund phrase used as subject). "She enjoys *swimming against the current"* (gerund phrase used as object of verb). "After *swimming against the current,* she was tired" (gerund phrase used as object of preposition).

4. *Absolute Phrase:* a noun and part of a predicate, usually a participle, that does not directly modify any particular word in a sentence. Examples: "*Their differences forgotten,* father and son embraced." "The actors accepted the ovation, *faces flushed with excitement and success."*

Point of view In discussions of imaginative literature, the term refers to the grammatical person used by the narrator, generally first or third person. *Point of view* can also refer to the mental position from which a writer views a subject. For example, the subject of whales might be viewed by a scientific researcher one way, by a member of a "Save the Whales" group in another way, and by a fisherman in still another way.

Predicate A verb and all its modifiers; it comments on the subject of the sentence. See **Clause.**

Premise A proposition from which a conclusion is drawn. For example, the proposition "All warm-blooded creatures are mammals" supports the conclusion that "Whales are mammals."

Red herring Something used to distract attention from the issue at hand (see page 295).

Refutation Proof or evidence offered against opposing arguments (see pages 286–287).

Repetition The repeated use of the same word or phrase to gain or heighten emphasis. Winston Churchill's "We shall fight on the beaches, we shall fight on the landing grounds, we shall fight in the fields and in the streets, we shall fight in the hills" is a famous example of effective repetition. (It is also a good example of **Parallelism.**) Used thoughtlessly or excessively, repetition can easily become a fault.

Rhetorical question A question asked for dramatic effect, one which usually assumes the answer. Example: "What shall it profit a man to gain the whole world if he loses his immortal soul?" In this question, as in most rhetorical questions, the answer is obvious. But sometimes the obvious or assumed answer is not the correct one.

Rhythm The regular or irregular, rising or falling stress patterns of prose (see pages 218–224). **Repetition,** variation of sentence length and pattern, **Parallelism,** and calculated imbalance contribute to the rhythms of prose. Example: "There was something rather 'doggy,' rather smart, rather acute and shrewd, and something wan, and something slightly contemptible about him."

Run-on sentence One which links main or independent clauses without using a coordinating conjunction or a semicolon (see page 206). Example: "Get your ticket, win the lottery today!" Although run-on sentences are usually identified as "errors" in textbooks, they are sometimes used deliberately by writers to create special effects.

Satire The use of irony, sarcasm, or wit to expose evil or folly.

Sentimentality The use of affected and/or exaggerated emotional appeals which are not justified by the situation or the subject (see pages 149–152).

Simile An explicit comparison between two typically unlike things. Examples: "Silence settled on the crowd like a thousand deaths." "Her voice was like honey over ice." "Ghostlike, they slipped into the room." Compare **Metaphor.**

Stereotype An idea or character cast into a conventional mold or form, without individuality. Stereotypes are most often based on oversimplification or prejudices (see pages 7, 18, and 68–73 for examples and discussion of stereotypes as well as of stereotypical language).

Stream of consciousness A technique by which a writer attempts to reflect the actual thought sequence of a character (see pages 224–226). To do so, the writer often uses **Fragments, Run-on sentences,** and lists of sense impressions, with little or no punctuation.

Subject A noun or its substitute, including modifiers, which acts as the topic of the verb. See **Clause.**

Subordinate clause See **Clause.**

Syllogism The rigidly organized structure of premises and conclusion used in scientific argument (see pages 269–274 for examples and explanation).

Symbol Representation of one thing (usually an abstraction) in terms of something else (usually a concrete object) (see pages 124–132). Examples: *crown* symbolizes royalty; the *wedding ring* symbolizes married love.

Synonym A word that has the same or very nearly the same meaning as another. Examples: *danger* and *hazard; noon* and *midday.*

Tone The total effect of a piece of writing, as achieved by language. Tone embodies the writer's stance and attitude toward his or her audience. It can be flippant, serious, angry, passionate, friendly, and so on. In general, it informs an entire piece of writing and helps determine a reader's response. See pages 111–112.

Topic sentence The statement which conveys the central idea of an expository paragraph. The topic sentence may appear in the paragraph, or it may be only implied by the content of the paragraph as a whole. Examples of topic sentences are found in the passages on pages 228–230.

Transfer device The technique of linking one idea or person or institution with another, in spite of the fact that the two may not be logically connected (see pages 291–293). Most "testimonial" advertisements use the transfer device, as in the case of a movie star who recommends a particular brand of costume jewelry. In this instance, the prestige and glamour of the star are supposedly "transferred" to the jewelry.

Transitions Words, phrases, sentences, or paragraphs used to relate ideas. Common transition devices include **Repetition, Synonyms,** pronouns referring to earlier nouns, directional words and phrases such as *next,* and logical connectors such as *consequently.* See **Coherence.**

Understatement (or **Litotes** or **Meiosis**) The presentation, for rhetorical effect, of an idea or object as of much less importance than it really is (see pages 146–147). Understatement and its counterpart, overstatement or **Hyperbole,** are often used as types of **Irony.** In the following sentence, the master ironist Jonathan Swift uses both figures: "After hurling a million profanities at his opponent, Jack ran mad with spleen, spite, and hatred; in short, here began a breach between the two." (The first clause exemplifies hyperbole; the second, understatement.)

Voice A grammatical term referring to a property of verbs (active or passive voice). The following paradigm exemplifies these two voices:

Tense	Active Voice	Passive Voice
Present	She questions.	She is questioned.
Past	She questioned.	She was questioned.
Future	She will question.	She will be questioned.
Present perfect	She has questioned.	She has been questioned.
Past perfect	She had questioned.	She had been questioned.
Future perfect	She will have questioned.	She will have been questioned.

For the relation of *voice* to **Tone,** see page 111, footnote.

SOURCES OF QUOTATIONS

The following pages list the sources of all quotations (except those from advertisements which are self-identifying and those whose sources are listed on the page on which they appear) in the text and the exercises. Illustrative and exercise materials not specifically attributed are the inventions of the authors.

Introduction

Page

xi–xii   "Mr. Chairman, Ladies and Gentlemen . . .": This speech has appeared in various publications, e.g. *Christian Century*, January 24, 1951. Its author was A. Parker Nevin.

xiii–xiv   "There is an immense and justified pride . . .": from a speech by Brand Blanshard, printed in the *Swarthmore College Bulletin*, 42 (July 1945). Reprinted by permission of the author and the *Swarthmore College Bulletin*.

xv   "If we consider men and women . . .": Mortimer Adler, *How to Read a Book* (1940). Reprinted by permission of Simon and Schuster, publishers.

xiii–xiv   "No doubt strong, silent men . . .": F. L. Lucas, "What Is Style?" *Holiday*, March, 1960.

xv   Carlyle's words are in "The Hero as Man of Letters" (1841).

Chapter One

1   *"Synonyms: sensuous, sensual . . .": The American Heritage Dictionary* (1976). © Houghton Mifflin Company. Reprinted with permission from *The American Heritage Dictionary of the English Language*.

2   *"Denote* implies all . . .": from *Webster's New Collegiate Dictionary*, copyright 1941, 1951, 1953 G. and C. Merriam Company. Reprinted by permission.

7   "When I hear the word *dropout* . . .": Bernard Lefkowitz, "Making it as a Dropout," *Psychology Today*, December 1980.

8   "It is a frigid February morning . . .": Ken Auletta, "The Underclass," *New Yorker*, November 23, 1981. Originally published in *The Underclass*. Copyright 1980 by Ken Auletta. Reprinted by permission of the author and Random House, Inc.

9   "You take my hand . . .": Margaret Atwood, "You Take My Hand," from *Power Politics* (Toronto: House of Anansi Press, 1971; New York: Harper and Row, 1971.) Reprinted by permission of Margaret Atwood, the House of Anansi Press, and Harper and Row, Publishers, Inc.

9–10   "I have known the inexorable . . .": Theodore Roethke, "Dolor." Copyright 1943 by Modern Poetry Association, Inc. From the *Collected Poems of Theodore Roethke*. Reprinted by permission of Doubleday and Company, Inc.

10   The writer is Paul Stevens (pen name for Carl Wrighter); his description of "weasel words" is found in *I Can Sell You Anything* (1972).

11   The words in the original cheese advertisement used in 1: *adds; zesty; mellow; lively; featuring; scrumptious*. Words in the original shoe advertisement used in 2: *duplicate; unique; look; benchcrafted; skilled*. Words in

Page

the original pen and pencil advertisement used in 3: *writing instrument; delicate; design; distinctive; cherished; handsomely; brochure.*

15-16   "One day last summer . . .": Alistair Cooke, "Justice Holmes and the Doffed Bikini," *The Americans* (1979). Originally delivered as a talk on the British Broadcasting Corporation. Reprinted by permission of Random House, Inc.

16-18   The letter from Representative Udall was printed in *The New Republic,* January 18, 1964.

19-20   "Now as I was young and easy . . .": Dylan Thomas, "Fern Hill," *Poems of Dylan Thomas.* Copyright 1954 by New Directions Publishing Corporation. Reprinted by permission of New Directions Publishing Corporation, J. M. Dent, and David Higham Associates, Ltd.

20   "This is the way the world ends . . .": Excerpt from "The Hollow Men" in *Collected Poems 1909-1962* by T. S. Eliot, copyright 1936 by Harcourt Brace Jovanovich, Inc.; copyright © 1963, 1964 by T. S. Eliot, printed by permission of the publisher.

21   "Your low voice . . .": Edwin Arlington Robinson, "Tristram," from the *Collected Poems* (1930). Reprinted by permission of The Macmillan Company, Publishers.

21   "You want to know what science . . .": "Letter to the author from the scientist" from Prologue in *An Imagined World: A Story of Scientific Discovery* by June Goodfield. Copyright © 1981 by June Goodfield. Reprinted by permission of June Goodfield and Harper and Row, Publishers, Inc.

22   "My soul is an enchanted Boat . . .": Shelley, *Prometheus Unbound,* Act II (1820).

23   "Workbench Analysis . . .": *Discover* Magazine, July, 1981. Reprinted by permission of Natalie Angier, *Discover* Magazine, © 1981 Time Inc.

24   "A creature not too bright or good . . .": Wordsworth, "She Was a Phantom of Delight" (1807).

28   "I had spent so many years . . .": Loren Eiseley, "The Creature from the Marsh," *The Night Country* (1971).

29   "It has not, however . . .": Henry James, *Partial Portraits* (1888).

Exercises

33   1.4: The list is based on Josephine Miles's *The Continuity of Poetic Language* (1951).

36-38   1.15:(1) Reprinted courtesy of Chevrolet Motor Division, General Motors Corporation. (2) Reprinted with permission of Pontiac Motor Division, General Motors Corporation. (3) Reprinted courtesy of Ford Motor Company.

38-39   1.16:(c) This parody appeared in the *New Yorker,* December 21, 1981. Reprinted by permission; © 1981 by Bruce McCall.

40   1.18: Senator Barry Goldwater, quoted in Ralph de Toledano, *The Winning Side* (1963).

40   1.19: The quotation is from Alfred M. Lee, *How to Understand Propaganda* (1952).

42-44   1.24:(1) George Starbuck, "Lamb," from "Translations from the English," *White Paper.* Copyright © 1965 by George Starbuck. First appeared in *The Atlantic.* By permission of Little, Brown and Company in association with

Chapter Two

Page

79   "I think I was in the first . . .": Tom Wicker, "The Assassination," *Times Talk*, December 1963. © 1963 by The New York Times Company. Reprinted by permission.

81   "There were the houses, too . . .": Reprinted with permission of the Macmillan Company from *Inishfallen, Fare Thee Well* by Sean O'Casey. Copyright 1949 by Sean O'Casey.

82   The anecdote about the plumber and the hydrochloric acid entered this book by way of a wire-service story in February, 1947. It is probably even older than that.

83   "The purpose of this article . . .": George Fisk, "Media Influence Reconsidered," *Public Opinion Quarterly*, 23 (Spring 1959).

83   "From a socio-psychological point . . .": William A. Scott, "Correlates of International Attitudes," *Public Opinion Quarterly*, 22 (Winter 1958–59).

Exercises

85   2.1:(16) Congreve, *Love for Love* (1695), III. iii. (17) "Smohalla Speaks," from *The Winged Serpent: An Anthology of American Indian Prose and Poetry*, ed. Margot Astrou (1946). (18) Demetrius Mavroundis, "UR Needs Courses on Morality in Its Broadest Sense," *The Collegian*, Thursday, April 15, 1982. (19) Dickens, *Bleak House* (1852–53), ch. 19.

86   2.2: "The czars exiled misfits to Siberia . . .": John McPhee, *Coming into the Country* (1977). Reprinted by permission of Farrar, Straus and Giroux, Inc. Excerpt from *Coming into the Country* by John McPhee. Copyright © 1976, 1977 by John McPhee. This material first appeared in the *New Yorker*.

87   2.4: "The floor where lives . . .": from a 1923 advertisement entitled "Floor with Maple, Beech, or Birch." Reprinted by permission of Andrews/Mautner, representing Maple Flooring Manufacturers Association.

88   2.8: Reprinted courtesy of Tom's of Maine, Inc., Kennebunk, Maine.

89–92   The two statements concerning plagiarism were composed by members of the freshman composition staff of the Ohio State University.

92–93   2.11: "If You Are Writing a Book" was issued by the Dryden Press, a division of CBS College Publishing.

95   2.12:(5) This sentence is quoted in Joseph Williams, *Style* (1981).

96   2.16: The "Hot enough to fry an egg" story is from Russell Baker's "Hot News," Vancouver *Province*, July 26, 1982.

102–103   2.28:(1) Ronald Melzack, "The Genesis of Emotional Behavior," *Journal of Comparative and Physiological Psychology*, 47 (1954). (2) Harold Mark and Kent P. Schwirian, "Ecological Position, Urban Central Place Function, and Community Population Growth," *American Journal of Sociology*, 73 (1967). (3) R. W. Sperry, "Optic Nerve Regeneration with Return of Vision," *Journal of Neurophysiology*, 7 (1944). (4) John D. McNeil, "Concomitants of Using Behavioral Objectives in the Assessment of Teacher Effectiveness," *Journal of Experimental Education*, 36 (1967).

103–104   2:29:(1) Thomas Cahill, Chief of Police in San Francisco, quoted in Julian Symons, *Crime and Detection* (1966).

105–106   2.30:(2) The speech as here rewritten by the *Workbench* computer program, in *Discover* Magazine, July 1981. Reprinted by permission of Natalie Angier, *Discover* Magazine, © Time, Inc. (5) Attributed to "Some-

Page

one in Washington": printed in *The New Republic*, June 17, 1957. The same jeu d'esprit has appeared in numerous other places (e.g., Dwight Macdonald, *Parodies* (1960), where it is attributed to Oliver Jensen). There are some textual variants in the various printings.

108–109   2.32.(1) A letter from George Bernard Shaw to the London *Times*, quoted (perhaps inaccurately) in *The Listener*, September 4, 1947. (2) A letter by Raymond Chandler, quoted in *The Pleasures of Publishing*, December 1958. (3) Cervantes, *Don Quixote* (1700–03; Motteux translation). (4) Jacques Barzun, *Teacher in America* (1945). (5) Ford Madox Ford, *Joseph Conrad* (1924). (6) Montaigne, *Essays* (Florio translation, originally published 1580), quoted in Sir Herbert Read, *English Prose Style* (1952).

109–110   2.33. from *The Idler* (1759), 36.

Chapter Three

112   "Where a satirist like Pope ...": William Golding, *A Moving Target* (1982).

113   "the metaphors of mind ...": Julian Jaynes, *The Origin of Consciousness in the Break-Down of the Bicameral Mind* (1976).

114   "Television is a vast ...": Jonathan Miller, "The Air," *New Yorker*, November 16, 1963. Reprinted with permission.

117   "The title 'The Uses of the Blues' ...": James Baldwin, "The Uses of the Blues," *Playboy*, January 1964.

117–118   "For millions of people ...": "Ah, How Sweet It Is!" *Time*, July 12, 1982. © Time Inc. All rights reserved. Reprinted by permission from *Time*.

118   "James Doohan (Scotty) was nothing ...": Susan Lerner, "Scotty Is Still Beaming," Vancouver *Province*, TV Times, July 9, 1982. Reprinted with permission of Susan Lerner and *TV Times*.

119   "The tulips are too red ...": stanza 6 from "Tulips" in *The Collected Poems* by Sylvia Plath. Edited by Ted Hughes. Copyright © 1962 by the estate of Sylvia Plath. Reprinted by permission of Harper and Row, Publishers, Inc. Also from *Ariel* by Sylvia Plath, published by Faber and Faber, London; copyright Ted Hughes, 1965.

119   "I remember when she opened ...": Carolyn Fireside, "Anything but Love," *Cosmopolitan*, July 1982.

120   "In those days time ...": quoted in Emery Neff, *Edwin Arlington Robinson* (1948).

121   "In a sense we have come ...": Martin Luther King's speech, "I Have a Dream," was delivered in Washington, D.C., on August 28, 1963.

121   "I made my song a coat ...": Reprinted with permission of Macmillan Publishing Co., Inc., Macmillan, London Ltd., M. B. Yeats and Anne Yeats from *The Collected Poems of William Butler Yeats*. Copyright 1916 by Macmillan Publishing Co., Inc., renewed 1944 by Bertha Georgie Yeats.

122–123   "I find the great thing ...": Oliver Wendell Holmes, *The Autocrat of the Breakfast Table* (1858), ch. 4.

124   "She cast that line ...": Jack Hodgins, *The Resurrection of Joseph Bourne* (1980).

124–126   "Whether 'tis nobler ...": *Hamlet*, III. i. 57–60. "Will all great Neptune's ...": *Macbeth*, II. ii. 61–64. "I do not know what ...": quoted in Horace Freeland Judson's "The Rage to Know," *The Atlantic*, April 1980. "Give me fullness of life ...": Richard Jefferies, *The Story of My Heart* (1883), ch. 6. "The waters were his winding sheet . . .": Richard Barnfield, epitaph on Sir John Hawkins, quoted in the preface to his *Encomion of Lady Pecuria* (1598). "Sunset and evening star . . .": Alfred, Lord Tennyson, "Crossing the Bar." "Whereto answering . . .": Walt Whitman, "Out of the Cradle Endlessly Rocking." "The people along the sand . . .": "Neither Out Far Nor In Deep," from *The Poetry of Robert Frost*, ed. by Edward Connery Lathem. Copyright 1916, 1923, 1960 by Holt, Rinehart and Winston. Copyright 1936, 1944, 1951 by Robert Frost. Copyright © 1961 by Lesley Frost Ballantine. Reprinted by permission of Holt, Rinehart and Winston, Publishers. "A current under sea . . .": Excerpt from "The Waste Land" in *Collected Poems 1909-1962* by T. S. Eliot, copyright 1936 by Harcourt Brace Jovanovich, Inc.; copyright © 1963, 1964 by T. S. Eliot, reprinted by permission of Harcourt Brace Jovanovich, Inc. and Faber and Faber Ltd.

127   "Why should the poor . . .": *Hamlet*, III. ii. 64–67.

128–130   "Nature's first green is gold . . .": Robert Frost, "Nothing Gold Can Stay," from *The Poetry of Robert Frost* edited by Edward Connery Lathem. Copyright 1916, 1923, © 1969 by Holt, Rinehart and Winston. Copyright 1936, 1944, 1951 by Robert Frost. Copyright © 1964 by Lesley Frost Ballantine. Reprinted by permission of Holt, Rinehart and Winston, Publishers. "O, swear not by the moon . . .": *Romeo and Juliet*, II. ii. 109–11. "We walked out late . . .": Robert Wallace, "Out for Stars," from *Ungainly Things*. Copyright 1968 by Robert Wallace. Reprinted by permission of the author. "Were you ever out . . .": Robert Service, "The Shooting of Dan McGrew," stanza 4. "Two roads diverged . . ." and "Some say the world . . .": Robert Frost, "The Road Not Taken" and "Fire and Ice" from *The Poetry of Robert Frost* edited by Edward Connery Lathem. Copyright 1916, 1923, © 1969 by Holt, Rinehart and Winston. Copyright 1936, 1944, 1951 by Robert Frost. Copyright © 1964 by Lesley Frost Ballantine. Reprinted by permission of Holt, Rinehart and Winston, Publishers.

130–131   "From too much love . . .": Swinburne, "The Garden of Proserpine" (1866). "Our revels now are ended . . .": *The Tempest*, IV. i. 148–157.

131–132   "To die—to sleep . . .": *Hamlet*, III. i. 60–69. "When you are old and grey . . .": W. B. Yeats, "When You are Old," reprinted with permission of Macmillan Publishing Company, Inc., Macmillan, London Ltd., M. B. Yeats and Anne Yeats from *Collected Poems of William Butler Yeats* (New York: Macmillan, 1956).

132   Christopher Marlowe, *Doctor Faustus* (1604).

133   "But strawberries were his real . . .": Wallace Stegner, "Turtle at Home," *Atlantic Monthly*, April, 1943. Reprinted by permission of Mr. Stegner and the *Atlantic Monthly*.

135   "Ariel, which rages unbounded . . .": Richard Lubbock, "Why I Love My Computer," *Quest*, June-July-August, 1981. "And what rough beast . . ." W. B. Yeats, "The Second Coming." Reprinted with permission of Macmillan Publishing Co., Inc., Macmillan, London Ltd., M. B. Yeats, and Anne Yeats from *The Collected Poems of William Butler Yeats.* Copyright 1924 by Macmillan Publishing Co., Inc., renewed 1952 by Bertha Georgie Yeats.

136   "I reached up to knock . . .": Andrew Ward, "They Also Wait Who Stand and Serve Themselves," *Atlantic Monthly*, May 1979. Reprinted by permission of *Atlantic Monthly*.

136   "Our Barbie doll president . . .": from *Rolling Stone*, September 12, 1974.

137   "McLuhan rose up . . .": Reprinted by permission of Farrar, Straus and Giroux, Inc.; excerpt from "What If He Is Right" from *The Pump House*

Page

Gang by Tom Wolfe. Copyright © 1965 by the *New York Herald Tribune*, Inc., Copyright © 1968 by Tom Wolfe.

138   "I look at my mama . . .": Ernest J. Gaines, "The Sky is Gray," *Bloodline* (1968).

138–139   "Man must teach himself . . .": William Faulkner, "On Receiving the Nobel Prize," in *The Faulkner Reader* (1954). Reprinted by permission of Random House, Inc.

139   "Isolt the abandoned one . . .": from a booklet issued by a chain of New England mortuaries.

140–141   "Today the fear of cops . . .": H. L. Mencken, *Happy Days* (1940).

141   "To manifest truth and beauty . . .": from William Buckley's *The Governor Listeth* (1970). © William F. Buckley. Reprinted by permission of G. P. Putnam's Sons.

142   "I was anxious to see . . .": from Washington Irving's "The Author's Account of Himself," *The Sketchbook* (1820).

142   "When I visited its headquarters . . .": Reprinted by permission of G. P. Putnam's Sons from "Fathers for Moral America," *And Then I Told the President*, by Art Buchwald. Copyright © 1964, 1965, 1966 by Art Buchwald.

143–44   "Being told I would be expected . . .": Samuel Clemens, "Advice to Youth" (1882).

145   "It occurs to me . . .": Muriel Spark, "Conversation Piece," *New Yorker*, November 23, 1981. Reprinted by permission of Harold Ober Associates Incorporated. Copyright © 1981 by Copyright Administration Limited.

146   "Until two weeks ago . . .": Stephen Leacock, *Further Foolishness* (1916).

147   "I am not disclosing any . . .": Conrad, "Heart of Darkness," from *Youth, and Other Stories* (1924). "It has not escaped our notice . . .": James Watson and Francis Crick, "Molecular Structure of Nucleic Acids," *Nature*, April 25, 1953. "Two monsters loomed on Cooper's . . .": D. H. Lawrence, "Fenimore Cooper's Leatherstocking Novels," *Studies in Classic American Literature* (1923).

148   "Napoleon Bonaparte, where are you . . .": Eric Nicol, in the Vancouver *Province*, July 14, 1982. Reprinted by permission of the author and the *Province*, Vancouver, B.C.

149   "Keeps His Mom-in-Law . . .": Tom Wolfe, "Pornoviolence." Reprinted by permission of Farrar, Straus and Giroux, Inc. Excerpt from "Pornoviolence" from *Mauve Gloves and Madmen, Clutter and Vine* by Tom Wolfe. Copyright © 1967, 1976 by Tom Wolfe.

152   "Now I lay me . . .": Dickens, *Dombey and Son* (1848), ch. 16.

153   "Albert Einstein was born . . .": Carl Sagan, "That World Which Beckons Like a Liberation," *Broca's Brain: Reflections on the Romance of Science* (1979). Copyright © 1979 by Carl Sagan. Reprinted by permission of Random House, Inc.

153–154   "The articles in the women's magazines . . .": from *Singin' and Swingin' and Gettin' Merry Like Christmas*, by Maya Angelou. Copyright © 1969 by Maya Angelou. Reprinted by permission of Random House, Inc.

155   "On moonlit heath . . .": from "A Shropshire Lad," *The Complete Poems of A. E. Housman*. Authorised Edition. Copyright 1939, 1940, © 1959 by Holt, Rinehart and Winston. Copyright © 1967, 1968 by Robert E. Symons. Reprinted by permission of Holt, Rinehart and Winston, Inc.

157   "So here they are now, three atoms. . . .": Thomas Wolfe, *Of Time and the*

Page

River. Reprinted with the permission of Charles Scribner's Sons; renewal copyright © 1963 Paul Gitlin.

158   "all the experiences in . . .": Bernard De Voto, *Forays and Rebuttals* (1936).

Exercises

159   3.2: 1, 2, 3, and 6 are quoted in H. L. Mencken, *The American Language*, 4th ed. (1936); they are from Carl Sandburg, Victor Hugo, Ambrose Bierce, and Walt Whitman, respectively. 4 is from James B. Greenough and George L. Kittredge, *Words and Their Ways in English Speech* (1914). 5 is from Emerson's journal, June 24, 1840. 7 is from Patrick Hartwell, *Open to Language* (1982).

160–163   3.3:(1) The Earl of Lytton ("Owen Meredith"), "Love and Sleep" (1861). (2) Arnold Bennett, *Your United States* (1912). (3) "What We Want" is reprinted from *Waiting For My Life, Poems* by Linda Pastan, by permission of W. W. Norton and Company. Copyright © 1981 by Linda Pastan. (4) W. S. Merwin, "The Unwritten," in *Writings to an Unfinished Accompaniment*. Copyright © 1973 by W. S. Merwin. Reprinted with permission of Atheneum Publishers. "The Unwritten" was first published in the *New Yorker*. (5) Melville, *Moby-Dick* (1851), ch. 87. (6) Reprinted with permission of Macmillan Publishing Company, Macmillan, London Ltd., M. B. Yeats and Anne Yeats from "Sailing to Byzantium," *The Collected Poems of William Butler Yeats*. Copyright 1928 by Macmillan Publishing Co., Inc.; renewed 1956 by Georgie Yeats. (7) Abridged from *An Imagined World: A Story of Scientific Discovery* by June Goodfield. Copyright © 1981 by June Goodfield. Reprinted by permission of June Goodfield and Harper and Row, Publishers, Inc. (8) Shakespeare, Sonnet 73. (9) Barbara Mikulski, quoted in the Chicago *Daily News*, March 1974. (10) H. L. Mencken, "Professor Veblen," *Prejudices, First Series* (1918). (11) Amy Lowell, "A Decade," *The Complete Poetical Works of Amy Lowell*. Copyright © 1955 by Houghton Mifflin Company. Reprinted by permission of Houghton Mifflin Company. (12) Vladimir Nabokov, "L'Envoi," *Lectures on Literature*, vol. 1 (1980).

163–164   3.4:(1) Jonathan Raban, "Work in Progress," *New York Times Book Review*, June 6, 1982. (2) From unidentified newspaper item. (3) Vladimir Nabokov, *Pnin* (1957). (4) Graduate student paper. (5) From *Cosmos* by Carl Sagan. Copyright © 1980 by Carl Sagan. Reprinted by permission of Random House, Inc. (6) George Meredith, *Modern Love*, I (1862). (7) Reviewer in the New York *Herald-Tribune*, quoted in the *New Yorker*, November 10, 1956. (8) Langston Hughes, "Harlem." Copyright 1951 by Langston Hughes. Reprinted from *The Selected Poems of Langston Hughes*, by Langston Hughes; by permission of Alfred A. Knopf, Inc. (9) Review of Robert Penn Warren's *The Cave*, London *Observer*, December 6, 1959. (10) *Prevention* magazine, June 1982.

165–166   3.5:(1) Sleeve copy for the Stuttgart Chamber Orchestra recording of the Brandenburg Concertos (1950). Reprinted by permission of London Records, Inc. (2) Ruskin, *Sesame and Lilies* (1865), lecture 1. (3) Lytton Strachey, "Traps and Peace Traps," *War and Peace*, June 1918; quoted in C. R. Sanders, *Lytton Strachey* (1957).

166–167   3.7:(1) John Donne, Meditation 27. (2) Justice Oliver Wendell Holmes, Jr., opinion in 245 U.S. 418. (3) Logan Pearsall Smith, *All Trivia* (1945). (4) George H. W. Rylands, *Words and Poetry* (1928). (5) James Russell Lowell,

Page

Introduction to *The Biglow Papers*, 2nd series (1867). (6) Martha Gies, "Camelot for a Day," *Oregon Magazine*, July 1982. (7) William K. Wimsatt and Cleanth Brooks, *Literary Criticism: A Short History* (1957). (8) From Philip Larkin's "Toads," reprinted from *The Less Deceived* (1955) by permission of the Marvell Press, England.

167–168   3.8:(1) From "Praise to the End" copyright 1950 by Theodore Roethke, from *The Collected Poems of Theodore Roethke*. Reprinted by permission of Doubleday and Company, Inc. (2) Wordsworth, "A Slumber Did My Spirit Seal" (1800). (3) Spenser, *The Faerie Queene* (1589–96), Bk. I, Canto IX, stanza 40. (4) John Masefield, "Sea Fever," *Poems* (1902). (5) "The Force That Through the Green Fuse Drives the Flower," Dylan Thomas, *Poems of Dylan Thomas*. Copyright 1954 by New Directions Publishing Corporation. Reprinted by permission of New Directions Publishing Corporation, J. M. Dent, and David Higham Associates Limited. (6) John Donne, "Death Be Not Proud," *Holy Sonnets* (1633). (7) *Hamlet*, IV. iii. 22–23. (8) *Romeo and Juliet*, III. i. 102–103.

169–170   3.10:(a) *Hamlet*, I. ii. 139–153. (2) sonnet by Wordsworth.

170–171   3.11:(1) From *Cosmos*, by Carl Sagan. Copyright © 1980 by Carl Sagan. Reprinted by permission of Random House, Inc. (11) Geneva Smitherman, *Talkin' and Testifyin'* (1977). (12) From an anonymous retelling of a Northwest Coast Indian myth. (13) Max Wyman, in a theatre review in the Vancouver *Province*, July 27, 1982. Reprinted by permission of the author and the *Province*. © 1982 Vancouver *Province*.

172–173   3.14:(1) Benjamin Disraeli, *Vivian Grey* (1826), Book V, ch. xv. "Shadeborn" is probably a mistake for "shard-borne" (*Macbeth*, III. ii. 42). (2) Excerpt from "The Last American Hero" from *The Kandy Kolored Tangerine Flake Streamline Baby* by Tom Wolfe. Reprinted by permission of Farrar, Straus and Giroux, Inc. Copyright © 1964 by The New York Herald Tribune, Inc. Copyright © by Thomas K. Wolfe, Jr. (3) Chief Seattle, "Address" (1854).

173–176   3.15:(1) Benjamin Franklin. (2) *Scientific Monthly*, 64 (1947). Quoted by permission of the author, Dr. Paul W. Merrill. (3) Art Buchwald, "Hurts Rent-a-Gun." Reprinted by permission of G. P. Putnam's Sons from *I Never Danced at the White House* (1973). Copyright © 1971, 1972, 1973 by Art Buchwald. (4) Ambrose Bierce, *The Devil's Dictionary* (1911). (5) Darrell Huff, *How to Lie With Statistics* (1954). (6) Jessica Mitford, "Behind the Formaldehyde Curtain," *The American Way of Death* (1963). (7) W. H. Auden, "The Unknown Citizen." Copyright 1940 and renewed 1968 by W. H. Auden. Reprinted from *W. H. Auden: Collected Poems*, by W. H. Auden, edited by Edward Mendelson, by permission of Random House, Inc. and by permission of Faber and Faber Ltd. (8) Letter to the Ohio State University *Lantern*, March 30, 1965. (9) "We Real Cool: The Pool Players. Seven at the Golden Shovel" from *The World of Gwendolyn Brooks* by Gwendolyn Brooks. Copyright © 1959 by Gwendolyn Brooks. Reprinted by permission of Harper and Row, Publishers, Inc.

177–178   3.17:(1) Vladimir Nabokov, *Speak, Memory* (1967). (2) Charles Lamb, "A Chapter on Ears" (1821). (3) Woody Allen, "The Allen Notebooks," *Without Feathers* (1975). (4) Jonathan Swift, "Digression in Praise of Digression," from *Tale of a Tub* (1710). (5) Dickens, *The Old Curiosity Shop* (1841), ch. 45. (6) Advertisement produced by Vickers and Benson, Ltd. for the Pollution Probe Foundation, a non-governmental, non-profit environmental organization located in Toronto, Canada. Reprinted by permission of Pollution Probe.

Page

179–181   3.18:(2) John Dos Passos, *Chosen Country* (1951). (3) Maya Angelou, "Graduation," from *I Know Why the Caged Bird Sings*, by Maya Angelou. Copyright © 1969 by Maya Angelou. Reprinted by permission of Random House, Inc. (4) W. B. Yeats, "Politics." Reprinted by permission of Macmillan Publishing Company, Inc., Macmillan London Ltd., M. B. Yeats and Anne Yeats from *Collected Poems of William Butler Yeats*. Copyright 1940 by Georgie Yeats, renewed 1968 by Bertha Georgie Yeats, Michael Butler Yeats and Anne Yeats. (5) Eliza Cook, "The Welcome Back." (6) James Lawton, "Critic's Choice," Vancouver *Sun*, July 23, 1982. Reprinted by permission of the author and the Vancouver *Sun*.

181–182   3.19:(a) From H. B. Irving, introduction to *The Trial of Mrs. Maybrick* (Notable British Trials Series, 1912). (b) From Naomi Weisstein, "Psychology Constructs the Female, or, The Fantasy Life of the Male Psychologist." Copyright © by Naomi Weisstein, 1971. Reprinted by permission of Naomi Weisstein.

182–186   3.20:(1) Thackeray, "Going to See a Man Hanged" (1840). (2) Thomas Hardy, *Tess of the d'Urbervilles* (1891), conclusion. (3) Ernest Hemingway, *In Our Time* (1924), ch. 17. (4) Rudyard Kipling, "Danny Deever," *Barrack-Room Ballads* (1892). (5) From *The Encyclopedia Britannica*, 11th ed. (1910–11), vol. 4. (6) James Anthony Froude, "The Execution of Queen Mary," *History of England from 1529 to the Death of Elizabeth* (1856–70), ch. 34.

187–189   3.21:(1) The opening of Jane Austen's *Pride and Prejudice* (1813). (2) From *Fifth Business* (1970) by Robertson Davies. Copyright © 1970 by Robertson Davies. Reprinted by permission of Robertson Davies and Viking Penguin, Inc. (3) Aldous Huxley, *Brave New World* (1932). (4) Anthony Burgess, *Earthly Powers* (1980).

190–191   3.23: Andrew Marvell, "To His Coy Mistress" (1681).

191–193   3.24:(1) James Burke, *Connections* (1978). (2) Adrienne Rich, "Living in Sin," reprinted from *Poems, Selected and New, 1950–1974*, by Adrienne Rich, by permission of W. W. Norton and Company, Inc. Copyright © 1975, 1973, 1971, 1969, 1966 by W. W. Norton and Company, Inc. Copyright © 1967, 1963, 1962, 1961, 1960, 1959, 1958, 1957, 1956, 1955, 1954, 1953, 1952, 1951 by Adrienne Rich. (3) Dylan Thomas, "Memories of Christmas," *Quite Early One Morning*. Reprinted by permission of J. M. Dent and David Higham Associates, Ltd. Published in slightly different form as "A Child's Christmas in Wales." Copyright 1939 by New Directions Publishing Corporation, 1945 by the Trustees for the Copyright of Dylan Thomas. Reprinted by permission of New Dirctions Publishing Corporation.

193–198   3.25:(1) Roderick Haig-Brown, "Let Them Eat Sawdust," *Measures of the Year* (1950). (2) Tillie Olsen, *Tell Me a Riddle* (1961). (3) Calvin Trillin, "Eating in Cincinnati," *American Fried* (1974). First published in the *New Yorker*, Feb. 3, 1973. Copyright © 1973 by Calvin Trillin. By permission of the publisher. (4) Stan Sanvel Rubin, "For My Daughter's Best Friend, the Night Before Moving," *Lost* (1981). Reprinted by permission of the author and State Street Press Chapbooks. (5) Annie Dillard, "Sight into Insight," *Harper's Magazine*, February 1974. (6) From *Cosmos*, by Carl Sagan. Copyright © 1980 by Carl Sagan. Reprinted by permission of Random House, Inc. (7) Margaret Atwood, "Death of a Young Son by Drowning." From *The Journals of Susanna Moodie* (1970) by Margaret Atwood. Copyright Oxford University Press, Canada; by permission of the publisher. (8) James Baldwin, "Dark Days," *Esquire*, October 1980. Copyright

Page

© 1980 James Baldwin. By permission of the publisher. (9) Joy Kogawa, "When I Was a Little Girl," *A Choice of Dreams* (1974). Reprinted by permission of Joy Kogawa. (10) Ursula K. LeGuin, "Winter's King," *The Wind's Twelve Quarters* (1976). (11) From "Poetry of Departures" by Philip Larkin, reprinted from *The Less Deceived* (1955) by permission of The Marvell Press, England.

Chapter Four

201   "One early morning . . .": *Jack and Jill*, June 1959. "It was just before hunting . . .": A. J. Doucet, *The Beaver and the Muskrat* (n.d.).

202   Advertisement for Valley Fresh, reprinted with permission of Valley Fresh, Inc.

203   "I touched the gun butt . . .": Raymond Chandler, *Farewell, My Lovely* (1940). "There you have a nice . . .": D. H. Lawrence, "Hawthorne's *Blithedale Romance*," *Studies in Classic American Literature* (1923).

204   "He began to confess . . .": James Joyce, *Portrait of the Artist as a Young Man* (1916). "Am I a Whig . . .": Benjamin Disraeli, quoted in Peter Stansky, "What Dizzy Did," *The Dial*, August 1982. "Of course, much that was once . . .": Lance Morrow, "Have We Abandoned Excellence?" *Time*, March 22, 1982.

205   "The present movement toward . . .": *War Times*, quoted in the *New Yorker*, July 1, 1945.

205–206   "All the Christmases roll down . . .": Dylan Thomas, "Memories of Christmas," *Quite Early One Morning*. Reprinted by permission of J. M. Dent and David Higham Associates Limited. Published in a slightly different form in "A Child's Christmas in Wales," copyright 1939 by New Directions Publishing Corporation; 1945, by the Trustees for the Copyright of Dylan Thomas. Reprinted by permission of New Directions Publishing Corporation.

207   "The virtue of a periodic . . .": Paull F. Baum, *The Other Harmony of Prose* (1952).

208   "Even as the eagle . . .": Roger Caras, *The Forest* (1979). "When Enrico Fermi . . .": James Burke, *Connections* (1978). "Although in many ways . . .": Herbert Warren Wind, "The Sporting Scene," *New Yorker*, July 14, 1980. "The supplicant, far from rebelling . . .": Imamu Amiri Baraka, "Soul Food," *Home: Social Essays* (1966).

209   "Over the next year . . .": adapted from Aaron T. Beck and Jeffrey E. Young, "College Blues," *Psychology Today*, September 1978. "Modern Houseboats being . . .": Hugh D. Whall, "A House Is Not a Hot Rod," *Sports Illustrated*, July 28, 1969; quoted in Virginia Tufte, *Grammar as Style* (1971). "The main clause, which may . . .": Francis Christensen, "A Generative Rhetoric of the Sentence," *College Composition and Communication*, October 1963.

210   "I watched this human ocean . . .": Loren Eiseley, "One Night's Dying," *The Night Country* (1971). "He could sail for hours . . .": Walter Van Tilburg Clark, *The Oxbow Incident* (1950). "The cumulative sentence in unskilled . . .": Francis Christensen, *Notes Toward a New Rhetoric* (1978).

211   "Though in many natural objects . . .": Melville, *Moby-Dick* (1851), ch. 42.

212   "Nothing was more common . . .": Lamb, "Christ's Hospital Five and Thirty Years Ago" (1820). "Then the cheers were loud . . .": Robertson

Page

Davies, *Fifth Business* (1970). Reprinted by permission of Robertson Davies and Viking Penguin, Inc. "Johnson's esthetic judgments ...": Lytton Strachey, *Books and Characters* (1922).

212–213   "And Julia's voice ...": Byron, *Don Juan* (1819), Canto I, stanza 117. "Here, therefore ... let me return ...": Alexander Pope, *Peri Bathous* (1728), ch. xvi.

214   "And oh! if e'er I should ...": Byron, *Don Juan* (1819), Canto II, stanza 19. "The emotional isolation ...": C. P. Snow, *The Search* (1958).

215   "Into this grey lake ...": Doris Lessing, *A Proper Marriage* (1970, New American Library edition). "Ah! you should keep dogs ...": Dickens, *Pickwick Papers* (1837), ch. 2. "To: Deep Well Oil Company ...": Winston Weathers, *An Alternate Style* (1980).

216   "Perhaps it is easy ...": "Letter from a Birmingham Jail," in *Why We Can't Wait* (1963) by Martin Luther King, Jr. Copyright © 1963 by Martin Luther King, Jr. By permission of Harper and Row, Publishers, Inc.

217   "Mankind must put an end ...": John F. Kennedy, United Nations speech, 1961. "Not only are they just ...": George Steiner, *The Death of Tragedy* (1961). "To learn what one can know ...": Roger Rosenblatt, "The Mind in the Machine," *Time*, May 3, 1982. "It is a sin ...": H. L. Mencken, *Prejudices, Second Series* (1920). "We observe today ...": John F. Kennedy, Inaugural Address (1960). "Hicks had no ...": Samuel Clemens.

219   "The period of reappraisal ...": George F. Kennan in the *New York Times Magazine*, September 12, 1954. "Society, through every fiber ...": Thomas Carlyle, essay on Croker's edition of Boswell's *Life of Johnson*. "And so no force ...": quoted by Baum, *The Other Harmony of Prose* (1952) from Edmund Gurney, *Tertium Quid*. As Baum points out, the sentence is often attributed to Archbishop Whately.

220   "I was staying at the time ...": Dylan Thomas, "A Story," *Quite Early One Morning* (1954). Copyright 1954 by New Directions Publishing Corporation. Reprinted by permission of New Directions Publishing Corporation, J. M. Dent, and David Higham Associates Limited.

221   "The young men ...": William Gass, *In the Heart of the Heart of the Country* (1968). "Underfoot crunches the oldest ...": Thomas Pynchon, *Gravity's Rainbow* (1973). "When I grow up there ain't ...": Alden Nowlan, "Hurt," *Miracle at Indian River* (1968).

221–222   "She must have felt ...": John Updike, "A&P," *Pigeon Feathers and Other Stories*. Reprinted by permission of Alfred A. Knopf, Inc.

222   "It was on the afternoon ...": Dylan Thomas, "A Child's Christmas in Wales," *Quite Early One Morning*. Copyright 1939 by New Directions Publication Corporation, 1945 by the Trustees for the Copyright of Dylan Thomas. Reprinted from "A Child's Christmas in Wales" by permission of New Directions Publishing Corporation and from "Memories of Christmas" by permission of J. M. Dent and David Higham Associates Limited.

224   "Who can say at what point ...": Courtesy of Security Mutual Life Insurance Company, Binghamton, New York.

225   "He crossed to the bright side ...": James Joyce, *Ulysses* (Modern Library edition). Copyright 1934. The Modern Library, Inc.

225–226   "what have I done ...": William Faulkner, *The Sound and the Fury* (1929). Random House, Inc. Copyright by William Faulkner.

226   "walk the streets ...": John Dos Passos, *The Big Money* (Part Three of *U.S.A.*; Modern Library edition).

226–227   "In the folds of the hills ...": Sheila Watson, *The Double Hook* (1969).

Page

228–229   "Few Americans stay put . . .": First four paragraphs of "On Friendship— August, 1966" from *A Way of Seeing* (1974) by Margaret Mead and Rhoda Metraux. Copyright © 1966 by Margaret Mead and Rhoda Metraux. By permission of William Morrow and Company. In the original, paragraphs begin with sentences 1, 4, 9, and 13.

229–230   "The most famous of all hotels . . .": Margaret Leech, *Reveille in Washington* (1941).

231   "He plunked the $5.00 . . .": The psychologist is Allan Collins, and he describes this experiment in "Inference in Text Understanding," ERIC document #ED150547 (1977).

232–233   "There was once a town . . .": "Preface," from *Silent Spring* (1962) by Rachel Carson. Copyright © 1962 by Rachel Carson. Reprinted by permission of Houghton Mifflin Company.

233–234   "Men tried to talk about it . . .": Carl Sandburg, *Abraham Lincoln: The War Years* (1939), IV. By permission of Harcourt, Brace and Company, publishers.

234   "Fear. How could it be otherwise . . .": "Other Balks, Encumbrances in Coming to One's Own Voice, Vision, Circumference," excerpted from *Silences* by Tillie Olsen. Copyright © 1965, 1978 by Tillie Olsen. Reprinted by permission of Delacorte Press/Seymour Lawrence.

Exercises

236   4.1:(1) Samuel Clemens, *Adventures of Huckleberry Finn* (1884), ch. 1. (2) James Joyce, *Portrait of the Artist as a Young Man* (1916). (3) Joyce Carol Oates, "Four Summers," *The Wheel of Love* (1970).

237–238   4.3:(1) Thoreau, *Walden* (1854), ch. 1. (2) Samuel Johnson, "Savage," *Lives of the Poets* (1780). (3) Washington Irving, "The Author's Account of Himself," *The Sketch Book* (1820). (4) John Morley, *Rousseau* (1873).

239   4.5:(1) Ernest Hemingway, "An Alpine Idyll," *Men Without Women* (1927). Charles Scribner's Sons. (2) William Faulkner, *absalom, absalom!* (1936).

241   4.9:(4) Frank Lloyd Wright, *Frank Lloyd Wright: Writings and Buildings* (1960).

241–242   4.10:(2) Aldo Leopold, *A Sand County Almanac* (1966). (4) Mary Ellen Chase, *This England* (1936). (5) Catalogue of an exhibition of banned and censored books, Kansas University Library, 1955. (6) Melville, *Typee* (1846), ch. 17. (7) F. Scott Fitzgerald, *The Great Gatsby* (1925).

243–245   4.13: Periodic Sentences: (1) Dylan Thomas, "The Lemon," *Adventures in the Skin Trade* (1955). (2) Edwin Way Teale, *The Lost Woods* (1945). (3) Adapted from Jane Howard, "A Woman," *Quest*, April 1981. (4) Frederick Raphael, preface to *Two for the Road* (1954). (5) Ralph Waldo Emerson, "Nature" (1836). (6) John Updike, "A&P," *Pigeon Feathers and Other Stories*. Cumulative Sentences: (1) Excerpt from "A Sunday Kind of Love" from *The Kandy Kolored Tangerine Flake Streamline Baby* (1965) by Tom Wolfe. Reprinted by permission of Farrar, Straus and Giroux, Inc. Copyright © 1964 by The New York *Herald Tribune*, Inc. Copyright © 1965 by Thomas K. Wolfe, Jr. (2) John Fowles, *The Magus* (1966). (3) Frank Trippett, "The Growing Battle of Books," *Time*, January 19, 1981. (4) Vladimir Nabokov, *Speak, Memory* (1966 revised edition). (5) Muriel Spark, *Memento Mori* (1959). (6) Frank Smith, *Writing and the Writer* (1982).

Page

245   4.14: "Doom. Doom!": D. H. Lawrence, "Herman Melville's *Moby-Dick,*" *Studies in Classic American Literature* (1923). 4.15:(1) J. R. R. Tolkien, *The Hobbit* (1937). (2) Brian Moore, *The Lonely Passion of Judith Hearn* (1965). (4) Truman Capote, *Other Voices, Other Rooms* (1955).

246   4:16:(1) Adapted from Aldo Leopold, *A Sand County Almanac* (1966). (4) Adapted from R. Z. Sheppard, "The First All-American Poet," *Time,* November 17, 1980.

246–248   4.18:(1) Reprinted by permission of Toyota Motor Sales U.S.A., Inc. Advertising Agency Dancer Fitzgerald Simple, Inc. (2) Reprinted by permission of Jaguar Rover Triumph Canada Inc. and R. T. Kelley, Inc.

248–249   4.19:(1) From a report of the State Capitol Historical Association of Washington State, quoted in the *New Yorker,* May 5, 1955. (The *New Yorker's* comment: "Exhale.") (2) From a speech by Sitting Bull, quoted in *Touch the Earth: A Self-Portrait of Indian Existence,* T. C. McLuhan, ed. (1971). (4) Matthew Arnold, Preface to *Poems* (1853).

249–250   4.20:(1) Thomas O'Toole, "The Eagle Has Landed: Two Men Walk on the Moon," Washington *Post,* July 21, 1969. Copyright © 1969 Washington *Post.* (2) William F. Buckley, "Moonstruck," Washington *Star,* July 24, 1969. Reprinted by permission of Washington *Star.* (3) Norman Mailer, *Of a Fire on the Moon* (1970).

250–252   4.21:(1) Winston Churchill, speech on the fall of Dunkirk (1940), in *Blood, Sweat, and Tears.* Copyright 1940 by Winston Churchill. (2) William Faulkner, "Nobel Prize Address" (1950); in *The Faulkner Reader* (1954). Copyright by William Faulkner. Reprinted by permission of Random House, Inc. (3) Chief Dan George, from a speech delivered on the occasion of Canada's centennial celebration (1967). Reprinted by permission of Mr. Leonard George.

252–254   4.23:(1) *The Art of Literary Research* (1963). (2) Calvin Trillin, *Alice, Let's Eat* (1979). (3) Macaulay, essay on Bacon. (5) Marcia Gillespie, "They're Playing My Music, but Burying My Dreams," *Ms.,* July-August, 1982. (6) Betty Edwards, *Drawing on the Right Side of the Brain* (1979). (7) Dickens, *Pickwick Papers* (1837), ch. 2.

254–255   4.24: Ohio State University *Lantern,* December 1, 1966.

256   4.26: Excerpt from *Disturbing the Universe* by Freeman Dyson. Copyright © 1979 by Freeman J. Dyson. Reprinted by permission of Harper and Row, Publishers, Inc.

256–257   4.27:(1) Leon Harrison, "Late for class? O.K., if the excuse is show business," *Smithsonian,* May 1982. (2) Paul and Karyn Pfarr, *Build Your Own Log Cabin* (1978).

257–258   4.28:(1) Aldo Leopold, *A Sand County Almanac* (1966). (2) "Still steaming . . . and clanging and tooting," *Sunset* magazine, August 1982. Reprinted by permission of *Sunset* magazine, Lane Publishing Company.

258–260   4.29(1): Mary Elsie Robertson, *The Clearing* (1982). (2) John Stuart Mill, *On Liberty* (1859), ch. 1. (3) William Appleman Williams, *The Contours of American History* (1961). (4) J. Robert Oppenheimer, *Science and the Common Understanding* (1954). (5) Dickens, *Bleak House* (1853), ch. 1. (6) "The Joy of Gardening," *Newsweek,* July 26, 1982. (7) Ernest Hemingway, *Men at War* (1942), introduction.

260, 263–264   4.31:(1) Adapted from Lillian Hellman, *Pentimento* (1973). (2) Also adapted from *Pentimento.* Hellman's original version: "Then, to save carfare, she walked the long distance to the end of Canal Street, where she carried shoe box stacks back and forth all day for the German merchant

Page

who ran a mean store for sailors off the wharves." (3) Adapted from Sherwood Anderson, "Death." Anderson's original version: "Doctor Reefy's office was as large as a barn. A stove with a round paunch sat in the middle of the room. Around its base was piled sawdust, held in place by heavy planks nailed to the floor. By the door stood a huge table that had once been a part of the furniture of Herrick's clothing store and that had been used for displaying custom made clothes. It was covered with books, bottles, and surgical instruments." (4) Adapted from Stephen Crane, "The Bride Comes to Yellow Sky." Crane's original version: "The bride was not very pretty, nor was she very young. She wore a dress of blue cashmere, with small reservations of velvet here and there, and with small buttons abounding. She continually twisted her head to regard her puff sleeves, very stiff, straight, and high. They embarrassed her."

261–262   (1) The Sweet 'n Low advertisement is reprinted by permission of HBM/Stiefel, Inc. (2) The Perrier advertisement is reprinted by permission of Perrier, Inc.

264–267   4.32:(1) Vladimir Nabokov, *Speak, Memory* (1966 revised edition). (2) Reprinted with permission of Susan K. James, copywriter, and The Hamilton Collection. (3) Stephen Crane, *The Red Badge of Courage* (1895), ch. 17. (4) Owen Gingerich, "The Galileo Affair," *Scientific American,* August 1982. Reprinted by permission. (5) Virginia Woolf, *The Waves* (1931). Quoted by permission of Harcourt, Brace & World.

Chapter Five

271   "Consider this syllogism . . .": From Owen Gingerich, "The Galileo Affair," *Scientific American,* August 1982. Quoted by permission.

274–275   "As a perceiver I am . . .": William J. Brandt, *The Rhetoric of Argumentation* (1970).

281   The story of the cobalt in the beer appeared in *Time,* January 20, 1967.

283   "Most people engaged in creative . . .": Howard Gardner, "On Becoming a Dictator," *Psychology To lay,* December 1980.

284   "The story of Steinbrenner . . .": Lance Morrow, "The Lessons of Steinbrennerism," *Time,* August 23, 1982. Copyright 1982 Time Inc. All rights reserved. Reprinted by permission from *Time.*

286   Stephen Toulmin's system is described in his *The Uses of Argument* (1958), and is used in his textbook, *An Introduction to Reasoning* (1982).

286–287   "The Burrowing Owl . . .": Reprinted through the courtesy of World Wildlife Fund Canada and Ogilvy and Mather Canada.

294   The material on Beard is from Samuel Eliot Morison, "History Through a Beard," *By Land and By Sea* (1953), where other examples of innuendo, rhetorical questions, and similar devices are used.

294–295   "a conventional rehash of cubist . . .": Quoted from Thomas Craven by Curtis D. MacDougall, *Understanding Public Opinion* (1952).

298   The opinions on *Boeing Boeing* were quoted in *Newsweek,* February 15, 1965.

300   "No week passes without . . .": Comment by A. H. Rankin in an article in the *New York Times Magazine,* June 11, 1967.

301   Emerson's words are in his essay "The American Scholar" (1837).

Exercises

Page

304   5.5:(a) Copyright 1982, by Newsweek, Inc. All rights reserved. Reprinted by permission.

311   5.12: Copyright 1982. Reprinted through the courtesy of Turner Broadcasting Company, Atlanta, Georgia.

313   Reprinted through the courtesy of Craig Van Note, Monitor Consortium, Washington, D.C.

314   Reprinted through the courtesy of Schenley Imports Company, New York.

315   Reprinted through the courtesy of Canon, U.S.A., Inc. and Ms. Austin.

316   5.21: Paul Goodman, *Growing Up Absurd* (1960).

318   5.26:(1) From a letter to *The New Republic*, May 9, 1964.

320   5.29: Letter to the Editor, by Craig Chapman, is reprinted by permission of the Corvallis (Oregon) *Gazette-Times* from its September 15, 1982 issue.

320–321   5.30: The communication is genuine, although the name of the "note-taking service" has been changed.

322   Copyright 1981 International Telephone and Telegraph Corporation. Reprinted through the courtesy of International Telephone and Telegraph Corporation.

323   Reprinted by permission of the Chemical Manufacturers Association.

324–325   5.33: John Skow, from *Time*, August 17, 1981. Copyright 1981 Time Inc. All rights reserved. Reprinted by permission from *Time*.

325–326   5.35:(1) Advertisement of the Magazine Publishers' Association, *Life*, July 7, 1967.

Glossary

327   Analogy: "If the aircraft . . .": from Hoo-min D. Toong and Amar Gupta, "Personal Computers," *Scientific American*, December 1982. Antithesis: "He for God . . .": Milton, *Paradise Lost*, Book IV, line 297.

328   Climax: "I think we have . . .": George Wald, "A Generation in Search of a Future" (1945). Cumulative Sentence: "Their trim boots . . .": James Joyce, *Portrait of the Artist as a Young Man* (1916).

329   Ellipsis: "At twenty years . . .": Benjamin Franklin, *Poor Richard's Almanack* (1741).

331   Periodic Sentence: "When a writer begins . . .": Van Wyck Brooks, *A Chilmark Miscellany* (1948).

332   Rhythm: "There was something rather 'doggy' . . .": D. H. Lawrence, *Sons and Lovers* (1913).

INDEX